Anthropological Locations

To Aila and Elias

Anthropological Locations

Boundaries and Grounds
of a Field Science

EDITED BY

Akhil Gupta and James Ferguson

UNIVERSITY OF CALIFORNIA PRESS
Berkeley   Los Angeles   London

University of California Press
Berkeley and Los Angeles, California

University of California Press, Ltd.
London, England

© 1997 by
The Regents of the University of California

Library of Congress Cataloging-in-Publication Data

Anthropological locations : boundaries and grounds of a field science
   edited by Akhil Gupta and James Ferguson.
      p.   cm.
   Includes bibliographical references and index.
   ISBN 0-520-20680-0 (pbk. : alk. paper)
      1. Anthropological—Field work.   2. Anthropology—Methodology.
   3. Anthropology—Philosophy.   I. Gupta, Akhil, 1959–   .
   II. Ferguson, James, 1959–   .
   GN34.3.F53A56   1997
   301'.07'23—dc21   96-46305
                                                              CIP

Printed in the United States of America

10   09   08   07   06   05   04   03   02
      10   9   8   7   6   5   4   3

The paper used in this publication meets the minimum requirements of
ANSI/NISO Z39.48-1992 (R 1997) (*Permanence of Paper*). ∞

CONTENTS

ACKNOWLEDGMENTS

This volume grows out of a conference, Anthropology and "the Field": Boundaries, Areas, and Grounds in the Constitution of a Discipline, which was held on February 19 and 20, 1994, at Stanford University and the University of California, Santa Cruz. The conference was sponsored chiefly by the Center of Cultural Studies at U.C. Santa Cruz and by the Department of Anthropology at Stanford, with additional funding provided by the School of Arts and Sciences, Stanford University, and the Department of Anthropology and the School of Social Sciences of U.C. Irvine. We are grateful for this support and would like to thank George Collier, chair of the Department of Anthropology, and Anne Peck, associate dean of social sciences, both of Stanford University, for supporting the conference.

We would also like to thank the many participants in the conference, who included (in addition to the contributors to this volume) Talal Asad, Paulla Ebron, Joan Fujimura, Mary Pratt, Lisa Rofel, Renato Rosaldo, George Stocking, and Anna Tsing. All made important contributions to the success of the conference and to the development of our own ideas about "the field." We would like to offer a special thanks to George Stocking, who—both at the conference and in personal correspondence—has very generously shared with us his remarkable knowledge of, and insight into, the history of the discipline of anthropology and has provided invaluable encouragement. We are also especially indebted to Diane Nelson, whose efforts in assisting the organization and logistics of the conference went far beyond the call of duty.

We would like the thank the following colleagues for their insightful and constructive comments on various drafts of the volume's introduction: George Bisharat, Teresa Caldeira, Jane Collier, Shelly Errington, Susan Greenhalgh, Liisa Malkki, George Stocking, Kath Weston, and Margery Wolf. Three additional colleagues read the entire volume at a late stage and provided innumerable important suggestions to us and to the other volume contributors: Don Brenneis, Ben Orlove, and Joan Vincent. We are grateful to them all for helping us to sharpen and clarify our project. Errors and deficiencies that remain, needless to say, are ours alone.

Finally, we wish to thank Monica McCormick, who has been an exemplary editor throughout the process. Her patience, support, and understanding for the project have been profoundly appreciated. We also are especially grateful for the assistance of Aradhana (Anu) Sharma in copyediting the manuscript and of Eric Kaldor for his help in preparing the index.

Akhil Gupta
Stanford, California

James Ferguson
Irvine, California

June 16, 1996

ONE

Discipline and Practice: "The Field" as Site, Method, and Location in Anthropology

Akhil Gupta and James Ferguson

I. INTRODUCTION

The practice of fieldwork, together with its associated genre, ethnography, has perhaps never been as central to the discipline of anthropology[1] as it is today, in terms of both intellectual principles and professional practices. Intellectually, ethnography has long ceased to be conceived of as "mere description," raw material for a natural science of human behavior. Whether via the literary turn (from "thick description" to "writing culture") or the historic one (political economy and the turn to regional social history), mainstream social/cultural anthropology as practiced in leading departments in the United States and the United Kingdom[2] has come to view ethnographic explication as a worthy and sufficient intellectual project in its own right. Indeed, it is striking that the generalist and comparativist theorists who dominated anthropology at midcentury (e.g., Radcliffe-Brown, Leslie White, and George Murdock) seem in the process of being mnemonically pruned from the anthropological family tree, while the work of those remembered as great fieldworkers (Malinowski, Boas, Evans-Pritchard, Leenhardt, etc.) continues to be much more widely discussed.

In terms of professional socialization and training, too, ethnographic fieldwork is at the core of what Stocking has called anthropology's fundamental "methodological values"—"the taken-for-granted, pretheoretical notions of what it is to do anthropology (and to be an anthropologist)" (1992a: 282). As all graduate students in social/cultural anthropology know, it is fieldwork that makes one a "real anthropologist," and truly anthropological knowledge is widely understood to be "based" (as we say) on fieldwork. Indeed, we would suggest that the single most significant factor determining whether a piece of research will be accepted as (that magical word) "anthropological" is the extent to which it depends on experience "in the field."

Yet this idea of "the field," although central to our intellectual and professional identities, remains a largely unexamined one in contemporary anthropology. The concept of culture has been vigorously critiqued and dissected in recent years (e.g., Wagner 1981; Clifford 1988; Rosaldo 1989a; Fox, ed., 1991); ethnography as a genre of writing has been made visible and critically analyzed (Clifford and Marcus 1986; Geertz 1988); the dialogic encounters that constitute fieldwork experience have been explored (Crapanzano 1980; Rabinow 1977; Dumont 1978; Tedlock 1983); even the peculiar textual genre of fieldnotes has been subjected to reflection and analysis (Sanjek 1990). But what of "the field" itself, the place where the distinctive work of "fieldwork" may be done, that taken-for-granted space in which an "Other" culture or society lies waiting to be observed and written? This mysterious space—not the "what" of anthropology but the "where"—has been left to common sense, beyond and below the threshold of reflexivity.

It is astonishing, but true, that most leading departments of anthropology in the United States provide no formal (and very little informal) training in fieldwork methods—as few as 20 percent of departments, according to one survey.[3] It is also true that most anthropological training programs provide little guidance in, and almost no critical reflection on, the selection of fieldwork sites and the considerations that deem some places but not others as suitable for the role of "the field." It is as if the mystique of fieldwork were too great in anthropology for the profession even to permit such obvious and practical issues to be seriously discussed, let alone to allow the idea of "the field" itself to be subjected to scrutiny and reflection.

In turning a critical eye to such questions, our aim is not to breach what amounts to a collectively sanctioned silence simply for the pleasure of upsetting traditions. Rather, our effort to open up this subject is motivated by two specific imperatives.

The first imperative follows from the way the idea of "the field" functions in the micropolitical academic practices through which anthropological work is distinguished from work in related disciplines such as history, sociology, political science, literature and literary criticism, religious studies, and (especially) cultural studies. The difference between anthropology and these other disciplines, it would be widely agreed, lies less in the topics studied (which, after all, overlap substantially) than in the distinctive method anthropologists employ, namely fieldwork based on participant observation. In other words, our difference from other specialists in academic institutions is constructed not just on the premise that we are specialists in difference, but on a specific methodology for uncovering or understanding that difference. Fieldwork thus helps define anthropology as a discipline in both senses of the word, constructing a space of possibilities while at the same time drawing the lines that confine that space. Far from being a mere research technique, fieldwork has become "the basic constituting experience both of anthropologists and of anthropological knowledge" (Stocking 1992a: 282).

Since fieldwork is increasingly the single constituent element of the anthropological tradition used to mark and police the boundaries of the discipline, it is impossible to rethink those boundaries or rework their contents without confronting the idea of "the field." "The field" of anthropology and "the field" of "fieldwork" are thus politically and epistemologically intertwined; to think critically about one requires a readiness to question the other. Exploring the possibilities and limitations of the idea of "the field" thus carries with it the opportunity—or, depending on one's point of view, the risk—of opening to question the meaning of our own professional and intellectual identities as anthropologists.

The second imperative for beginning to discuss the idea of "the field" in anthropology follows from a now widely expressed doubt about the adequacy of traditional ethnographic methods and concepts to the intellectual and political challenges of the contemporary postcolonial world. Concern about the lack of fit between the problems raised by a mobile, changing, globalizing world, on the one hand, and the resources provided by a method originally developed for studying supposedly small-scale societies, on the other, has of course been evident in anthropological circles for some time (see, for instance, Hymes 1972; Asad 1973). In recent years, however, questioning of the traditional fieldwork ideal has become both more widespread and more far-reaching. Some critics have pointed to problems in the construction of ethnographic texts (Clifford and Marcus 1986), some to the structures and practices through which relationships are established between ethnographers and their "informants" in the field (Crapanzano 1980; Dumont 1978; cf. Harrison, ed., 1991). Others have suggested that the problem lies as much in the fact that the world being described by ethnographers has changed dramatically without a corresponding shift in disciplinary practices since "fieldwork" became hegemonic in anthropology. Appadurai has posed the problem in the following terms:

> As groups migrate, regroup in new locations, reconstruct their histories, and reconfigure their ethnic "projects," the *ethno* in ethnography takes on a slippery, nonlocalized quality, to which the descriptive practices of anthropology will have to respond. The landscapes of group identity—the ethnoscapes—around the world are no longer familiar anthropological objects, insofar as groups are no longer tightly territorialized, spatially bounded, historically self-conscious, or culturally homogeneous. . . . The task of ethnography now becomes the unraveling of a conundrum: what is the nature of locality, as a lived experience, in a globalized, deterritorialized world? (Appadurai 1991: 191, 196)[4]

In what follows, we will further explore the challenge of coming to terms with the changed context of ethnographic work. For now, it is sufficient to note a certain contradiction. On the one hand, anthropology appears determined to give up its old ideas of territorially fixed communities and stable, localized cultures, and to apprehend an interconnected world in which people, objects, and ideas are rapidly shifting and refuse to stay in place. At the same time, though, in a defensive response to challenges to its "turf" from other disciplines, anthropology has come to lean more heavily than ever on a methodological commitment to spend long periods in one localized setting. What are we to do with a discipline that loudly rejects received ideas of "the local," even while ever more firmly insisting on a method that takes it for granted? A productive rethinking of such eminently practical problems in anthropological methodology, we suggest, will require a thoroughgoing reevaluation of the idea of the anthropological "field" itself, as well as the privileged status it occupies in the construction of anthropological knowledge.

This book therefore explores the idea of "the field" at each of the two levels described above. Some of the authors investigate how "the field" came to be part of the commonsense and professional practice of anthropology, and view this development in the contexts both of wider social and political developments and of the academy's micropolitics. Other authors, researchers whose own work stretches the conventional boundaries of "fieldwork," reflect on how the idea of "the field" has bounded and normalized the practice of anthropology—how it enables certain kinds of knowledge while blocking off others, authorizes some objects of study and methods of analysis while excluding others; how, in short, the idea of "the field" helps to define and patrol the boundaries of what is often knowingly referred to as "real anthropology."

In the remaining sections of this chapter, we develop some general observations about how the idea of "the field" has been historically constructed and constituted in anthropology (Part II) and trace some key effects and consequences of this dominant concept of "the field" for professional and intellectual practices (Part III). We want not only to describe the configurations of field and discipline that have prevailed in the past but also to help rework these configurations to meet the needs of the present and the future better. "The field" is a (arguably *the*) central component of the anthropological tradition, to be sure; but anthropology also teaches that traditions are always reworked and even reinvented as needed. With this in mind, we search (in Part IV) for intellectual resources and alternative disciplinary practices that might aid in such a reconstruction of tradition, which we provisionally locate both in certain forgotten and devalued elements of the anthropological past and in various marginalized sites on the geographical and disciplinary peripheries of anthropology. Finally, in Part V, we propose a reformulation of the anthropological fieldwork tradition that would decenter and defetishize the concept of "the field," while developing methodological and epistemological strategies that foreground questions of location, intervention, and the construction of situated knowledges.

Whether anthropology *ought* to have a unique or distinctive approach that sets it apart from other disciplines is not a question of great intrinsic interest to us. Certainly, there are many more interesting questions to ask about any given piece of work than whether or not it "belongs" within anthropology. But we accept James Clifford's point (chapter 10 in this book) that as long as the current configuration of disciplines obtains,[5] the slot labeled "anthropology" will be obliged, in one way or another, to distinguish and justify itself. We agree, too, that the anthropological "trademark" of fieldwork seems certain to be central to any such disciplinary strategies of self-definition and legitimation, at least in the near future. With this in mind, it seems most useful to us to attempt to redefine the fieldwork "trademark" not with a time-honored commitment to the *local* but with an attentiveness to social, cultural, and political *location* and a willingness to work self-consciously at shifting or realigning our own location while building epistemological and political links with other locations (an idea that we develop in Part V). Such "location-work," we suggest, is central to many of the most innovative reconceptualizations of anthropological fieldwork practices in recent years, some of which are illustrated in this book. The fact that such work fits only uneasily within the traditional disciplinary bounds of a "real anthropology" defined by "real fieldwork" has caused a good many recent tensions within the discipline. A serious consideration of what the conventional anthropological commitment to "field" and "fieldwork" entails, and a willingness to rethink how such a commitment might be conceptualized, could contribute to a better understanding of such tensions and ways in which they might be addressed constructively.

II. GENEALOGY OF A "FIELD SCIENCE"

Anyone who has done fieldwork, or studied the phenomenon, knows that one does not just wander onto a "field site" to engage in a deep and meaningful relationship with "the natives." "The field" is a clearing whose deceptive transparency obscures the complex processes that go into constructing it. In fact, it is a highly overdetermined setting for the discovery of difference. To begin with, it is the prior conceptual segmentation of the world into different cultures, areas, and sites that makes the enterprise of fieldwork possible. How does this territorialization take place? Through what conventions and inherited assumptions is it possible for the world to appear, through the anthropological lens, as an array of field sites?

Natural History and the Malinowskian "Field"

One place to begin thinking about these questions is to note how the idea of "the field" entered the discipline. We do not aim here to construct a full intellectual history of the idea of "the field," nor do we possess the historiographical expertise to do so, though scholars of the history of anthropology such as George Stocking (ed., 1983, 1991, 1992a), Henrika Kuklick (1991, and chapter 2 of this book), and Joan Vincent (1990) have already made important contributions toward that task. Instead, we wish to raise, in a genealogical spirit, a more restricted and focused set of questions about the key relationships that led to the constitution of anthropology as a field of knowledge that depends on fieldwork as the distinctive mode of gathering knowledge.[6]

In this spirit, it is interesting to note that the term *fieldwork*, apparently introduced into anthropology by the former zoologist A. C. Haddon, was derived from the discourse of field naturalists (Stocking 1992a; Kuklick, chapter 2). As Stocking observes, Haddon conceived his first fieldwork in the Torres Straits squarely within the terms of natural history: "to study the fauna, the structure, and the mode of formation of coral reefs" (1992a: 21). Indeed, Kuklick (chapter 2) vividly demonstrates that the anthropological "discovery" of fieldwork needs to be set in the context of a more general set of transformations in the late nineteenth- and early twentieth-century practices of *all* naturalists. Like other "field sciences," such as zoology, botany, and geology, anthropology at the start of the century found both its distinctive object and its distinctive method in "the detailed study of limited areas" (Kuklick, chapter 2; cf. Stocking 1992a). Anthropology's origin as a naturalistic science of the early human is therefore closely tied to the eventual role of fieldwork as its dominant disciplinary practice. To do fieldwork was, in the beginning, to engage in a branch of natural history; the object to be studied, both intensively and in a limited area, was primitive humanity in its natural state.[7]

Many early twentieth-century fieldworkers explicitly recognized, of course, that their subjects were in fact *not* living in a pristine, "natural" condition; so-called "salvage anthropology" was a self-conscious attempt to reconstruct such a state from the observation and questioning of natives living under the patently "unnatural" conditions of a postconquest colonial world. David Tomas (1991) shows, for example, how Radcliffe-Brown complained that the informants he met on a penal settlement (established by the colonial government in the Andaman Islands to imprison those who rose against it in the Great Indian Mutiny of 1857) no longer remembered "the things of the old time"; he therefore tried to interview others who "do not know a single word of any language but their own" (in Tomas 1991: 96). His eventual plan was to go to the Nicobars where the data were less likely to be contaminated by the natives' previous contact with white people like himself (Tomas 1991: 95–96). The early Boasians in the United States faced similar difficulties in seeking to build comprehensive descriptions of peoples and societies that had been substantially decimated by conquest, genocide, and disease.

With the Malinowskian revolution in fieldwork,[8] anthropological naturalism came to be asserted in an even stronger form. Through an active forgetting of conquest and colonialism, fieldworkers increasingly claimed not simply to *reconstruct* the natural state of the primitive, but to *observe* it directly. Thus did social anthropology become defined as "the study of small-scale society—ahistorical, *ethno*-graphic, and comparative," with extended participant observation its distinctive method (Vincent 1991: 55). Yet it is worth remembering just how late a development this was. It is not only that, as Kuklick shows (chapter 2), the gentlemen-scholars of the nineteenth century scorned the idea of actually going to "the field" (regarding the "collection" of data as a task for unskilled and low-status workers—in some places, for slaves). For even *after* the Trobriand Islanders provided anthropology with its mythic fieldwork charter, many of Malinowski's own students (according to George Stocking, personal communication, 10 November 1993) did library dissertations before ever going into "the field," as did their Boasian contemporaries (and, indeed, Malinowski himself). As Stocking has shown, it was Malinowski's ambition and "entrepreneurial talent," rather than simply the intrinsic intellectual merits of his program, that enabled him to secure the support of the Rockefeller Foundation for his vision of anthropology, which only then (i.e., after 1930) enabled him to institutionalize his perspective. (For example, all Rockefeller-funded fieldworkers of the International African Institute were required to spend a year in Malinowski's seminar [Stocking 1992a]). Malinowski's success in normalizing "his method" may have owed more to his institutional skills and to the leaving of progeny who continued his legacy than to anything inherent in extended participant observation itself (cf. Kuklick 1991; Vincent 1990).

A key result of the Malinowskian triumph, however, was that a naturalistic ideal that had been dismissed as impractical in the actual fieldwork of such founding fathers as Radcliffe-Brown and Boas came to be retrospectively asserted as the discipline's foundational methodological strategy. Fieldwork in sociocultural anthropology in this way came to share with fields such as primatology the requirement that its subjects be directly observed in their natural surroundings (see Haraway 1989). Those living outside their native state (for example, Native Americans working in towns; Aborigines employed on ranches; or, in Radcliffe-Brown's case cited above, prisoners forcibly held in a penal settlement) came to be considered less suitable anthropological objects because they were outside "the field," just as zoological studies of animals in captivity came to be considered inferior to those conducted on animals in the wild. The naturalistic genre of ethnography was an attempt to recreate that natural state textually, just as the dioramas painstakingly constructed in natural history museums aimed not only to describe but also to recreate the natural surroundings of primates and other animals (Haraway 1989: 26–58). Thus, when Ulf Hannerz (1986) complained that ethnography was still obsessed with "the most *other* of others," he was critiquing a long-standing ethnographic attitude that those most Other, and most isolated from "ourselves," are those most authentically rooted in their "natural" settings (cf. Malkki 1992).

This conception, of course, was and is undergirded by the metaphor of the "field" to denote the sites where anthropologists do their research. The word *field* connotes a place set apart from the urban—opposed not so much to the transnational metropolises of late capitalism as to the industrial cities of the era of competitive capitalism, as befits the word's period of origin (Fox 1991b). Going to the "field" suggests a trip to a place that is agrarian, pastoral, or maybe even "wild"; it implies a place that is perhaps cultivated (a site of culture), but that certainly does not stray too far from nature. What stands metaphorically opposed to work in the field is work in industrial places: in labs, in offices, in factories, in urban settings—in short, in civilized spaces that have lost their connection with nature. As a metaphor we work by, "the field" thus reveals many of the unspoken assumptions of anthropology. This is not, of course, to say that anthropologists do not work in industrial or urban settings, or that they do not call those sites "fields"—we are not being literalist, merely noting that it is not just coincidence that pastoral and agrarian metaphors shepherd anthropologists in their daily tasks.[9]

Areas and Sites

Anthropology, more than perhaps any other discipline, is a body of knowledge constructed on regional specialization, and it is within regionally circumscribed epistemic communities that many of the discipline's key concepts and debates have been developed (Fardon 1990; Appadurai 1988b). More than comparativists in other fields—political science, sociology, literature, history, law, religion, and business—anthropologists combine language learning and regional scholarship with long-term residence in "the field." Regional expertise is thus built into the anthropological project, constituting the other face of a discipline (at least implicitly) predicated on cultural comparison (Marcus and Fischer 1986). As we have argued elsewhere (Gupta and Ferguson 1992, 1997), it is precisely the naturalization of cultural difference as inhering in different geographical locales that makes anthropology such a regional science. From this, too, there follows the built-in necessity of travel: one can only encounter difference by going elsewhere, by going to "the field."

It is possible to situate "the field" more precisely as a site constructed through the shifting entanglements of anthropological notions of "culture

areas," the institutional politics of "area studies," and the global order of nation-states. The notion of culture areas, supplemented by ideas such as peo-
plehood and ethnicity (e.g., "the Kurds"), religion (e.g., "the Islamic world"),
language (e.g., "Bantu-speaking Africa"), and race (e.g., "Melanesia" [see
Thomas 1989a] or "Black Africa" [see Amory chapter 5]), attempted to relate a set of societies with common traits to each other. Thus the Mediterranean with its honor-and-shame complex constituted one culture area
(Herzfeld 1987; Passaro chapter 8), while South Asia with the institution of
caste hierarchy formed another (Appadurai 1988b), and Polynesia with its
centralized chiefdoms constituted a third (Thomas 1989a). Although we anthropologists devote far less attention today to mapping "culture regions"
than we used to (e.g., Wissler 1923; Murdock 1967; but cf. Burton et al. 1996),
the culture area remains a central disciplinary concept that implicitly structures the way in which we make connections between the particular groups
of people we study and the groups that other ethnographers study (cf. Fardon 1990; Thomas 1989a).[10]

However, and this is where issues become more complicated, ideas about
culture areas in the anthropological literature are refracted, altered, and
sometimes undermined by the institutional mechanisms that provide the intellectual legitimacy and financial support for doing fieldwork. To take but
one example, the setting up of area studies centers in American universities
has long been underwritten by the U.S. government. The definition of areas, the emphasis placed on various activities, and the importance of particular topics as research priorities have mostly been thinly disguised (if that)
projections of the state's strategic and geopolitical priorities. As the state's
interests shift, so do funding priorities and the definition of areas themselves.
A few years ago, for instance, there was an effort to carve out a new area, "In-
ner Asia," which would be distinct from Eastern Europe and Soviet studies
on the one hand, and the Middle East and China on the other. The timing
of this development remains mysterious unless one understands the concern
with the war in Afghanistan and the fear of the possible ascendance of "Islamic republics" in the regions adjacent to what was then the Soviet Union.

As the institutional mechanisms that define areas, fund research, and support scholarship change, they intersect in complicated ways with changing
ideas about "culture areas" to produce "fields" that are available for research.
Thus, no major funding agency supports research on "the Mediterranean"
or "the Caribbean." Some parts of the Mediterranean culture area are funded
by European area studies and the others by Middle Eastern area studies. The
more culturally exotic and geostrategically embattled parts thus become
proper "anthropological" field sites, whereas Western Europe (which, besides
having "less culture" [cf. Rosaldo 1988], is part of NATO) is a less appropriate "field," as the many Europeanists who struggle to find jobs in anthropology departments can attest.[11]

Similarly, anthropological ideas about culture areas and geographical specializations have been transformed by their encounter with the rude realities of decolonization. For instance, anthropologists working in Africa today
normally construct their regional specializations in national terms that
would have made no sense prior to the 1960s. Thus Victor Turner was not,
as he would be styled today, a "Zambianist" but an "Africanist"; his *Schism and
Continuity in an African Society* was "A Study of Ndembu Village Life," and the
reader would have to comb the text with some care to find out that the study
was in fact conducted in what was then northern Rhodesia. Evans-Pritchard's
research freely crossed between the Belgian Congo (Azande), the Anglo-
Egyptian Sudan (Nuer), and British East Africa (Luo); his regional specialization was not defined by such political territorializations. Yet just as Evans-
Pritchard's work was enabled by the brute fact of colonial conquest,[12] so, too,
the field sites in which contemporary anthropologists work are shaped by
the geopolitics of the postcolonial, imperial world. Decolonization has transformed field sites not merely by making it difficult, if not impossible, to move
across national borders, but by affecting a whole host of mechanisms, from
the location of archives to the granting of visas and research clearance. The
institutions that organized knowledge along colonial lines have yielded to
ones that organize it along national ones.[13]

A "good" field site is made, however, not only by considerations of funding and clearance, but by its suitability for addressing issues and debates that
matter to the discipline. As Jane Collier shows (chapter 6), the idea of sub-
stantive "subfields" such as "legal anthropology," "economic anthropology,"
"psychological anthropology," and so on was until recently a key device
through which such issues and debates were constituted. The problematics
and conventions of such subfields helped to shape not only the topic of investigation, but also the conception of the field site itself, in a number of
ways. First, as we have noted, culture areas have long been linked to subject
areas; thus India, with its ideologies of caste and purity, was long taken to be
an especially good site for an anthropologist of religion (Appadurai 1988b),
and Africa (with its segmentary lineages) was thought ideal for the political
anthropologist, just as Melanesia (with its elaborate systems of exchange) invited economic anthropologists (cf. Fardon 1990). But subfields have also
carried more specific assumptions about fieldwork and methodology. The
"fieldwork" of a legal anthropologist, for instance, might be expected to include the examination of written court records, while that of a psychological anthropologist working in the same area likely would not; in this manner, different subfields could construct the site to be studied in different ways.
As Collier shows, however, the very idea of coherent "subfields" has broken
down in recent years. The growing willingness to question received ideas of
"field" and "fieldwork" may well be related to the recent decline of the well-
defined subfields that once helped to define and bound field sites.

Field sites thus end up being defined by the crosshatched intersection of visa and clearance procedures,[14] the interests of funding agencies, and intellectual debates within the discipline and its subfields. Once defined in this way, field sites appear simply as a natural array of choices facing graduate students preparing for professional careers. The question becomes one of choosing an appropriate site, that is, choosing a place where intellectual interests, personal predilections, and career outcomes can most happily intersect. This is to be expected. What is more surprising is the recurrence of anecdotes in which experienced fieldworkers relate how they "stumbled" on to their field sites entirely "by chance."[15] Just as the culturally sanctioned discourse of "hard work" and "enterprise" enables the structurally patterned outcomes of career choice in competitive capitalism to disappear from view, so do the repeated narratives of discovering field sites "by chance" prevent any systematic inquiry into how those field sites came to be good places for doing fieldwork in the first instance. The very significant premises and assumptions built into the anthropological idea of "the field" are in this way protected from critical scrutiny, even as they are smuggled into the discipline's most central practices of induction, socialization, and professional reproduction.

III. IMPLICATIONS OF AN ARCHETYPE

As Stocking has pointed out (1992a: 59), the classical Malinowskian image of fieldwork (the lone, white, male fieldworker living for a year or more among the native villagers) functions as an *archetype* for normal anthropological practice.[16] Because an archetype is never a concrete and specific set of rules, this ideal of fieldwork need not carry with it any specific set of prescriptions; its link to practice is looser than this, and more complex. Since the archetypal image is today often invoked ironically and parodically, it can easily be made to appear an anachronism—a caricature that everyone knows, but nobody really takes seriously anymore. Yet such easy dismissals may be premature. After all, archetypes function not by claiming to be accurate, literal descriptions of things as they are, but by offering a compelling glimpse of things as they should be, at their purest and most essential. In the contemporary United States, for instance, the image of the so-called "all-American" look (healthy, wholesome, and white) has the power of an archetype. Americans know, of course, that most Americans do not look like this. If asked, most would surely say that dark-skinned Americans are every bit as "American" as light-skinned ones. Yet at a more fundamental and spontaneous level, when people think of "an American"—a "*real* American"—it is the "all-American" image that is likely to come to mind. Such archetypes operate ideologically in a way that is peculiarly hard to pin down; their effects are simultaneously ineffable and pervasive. Yet it is impossible to understand the full implications of the anthropological concept of "the field" without taking account of the deep-seated images of the "real fieldworker," the "real anthropologist," that constitute a significant part of the "common sense" (in the Gramscian usage of the term) of the discipline.

In sketching some of the key consequences of the construction of the field of anthropology through the practice of fieldwork, we focus on three themes in particular: first, the radical separation of "the field" from "home," and the related creation of a hierarchy of purity of field sites; second, the valorization of certain kinds of knowledge to the exclusion of other kinds; and third, the construction of a normative anthropological subject, an anthropological "self" against which anthropology sets its "Others." We emphasize, again, that these are not simply historical associations, but archetypal ones that subtly but powerfully construct the very idea of what anthropology is. We will argue that even *ideas* about "the field" that are explicitly disavowed by contemporary anthropologists in intellectual terms continue to be deeply embedded in our professional *practices*.

"Field" and "Home"

The distinction between "the field" and "home" rests on their spatial separation.[17] This separation is manifested in two central anthropological contrasts. The first differentiates the site where data are collected from the place where analysis is conducted and the ethnography is "written up." To do ethnographic work is thus to do two distinct types of writing. One kind is done "in the field." These "fieldnotes" are close to experience, textually fragmentary, consisting of detailed "raw" documentation of interviews and observations as well as spontaneous subjective reactions (Sanjek 1990). The other sort, done "at home," is reflective, polished, theoretical, intertextual, a textual whole—this is the writing of ethnographic papers and monographs. The former is done in isolation, sometimes on primitive equipment, in difficult conditions, with people talking or peering over one's shoulder; writing at "home" is done in the academy, in libraries or studies, surrounded by other texts, in the midst of theoretical conversation with others of one's kind. Moreover, the two forms of activity are not only distinct, but sequential: one commonly "writes up" after coming back from "the field." Temporal succession therefore traces the natural sequence of sites that completes a spatial journey into Otherness.

The second place the sharp contrast between "field" and "home" is expressed is in the standard anthropological tropes of entry into and exit from "the field." Stories of entry and exit usually appear on the margins of texts, providing the narrative with uncertainty and expectation at the beginning and closure at the end. According to Mary Louise Pratt (1986), the function of narratives of entry and exit is to authenticate and authorize the material that follows, most of which used to be written from the standpoint of an objective, distanced, observer.[18] Such stories also form a key piece of the informal lore of fieldwork that is so much a part of socialization into the discipline. Colonial-style heroic tales of adventurers battling the fierce tropics are, of course, out of favor nowadays, and the usual cliches of anthropological arrival are perhaps more often invoked today in a self-consciously ironic mode. But what needs to be emphasized is that *all* tropes of entry and exit, however playful, parodic, or self-conscious, may still function to construct the difference between "the field" and "home." The image of arriving in "another world" whose difference is enacted in the descriptions that follow, tends to minimize, if not make invisible, the multiple ways in which colonialism, imperialism, missionization, multinational capital, global cultural flows, and travel bind these spaces together. Again, most anthropologists today recognize this, but even as we reject ideas of isolated peoples living in separate worlds, the tropes of entry and exit and the idea of a separation of "fieldwork" from "writing up" continue to structure most contemporary ethnography.[19]

The very distinction between "field" and "home" leads directly to what we call a *hierarchy of purity* of field sites. After all, if "the field" is most appropriately a place that is "not home," then some places will necessarily be *more* "not home" than others, and hence more appropriate, more "fieldlike." All ethnographic research is thus done "in the field," but some "fields" are more equal than others—specifically, those that are understood to be distant, exotic, and strange. Here the parallel is striking with the older conception of anthropology as a field science, in which some sites offered better approximations of "the natural state" than others and were therefore preferred. Although anthropologists no longer think in terms of natural or undisturbed states, it remains evident that what many would deny in theory continues to be true in practice: some places are much more "anthropological" than others (e.g., Africa more than Europe, southern Europe more than northern Europe, villages more than cities) according to the degree of Otherness from an archetypal anthropological "home."

Largely because the idea of "the field" remains uninterrogated, such hierarchies of field sites live on in our professional practices. Among anthropologists who have done fieldwork, for instance, some are still understood to have done what is knowingly referred to as "real fieldwork"—that is, worked for a long time in an isolated area, with people who speak a non-European language, lived in "a community," preferably small, in authentic, "local" dwellings—while others have less pure field sites and thus are less fully anthropological. Anyone who doubts that such thinking continues to operate in the discipline should take a close look at anthropological job searches, where the question of who has or has not done "real fieldwork" (presumably in the "real field") is often decisive. Indeed, it is worth noting that the geographical categories by which such searches usually proceed[20] rule out from the start many outstanding job candidates who do not work, say, "in Africa" or "in Mesoamerica," but on such things as whiteness in the U.S. (Frankenberg 1993b) or on the practices of transnational "development" agencies (Escobar 1994). That anthropology's archetypal "home" (the dominant, majority culture of the contemporary United States) is still considered only a poor approximation of "the field" is shown perhaps most clearly by the fact that when job advertisements offer a position for a "North Americanist," what is called for is nearly always a specialist on ethnic and racial minorities, most often on those who occupy a special place in white North American "imperialist nostalgia" (Rosaldo 1989b), namely Native Americans.[21]

A very large number of anthropologists, of course, do work in the United States, and by no means all of them focus on Native Americans or minorities. Yet working in the United States has long had a low status in the field, and even a certain stigma attached to it. Exotic fieldwork, Kuklick points out (chapter 2), has been a "gatekeeper" in Anglo-American anthropology. Since it requires external funding, not everyone can do it, and those who can are therefore marked as a select group. Indeed, one of us was actually told in graduate school that fieldwork in the United States was "for people who don't get grants." Such prejudices may have diminished in recent years, but they have hardly disappeared. The fact that today more high-status American anthropologists (the ones who *do* get the grants) are working "at home" is significant, but it should also be noted that they are mostly anthropologists whose careers are already established and who take on second field sites closer to home (a pattern often remarked to fit well with considerations both of tenure and of child rearing). It remains extremely difficult for students who do their dissertation fieldwork entirely within the United States to get jobs at top departments. A quick survey of ten top American departments of anthropology reveals only 8 anthropologists (out of a total of 189) who claim a primary specialization in the nonnative United States. Only 1 of these 8 had received a Ph.D. within the last fifteen years.[22] (See also the personal testimony of Passaro and Weston in chapters 8 and 9.)

In pointing out the existence of such a hierarchy of field sites, we do not mean to suggest that anthropologists ought to give up working "abroad," or that the only fieldwork worth doing is "at home." On the contrary, many of the reasons that have led anthropologists to leave their homes for faraway field sites seem to us excellent ones. If nothing else, the anthropological insistence that "out of the way places" matter (Tsing 1993, 1994b) has done much to counter the Eurocentric and parochial understandings of culture and society that dominate most Western universities. What we object to is not the leaving of "home," but the uncritical mapping of "difference" onto exotic sites (as if "home," however defined, were not also a site of difference [cf. chapters 8 through 10; cf. also Greenhouse 1985]) as well as the implicit presumption that "Otherness" means difference from an unmarked, white Western "self" (which has the effect of constructing the anthropologist as a very particular sort of subject, as we discuss below). The issue, then, is not whether anthropologists should work "abroad" or "at home," but precisely the radical separation between the two that is taken for granted as much by those who would insist that anthropology remain "at home" as by those who would restrict its mission to fieldwork "abroad."

Fieldwork-Based Knowledge

A second consequence of anthropology's emphasis on "the field" is that it enables certain forms of knowledge, but blocks off others. With the idea that knowledge derived from experience in "the field" is privileged comes a fore-grounding of face-to-face relations of community, while other, less localized relations disappear from view (see Thomas 1991). Ethnographic knowledge is heavily dependent on the presence and experience of the fieldworker. More than any other discipline, the truths of anthropology are grounded in the experience of the participant observer. This experience yields much that is valuable, but also severely circumscribes the knowledge obtained. Why, for instance, has there been so little anthropological work on the translocal aspects of transnational corporations and multilateral institutions (cf. Nash 1979; Ghosh 1994)? Why are there so few ethnographic treatments of the mass media?[23] More generally, why do translocal phenomena of various kinds evade classical methods of participant observation?

Though anthropologists often picture themselves as specialists in "the local," we suggest that the idea of locality in anthropology is not well thought out. Clearly geographical contiguity and boundedness are insufficient to define a "local community"; otherwise, high-rise buildings in urban metropolises would automatically qualify, and office-dwellers crammed together for large parts of the day would constitute ideal subjects for fieldwork. That we don't readily think of these "localities" as field sites should give us pause. Is the idea of the local a way of smuggling back in assumptions about small-scale societies and face-to-face communities that we thought we had left behind? Why is it that, for example, local politics is so anthropological, whereas national or international politics is not ("natives" as political actors are rarely described in terms that would situate them within a political world we share —"left-wing," "rightist," or "Social Democrat")?[24] Similarly, the household economy has long been considered eminently anthropological, but the study of labor unions or international finance much less so. One can, of course, use a "local" site to study a "nonlocal" phenomenon. But what makes a site "local" in the first place? In an oft-cited passage, Geertz has pointed out that "Anthropologists don't study villages (tribes, towns, neighborhoods . . .); they study *in* villages" (1973a: 22). But what remains unasked, conspicuously, is *why* we study "in villages" in the first place.[25]

As with field sites, then, there is clearly also a hierarchy of topics or objects of study, ranked according to their anthropological-ness. Things that are unfamiliar, "different," and "local" (read: not like at home) become defined as suitable anthropological objects, whereas phenomena and objects that are similar to "home" or already in some way familiar are deemed to be less worthy of ethnographic scrutiny. Thus an account of an indigenous ritual, especially if it is strange, exotic, and colorful, is almost automatically "anthropological," and eminently suited to publication in a leading anthropological journal; television viewing, meanwhile, has remained until recently largely terra incognita for anthropology.[26] Even if one were to accept the problematic idea that anthropology's mission is that of "cultural critique," the topics that are deemed suitably "anthropological" already circumscribe the form and scope of that critique.

The Fieldworker as Anthropological Subject

We now turn to the third of our themes, the construction of an archetypal fieldworker and the consequent ordering of the identities of ethnographers. Anthropologists often speak, sometimes half-jokingly, of fieldwork as a "rite of passage," a ritual of initiation into a mature professional identity. We suggest that it would be useful to take this formulation seriously, instead of allowing it to pass as a joke, by asking precisely what kind of a social being such a ritual of initiation produces. If a heroized journey into Otherness is indeed a rite of passage, what sort of subject might we expect to be formed by such a rite?

We have seen that ideas about Otherness remain remarkably central to the fieldwork ritual. But any conception of an Other, of course, has implications for the identity of the self. We will argue that even in an era when significant numbers of women, minorities, and Third World scholars have entered the discipline, the self that is implied in the central anthropological ritual of encountering "the Other" in the field remains that of a Euro-American, white, middle-class male. We will demonstrate how this unmarked category is constructed through an examination of disciplinary practices that endow certain kinds of research questions, methods, and textual production with "excellence."

The rhetoric of meritocracy, with its powerful roots in capitalist ideology and the competitive conditions of academic production, and its seeming objectivity, appears to be socially neutral in the sense that it does not automatically privilege certain groups of people. Who wouldn't agree with the goal of hiring the best scholars, rewarding the best researchers, and training students so that they become the best anthropologists? The problem is, of course, that there is no neutral grid through which such judgments can be made.[27] The hierarchy of field sites noted above assigns positions based on degrees of Otherness. But Otherness from whom? Is Africa more Other than Europe for a Third World anthropologist? For an African American? For whom are minority populations in the United States more worthy anthropological objects? The hierarchy of field sites privileges those places most Other for Euro-Americans and those that stand most clearly opposed to a middle-class self. Similarly, the notion of going to "the field" from which one returns "home" becomes problematic for those minorities, postcolonials, and "halfies"[28] for whom the anthropological project is *not* an exploration of Otherness. Such people often find themselves in a double bind: some anthropologists regard them with suspicion, as people who lack the distance necessary to conduct good fieldwork; on the other hand, well-intentioned colleagues thrust on them the responsibility of speaking their identity, thus inadvertently forcing them into the prison-house of essentialism (cf. chapter 9).

Amory (chapter 5) shows how ideas about Otherness, and the taking for granted of an unmarked, white subject, have helped to shape the field of African studies in the United States, and to produce a durable division between it and Afro-American studies. She shows that African American scholars were discouraged from working in Africa, on the grounds that they were "too close" and would not manage to be "objective," while white scholars were judged to have the appropriate distance from the black "Other." This helps to explain the fact that the contemporary field of African studies (like the field of anthropology itself) contains remarkably few black American scholars.[29] Unexamined assumptions about Otherness that came along with the idea of "a good field site" thus turned out to be racially exclusionary.

Likewise, the implicit standard against which "good fieldwork" often continues to be judged is highly gendered. The archetypal ideal of the lone, manly anthropologist out in the bush, far away from the creature comforts of First World life, derives, as Kuklick notes, from Romantic notions of (implicitly masculine) personal growth through travel to unfamiliar places and endurance of physical hardship (chapter 2). To be sure, women as well as men have over the years credentialed themselves—and even become powerful figures in the discipline—through the fieldwork rite of passage, and anthropology has historically been less closed to women than many other disciplines. Indeed, a certain romantic image of the female anthropologist seems to have a fairly prominent place in the American public imagination (probably due largely to the celebrity of primatologists such as Jane Goodall and Diane Fossey—though it is worth remembering that Margaret Mead was also a highly visible and influential public figure in her time). But it is no slight to the achievements of such women to say that they established themselves as "real anthropologists" only by beating the boys at their own (fieldwork) game. Many other women were not so lucky; historically, a very high proportion of women trained in anthropology have failed to secure institutional positions appropriate to their training (Behar and Gordon 1995).

Passaro (chapter 8) suggests that the image of field research as heroic adventure or quest remains with us today in the widespread, if often implicit, expectation that authentic fieldwork ought to involve physical hardship and even danger. Such expectations are far from neutral in gender terms.[30] For example, young women are discouraged from attempting "difficult" rural fieldwork in some areas of North India, because of the ever-present threat of rape and sexual violence; later, in the Western academy, their failure to spend long periods in rural areas where the "real" India lives is construed to show the absence of "good fieldwork"—a question of merit, not gender discrimination.

Similarly, the notion that field sites should be selected solely for disinterested scholarly reasons continues to be highly influential. Although it is widely recognized that this is not how most of us choose our field sites, the vocabulary of justification employed in grant proposals, books, and research reports requires that such choices be cast in terms of the theoretical problems that the research site was especially suited to think about. Such a view privileges those who have no compelling reason to work in particular localities or with particular communities other than intellectual interest. For those interested in working with their "own" communities, engaged in activist organizing, or responsible for supporting financially strapped, extended families, exoticism has no inherent value. Leaving their commitments and responsibilities for the sake of untethered "research interests" is for many anthropologists a Faustian bargain, a betrayal of those people whose lives and livelihoods are inextricably linked to their own. Once again, what pass for universal, meritocratic norms end up supporting a particular structural and ideological location, one occupied most often by white, middle-class men.[31] In this context, we might understand the recent figures showing that, as of the 1992–1993 academic year, fully 90 percent of all full-time anthropology faculty in the United States were white, and 70 percent were male (American Anthropological Association 1994: 288, 291).

We do not want to be misunderstood as suggesting that an academic discipline can or should attempt to do without standards of excellence. Our point is only that the social and political implications that any such standards must contain ought to be made explicit and open to debate and negotiation. The alternative to evaluating anthropologists according to prevailing norms of fieldwork is not to forgo all evaluation (which would be neither possible nor desirable), but to develop different and better-justified criteria of evaluation, based on a different conception of what should count as "good work" in anthropology. Where might such a conception come from, and how might it be legitimated? It is with such questions in mind that we briefly survey some alternative traditions of "field" and "fieldwork" on which it might be possible to draw.

IV. HETERODOXIES AND HEGEMONIES:
ALTERNATIVE TRADITIONS OF "FIELD" AND "FIELDWORK"

Thus far, we have emphasized the constitutive role of a certain dominant tradition of "the field" (what we have called the Malinowskian tradition) in shaping the bounds of anthropology and defining what sorts of work will be permitted within that disciplinary space. What we have left unmentioned in tracing the dominant Malinowskian orthodoxy and its effects are the various heterodox practices of "field" and "fieldwork" that have existed in different ways both within and, as it were, adjacent to the constituted field of anthropology. Lacking the space to explore this issue in depth, we will simply point to, and give brief examples of, three different kinds of heterodoxy. First, we will discuss the diversity of actual practices and conceptions of "the field" submerged in the history of the dominant Anglo-American stream of anthropology. Second, we will briefly address the heterodoxy of practices of "the field" in various national and geographical sites that lie at some distance from anthropology's hegemonic geopolitical "core" (i.e., national traditions other than those in the U.S., U.K., and France, and the issue of "Third World" anthropologies). Finally, we will consider the way that anthropological practices of "the field" have maintained their distinctiveness in relation to "fieldwork-like" practices in other genres of representation, such as folklore and ethnic studies, realist novels of experience, and "insider ethnography." By pointing to the existence of such heterogeneity, we hope both to complicate our so-far oversimple picture of anthropology's practices and conventions of "the field," and to suggest that it may be possible to draw on such heterodoxies as resources for the disciplinary rethinking that, as we argue in Part V, is both urgently needed and already well under way.[32]

Hidden Heterodoxies: Rereading Anglo-American Anthropology

In the usual renditions of the history of anthropology, the triumph of the Malinowskian fieldwork revolution is set against a backdrop of theoretical and methodological darkness called "diffusionism." Students are rarely called upon to *read* any of the early twentieth-century diffusionists, but are often treated to derogatory accounts of the "hyper-diffusionism" of such figures as Grafton Elliot Smith and William Perry, whose "speculative" schemes, "conjectural" history, and lack of "real" fieldwork experience are used as foils against which to set the Malinowskian achievement.

Joan Vincent (1990, 1991) has recently developed a provocative argument that diffusionism's poor reputation is largely undeserved, and that many of anthropology's later failings may be traced to the turn that led away from key questions of history and culture contact in the early decades of the century. The "fieldwork revolution," in this view, was a mixed blessing. To be sure, it brought certain objects into view, and established an empirical basis for a certain kind of anthropological inquiry. But at the same time, it shifted attention away from some of the crucial issues with which diffusionists had been most concerned.[33]

While Malinowski, for instance, was constructing an image of the Trobriands as an isolated and self-contained natural laboratory, the diffusionist Rivers was conspicuously concerned with just the thing that Malinowski seemed to be (until late in his career) so determined to ignore: the "rapid and destructive change" that the new imperialisms were inflicting on the peoples of Melanesia and elsewhere (Vincent 1990: 120). Rivers's edited work *Essays on the Depopulation of Melanesia* (1922) was meant to document such effects of "culture contact" as "blackbirding," the abusive form of labor recruitment in which some 100,000 Pacific Islanders were removed and forced to work as indentured plantation laborers (Vincent 1990: 120, 122, 198). According to Vincent (1991: 54), for a historically oriented scholar such as Wheeler, diffusionism meant not wild speculative schemes, but "an ethnology that was historical, that dealt with complex as well as primitive societies and that recognized culture contact, movement, and change." Even the much-abused arch-diffusionist Elliot Smith seems, from the vantage point of the 1990s, surprisingly ahead of his time, since (as Elkin put it) he "saw the whole civilized world as one Oikoumene (using Kroeber's term), of which diffusion, or the interpenetration of culture traits and complexes, was the means of ensuring continuity in space and time" (cited in Vincent 1990: 123). Given such interests, it is only natural that Elliot Smith should have been wary of the narrowing scope implied by "the fieldwork revolution," irreverently demanding to know why "the sole method of studying mankind is to sit on a Melanesian island for a couple of years and listen to the gossip of the villagers" (cited in Stocking 1992a: 58).

No doubt, the virtues of Edwardian diffusionism can be exaggerated, and Vincent may be stretching a point when she claims for diffusionist theory a "latent function in countering the dehistoricization of a dominated people" (1990: 123). But, whatever its faults, diffusionism did show an interest in larger political and economic contexts and dynamic historical sequences that would be rediscovered much later. And Vincent is surely right to insist that it was not only functionalism as a theory, but fieldwork as a hegemonic method, that helped to drive such questions out of the anthropological mainstream for so many years. As she points out in showing how the British methodology handbook *Notes and Queries* constructed the domain of "politics" on the eve of the "fieldwork revolution," "the *method* of study—close and prolonged observation—was beginning to shape the *field* of study; the closed system was in the making" (Vincent 1990: 116).

The Boasian tradition in the United States had a significantly different orientation, and the emphasis on culture history and the collection of texts and text-analogues gave early twentieth-century American anthropology a relationship to "the field" that was initially quite different from the British natural history approach. Boas himself conceived of the anthropological task less in terms of observing functioning societies, and more as a matter of compiling documentation for disappearing cultures, with the aim both of reconstructing histories of migration and diffusion and of assembling an archive of primary materials so that the indigenous cultures of the Americas might live on in libraries and museums, much as the ancient and premodern cultures of Europe did (Stocking 1992a: 62–63). While there is much to object to in this paradigm (not least the fatalistic indifference to the contemporary struggles and predicaments of actually existing Native Americans [cf. Stocking 1992a: 163]), it is also worth noting that this approach implied a healthy skepticism about the idea of encountering intact, observable "primitive societies" that could be holistically described through the direct experience of participant observation. Methodologically, Boasian "salvage anthropology" was eclectic, combining firsthand interviews and observations with the analysis of historical texts, folklore, archaeological materials, oral history, and the recollections and expert knowledge of key informants.

As American anthropology outgrew its "salvage" phase, two different paths seem to have been available. One was to adopt the Malinowskian model of direct observation of contemporary (and exotic) "primitive societies." Here, the highly visible figure of Margaret Mead in her pioneering work in Samoa and New Guinea marked a major turn away from the historicist concerns of early Boasian anthropology and toward a model of fieldwork that converged with British practice.[34] The other, less celebrated path did not lead out from the United States to new, "primitive" sites abroad, but out from the Indian reservation and into the larger American society, via the question of "acculturation."

Like diffusionism, acculturation studies involved the blurring of "here" and "there," and challenged the idea of a clearly demarcated space of Otherness. Acculturation was the domain of "creole" cultures, of what Sidney Mintz (1970: 14) once described (speaking of the Afro-American diaspora) as "not the things anthropologists' dreams are made of":

> Houses constructed of old Coca-Cola signs, a cuisine littered with canned corned beef and imported Spanish olives, ritual shot through with the cross and the palm leaf, languages seemingly pasted together with "ungrammatical" Indo-European usages, all observed within the reach of radio and television.

Like diffusionism, acculturation studies have long suffered from a bad reputation within the discipline. In the 1930s, the editor of the *American Anthropologist* even opined that acculturation studies were not in fact anthropology at all, belonging instead in political science (Vincent 1990: 198; Spicer 1968: 22). Even today, the very word *acculturation* is likely to elicit yawns (if not shudders) from contemporary anthropologists trained to critique the functionalist, depoliticized acculturation studies of the 1950s and 1960s (cf. Spicer 1968).[35] Yet much of the early work on acculturation was an attempt to bring anthropology to bear on contemporary domestic social problems and to engage anthropological expertise with political issues such as racism and immigration (Vincent 1990: 197–222). Indeed, Vincent goes so far as to claim early acculturation theory as part of a "subterranean trend within the discipline" that "contained, albeit implicitly, [an] attack on racial domination, imperialism, and monopoly capitalism" (1990: 222). This may overstate the case. But given anthropology's current theoretical problems and political commitments, it is far from clear that this is an area of the disciplinary history that ought to be despised or ignored. Indeed, at least some of the heterodox forms of anthropology that flourished in the problem-oriented work of the 1930s and 1940s would seem to be of considerable contemporary relevance.[36]

The Depression, of course, put domestic poverty and social issues on the anthropological map. Anthropologists were led to study not only minority groups and questions of "assimilation" and "culture clash," but also aspects of "mainstream America" that had conventionally been considered to lie beyond the bounds of the discipline. Thus Walter Goldschmidt, for example, originally trained as a Native Americanist in the Boasian tradition, shifted his attention to agribusiness and changing class structure in a California farming town (Goldschmidt 1947). Other anthropologists were similarly inspired to apply anthropology to domestic social problems by new social programs such as the Works Progress Administration, which funded a wide range of social research with the twin aims of creating a base of knowledge to support "New Deal"–style social reforms, and creating research projects in which the unemployed could be given jobs. A full study of the impact of such programs on anthropological practice has yet to be completed. But it is clear that this form of anthropological intervention did involve some significant heterodoxy, not only in the selection of research topics, but (our particular concern here) in practices of "the field."

One example of such heterodoxy is Paul Radin's ethnography *The Italians of San Francisco: Their Adjustment and Acculturation* (Radin 1970 [1935]).[37] First published in 1935, in the midst of the Depression, this project is a vivid illustration of a road not taken in mainstream American anthropology. The study is unconventional in a number of ways, perhaps most notably in its explicit left politics, its strong commitment to a historical account, and its concern to present the voices and life stories of informants. Indeed, the text reads in some ways more like a leftist social history from the 1960s than a Boasian ethnography of the 1930s. But Radin's study is of special interest to us here for its heterodox experimentation with "field methods." Radin, a student of Boas's and friend of Sapir's, was one of the most meticulous of the Boasian fieldworkers.[38] But this was a large-scale study, requiring large numbers of investigators, instead of the usual lone anthropologist. What is more, since this was an employment project, "the investigators had to be taken from the county relief rolls" (1970: 5). Much as Malinowski had once made a virtue of necessity by treating his imposed lengthy isolation on the Trobriands as a methodological breakthrough, Radin (1970: 5–6) explains:

> The limitations thus imposed, far from militating against the accuracy of the information, actually increased it, for academically and professionally quali-fied observers are often the worst people to send out to secure sociological ma-terial. Their very training erects an undesirable barrier between themselves and the persons to be interrogated and this barrier is increased by the fact that they have frequently no experience in establishing contacts with strangers.

Here, Radin directly contradicts the most sacred premise of a newly profes-sionalized anthropology, the premise that only professionally trained ob-servers could be trusted to collect ethnographic data. On the contrary, Radin claims, intellectually elite and socially aloof Ph.D.s, by virtue of their social distance, made very poor interviewers of working-class Italians, while many of his unemployed research assistants were much better qualified:

> The essential qualification for an observer is that he possess the gift for es-tablishing a direct and immediate contact with his source of information in as unobtrusive as possible a manner. The persons almost ideally adapted for bring-ing about such a relation are salesmen and business solicitors such as insur-ance agents, real estate agents, etc. (1970: 6)

The anthropological heresy is complete: the real secret of ethnographic rap-port is to have the fieldwork done by unemployed insurance salesmen and real estate agents! One could hardly ask for a more vivid illustration of the point that conventions of fieldwork are shaped not simply by intrinsic methodological merits, but by the institutional conditions of intellectual pro-duction.

It is easy enough to laugh at the image of the insurance salesman as wel-fare-fieldworker. But the issues raised by Radin's heterodoxy are serious ones. After all, how many of the "lone anthropologists" doing fieldwork in "other cultures" have actually worked alone? What does the heavy reliance of so many ethnographers on "native" research assistants do to our conceits about the intrinsic virtues of the "professionally trained observer"? Radin's strategy neatly reverses the hard-won Malinowskian/Boasian dogma that only people with university degrees in anthropology can really get the facts right. Radin argues, plausibly enough, that such professionals are socially separated from those they would understand by their very training, and that local intellectuals or specialists may be better positioned, at least for certain sorts of data collection.

How different might anthropology look today if the academic mainstream had accepted Radin's argument that inexperienced and often socially awkward First World graduate students are not necessarily the best of all possible observers? What different ways of theorizing the relation between professional researcher and local expert might have been developed? What relevance might this have for the contemporary anthropological task of forging new and less colonial modes of engagement between anthropologists and the intellectuals who inhabit the societies they study?[39] There may well lie some questions worth going back to in the forgotten corners of the history of heterodox anthropological fieldwork.

Another form of heterodoxy, of course, appeared in the 1960s and early 1970s, with the rise of a host of politically engaged challenges to anthropology-as-usual (e.g., Hymes 1972; Gough 1967, 1968; Asad, ed., 1973; Tax 1975; Huizer and Mannheim 1979). In some cases, it seems to us, the political radicalism of such projects was hindered by a conventional conception of the relation of anthropologist to "the field"; thus, the programs of "action anthropology" (cf. Tax 1975) too often tended to assume a white, middle-class anthropologist who would go "there," into "the field," and be a catalyst, organizer, or broker for "the local people." As we will suggest in Part V, a questioning of the neat separation of "here" and "there," "home" and "field," can suggest other, more complex models of political engagement.

But it is also striking that many of the critics of the 1960s and early 1970s did call into question not only the usual anthropological focus on the "Other," the different and the exotic (what Mintz [cited in Hymes 1972: 30] called the "preoccupation with purity"), but also at least some of the taken-for-granted conventions of "field" and "fieldwork" (e.g., Hymes 1972: 32; Willis 1972: 148). Yet while the political challenges of the 1960s radicals provoked a vigorous disciplinary discussion of anthropology's political commitments, its relations to imperialism and colonialism, the possibility of a Marxist anthropology, and so on, the received ideas of field and fieldwork remained mostly above the fray.

For many who worked in this vein, to be sure, the anthropological world of "peoples and cultures" was reconceptualized as an interconnected capitalist world system characterized by relations of exploitation. With such a perspective, one might aim to study not this or that isolated, traditional society, but such things as the impact of multinational capital on this or that community, or the articulation of local production systems with migrant labor or cash cropping. But that an anthropological dissertation would normally involve an ethnographic study of a *local community* (however "linked" it might be with a wider system), and that such a study would make use of the usual fieldwork methodology (stereotypically, "twelve months in a village"), appropriately supplemented with historical "background," remained the common sense of the discipline.[40]

This development, the ultimate triumph of a version of the hegemonic "Malinowskian" practice of "the field," brings our discussion back to where we began. For it is necessary to remember that the heterodoxies we have briefly sketched here, however interesting or provocative, remained heterodox; ultimately, all were marginalized and contained. We have revisited them here with the aim less of rewriting the anthropological past than of rereading it—combing our disciplinary history for resources that might contribute to a "reinvention" of the fieldwork tradition. It should be clear that we are not advocating the wholesale adoption of any of the various heterodox fieldwork practices we have discussed—neither a return to Edwardian diffusionism nor a resurrection of WPA anthropology is what we have in mind. Our aim is not to propose a single alternative to the conventional image of "the field," but only to denaturalize the Malinowskian model, and to rediscover it—not as the necessary methodological foundation of all anthropology, but as one methodological possibility that, in its striking academic-political success, has allowed us to forget the existence, within our own disciplinary history, of alternatives.

From the Margins: Alternative Regional and National Traditions of Field and Fieldwork

In his recent memoir *After the Fact* (1995), Clifford Geertz, whose reputation as a fieldworker has attained near-mythic proportions, provides a vivid description of his first fieldwork experience. After experiencing the normal graduate student anxiety over the choice of a fieldsite ("Where was our Trobriands, our Nuerland, our Tepoztlan to be?" [1995: 101–102]), he was recruited quite "accidentally" to be part of a multidisciplinary nine-member team led by a professor in Harvard's Social Relations Department. Their destination was Java, where they were to be paired with counterparts from an Indonesian university.

The three professors directing the project on the Indonesian side wanted to use the opportunity to train some of their own students to do anthropological research. According to Geertz, the Indonesians had the "unworkable" idea, learned from the Dutch, that field research might be conducted out of an old Dutch resort hotel, calling people in from the countryside to be interviewed in groups and asking them questions from a prepared schedule of topics. "It would be hard to conceive an image of social research more entirely opposed to our notions," Geertz observes, ". . . than this extraordinary reincarnation of the pith-helmet procedures of colonial ethnology" (1995: 105). "Caught between academic mentalities, one ambitious, confident, and ultramodern, one nostalgic, defensive, and obsolescent" (1995: 105–106), the Americans sought to evade the demands of their hosts, given their "conviction that what [they] wanted to do demanded free, intimate, and long-term relations with those [they] were studying, isolated from external oversight and the attentions of the state," a "maximally uncontrolled situation: the Trobriands in Java" (1995: 106). In the end, the Indonesians yielded (though not before the minister of culture had delivered "a three hour harangue about arrogance, faithlessness, and the fact that the world was changing and whites had damn better realize it" [1995: 108]), and the Americans were able to settle into a "local community" favorably situated "much too far for anyone to commute, much too rustic for anyone to want to" (1995: 107). The anthropologists, now free from both supervision and the need to collaborate, were left alone at last: "here, finally, was 'the field'" (1995: 109).

What this extraordinary account makes clear is that the chief division between the Indonesians and the Americans lay less in their theoretical orientation than in their conceptions of what constituted "the field" and how one was to go about doing fieldwork. Instead of responding to their hosts' expressed desire to train students and work collaboratively, the Americans reacted in horror to field methods different from their own, dismissing them as leftovers of colonial ethnology. It is easy to agree with Geertz that the Indonesians' proposed approach might not be the best way to build the rapport, trust, and informal understanding that conventional Malinowskian fieldwork at its best can create. And there are indeed often compelling reasons for anthropologists to wish to speak to their informants informally, alone, and in confidence—and, indeed, to seek to evade "the attentions of the state." But there remains a certain irony in the dismissal of a methodological proposal that included nationalist demands for student training and local collaboration as "pith-helmet procedures of colonial ethnography," particularly when we bear in mind the baldly neocolonial relations that allowed a team of Ford Foundation–funded American graduate students to descend upon the newly independent nation of Indonesia in 1951 and proceed to disregard completely the conditions of research that had been set by local academics. As Geertz makes clear, the Americans sought "free, intimate, and long-term relations" not with Indonesian scholars, but with Indonesian natives; thus the U.S. team sought to break away from their "hosts" as quickly and completely as possible. In this way, the Americans attained the archetypal anthropological "field"—a space of freedom in which they might study the natives in an environment undisturbed by the presence of educated, urban Javanese.

Our point is not to find fault with Geertz's conduct in this episode. On the contrary, our analysis leads us to regard with some sympathy the discomfort and distress of a U.S.-trained anthropology graduate student denied the right to do "fieldwork" in the recognizable Malinowskian fashion. As we have insisted, on such points are careers made and broken. And nothing we have said is meant to detract from Geertz's justly celebrated achievements as a fieldworker. Indeed, we believe that Geertz, in the incident described, did only what any good fieldworker of the time would have done. Our interest in his case lies in the fact that he has given us an unusually explicit description of what being a "good fieldworker" entailed: namely, constructing "a good field." It is here that his account is so telling, for it allows us to see with special clarity how a certain dominant practice of "the field" asserted itself, and to what effect. Faced with a situation that might have led to an interrogation of their methods, and even to constructive and creative ways to bridge the gap that separated them from their Indonesian counterparts, the American scholars could only react with disbelief at the "nostalgic, defensive, and obsolescent" views of their hosts. It is important for the purposes of our argument to note that it was differences of field methods, and not of theories and subject matter, that in this instance most firmly divided the American ethnographers from their Indonesian counterparts. For all the anthropological devotion to the understanding of difference, this was one difference that proved insurmountable.

As this episode suggests, a detailed study of regional "anthropologies" could contribute much to understanding the different ways in which "the field" has been constituted, and instituted, in diverse locations. In most standard accounts of the history of anthropological theory, the canonical narrative examines the relationship between national traditions of anthropology only in the United States, Britain, and France. Other national traditions are marginalized by the workings of geopolitical hegemony, experienced as a naturalized common sense of academic "center" and "periphery." Anthropologists working at the "center" learn quickly that they can ignore what is done in peripheral sites at little or no professional cost, while any peripheral anthropologist who similarly ignores the "center" puts his or her professional competence at issue ("They're so out of it, they haven't even heard of x").[41]

If a diversity of practices and conventions of "field" and "fieldwork" exists in such "peripheries," as we suspect, there might be much to learn from comparing the different fields of knowledge that such different practices and conventions open up. Most anthropologists working in the U.S. or U.K. (and we include ourselves here) know very little about the history of anthropology (and such related fields as ethnology and folklore), even in such strong and long-established "national" traditions as those of Mexico, Brazil, Germany, Russia, or India. We do not propose (nor do we consider ourselves qualified) to discuss these traditions in any depth here. And it is no doubt misleading to imagine discrete and autonomous "national" traditions in an academic world structured around the global hegemony of a North Atlantic center, which often does give the universities of the periphery and semiperiphery a derivative character.[42] But it seems clear that, in spite of homogenizing tendencies rooted in colonial and neocolonial histories, practices of "the field" and definitions of the discipline are indeed significantly different away from the hegemonic centers of intellectual production.

Asked about his experiences in Mexico, the United States, and France, the Brazilian anthropologist Cardoso de Oliveira (Correa 1991) spoke enthusiastically about his intellectual exchanges with his Mexican colleagues in contrast to his description of the wonderful *facilities* for research at Harvard and Paris. Apparently, the situation in which Brazilian anthropologists found themselves doing "fieldwork" in their own country had more in common with the problems and dilemmas faced by Mexican anthropologists than those anthropologists located in First World institutions. At a time when British and American theories of ethnicity were emphasizing more depoliticized conceptions of "social change" and "acculturation" respectively, Cardoso de Oliveira was developing his theories of "interethnic friction," which were in turn influenced by Rodolfo Stavenhagen's important theories of "internal colonialism" in Mexico (Correa 1991: 340; de Alcantara 1984: 113–116).[43] In like manner a generation earlier, Fernando Ortiz had found that, in writing from and about Cuba, it was useful to replace the concept of "acculturation" with a notion of "transculturation" to capture the "counterpoint" through which change occurred not simply "in a culture," but between and across interconnected cultures. Ortiz's "field" was not a bounded localized community, but (in a conception that foreshadows both Mintz 1985 and Gilroy 1993) a multistranded transatlantic traffic of commodities, people, and ideas that shaped a Cuban experience conceived as a "history of . . . intermeshed transculturations" (Ortiz 1995: 98; cf. Coronil 1995).

The regional heterogeneity of "anthropology," then, is not only a matter of diverging politics and histories, of different divisions of academic labor and distinctive institutional configurations. It is also, and at the same time, a matter of different conventions and practices of the field, with corresponding implications for the way anthropology is constituted and bounded as a discipline. In central and eastern Europe, for example, ethnography comes out of a tradition of national ethnology and folklore studies, and fieldwork is focused on the rural and "folk" cultures of the ethnographer's own society. "The field" is therefore always nearby and easy to visit; researchers spend a few weeks in rural areas collecting data and then come back to analyze them. Institutions are neither set up to grant research leaves of one year or more, nor are there funding agencies to support such "fieldwork." Furthermore, there is no assumption that after researchers return from "the field," their contacts with subjects will cease (Hofer 1968; Halpern and Ham-

mel 1969; Jakubowska 1993). In many African universities, meanwhile, anthropology departments are nonexistent (thanks largely to the discipline's
"colonialist" reputation), and anthropological research must be done (if at
all) in affiliation with sociology, history, or economics departments, or in the
guise of studying oral literature, or through externally funded development
projects. In each case, anthropologists are obliged to come to terms with different norms and expectations about what kind of fieldwork is appropriate,
how long it may last, and what sort of team organization, use of assistants,
and so on are required.

In pointing to the existence of such diversity in fieldwork traditions, we
are not advocating that North American anthropologists simply ought to
adopt the fieldwork conventions of other national or regional practices of
anthropology. Indeed, we would agree that there are often compelling reasons not to do so.[44] The point is not to valorize blindly such nondominant
fieldwork traditions, but only to suggest that our discipline's much vaunted
respect for cultural "difference" should include the recognition that anthropological methods that differ from one's own are not inherently suspect
or inferior. Instead of decrying the "lack of professionalism" or "backward-
ness" of the discipline in other geographical contexts, we need to ask what
kinds of knowledges these other practices of "the field" make possible. For
those of us based in North American universities, what are our responsibilities when faced with practices of "the field" that are very different from our
own? Is the only appropriate response to flee from those differences in the
name of an "authentically anthropological" methodology, as Geertz's team
did in Java?[45] And, if not, what would it mean to arrive at a "re-formed"
method? Might such practical reworkings help bridge the rather conspicuous contemporary gap between our ambitious theoretical aspirations and
our remarkably unreconstructed methodological habits?

Other Genres, Other Fields?

By definition, the borders of the discipline constitute those spaces where the
hegemonic hold of canonical methods and disciplinary formations has been
the weakest. These borders are not merely geographic, but can be seen in
the heterogeneity of ethnographic representations that threaten to overrun
the well-policed boundaries of anthropology. We will not deal with those obvious suspects that anthropology struggled to distinguish itself from at the
beginning of the formation of the discipline, namely, travelogues, missionary reports, the narratives produced by colonial bureaucracies, and so forth.
Rather, we wish to highlight a congeries of practices and representions of
the field that interrupt the mutual constitution of the "field" as a specific
empirical practice and the "field" as a discipline.

Although we cannot pursue this topic in any detail here, we have relied heavily on some of the excellent research already done in order to draw attention to three of these borders: the disciplinary challenge posed by folklore, sociology, and ethnic studies; the questions posed by heterodox representations of fieldwork such as novels of the field, novels by "natives," and nonrealist ethnographies; and, finally, the difficulties raised by heterodox "fieldwork" such as "insider" ethnography, or the use in ethnography of observations derived from the experience of growing up in "a culture."[46]

Folklore's ambivalent status in American anthropology is institutionally visible in its occasional inclusion in anthropology departments, history or literature departments, and at times in a separate program. Whereas collecting "folklore" was an intrinsic part of the Boasian method, its status may have diminished as participant observation became the regnant method in anthropology: a narrative based on what one observed and experienced was more "direct" (hence closer to the truth?) than a narrative based on collected texts or stories. The marginal status of folklore was accentuated when it intersected sociology and that genre of research that we now label "ethnic studies," as is painfully evident from the low status accorded to the pioneering researches of Zora Neale Hurston during her lifetime, and the continuing neglect of scholars such as Americo Paredes in the teaching of the anthropological canon. Similarly, the ethnographic and ethnohistorical research of scholars such as W. E. B. Du Bois, C. L. R. James, and St. Clair Drake is rarely mentioned in the same breath as that of Boas, Radcliffe-Brown, and Malinowski (cf. chapter 5).[47] Is it merely coincidence that anthropology's boundaries against folklore, ethnic studies, and sociology are constructed in such a way that scholars of color so often fall outside the boundaries of what is considered to be "real" anthropology? This is one place in which the consequences of using largely implicit standards to determine what is appropriate "fieldwork," and who its implied subject is, are clearly evident.

A second border that threatens to undo the self-evident connections between the discipline, field methods, and subject-formation is that constituted by heterodox representations of fieldwork. There has already been a fair amount of interest in novels of the field, often written by those denied the institutional legitimacy accorded to archetypal male fieldworkers out in the bush—their wives. The ethnographic novel, however, has also been a preferred form of representation by those (mostly women) for whom academic positions were impossible to attain (Zora Neale Hurston, Ella Deloria), or by those who wanted to reach a wider, genuinely popular audience for their work (Behar and Gordon 1995; Visweswaran 1994; Lamphere 1992). Ethnography, as a genre of realist description, has always drawn inspiration from fiction (Malinowski, for example, boasted of his ambition to be "the Conrad of anthropology" and read voraciously in "the field"). Writing ethnography novelistically is considered acceptable, as long as it does not go "too far"; elegant writing is a virtue, but becoming "too literary" is a serious fault

(cf. Landes 1994 [1947]). But many anthropologists are uneasy about reading realist novels ethnographically (cf. Handler and Segal 1990). For our
purposes here, we will employ one example to help show the difficulties involved in maintaining this distinction.

Adwaita Mallabarman's *A River Called Titash* was originally published in
Bengali in 1956, and Kalpana Bardhan has recently (1993) translated it into
English. Mallabarman was born in 1914 of a Hindu fishing caste called the
Malos in what is now Bangladesh. He was the first person of his caste to receive a high school education, then went on to a career in literary magazines
and journalism. *A River Called Titash* is a loving recreation of the everyday
practices and rituals of the Malo community and the Malo way of life, which,
by the time the novel was completed in 1951, had been dismantled by the
conflicts surrounding the partition of the subcontinent a few years earlier.
The novel is a truly hybrid form, a curious mixture of ethnographic detail
and conventional narrative. Sections that might easily have been lifted from
a canonical ethnography are overlaid on a plot, much as the narrative fictions employed in ethnographies describe "a day in the life" of an ordinary
villager or a "typical" rendering of a ritual. The excessively lyrical descriptions of the river rival Malinowski's vivid sketches of the play of color in the
Trobriands (Stein 1995). Mallabarman was not trained as an anthropologist
and did not write the novel as an "alternative" version of "his people" to op-
pose representations created by anthropologists. Yet he too was engaged in
salvage ethnography by recording the Malo's lifeways, struggles, and rituals
at a time when the enormous political changes that swept the subcontinent
were destroying this existence. Novels such as *A River Called Titash* blur the
boundary between "novel" and "ethnography" (cf. Michaels 1994). If the call
to "decolonize" anthropology is to be taken seriously, why should we not jux-
tapose "natives'" representations of "themselves" and ethnographies written
by those serving the colonial government? In this spirit, it would make sense
to read *A River Called Titash* alongside a "professional" account written at that
time, such as Leach's *Political Systems of Highland Burma* (1954).

Mallabarman's novel helps us to challenge a third border, that which separates "fieldwork" from other forms of dwelling (cf. Clifford 1992, and chapter 10 of this book). Is growing up in "a culture" a heterodox form of "fieldwork"? Mallabarman obviously draws on the knowledge and experience
gained from living within a fishing community to paint a remarkably rich
picture of village life, with an accretion of the subtle detail so necessary for
"thick description" that could only have been acquired from a lifetime of
"fieldwork." "Insider" ethnography[48] most clearly challenges the unspoken
assumptions about what makes a site a "field" in anthropology. "Fieldwork"
is a form of dwelling that legitimizes knowledge production by the familiarity
that the fieldworker gains with the ways of life of a group of people. Unlike
travelers and tourists, the fieldworker has experience, obtained by staying a

long time, learning the language well, and participating in everyday life, which authorizes his or her discourse. Yet, paradoxically, if that experience is gained outside the institutional framework of a doctoral program in anthropology, it is consistently devalued. To argue that a "trained" observer is likely to "see" different things than an "untrained" observer is to state the obvious; yet, surely the claim that training enables certain things to come into light begs the question of what "training" might prevent one from seeing. A discipline in which "experience" is so central has been surprisingly unfriendly to the notion that "experience" is constantly reconfigured by memory. If an anthropologist can "write up" an ethnography based on data collected during doctoral fieldwork twenty or thirty years ago, why should it not be possible for "natives" to "write up" an ethnography based on their lives? In what sense might we think of one's "background"—growing up, as it were, in "the field"—as a kind of extended participant observation? In posing such questions, we do not mean to deny the evident differences between the two kinds of experience; we intend only to ask what the consequences are of treating such differences as both absolute and absolutely definitive of anthropology's disciplinary identity.

V. REINVENTING "THE FIELD": METHODOLOGY AND LOCATION

It is clear that anthropologists have in recent years been more and more inclined to depart from the conventions of archetypal fieldwork as they have taken on research projects not easily approached via the traditional model of immersion within a community (cf. chapter 10). Reflecting on their experiences of testing and even transgressing the disciplinary boundaries set by the expectations of "real fieldwork," several of the contributors to this book help point the way toward developing of new practices and conventions for the field. In this section, we will first briefly discuss how Weston, Passaro, Malkki, Des Chene, and Martin have contributed to a rethinking of field and fieldwork. We will then offer a general reformulation of the fieldwork tradition that we believe can preserve what is most vital and valuable in it, while not only leaving room for but properly valuing and legitimating the diverse and innovative new practices of the field that are evident in the contributions to this book and elsewhere.

Toward New Practices of the Field: Problems and Strategies

One of the most profound issues raised by recent work in anthropology is the question of the spatialization of difference. The unspoken premise that "home" is a place of cultural sameness and that difference is to be found "abroad" has long been part of the common sense of anthropology. Yet some of our contributors, drawing on recent work on gender and sexuality, begin their "fieldwork" with the opposite premise—that "home" is from the start a place of difference.

In chapter 9, Kath Weston points out that studying such "difference at home" as gay and lesbian communities in the United States profoundly unsettles anthropological sensibilities. Who is the native and who is the ethnographer when "queers study queers"? Trying to speak as a professionally qualified ethnographer of gays and lesbians, Weston finds that she is heard as a "native"—speaking for "her own people," maybe even "an advocate" (cf. Narayan 1993). As a "Native Ethnographer," she must alternate between "I, Native" and "I, Ethnographer," losing "the nuance of the two as they are bound up together," the hybridity of the Native Ethnographer positioning. The reason, of course, is that the position "Native Ethnographer" itself blurs the subject/object distinction on which ethnography is conventionally founded. Speaking from such a position, at least within the discipline as currently constituted, implies not simply exclusion, but something more complicated that Weston calls "virtuality": a condition in which one is an anthropologist, but not "a real anthropologist," in which one has done fieldwork, but not "real fieldwork." The virtual anthropologist, Weston argues, must always be the one who lacks an authentic Other—unless she speaks *as* an authentic Other, in which case she ceases to be an authentic *anthropologist*. Yet, significantly, Weston suggests that the very studies that are most suspect in these terms are the ones that "could complicate [the] dichotomy between Us and Them in useful ways"; the virtual anthropologist may be the one who can contribute most to "the thoroughgoing reevaluation of the anthropological project that an understanding of hybridity entails."

Joanne Passaro's research (chapter 8) among the homeless in New York City raises some related issues. Like Weston, she reports encountering skepticism that researching the lives of homeless, transient people in her "own" society could constitute "real fieldwork." Well-meaning advisors pressed her to adopt a nativizing community-study model ("That family shelter sounds fascinating. Why not stay there and do an ethnography of it?"), imagining a stable territorial community even for people defined in the first place by their mobility, marginality, and lack of any stable "home." Tellingly, Passaro reports, "I often felt that my various disciplinary interrogators would be happiest if I discovered some sort of secret communication system among homeless people like the codes of hoboes earlier in the century," in which case a suitable "subculture" would have been found in which one could immerse oneself! Yet Passaro resisted the temptation to construct "a homeless village," and developed instead an innovative, hybrid methodology that involved a number of "sites that would afford . . . positionalities at varying points along a participant-observer continuum." Combining different sites and styles of "fieldwork" with various kinds of volunteer and advocacy work provided a successful, if unorthodox, methodological strategy for an ethnographic study that ended up yielding powerful and surprising insights into the predicaments of homeless people (cf. Passaro 1996).

In chapter 4, Liisa Malkki discusses a different way in which the methodological demands of one's research may require a reconfiguring of "the field." Her research among Hutu refugees in Tanzania led her to question one aspect of the fieldwork tradition that is commonly celebrated as a great virtue—its emphasis on the ordinary, the everyday, and the routine. As she points out, such an emphasis tends to direct attention away from those things that the refugees she worked with cared about most—the extraordinary and exceptional events that had made refugees of them, and the atypical and transitory circumstances of their lives in a refugee camp. She observes that a division of labor between anthropology and journalism has made all big, extraordinary happenings into "stories" to be covered by journalists, while the durable, ordinary, everyday occurrences are to be found in "sites" suitable for long-term anthropological fieldwork. What would it mean, she asks, to direct an anthropological gaze on singular, exceptional, and extraordinary events? What sorts of fieldwork would be appropriate to studying the "communities of memory" formed in the aftermath of such events? A different sort of engagement than that of the usual "anthropological investigation" of a geographical "field site" might, she suggests, be warranted.

For Mary Des Chene in chapter 3, the issue is the relation between fieldwork and history, and the way knowledge gained through archival research is received and valued within anthropology. As she points out, historical material is widely valued in anthropology as a supplement to "real fieldwork," but considerable anxiety is provoked if it begins to take center stage. Des Chene asks how different the two modes of acquiring knowledge really are, skillfully distinguishing the real differences from the mythology that valorizes fieldwork-based knowledge as necessarily truer or less mediated than other types. She also confronts the question of how ethnographic methods can be adapted for studying spatially dispersed phenomena, raising the issue of multisite ethnography (cf. Marcus 1995; Hastrup and Olwig 1996).

Finally, in chapter 7, Emily Martin also takes up the question of social and cultural processes that are not well localized spatially. She points out that even many ethnographers of science have retained an idea of a "scientific community" as spatially bounded, to be examined through the traditional methods of the community study. The reaction of one such traditionalist to Martin's own multisite methods ("Don't you know how to stay put?") tells us that the localizing conventions of "the field" remain strong even in an area such as the ethnography of science, which one might expect to have traveled far from the Malinowskian archetype. But Martin insists that key developments in science are also occurring simultaneously elsewhere in society and that we need different models and metaphors than those provided by "the field" to grasp such changes. She proposes several new metaphors and shows how she used them in her own research, laying out a "tool kit" for exploring processes that occur neither in a single field site nor in some unlocated global space, but in many different spaces that are discontinuous from each other.

Retheorizing Fieldwork: From Spatial Sites to Political Locations

We begin our own efforts to rethink "the field" by building on recent critical reflections about how place has figured in anthropological conceptions of culture (cf. Gupta and Ferguson, eds., 1992, 1997; Appadurai 1988a). We have argued that the passage in and out of "the field" rests on the idea that different cultures inhere in discrete and separate places. Therefore, to go into "the field" is to travel to another place with its own distinctive culture, to live there is to enter another world, and to come back from "the field" is to leave that world and arrive in this one—the one in which the academy is located.[49] To challenge this picture of the world, one made up of discrete, originally separate cultures, is also to challenge the image of fieldwork as involving the movement in and out of "the field." "Where is the field?" D'Amico-Samuels (1991: 69) asks, when one studies gender, color, and class in Jamaica, writes about those experiences in New York, and participates in a seminar in Trinidad. "Which if any of these three experiences was fieldwork? Does fieldwork still carry the connotation of colonial geography—so that only activities in a Third World setting apply? . . . Do we think still of fieldwork in the archetype of the white-faced ethnographer in a sea of black or brown faces?" (1991: 72). Perhaps we should say that, in an interconnected world, we are never really "out of the field." Yet, if this is true, then what does change when anthropologists go from (usually) First World universities to various destinations around the world?

Ethnography's great strength has always been its explicit and well-developed sense of location, of being set here-and-not-elsewhere. This strength becomes a liability when notions of "here" and "elsewhere" are assumed to be features of geography, rather than sites constructed in fields of unequal power relations. But it is precisely this sense of location that is missing in a great deal of universalizing and positivist social science. Ethnography has always contained at least some recognition that knowledge is inevitably both "about somewhere" and "from somewhere," and that the knower's location and life experience are somehow central to the kind of knowledge produced. Yet, through the anthropological notion of "the field," this sense of location has too often been elided with locality, and a shift of location has been reduced to the idea of going "elsewhere" to look at "another society."

Taking as a point of departure the idea of "location" that has been developed in recent feminist scholarship,[50] we believe that it is possible to rethink the anthropological fieldwork tradition in quite a fundamental way, while preserving what we think are its real virtues. We wish to be clear that, however significant the problems with "the field" are, there remain many aspects of the fieldwork tradition that we continue to value—aspects that have allowed ethnographically oriented work in sociocultural anthropology (with all its faults) to serve as an extraordinarily useful corrective to the Eurocentrism and positivism that so often afflict the social sciences. We believe a well-developed attentiveness to location would preserve and build upon these aspects of the fieldwork tradition, which we will now discuss individually.

1. The fieldwork tradition counters Western ethnocentrism and values detailed and intimate knowledge of economically and politically marginalized places, peoples, histories, and social locations. Such marginalized locations enable critiques and resistances that would otherwise never be articulated (hooks 1990; Spivak 1988). Since anthropology departments continue to be among the few places in the Western academy not devoted exclusively or largely to the study of the lives and policies of elites, they constitute potentially important nodes for politically engaged intervention in many forms of symbolic and epistemic domination. We emphasize once again that our analysis of anthropology's "hierarchy of purity" of field sites is *not* meant to suggest that anthropologists should no longer work in far-flung and peripheral places—only that it is necessary to question the way that dominant conceptions and practices of "the field" have constructed such places. As Anna Tsing (1993) has recently demonstrated, by bringing marginality itself under the anthropological lens, instead of simply taking it for granted, it is possible to write about "out-of-the-way places" without distancing, romanticizing, or exoticizing them.

2. Fieldwork's stress on taken-for-granted social routines, informal knowledge, and embodied practices can yield understanding that cannot be obtained either through standardized social science research methods (e.g., surveys) or through decontextualized readings of cultural products (e.g., text-based criticism). One does not need to mystify or fetishize knowledge gained through long-term immersion in a social milieu to recognize its importance and value. Nor does one need to grant an unwarranted epistemological privilege to face-to-face interaction in order to appreciate the virtues of a research tradition that requires its practitioners to *listen* to those they would study, and to take seriously what they have to say.

3. Fieldwork reveals that a self-conscious shifting of social and geographical location can be an extraordinarily valuable methodology for understanding social and cultural life, both through the discovery of

phenomena that would otherwise remain invisible and through the acquisition of new perspectives on things we thought we already understood. Fieldwork, in this light, may be understood as a form of motivated and stylized dislocation. Rather than a set of labels that pins down one's identity and perspective, location becomes visible here as an ongoing project. As in coalition politics a location is not just something one ascriptively *has* (white middle-class male, Asian American woman, etc.)—it is something one strategically *works* at. We would emphasize, however, that (as in coalition politics) shifting location for its own sake has no special virtue. Instead, the question of what might be called location work must be connected to the logic of one's larger project and ultimately to one's political practice. Why do we *want* to shift locations? *Who* wants to shift? Why? (D. Gordon 1993; Visweswaran 1994: 95–113; Enslin 1994).

What emerges, then, is a set of possibilities for rethought and revitalized forms of fieldwork. We are not advocating the abandonment of the practice of fieldwork, but rather its reconstruction—decentering "the field" as the one, privileged site of anthropological knowledge, then recovering it as one element in a multistranded methodology for the construction of what Donna Haraway (1988) has called "situated knowledges." We might emerge from such a move with less of a sense of "the field" (in the "among the so-and-so" sense) and more of a sense of a mode of study that cares about, and pays attention to, the interlocking of multiple social-political sites and locations.

Such a reconstruction of the fieldwork tradition is, as we have emphasized, already well under way in anthropological practice. Participant observation continues to be a major part of positioned anthropological methodologies, but it is ceasing to be fetishized; talking to and living with the members of a community are increasingly taking their place alongside reading newspapers, analyzing government documents, observing the activities of governing elites, and tracking the internal logic of transnational development agencies and corporations. Instead of a royal road to holistic knowledge of "another society," ethnography is beginning to become recognizable as a flexible and opportunistic strategy for diversifying and making more complex our understanding of various places, people, and predicaments through an attentiveness to the different forms of knowledge available from different social and political locations. Although more and more ethnography today is proceeding along these lines, however, the institutionalized disciplinary framework of reception and evaluation too often continues to see experiential, "field-based" knowledge as the privileged core of an ethnographic work that is then "fleshed out" with supplementary materials (cf. chapter 3).

Any serious decentering of "the field" has the effect, of course, of further softening the division between ethnographic knowledge and other forms of representation flowing out of archival research, the analysis of public discourse, interviewing, journalism, fiction, or statistical representations of collectivities. Genres seem destined to continue to blur. Yet instead of assuming that truly anthropological truths are only revealed in "the field," and attempting to seal off the borders of anthropology from the incursions of cultural studies and other disciplines, it might be a far healthier response to rethink "the field" of anthropology by reconsidering what our commitment to fieldwork entails.

Such a rethinking of the idea of "the field," coupled with an explicit attentiveness to location, might open the way for both a different kind of anthropological knowledge and a different kind of anthropological subject. We have attempted to demonstrate that the uncritical loyalty to "the field" in anthropology has long authorized a certain positionality, a particular location from which to speak about Others. Without an explicit consideration of the kind of subject and the kind of knowledge that ethnographic work produces—by what method? for whom? about whom? by whom? to what end?—we anthropologists will continue to valorize, in the universalizing language of meritocracy, a very particular social, racial, gendered, and sexual location. Practicing decolonized anthropology in a deterritorialized world means as a first step doing away with the distancing and exoticization of the conventional anthropological "field," and foregrounding the ways in which we anthropologists are historically and socially (not just biographically) linked with the areas we study (E. Gordon 1991). In other words, we have to move beyond well-intentioned place-marking devices such as "Western, white anthropologist," which too often substitute a gesture of expiation for a more historical and structural understanding of location. It also means taking away lingering evolutionist and colonialist ideas of "natives in their natural state," and denying the anthropological hierarchy of field sites that devalues work in so many intellectually and politically crucial areas (homelessness, AIDS, sexuality, the media) that are often deemed insufficiently "anthropological." But a heightened sense of location means most of all a recognition that the topics we study and the methods we employ are inextricably bound up with political practice (Bourgois 1991).

The traditional commitment to "the field" has entailed, we have argued, its own form of political engagement, in terms of both the knowledge it has produced and the kind of disciplinary subject it has created. Our focus on *shifting locations* rather than *bounded fields* is linked to a different political vision, one that sees anthropological knowledge as a form of situated intervention. Rather than viewing ethnographic intervention as a disinterested search for truth in the service of universal humanistic knowledge, we see it as a way of pursuing specific political aims while simultaneously seeking lines of common political purpose with allies who stand elsewhere—a mode of building what Haraway (1988) has termed "web-like interconnections" between different social and cultural locations. Applied anthropology and especially activist anthropology have long had the virtue of linking ethnographic practice to a specific and explicit political project. Partly for this reason, they have been consistently devalued in the domain of academic anthropology (cf. Ferguson forthcoming). Yet we would emphasize that associating one's research with a political position does not by itself call into question the location of the activist-anthropologist in the way that we have suggested is necessary, since even the most politically engaged "experts" may still conceive of themselves as occupying an external and epistemologically privileged position. Rather than viewing anthropologists as possessing unique knowledge and insights that they can then share with or put to work for various "ordinary people," our approach insists that anthropological knowledge coexists with other forms of knowledge. We see the political task not as "sharing" knowledge with those who lack it, but as forging links between *different* knowledges that are possible from different locations and tracing lines of possible alliance and common purpose between them. In this sense, we view a research area less as a "field" for the collection of data than as a site for strategic intervention.

The idea that anthropology's distinctive trademark might be found not in its commitment to "the local" but in its attentiveness to epistemological and political issues of location surely takes us far from the classical natural history model of fieldwork as "the detailed study of a limited area." It may be objected, in fact, that it takes us *too* far—that such a reformulation of the fieldwork tradition leaves too little that is recognizable of the old Malinowskian archetype on which the discipline has for so long relied for its self-image and legitimation. At a time of rapid and contentious disciplinary change, it might be argued, such a reworking of one of the few apparently solid points of common reference can only exacerbate the confusion. But what such worries ignore is the fact that the classical idea of "the field" is *already* being challenged, undermined, and reworked in countless ways in ethnographic practice, as several of the chapters in this book, along with other works discussed in this chapter (and in chapter 10) illustrate. An unyielding commitment to the virtues of an unreconstructed Malinowskian "field" cannot reverse this transformation, though it can do much to misunderstand it. Indeed, if, as we have suggested, much of the best new work in the discipline challenges existing conventions of "field" and "fieldwork," the refusal to interrogate those conventions seems less likely to prevent disciplinary confusion and discord than to generate it. Like any tradition valued by a community, anthropology's fieldwork tradition will manage to secure its continuity only if it is able to change to accommodate new circumstances. For that to happen, as Malinowski himself pointed out, such a tradition must be aggressively and imaginatively reinterpreted to meet the needs of the present.

NOTES

1. Here and throughout this chapter we use "anthropology" as a shorthand for sociocultural anthropology, leaving to one side the very interesting issues raised by the roles of "field" and "fieldwork" in the other subfields of anthropology: archaeology and biological anthropology.

2. Our focus on what one might call the hegemonic centers of the discipline is deliberate and motivated. Since we are concerned, above all, with the mechanisms through which dominant disciplinary norms and conventions are established, we believe there is good reason for paying special attention to those institutional sites and national contexts that, in practice, enjoy a disproportionate say in setting theoretical and methodological agendas and in defining what will (and will not) count as "real anthropology," not only in the U.S. or U.K. but throughout the anthropological world. This choice of focus is not intended to diminish the importance and vitality of a variety of peripheral, heterodox, or subordinated sites and contexts of anthropological practice, which we discuss briefly in Part IV of this chapter. The point, on the contrary, is to explore how and why such alternative traditions have been marginalized and ignored, and with what consequences.

3. The survey is cited in Stocking 1992a: 14.

4. The observation that peoples and cultures are nowadays less localized is not meant to imply that in the past, groups were somehow naturally bounded, anchored in space, or unaffected by mass migrations or cultural flows. As we will emphasize later, processes of migration and cultural "diffusion" are far from new, and anthropology has a long (if often underappreciated) history of attention to them (cf. Gupta and Ferguson, eds., forthcoming).

5. It can be argued that the inherited division of conventional academic disciplines is part of the problem here, pressing the intellectual practices of the present into the Procrustean bed of outdated conceptual categories. This is certainly the case with respect to anthropology's perennial embarrassment over the issue of the (non)unity of its "subfields." The periodic trumpeting of the virtues of an "integrated," "holistic," "four-field" anthropology cannot disguise the obvious fact that the lumping of social and cultural studies of Third World peoples together in a single discipline with such things as behavioral studies of baboons and archaeological excavations of human fossils can only be understood as a legacy of nineteenth-century evolutionist thought, persisting (as a "survival," one might say) only thanks to the ossified institutional structure of the modern university. Indeed, Boas himself understood the shape of the anthropological discipline as a historical accident originating in the fact that "other sciences occupied part of the ground before the development of modern anthropology" (Stocking, ed., 1974: 269). The "four-field" structure, he predicted, would be dissolved in time, once other sciences such as linguistics and biology matured to the point where they would deal with "the work that we are doing now because no one else cares for it" (Stocking, ed., 1974: 35; cf. Stocking 1988).

It should be noted, however, that the predicament of finding one's disciplinary bounds at odds with current thinking is not unique to anthropologists. As Kuklick (chapter 2) points out, it was institutionalization in universities that gave *all* the disciplines the mixed blessing of stability, "imparting to each field the quasi-natural status that has become increasingly problematic for virtually all of them." But if the *form* of the disciplinary division of labor is, thanks to such institutionalization, fairly fixed, its *content* is not. Because disciplinary traditions and subject matters are continually reworked and reinvented, quite fundamental changes can occur even in the absence of disciplinary reorganization.

6. Again, we concentrate here on the dominant Anglo-American tradition (cf. note 2).

7. Kuklick is discussing the British tradition, which is essential to grasping the roots of the "Malinowskian revolution." The American Boasian orientation to the field was significantly different, however, as will be discussed below.

8. Vincent (1990: 106) has argued that the "fieldwork revolution" preceded Malinowski's self-promoting "discovery" of it, and might more properly be credited to Rivers. On the American side, a key role in the development of "fieldwork" has often been attributed to Boas, while Lewis Henry Morgan's researches among the Seneca provide an even earlier point of reference. A more complete account would also have to include (among many others) figures such as Henry Rowe Schoolcraft, Frank Hamilton Cushing, and Ely Parker. Kuklick (chapter 2) shows more fundamentally that the turn to field observation was not a uniquely anthropological move at all, but part of a general development within *all* of the natural history sciences in the late nineteenth and early twentieth centuries. However, as Malinowski would surely agree, foundation myths need have no necessary relation to actual historical sequences. Since our concern here is more with the received tradition of fieldwork than with its actual genesis, we are content to continue speaking of the "revolution" as Malinowskian (cf. Stocking 1992a: 281).

9. Akhil Gupta wishes to thank Marilyn Ivy for the stimulating conversation within which some of these ideas first arose. "The field" has, of course, other connotations as well; most interestingly, perhaps, the idea of a "field" of interacting forces, as in physics, as Roger Rouse and Emily Martin have both pointed out to us. Yet anthropology's "field," it seems to us, has more often been grasped as a place of terrestrial concreteness than as an abstract space within which invisible forces might meet. Anthropologists going to the field expect to get mud on their boots; like other "field scientists," they have aimed to discover not disembodied fields of force, but a reality repeatedly described by such adjectives as *messy, flesh-and-blood,* and *on-the-ground.*

10. As Thomas notes, the fact that "there is virtually no discussion now of what regions are, [and] of what status they are supposed to have as entities in anthropological talk" (1989: 27) shows not that anthropology no longer relies on culture areas, but that it relies on unacknowledged, untheorized, and taken-for-granted territorializations of cultural difference. The uncritical use of such mappings, Thomas shows, may unwittingly perpetuate evolutionist and racist assumptions inherited from the colonial past. For an attempt to locate an empirical basis for the division of the world into culture areas, see Burton et al. (1996).

11. It seems to be the case that doing fieldwork in Europe is much more acceptable in anthropology when it is a second field site developed later in the career, rather than a dissertation site (see the discussion of fieldwork in the United States, below).

It is also true that southern and eastern Europe seem to be distinctly more "anthropological" than northern and western Europe. Herzfeld (1987) shows that the "anthropological-ness" of Greece, like its "European-ness," is historically variable and subject to contestation and debate.

12. It does not follow from this that Evans-Pritchard therefore worked in the service of colonial rule—that is a different proposition requiring independent demonstration.

13. We realize that these categories are not as neatly opposed as this formulation might seem to imply. Much of the creation of knowledge about Third World nation-states continues to occur in, and through, former colonial centers.

14. We use the term *visa procedures* here as shorthand for the whole complex of mechanisms used to regulate the production of knowledge within and about nation-states.

15. We are reminded of Bellah et al.'s analysis (1985) of the systematic patterns by which people fall in love, each supposing their love to be entirely unique.

16. We borrow the term *archetype* from Stocking, but it should be noted that we develop it in ways that probably depart from his intended meaning.

17. Visweswaran (1994: 95–130) has discussed this constrast.

18. "Even in the absence of a separate autobiographical volume, personal narrative is a conventional component of ethnographies. It turns up almost invariably in introductions or first chapters, where opening narratives commonly recount the writer's arrival at the field site, for instance, the initial reception by the inhabitants, the slow, agonizing process of learning the language and overcoming rejection, the anguish and loss of leaving. Though they exist only on the margins of the formal ethnographic description, these conventional opening narratives are not trivial. They play the crucial role of anchoring that description in the intense and authority-giving personal experience of fieldwork. . . . Always they are responsible for setting up the initial positionings of the subjects of the ethnographic text: the ethnographer, the native, and the reader" (Pratt 1986: 31–32). See the thoughtful discussion of anthropological arrivals in Tsing (1993).

19. The phrase "writing up" is itself suggestive of a hierarchy of texts mapping itself onto a hierarchy of spaces. One "writes up" the disjointed, fragmented, immanent text found in fieldnotes into something more complete and polished. One also "writes up" in a space that is superior, more conducive to reflection and the higher arts of theoretical and mental work.

20. A survey of job ads for sociocultural anthropologists that appeared in the *Anthropology Newsletter* between September 1994 and April 1996 showed that most advertised positions (100 out of 178) specified preferred geographical areas (25 Asia, 37 Latin America, 37 North America, 15 Sub-Saharan Africa, 10 Caribbean, 3 Middle East, 3 Oceania, 2 Europe), while another 11 specified a geographical area negatively (e.g., "non-West" or "non-U.S."). (Note that the figures for the different areas add up to more than the total number of area-based positions, because some jobs mention more than one area.) Of the positions, 65 did not refer to area, and 2 referred to specific diasporic groups.

21. In the survey discussed in note 20, we found that of the 37 ads that included a call for a North America area focus (sometimes as one of several possible areas), 16 specifically called for a specialization on Native Americans. Another 10 requested

African American specialists, along with 2 for Asian American specialists, and 1 for Asian American/Chicano. Of the 8 remaining positions, 4 were described in regional terms (e.g., "Southeastern U.S.," "U.S. Southwest"), leaving only 4 jobs that were unqualified by ethnic or regional descriptors. These results are generally consistent with those of another, slightly different employment survey carried out by Judith Goode of the Society for the Anthropology of North America (SANA 1996), which found that out of 730 job listings (all subfields) sampled between 1986 and 1994, 64 were specifically designated as North Americanist positions, of which 45 required specialization on a specific U.S. ethnic group (SANA 1996: 31).

By pointing out such hiring patterns, we do not mean to imply that anthropologists should not focus on Native Americans or minority groups, but only to insist that the casting of the anthropological net to include sites ranging from "Samoa to South Central" (as a recent anthropological video catalogue from Filmmakers Library put it) does not displace the old conventions that locate the subject matter of anthropology in terms of white, Western, middle-class alterity. (The no-doubt-unintended primitivizing effects of such disciplinary definitions are made particularly clear when we open the Filmmakers Library brochure and find the "South Central" film located just opposite the "Primate Social Behavior" section.)

22. The "top ten" departments were taken from the recent National Research Council study of U.S. doctorate programs (Goldberger, Maher, and Flattau 1995: 475) and included: Michigan, Chicago, Berkeley, Harvard, Arizona, Pennsylvania, Stanford, Yale, UCLA, and UCSD. For each department, we counted all social-cultural anthropologists (including linguistic anthropologists) listed in the *AAA Guide to Departments of Anthropology* as "Full-time Faculty"—including joint appointment faculty, but not "Anthropologists in Other Departments" or courtesy (secondary) appointments. We found a total of 189 social-cultural anthropologists, of which 184 stated area specializations. We found that 23 of these anthropologists listed North America or the United States as their primary area (i.e., listed it first, in cases of more than one area focus), of which 15 could be determined to be specialists on Native Americans, leaving 8 primary specialists in nonnative North America. We found an additional 26 anthropologists who listed North America or the United States as a secondary area interest (i.e., listed it, but did not put it first).

23. Some who have ventured to examine the mass media ethnographically are: Heide 1995; Ang 1985 (1982); Morley 1980, 1986; Powdermaker 1950; Seiter et al. 1989; Abu-Lughod 1993; Mankekar 1993a, 1993b; Dickey 1993; Spitulnik 1994. See Spitulnik 1993 for a full review and discussion.

24. The reason for this historical tendency, we suggest, cannot simply be that such supralocal political identifications have developed only recently. For instance, during Robert Redfield's classic 1927 fieldwork (to take only one of many possible examples), the ethnographer witnessed "Bolsheviks" fighting in the streets of Tepoztlan as part of a Zapatista uprising, and he described the local people he knew as "very Zapatista in sentiment." But we know this from his personal papers and his wife's diary; his ethnography painted a very different picture of peaceful villagers living local lives with little interest in national or international politics (Vincent 1990: 206–207).

25. In posing this question, we do not mean to imply that there are not often excellent reasons for choosing to work in villages. Indeed, we have each carried out vil-

lage-level fieldwork in our own studies and appreciate fully the methodological opportunities and advantages often provided by such settings. Our point is only to question the conventional mapping of "field site" onto exotic "local community" that is
so economically expressed in the archetypal anthropological image of "the village."

26. Indeed, even much older communications technologies such as telephones
remain strikingly underresearched in anthropology, as Orvar Löfgren has pointed
out recently (Löfgren 1995).

27. This does not mean, of course, that judgments of excellence cannot or should
not be made, but only that (1) such judgments must always be made in terms of standards and principles that are never the only ones possible, and (2) every choice of
a set of standards and principles for judgment will have social and political implications; the "grid" will not in this sense be "neutral."

28. The term is Kirin Narayan's (cited in Abu-Lughod 1991).

29. It is also interesting to note how few Africans are involved in the anthropological study of Africa. Jane Guyer(1996: 30) has recently surveyed the percentage
of dissertations on Africa written by African-surnamed authors, and found that of
eighteen surveyed disciplines, anthropology had by far the lowest percentage of
African authors (only 18 percent of anthropology dissertations on Africa were written by authors with African surnames, compared with, e.g., 54 percent in political
science, 70 percent in sociology, and 33 percent in history). See also her thoughtful
remarks on the fieldwork tradition and its future in African studies (1996: 78–80).

30. Bell, Caplan, and Karim (1993) explore the myriad ways in which supposedly
gender-neutral norms of fieldwork clash with highly gendered actual experiences of
fieldwork.

31. In our discussion so far, we have not even touched on those micropractices
of the academy that screen candidates in the name of "collegiality" and "suitability"
for class, race, and sex (see Rabinow 1991).

32. We are grateful to Anna Tsing for pointing out to us the importance of exploring heterodox traditions of "the field."

33. Kuklick argues (chapter 2) that "a neglect of comparative, historical analysis" accompanied the rise of fieldwork not only in anthropology but in all of the field
sciences. Anthropologists, she suggests, "might derive some consolation from the
knowledge that the turn to the synchronic was not their field's alone."

34. Mead herself, of course, was also a leading figure in the study of "acculturation" and "modernization," especially (but not only) in her later work.

35. The kindred distaste that mainstream anthropology shows for the similarly
"impure" field of "development anthropology" is analyzed in Ferguson forthcoming.

36. The period of the 1930s and 1940s saw a good deal of politically engaged work
on "social problems" in British anthropology as well. Godfrey Wilson's "Essay on the
Economics of Detribalization in Northern Rhodesia" (1941–1942), for instance, was
a precocious analysis of labor migration, rural poverty, and what would later be called
"underdevelopment" in a colonial setting, which insisted on linking poverty and
famine in rural northern Rhodesia both to urban mining development and to a wider
world economy. Works such as this certainly challenged the prevailing assumptions
of academic anthropology in a number of ways. Since most of the British studies of
"culture contact" and "social change" were set in "the colonies," however, they did
not call into question the "home"/"field" division in the same way that work on ac-

culturation and poverty in the U.S. did. (Note, however, that some of the work on "culture contact" in South Africa had a similar blurring effect. For white South African anthropologists, the "field" that contained the "pure" natives was safely off in the reserves, but in the study of acculturation, "the field" came much closer to home. See Monica Hunter Wilson's extraordinary monograph in the "culture contact" tradition, *Reaction to Conquest: Effects of Contact with Europeans on the Pondo of South Africa* [1936].)

37. Radin's study was funded by the California State Emergency Relief Administration (SERA), Project 2-F2-98 (3-F2-145), Cultural Anthropology.

38. Radin's lifelong study of the Winnebago Indians left us with what has been called "perhaps the most complete and detailed long-term record in monographs and field notes that we have of a primitive society as seen by a single observer through all the stages of his own intellectual history" (Vidich 1966 [1933]: xiv). Radin chided Margaret Mead for drawing ethnographic conclusions on the basis of less than a year of fieldwork that would properly require "a long and protracted residence and a complete command of the language." A year or two, he suggested, was not nearly long enough for deep cultural understanding: "What one gets within a year, or for that matter within five years . . . is bound to be superficial" (Radin 1966 [1933]: 178–179).

39. The recent work of Rosaldo (1993, 1994) addresses similar questions regarding the political implications of heterodox anthropological methodologies.

40. Mafhoud Bennoune has described coming to the U.S. in the early 1970s to study anthropology from a background as an Algerian revolutionary and finding that his plans to study "the causes and consequences of labor migration" of Algerian workers to France were frustrated by being forced into a "community study" model. Bennoune recounts how the director of the research center with which his dissertation research was affiliated (and the "manager" of his Ford Foundation funds) demanded that he focus on firsthand observations within a community ("Mohammed A. and Mustafa B. and Musa C."), while giving documentary research only "very secondary consideration." Bennoune understood his director to be ordering him "in a very explicit manner to study only a small group of migrant workers in complete isolation from the historical, social, and economic context of colonialism and imperialism" (Bennoune 1985: 362–363).

41. Dipesh Chakrabarty (1992: 2) has pointed out a similar situation in the field of history, where historians of Europe feel no need to refer to non-Western, Third World histories: "'They' produce their work in relative ignorance of non-Western histories, and this does not seem to affect the quality of their work. This is a gesture, however, that 'we' cannot return. We cannot even afford an equality or symmetry of ignorance at this level without taking the risk of appearing 'old-fashioned' or 'outdated.'"

42. The interaction of metropolitan anthropology with the discipline's local representatives in peripheral settings is complex. Local anthropologists may exercise varying degrees of influence on the topics and methods used by Western ethnographers. But intellectual production in many such settings is itself heavily colonized. Discrepancies of funding and resources also endow First World ethnographers with distinct advantages in the space of representation. For example, graduate students funded from U.S. sources and doing fieldwork in India are paid at least twice as much as full professors in Indian universities. Journals in which First World ethnographers publish are not available in most libraries, and are much more expensive to subscribe

to from foreign countries, even poorer ones. In 1991, libraries in New Delhi cut back journal runs because the new fiscal regime imposed by the IMF raised the exchange rate, making journals prohibitively expensive. These circumstances make a mockery of the notion that the space of representation can be a truly dialogic one. Indian anthropologists have complained, for example, that First World ethnographers who pay large sums (by local standards) to "informants" effectively prevent any native ethnographers from working in the vicinity, as certain expectations of payment are set which local scholars are unable to meet.

43. De Lima (1992) has given a vivid account of the encounter between Brazilian and U.S. anthropological norms in the context of his own graduate education. While he does not discuss practices of the field, he has a great deal to say about the way that taken-for-granted and supposedly "neutral" academic forms—from "clear," "well-structured" essays and carefully timed oral presentations read from written texts to formal job searches ("they look for a professor the same way they look for a roommate")—in fact work to enforce American cultural premises.

44. We are convinced, for example, by Tishkov's critical appraisal (1992) of Soviet ethnography, which laments the lack of extended fieldwork among a younger generation of scholars. Yet Tishkov's essay also makes one realize how acutely the hegemony of Anglo-American norms is felt: "In world anthropology, at least a year's fieldwork with a community or group is considered the norm for everyone from the postgraduate student to the leading professional" (1992: 374).

45. Since we have relied entirely on Geertz's description of the encounter between the Harvard team and their Indonesian counterparts, we may have been misled by the dramatic presentation of the episode to overstate the apparent lack of negotiation between the Americans and their hosts.

46. Another important "border" of this kind is one that separates anthropology from journalism. This is explored at some length in chapter 4.

47. For a small sample of the work of these scholars, see:
   a. Hurston 1935, 1969 (1942), 1978 (1937); Hernandez 1993; Dorst 1987;
   b. Paredes 1958, 1993; Rosaldo 1987;
   c. Du Bois 1967 (1899), 1961 (1903), 1964 (1935); see also the excellent special issue of *Critique of Anthropology* (Harrison and Nonini, eds., 1992);
   d. James 1963 (1938), 1969, 1983 (1963); Grimshaw and Hart 1991;
   e. Drake 1966, 1987, 1990; Drake and Cayton 1993 (1945); Harrison and Nonini, 1992.

48. The status of "insider" is of course a complicated matter, since there are as many ways of being "inside" or "outside" as there are of defining a community (cf. Hurston 1935; Bell, Caplan, and Karim 1993; Narayan 1993).

49. Deborah D'Amico-Samuels (1991: 75) has put it very well: "The real distancing effects of the field are masked in the term 'back from the field.' These words perpetuate the notion that ethnographers and those who provide their data live in worlds that are different and separate, rather than different and unequal in ways which tie the subordination of one to the power of the other."

50. On the politics of location, see Rich (1986), Anzaldúa (1987), Spivak (1988), Pratt (1984), Martin and Mohanty (1986), Reagon (1983), Wallace (1989), Haraway (1988), Lorde (1984), Kaplan (forthcoming), Nicholson (1990).

TWO

After Ishmael: The Fieldwork Tradition and Its Future

Henrika Kuklick

"The naturalist who wishes to inflict his tale on a patient reader ought to have one at least of these three excuses," wrote J. C. Moulton in an article describing his 1914 collecting expedition in Borneo. These were "a real gift for observing and recording the wonders of Nature; a comparatively unknown or distant country to write about; or a region of some historic interest" (Moulton 1914: 362). In this chapter I intend to satisfy Moulton's standards of authorial craft. I will cover what may seem to be familiar historical ground—the emergence of fieldwork as central to the practice of anthropology—but I will emphasize comparatively unknown features of the terrain. These features denote a seismic shift in the orientation of those who worked to observe and record the wonders of nature, a shift that occurred toward the end of the nineteenth century. As I will show, developments in anthropology at that time can best be understood if we situate its practitioners within a larger community of scientists, who represent the dominant (if not the only) parental strain in anthropology's intellectual ancestry.[1] Along with others of their kind, anthropologists then embraced field methods as one element in their strategy of adaptive accommodation to the intellectual ecology of the day.

It is therefore appropriate to my purposes that I have begun by quoting a naturalist. He was a naturalist of the genus zoologist, and his paper appeared in a journal called *The Zoologist*, but by today's standards it would not be recognized as the work of a specialist. Reporting observations he made while retracing a journey earlier undertaken by the great evolutionary thinker Alfred Russel Wallace, Moulton wrote an account attending to all the phenomena that interested the scientific family of naturalists: characteristics of land and water affecting travel and settlement; area-specific plant and animal species; and last but hardly least, the distinctive appearance and behavior of the human inhabitants of the places he visited. Significantly, however, the journal in which his piece appeared in 1914 ceased publication two years later, ending a run begun in 1843. *The Zoologist* had once been a thriving monthly, but it had ceased to be viable both because its authors had been drawn from a literally moribund breed of writers and because its subscription list had dwindled to the vanishing point (see Distant 1912: iii–iv; Finn 1916: iii).

Nevertheless, the demise of *The Zoologist* did not indicate that breeds of omnivore naturalists had become extinct among the consumers of upper-middle-brow popular culture. They continued to flourish, their curiosities fed by all manner of publications, of which the *National Geographic* may be the most notable by virtue of its sheer durability.[2] At this moment, however, we need not consider how such publications have managed their production and circulation tasks. This chapter is not intended to explicate the intricate and changing relationships that have obtained between specialists and amateur enthusiasts from the late nineteenth century to the present. Certainly, these relationships are significant. There is no denying that the natural history sciences have been and continue to be affected in complex ways by developments outside their circles of committed practitioners. Perhaps most important, anthropologists share with other field scientists a behavioral ideal derived from a general cultural matrix; in particular, the cult of fieldwork could not have developed without Victorian-era expectations that personal growth (of an implicitly masculine sort) could be effected through pilgrimages to unfamiliar places, where the European traveler endured physical discomfort and (genuine or imagined) danger (e.g., Robbins 1987). And perhaps more than other field scientists, anthropologists have been obliged to respond to popular stereotypes about their subject matter, if only because these notions shape students' approaches to the discipline (e.g., Price 1989: esp. 37–55). For all of the field sciences, however, the boundaries between esoteric and popular understanding of natural phenomena remain blurred. Indeed, if one notes the attention currently given in print and broadcast journalism to stories about nature, as well as the extraordinary expansion of the sector of the travel industry known as ecotourism, one may judge that popular interest in field-based scientific inquiries is now reaching new heights. The mass media as well as guided tours are exposing members of the public to ostensibly unspoiled natural wonders, often in developing countries, as well as to exotic peoples who live in conditions advertised as close to nature; thus, notions academics have worked hard to discredit are gaining circulation—and public support for research is bound to be affected somehow (see, e.g., Allen 1995; Mason 1994). But no matter how fascinating the relationship between anthropological ideas and popular culture may be, its explication lies outside the scope of this chapter.

When naturalists made experience in the field a defining property of membership in their disciplinary communities, they were setting fundamental standards of scientific craft. Explaining this development requires attention to the internal dynamics of disciplinary change. One must stress that the very notion that a field's development can be internally generated rests on an understanding of its place in the general social scheme of things. A disciplinary community becomes a coherent group, its members looking primarily to their peers for confirmation of the merits of their efforts, only when it enjoys both institutionalized positions for the practice of its tasks and routinized patterns of recruitment to its ranks. And in all scientific communities peers may be arbiters of theoretical and methodological rigor, but the problems they choose inevitably have some—however remote—antecedents in widespread social trends that affect specialists no differently from many of their contemporaries. Bearing such qualifications in mind, we can observe that the demise of such journals as *The Zoologist* signaled a critical moment in the history of scholarly practice: a point of separation between esoteric and popular cultural spheres. Although writers for such journals were clearly not averse to providing entertainment as well as enlightenment, they were accustomed to thinking of themselves as contributors to scientific knowledge. And I am concerned here to describe the modifications in behavioral expectations effected at the turn of the century among those naturalists who were committed to identities as serious scientists.

FROM THE STUDY TO THE FIELD

The most obvious change in the behavior of naturalists dedicated to serious scientific inquiry was their increasing propensity to specialize, to focus on narrow sectors within the range of phenomena that constituted the erstwhile province of natural history. Persons such as Moulton represented intermediate life forms in the evolution of the natural history sciences. One can trace the progressive differentiation of labor among the various types of naturalists —from anthropologists to zoologists—to the second third of the nineteenth century, if not earlier. But the end of the century was the moment at which quantitative change became qualitative, the time when the disciplines we now recognize emerged and individuals' scientific interests were delimited by disciplinary boundaries.[3] Moreover, as the natural history specialties differentiated, their practitioners determined that naturalists must break their long-established habit of relying on theories articulated by armchair scholars, that scientists could not do credible analysis unless they had themselves gathered the data on which their generalizations rested.

In biology, for example, institution formation indicates the emergence of organized fieldwork in the 1870s. The field stations serving an international community of scientists were established in Europe in 1872 in Naples, Italy, and in 1873 in the United States on Penikese Island, off the coast of

New England (Haila 1992: 239). Working in these stations, scientists were able to examine living creatures instead of the preserved specimens that had previously provided the material basis for their generalizations; they soon determined that they should not be content with inspection of live organisms on their laboratory tables, but had to go into the field to see how their subjects behaved in their natural habitats. It is significant that immediately following his graduation from Cambridge University with a First Class Honours degree in natural sciences, the young A. C. Haddon spent six months at the Naples Zoological Station in 1879, at the moment when field biology was being self-consciously developed (British Association for the Advancement of Science [BAAS] 1879: 170). Then ambitious to build a career as a marine biologist, Haddon would a decade later translate the investigative techniques favored at Naples into sociocultural anthropological terms, seeking to explain variations within the human species as adaptations to geographical conditions. We should also note a formative experience in the life of a young German scientist, Franz Boas, who was to make a career in the United States as an anthropologist; trained as a geographer, he undertook his baptismal fieldwork in Baffinland in 1883 with expectations similar to Haddon's (see Stocking, 1968; Stocking, ed., 1983).[4]

Evidently, the naturalist disciplines became differentiated, but their newly distinct fields nevertheless moved (nearly in unison) toward a common commitment to fieldwork method. And the disciplines' shared research approach entailed more than faith in the merits of fieldwork per se. Anthropologists looking to the roots of their professional identity may recall such rallying cries as Haddon's 1890 plea for "detailed study of a single tribe or natural assemblage of people," which announced his intention to organize the Cambridge anthropological expedition to Torres Straits—the 1898 venture that took British anthropologists into the field (Haddon 1890: 638). But anthropologists will probably be unaware that other specialties responded to similar directives at the same time. For example, in 1897, the method of detailed ecological analysis of the life forms of strictly delimited geographical areas was contrived in Nebraska by the pioneering ecologist Frederick Clements and his student Roscoe Pound (Tobey 1981: 48–75).[5] British ecologists shortly adopted methods similar to Clements's and Pound's of investigating circumscribed natural communities (Tansley 1947). These examples are not isolated instances. The detailed study of a limited area became the characteristic research approach of natural history fields as remote from anthropology as oceanography (Rozwadowski 1996). Moreover, for every field that embraced this approach, intensive study was conducive to neglect of comparative, historical analysis and to an emphasis on synchronic interpretation.[6] The many anthropologists who have lamented the intellectual bankruptcy of ahistoric analysis might derive some consolation from the knowledge that the turn to the synchronic was not their field's alone.

Furthermore, the geopolitical conditions that permitted anthropologists to go into the field also shaped the practices of other natural history sciences. For example, when late-nineteenth-century American and European astrophysicists traveled to distant parts to make their observations, they had to work under conditions very similar to those anthropologists have faced: they pitched camp in surroundings possessing none of the comforts of home, and relied on guides and assistants whose behavior appeared alarmingly unpredictable by Eurocentric standards. No wonder that when early fieldworkers, whether astrophysicists or anthropologists, journeyed to remote locations to record phenomena unique to—or best observed in—exotic places, they preferred to work in the relative security of territories that seemed firmly fixed under colonial control (see Pang 1993). No matter how compromised anthropology may be because it depended on colonialism while being organized, anthropology is but one of the field sciences that owes much to the (remote or direct) protection of colonial authorities.

At base, however, naturalists' move to detailed studies of delimited areas, a move contingent on their commitment to sustain their research over long periods, was made possible by the changed character of intellectual life in both Europe and America at the end of the nineteenth century. Then, newly professionalized university systems admitted the disciplinary specialization naturalists embraced (and institutionalization in universities gave the disciplines stability in bureaucratized academic structures, imparting to each field the quasi-natural status that has become increasingly problematic for virtually all of them). The basic infrastructure of routine support for research was in place—funds provided by government agencies, science-based industries, and private philanthropies permitted the creation of the modern university. For academic naturalists, in particular, available financial patronage meant that they could do stints of prolonged fieldwork at various stages in their careers. And for all of the intellectual specialists housed within the university, not just for naturalists, institutional change facilitated enclosure of self-referential scholarly communities. Security within the university permitted their fields to follow the course that students of professionalization too numerous to mention have described. The authority to direct the disciplines' development came to be (largely) restricted to formally trained practitioners whose remunerated careers followed one of the standardized occupational paths accessible only to certified persons.

Professional scientific careers were also made possible by the creation of occupational niches outside the university—although these would in time require academic credentials. For naturalists, professionalization arguably began with the institutionalization of careers for geologists working for government geological surveys in the United States, Britain, and the Continent during the first half of the nineteenth century (see, e.g., J. A. Secord 1986). And as the century progressed, positions also multiplied in such venues as museums, botanical gardens, and zoos (it is worth noting that zoos developed less as the places of entertainment they are at least publicly today than as sites for scientific investigation of such matters as comparative anatomy and comparative psychology [see Mehos n.d.]). The museum, the botanical garden, and the zoo often (if not invariably) featured the captured booty of imperial adventure, and it can be argued that geologists' findings were valuable, though not necessarily indispensable, to those Europeans who wished to justify imperial expansion (see Stafford 1984).

Nevertheless, it was the perceived utility of natural knowledge for efficient exploitation of resources (animal, vegetable, mineral, and human) within the borders of the metropoles that provided the initial impetus to establish remunerated positions for practitioners of the natural history sciences (see, e.g., Goetzman 1967: 182; J. A. Secord 1986). It is unquestionably the case that both occupational structures and practical objectives were first developed in colonial territories for various types of scientists who were concerned to manage natural resources, and that until the era of decolonization, all manner of innovations derived from formal knowledge were more easily effected in subject territories than in the metropoles (e.g., Grove 1993; Wright 1987). But one must emphasize that the primary justification for colonial ventures was the benefits they were expected to bring home. Thus, anthropologists were sounding familiar refrains when they made their initial claims to professional status based on the value of their expertise in resolving practical dilemmas posed in both domestic and colonial situations (see Kuklick 1991: 27–74, 182–209; McGee 1897).

With professionalization, naturalists of every stripe embraced a new scientific creed. This was, not surprisingly, defined in opposition to the ethos of the professionals' amateur predecessors. The new creed was a distinctly middle-class one, embodying the aspirations of those sectors of various European and American populations whose interests were served by the professionalization of those occupations that remain a base of middle-class status. In the United States, where there was no hereditary aristocracy, the contrast between the pre- and postprofessional eras in intellectual life was less stark; indeed, historians have typically portrayed the middle-class reformers who created the modern university as members of the class who had before the Civil War upheld the genteel tradition of learning. They acted to establish a new basis for their moral authority because they felt threatened by the power of those who profited from postwar economic development (see, e.g., Haskell 1977: 51–85). Overall, however, it is safe to generalize that so long as amateurs dominated natural history, the scientific elite were drawn from the wealthier classes and had aristocratic pretensions, if not status. Committed naturalists were drawn from the lower-middle and working classes, and they organized their research efforts in a relatively democratic fashion, which seems—at least superficially—more closely akin to contemporary modes of scientific inquiry than does the scholarly style of their gentlemanly contemporaries (see A. Secord 1994). But until the late nineteenth century, it was only the very rare person of working-class origins who managed to achieve eminence in the elite circles of formally organized scientific activity.[7]

GENTLEMEN AND SCHOLARS

Aristocratically conceived natural history was predicated on the assumption that scientific labor should be divided along class lines, with naturalists from every class performing roles appropriate to their respective stations in life. Of these roles, the necessary one of fieldwork was unpleasant and inglorious. It was physical, dirty work. Some of it was inherently dangerous, such as investigations conducted on mountains, in caves, and underground. Some fieldwork—such as investigations in exotic places—was fraught with fear of unknown perils. Some of it was outright distasteful—such as the killing of insects, birds, and other creatures whose anatomical structures could not be detailed from examination of live specimens. And if certain fieldwork tasks were recognized as extraordinarily delicate procedures—such as killing insects without mutilating them—many others were supposed to require so little skill that they could safely be entrusted to virtually anyone. In sum, fieldwork was not gentlemanly activity.

The intellectual elite arrogated to themselves the labor of articulating theories to account for the diversity of nature. Notwithstanding the journeys of observational exploration undertaken by some of the pioneering intellectual giants of comprehensive natural history—the most notable of whom were Alexander von Humboldt, who traveled through Latin America at the turn of the nineteenth century, and Charles Darwin, who cruised the Pacific in the 1830s—the theoretical aspect of scientific work was for the mass of gentlemen-naturalists a comfortable task, performed within the familiar confines of their studies (see, e.g., Browne 1983: 42–43). Whether elite scholars were concerned to classify and explain flower, insect, or human variation, they confidently based their generalizations on data gathered by a congeries of collectors. These collectors supplied written descriptions, physical specimens, and drawn representations (which were characteristic yields of every significant expedition from the dawn of the age of exploration, and, until photography became common, were routine features of naturalists' practice, not just the products of specialist artists). The act of analyzing data collected by others was believed to be so straightforward that knowledge of scientific materials' provenance was considered virtually irrelevant to their interpretation.

Consider, for example, the case of one Rev. William Kirby, who was very active in early nineteenth-century zoological circles. At a London auction in 1818, he bought a large number of beetles, described in the auctioneer's catalogue as part of the "Very Superb and Celebrated Collection of Foreign Insects of the Late John Francillon, Esq." It is obvious to us today that such a collection should be recognized as highly problematic for scientific purposes—since it could constitute a very distorted sample of the beetle population. Kirby and his audience were untroubled by any such considerations, however, and he published his claim that he was able to identify several previously unknown genera after inspecting his new possessions (Larsen 1993: 277–278).

Indeed, a strict division of labor between theorists and fieldworkers was often advertised as conducive to superior science. In the field, the argument ran, unsophisticated workers would not be tempted to select only such evidence as would confirm specific theories, since they were ignorant of the possible implications of their findings. In the study, theorists could evaluate impartially the material at their disposition, since they had no personal stake in data they had not themselves collected. Although such eminent naturalists as Charles Darwin privately observed to their close colleagues that the notion of observation uncontaminated by any sort of bias was a fiction, these naturalists sustained their enterprise's conventional wisdom in public (noted in Novick 1988: 35–36). And this wisdom remained conventional so long as armchair scholars remained unrepentant about their method—as some anthropologists did well into the twentieth century (see, e.g., Frazer 1932: 918).

Dependent as they were on others' investigative efforts, elite amateur naturalists participated in thoroughly international communities of inquiry. In contrast, the careers of their professional successors have depended on satisfying disciplinary performance expectations that have varied from one national context to another (the internationalist ideology of modern science notwithstanding). And amateur communities were, in the ideal scheme of things, constituted wholly voluntarily: armchair scholars freely traded both information and specimens among themselves, and collectors supplied them with necessary materials. Sometimes collectors followed charges particular scientists gave them personally, and sometimes they spontaneously responded to the circulated questionnaires and published lists of informational lacunae that began to become routine features of natural scientific inquiry at the end of the seventeenth century.

Examination of naturalists' behavior, however, reveals considerable departure from their voluntarist ideal. When Kirby purchased his specimens, he was following the commercial mode of data collection that was, in fact, more common than exceptional in his enterprise. Trade in natural history specimens was integrated with trade in the material goods of conspicuous consumption that displayed the wealth of the prosperous who were (or wanted to be) members of fashionable society. In many instances, specimens were sold on the same premises as art, fine furniture, and jewelry. Indeed, because natural history artworks both reflected and influenced stylistic innovations in indisputably high art, it is hardly surprising that they figured into the art market (see, e.g., Smith 1960: esp. 14–76). Until museums received significant state and private philanthropic support at the end of the nineteenth century, even the most valuable natural history commodities were most likely to be housed in private residences.

Moreover, as should be intuitively obvious, the contemplation of the subjects of natural history in sites different from their field habitats had significant interpretive consequences. Consider, for example, the travels of sea creatures collected by nineteenth-century British and French naturalists. In Britain, they were displayed in drawing rooms; preserved in dried form, and thus rendered suitable for appearance in polite society, they were described in taxonomic terms derived from those features that survived processing. In France, they were housed in museums, where they were preserved in spirits; thus, French naturalists developed classificatory schemes that incorporated distinctions based on characteristics of soft tissues (Larsen, 1995). Or consider the careers of the non-Western peoples brought to Europe and America when anthropology was still a nascent discipline; exhibited as individuals to learned societies, grouped in mock villages constructed for fairs, or even in one notably scandalous instance put on display in the monkey house of the Bronx Zoo, they were implicitly treated as lesser humans than Europeans and Euro-Americans (Coombes 1994: 85–108; Bradford and Blume 1992: 169–190).

The history of the so-called "comparative method" in anthropology lacks sensational interest, but likewise demonstrates the link between the social and intellectual features of disciplinary practice: the method persisted so long as the armchair was the principal locus of research. Anthropologists engaged in theoretical generalization were able to make sense of the material they acquired from diverse sources by postulating that human development everywhere followed an invariant sequence of progressive stages, and that lacunae in their knowledge of any given people could be filled with information about any other population judged to be in an equivalent stage. Some of these anthropologists, such as Lewis Henry Morgan, might have done considerable fieldwork, but they nevertheless embraced the prevailing paradigm by assuming that the point of anthropological research was to derive universal laws of social evolution from comparative data, however much they disputed the details of these laws (see, e.g., Kuklick 1991: 88–91; Lubbock 1871; Morgan 1963 [1877]). Certainly, anthropologists' efforts to locate all of the world's peoples on a single developmental scale was an exercise typical of nineteenth-century natural history; naturalists of every description were concerned to identify apparently distinct life-forms as merely different phases in given organisms' life cycles. But the direct observation required to specify the life cycle of the butterfly, say, was unnecessary for anthropologists who accepted the axioms of the comparative method, and their studies were therefore appropriate venues for their work.

The social relations of nineteenth-century natural historians are also rendered more intelligible through examination of the economics of their enterprise. One can argue that natural objects were increasingly likely to be appreciated as scientific materials, rather than traded as consumer goods, during the second third of the nineteenth century. This shift coincided with the development of the very possibility of science as the basis for a respected career. In Britain, for example, the changed status of natural objects was evidenced by the 1824 repeal of the nearly prohibitive customs duties that had earlier been levied on them, and by sharp declines in their purchase prices at this time (Larsen 1993: 257). But even at the end of the century the naturalist who went into the field did not feel above exploiting any commercial opportunities presented to him, which is to say that he might make a virtue of necessity. For example, when Haddon paid his first visit to the islands of Torres Strait in 1888, pursuing his original career as a marine zoologist, he collected the art and artifacts of the islanders so that he might sell them to museums in Britain to supplement the small grant he had received for his biological research (Quiggin 1942: 82).

We can perhaps best appreciate the character of nineteenth-century scientific commercial life by contrasting it to the contemporary situation. Analogues and equivalents to the objects that nineteenth-century natural historians traded are bought and sold today. When biological organisms are marketed, however, they are supplied by specialized businesses. Scientists cannot finance their research as Haddon did, lest they lose face—or worse, find themselves treated as amateurs rather than professionals—since such behavior would be presumptive evidence that their work was of such low caliber that they could not secure support from established patrons.[8] The markets for scientific and decorative objects have become almost completely differentiated, save for the very humble or very important specimens; minerals and shells of no particular scientific interest grace many homes, for example, while such fossils as dinosaur remains loom so large in the popular imagination that private collectors have driven their prices to exorbitant levels in their competition with scholarly institutions to acquire them (Browne 1994).

Through the nineteenth century, however, gentlemanly disdain for the dirty work field research entailed was reinforced by the commodification of natural objects and by the crudely commercial relationships armchair scholars had with the suppliers of their materials. Collectors could, at best, be regarded as consummate craftsmen-tradesmen. A highly skilled fieldworker such as the British Thomas Drummond could sell his services relatively dearly for gentlemen's expensive projects. In 1831, for example, he was hired by a consortium of naturalists who wanted evidence from the United States and Mexico. They not only equipped, shipped, and paid him for a collecting expedition, but also supported his wife and children during his absence. Upon Drummond's death in 1835, however, his lowly status among the population of naturalists was made clear when he was eulogized as having "walk[ed] in science far beneath the lofty platform which Cuvier constructed," albeit "unrivaled in the path [he] chose" (quoted in Larsen 1993: 256). Or, consider the case of Paul du Chaillu, a French-born American who traveled to equatorial Africa in the middle of the nineteenth century. His exploration financed by the Academy of Natural Sciences of Philadelphia, he produced reports of African peoples and their natural environment, which were particularly notable because they reported his observations of the gorilla. But du Chaillu's accounts were not accepted as authentic until gentlemen-scientists attested to their veracity (McCook 1996). Thus, mediating agents among the scientific elite were required to disseminate the information accumulated by men such as Drummond and du Chaillu; in scientific communications, these agents' social status counted more than the authority of direct experience.

Drummond and du Chaillu were exceptional among collectors, because they commanded relatively high respect from the elite arbiters of scientific judgment; they evidently had considerable latitude in the exercise of their commissions. Other sorts of collectors, residents of exotic places, also had a measure of independence, earning their livelihoods by establishing steady relationships with European buyers of natural history specimens (see, e.g., Haddon 1900: 280). It was common practice, however, for ordinary collectors to be paid piece rates for their finds, and to receive specific instructions to acquire particular specimens that they might chance upon while pursuing their regular occupations at home or abroad. Some collectors were actually forced laborers. From a few tantalizingly elusive records, it is possible to infer that in such places as Australia it was considered appropriate to impress prisoners into scientific service. There is also clear documentation that slaves were purchased in various foreign parts for the specific purpose of having them gather scientific data (see, e.g., Larsen 1993: chapters 4 and 6; Shortland 1994: 38–39). The mere existence of slave-collectors demonstrates the low esteem in which fieldwork was held.

This is not to say that the arguments for the superiority of accounts based on direct observation were not rehearsed well before the end of the nineteenth century. The centuries-long debate over the existence of a great continent in the South Pacific provides a particularly compelling example, not the least because it stands at the origin of the fieldwork tradition. Armchair geographers, extrapolating from first principles, postulated an undiscovered continent rich in minerals; the continent of South America was filled with gold and silver, and it therefore followed that a comparable land mass existed in similar latitudes elsewhere. Capt. James Cook's mid-eighteenth-century voyages around Australia and New Zealand ought to have put an end to such speculations, but there were those who refused to accept the evidence that he and subsequent explorers provided, most notably the Frenchmen who believed the British and Dutch to be deliberately concealing the existence of a great southern continent because they wished to exploit its riches without competition from them (Mackay 1993: esp. 266–272). French conjectural biogeography similarly postulated that the new world of North America was literally new—its indigenous animal, vegetable, and human species immature variants of European types—inspiring early American naturalists to document the superiority of American flora and fauna in order to validate their claims that an ideal society could arise within it (White 1992: 886).

By the middle of the nineteenth century, debates over the value of field observations were explicitly framed by claims about rival modes of scientific practice. When James David Forbes, professor of natural philosophy at Edinburgh, went to the Alps to study glaciers, for example, his defense of his method was of the genre anthropologists would later elaborate: "People who visit a glacier and return to the civilized world at night think they get a good idea of it," he wrote in 1841, "but it is only a protracted residence amongst the Icy Solitudes which imbues one truly with their spirit [and] enables one to reason confidently concerning things so widely rumored from common experience." But for two decades Forbes confronted the opposition of the Cambridge mathematical theorist William Hopkins, who deduced the physics of glacier motion from mathematical models and laboratory investigations of the effects of force on solids and fluids (quoted and discussed in Hevly 1996).

Disputes such as that between Forbes and Hopkins are significant because they represent a recurrent debate in scientific circles. At issue in their contest was nothing less than the relative merits of antithetical ways of knowing: deductive reasoning, based on eternal truths intuitively understood by superior minds—a style of scientific inquiry often associated with a defense of aristocratic authority; and inductive reasoning, based on experience and leading to progressively improved interpretations of empirical evidence—a style of science endorsed by (relatively) democratically constituted communities of practitioners, which has often been associated with advocacy of meritocratic social ideals (see, e.g., Richards 1986). In no small part, the expansion of university systems at the end of the nineteenth century represented expression of the latter ideal, which entailed both repudiation of the didactic method once typical of higher education and pursuit of empirical research that might serve practical ends. The best place for scientific instruction was no longer to be the lecture hall but the site of direct inquiry—whether this was the laboratory or the field (see, e.g., Owens 1985). And the scientist whose lectures described phenomena he had never seen would feel himself something of a fraud, a man accustomed to "retailing second-hand goods over the counter" (Haddon quoted in Quiggin 1942: 77).

Thus, it is hardly surprising that when the restructured universities provided actual or aspiring members of the middle classes with opportunities for professional careers in the natural history sciences, the new professionals inverted the prestige hierarchy of gentlemen-naturalists. They declared that armchair theorists, innocent of both scientific training and personal experience of the substance of their speculations, were incapable of appreciating the significance of whatever empirical materials came their way. Furthermore, untrained collectors casually gathering information while passing through foreign parts could not possibly identify data of scientific significance, since sustained observation was required to appreciate the situational context within which evidence had meaning (see, e.g., Read in Garson and Read 1892: 87). Articulating the perspective of fieldworkers of every type, A. C. Haddon wrote that only from direct inspection could the anthropologist understand "native actions . . . from a native and not from an [sic] European point of view" (Haddon 1893: 131).[9] Moreover, he noted that the fusion of the roles of observer and theorist that he recommended to anthropologists had already been effected in kindred scientific fields with admirable results (Haddon 1905: 511–512).

Given the transformed character of the university, it is also not surprising that the new professional creed represented the introduction of practical concerns into the academy, as well as the extension of an age-old philosophic conflict. When, for example, the colonial official and travel writer H. H. Romilly argued in 1887 that it was impossible for "students of savage races" to grasp "the social laws by which they are governed" without residence "of considerable duration" among them, he was voicing a view common among self-styled "practical men": the scholar in the study could not achieve through abstract speculation an understanding equal to the knowledge gained through action (Romilly 1887: 8; and see Kuklick 1991: esp. 191–199). Appeals to concrete experience became routine among practitioners of subjects newly established in the university—a congeries of putatively utilitarian enterprises, of which the natural history sciences were only a fraction.

Thus twentieth-century naturalists dismissed their predecessors' disdain for the ungentlemanly labors fieldwork entailed. Indeed, they so glorified the erstwhile collectors' role that they often seemed to have embraced the epistemological premises on which it rested, representing their observations as unmediated by any theoretical framework. This was not the case, however, and not just because unqualified empiricism is an intellectual impossibility. Theorizing continued to be a high-status activity, serving as the medium of communication among specialists devoted to studying particular species and places. But the experience of fieldwork became the defining property of truly scientific research. That experience was represented in the heroic terms that still persist among all varieties of fieldworkers, as an ordeal that perforce sharpens the worker's observational powers. Furthermore, the venture into the field became a rite of passage of disciplinary socialization for extrinsic as well as intrinsic reasons, as I intimated earlier. That is, one could not do fieldwork without first acquiring the wherewithal to do so. Therefore, to have convinced the financial gatekeepers of one's discipline that one was a worthy candidate for initiation into the mysteries of the field was to have proven oneself a qualified candidate for full professional status.

PROOF AND PERSUASION

That scientists had suffered the character-building rigors of fieldwork did not, however, suffice to confer presumptive plausibility on their reports. Like Ishmael in Melville's *Moby Dick*, they addressed their audiences from a peculiar position: they claimed the status of privileged witnesses to the phenomena they described. Of course, as the only survivor of the wreck of the *Pequod*, Ishmael can be our only source of information about the crew's experience. But fieldworkers reporting their observations to fellow scholars have assumed a similar role, since they have been obliged to impress audiences whose members cannot independently corroborate workers' accounts. Thus, fieldworkers of every disciplinary variety have followed a recognizable strategy. Drawings and photographs of the scientists' subjects, narratives full of vivid details of particular places and incidents—these have been the devices by which fieldworkers have imparted an authoritative authenticity to their descriptions, and thereby (presumably) persuaded readers of the soundness of their judgments.

It is arguably the case that fieldworkers' literary technology has been little different from that deployed by laboratory scientists, who have from the earliest days of experimental research sought to describe their results in a fashion sufficiently detailed to render their readers "virtual witnesses" to experimental work (Shapin 1984). Laboratories are, after all, dedicated spaces, accessible just to skilled practitioners, whose reports are persuasive only if they adhere to the formal conventions of their genre. But it has been axiomatic to the practice of laboratory science that its findings are credible only if reproducible, that there is nothing peculiar to a time or place at which an experiment is performed that cannot be recreated (pace the recent efforts by sociologists of science to discredit the ideology of reproducibility [see, e.g., Knorr Cetina 1992]). In significant contrast, fieldworkers from nineteenth-century glaciologists to contemporary field biologists have resisted suggestions that the questions they ask can be even partially answered with reproducible laboratory procedures: the phenomena they study, which are situationally specific and historically contingent, cannot be simulated in the laboratory (see, e.g., Haila 1992: 234–235).

It is worth emphasizing that this argument is not restricted to practitioners of the human sciences, although the potted philosophy of science that frequently figures in social science texts often proclaims that the human sciences are to be distinguished from the natural sciences by the historicity of their subject matter. Among the phenomena studied by all manner of fieldworkers, those considered by anthropology are perhaps intrinsically the most evanescent, possibly equaled in their historical specificity only by the subjects of field biology; and anthropologists have, furthermore, emphasized the urgency of recording vanishing manifestations of human diversity—although other sorts of naturalists have also aggressively pursued species nearing extinction. Thus, though all fieldworkers have been obliged to account for their conclusions in narratives that are strategically phrased to persuade (if not necessarily eloquent in terms of canonical literary standards), anthropologists in particular have placed a premium on the literary skill necessary to convey verisimilitude. Rather than imagining anthropologists' literary practices to be unique, however, we ought to locate them on a continuum of descriptive techniques employed by every variety of scientist.

Nevertheless, there has been and is an important difference between the field practices of anthropologists and the practices of other sorts of naturalists, and that may be the most important feature of anthropological fieldwork. The difference is obvious: unlike those of other sorts of naturalists, anthropologists' subjects have been persons like themselves. Other sorts of naturalists indulge in anthropomorphic projections, imputing thoughts and feelings to their subjects—seeing political order in insect colonies, altruistic behavior among plants, and conscious calculation among marine organisms, for example. Indeed, these naturalists may be troubled by their conceptual habits, and may wonder, as at least some cell biologists do, whether the systematic relationships they observe in the basic structures of living organisms might not be translations of the indefensible inequalities of gender and class that continue to plague our society—and that biologists are therefore generating ill-considered normative political theory as well as bad science (see, e.g., Gilbert 1988). But no scientists, not even physicists, can construct theories devoid of comparisons (implicit or explicit) between the behavior of the phenomena they study and human relationships (see, e.g., Krieger 1992: 56–61). Other sorts of scientists insist that the social metaphors that guide their inquiries are merely necessary heuristic devices, disaggregating the results they achieve from the theories that have informed their work. That is, they dismiss their anthropomorphic projections as fanciful glosses that are practically irrelevant. In contrast, the equivalents of these fanciful glosses among anthropologists are the substance of their stories.

Moreover, anthropologists' method is problematic in contrast to that of other field naturalists because anthropologists cannot delimit clear boundaries between the professional tasks they undertake in the field and other aspects of their existence there. Consider E. E. Evans-Pritchard's famous complaint that while he was living among the Nuer of the Sudan he suffered from "Nuerosis," brought on by their refusal to accept that some features of his life were none of their business (Evans-Pritchard 1940: 13). As Robert LeVine has observed, everything the anthropologist does in the field is fieldwork, as "he lives with or near his subjects all day long and has varied contacts with them as interviewer, visitor, friend, sometime employer, dispenser of medicine, driver, fictive kinsman" (LeVine 1973: 207).

How did anthropologists come to defend their method of understanding their subjects' modes of thinking and feeling? Formal rationales of intensive fieldwork are by no means identical, but one can argue that at base they all reflect the assumption that participant observation is effective because anthropologists can themselves become experimental instruments. Following unfamiliar ways of life, anthropologists supposedly almost involuntarily come to resemble their subjects, although they retain sufficient intellectual distance to be able to describe their sensations. The supposition underlying a method may never be so clearly articulated as during the early stages of that method's development, and so I offer as evidence of it the 1897 report of a German explorer, K. E. Ranke, who for a time lived among a Brazilian people and imitated their behavior.

Ranke's personal history revealed to him the psycho-physical dynamic of how each individual allocated energies, which resulted in the maintenance of high and low cultures. Assiduously cultivating in himself those habits he understood to be distinctive features of the aboriginal way of life, habits of attention he conceptualized as those necessary for survival in an unimproved environment, he developed formidable skills of vision, hearing, and smell. Such skills had long figured in travelers' marvelous tales of supposedly savage behavior, and through the experience of acquiring them, Ranke believed that he had learned why one person could not simultaneously sustain the habits of savagery and civilization; at the same time as he developed his sensory powers, he "lost his capacity for the aesthetic enjoyment of scenery" and for contemplating "the more serious problems of life" (described by Rivers in Haddon 1901, 1903: 45, 70).

The assumption that the fieldworker was an instrument persisted, although none of the conditions that prompted its acceptance did. With professionalization, anthropology ceased to recruit from the ranks of medical practitioners, whose technique of autoexperimentation arguably inspired the method of participant observation (see, e.g., Rivers 1908: esp. 102–107). Anthropologists (and others) moved away from the nineteenth century's obsession with the laws of energy as expressed in the science of thermodynamics; translated into individual terms by Herbert Spencer and his followers among students of human psychology, these laws provided a plausible explanation for experiences such as Ranke's, permitting the conceptualization of each individual as a closed system endowed with a fixed portion of energy. And, of course, anthropology abandoned the theory Ranke's autoexperiment addressed, premised on the assumption that differences among types of societies could be described in qualitative, hierarchical terms.

To contemporary anthropologists pondering the future of their discipline, then, it may seem that basing the definition of their enterprise on the classical fieldwork tradition is at the heart of its problematic identity. The point of this cursory history of the field method's emergence among the entire family of natural history sciences is that it is the experience of the worker in the field, not the field site as such, that is problematic. Certainly, the association of fieldwork with manly heroism that became conventional during the nineteenth century has persisted in all sciences of the field. All of these sciences have invoked narratives of stoic endurance and daring exploits when socializing aspiring practitioners in their disciplinary identities; the field as proving ground looms large in the self-images of many field scientists. Nevertheless, many field scientists are likely to represent their field experiences primarily as the necessary means of collecting evidence. Botanists who now want to inventory the vanishing species of the shrinking Amazonian rain forest, say, obviously cannot do their research without going into the field. The advent of the video camera has allowed at least some primatologists to assume a stance reminiscent of nineteenth-century armchair anthropologists; these primatologists maintain that they can base their analyses of primate behavior on filmed records rather than on their own observations in the field (Brody 1996). Anthropologists, by contrast, have made fieldwork an end in itself, assuming that their observational powers are magnified when they interact with their subjects; if their creed is not unique, it is perhaps particularly fervent. But critical examination of anthropologists' methodological commitment involves far more than consideration of the parlous political position that many ascribe to anthropology, a position putatively entailing a problematic ethical orientation to research subjects that has also troubled practitioners of other human sciences.

In the final analysis, then, anthropology is distinguished from the other human sciences by its methodological stance of privileged witnessing. In the charter myth that has sustained the discipline for much of this century, the field assumed its distinctive character when individual anthropologists began to spend long periods in residence among peoples who had never before been subjected to scientific scrutiny—each of whom would thereafter be identified with the single anthropologist who had captured a record of their culture. As a historical description, this myth is flawed in every particular, but it remains the basis for the discipline's understanding of the purest expression of its mission. I do not for a moment wish to decry the value associated with the realization of this mission—identification of the diversity of social forms possible to humankind—for anthropology has performed a liberating role (even a subversive one) through sheer multiplication of instances of the variety of means by which peoples have achieved ways of life they find meaningful. As well as any form of scholarship can, anthropology has served to expand our notions of ourselves, suspending our taken-for-granted worlds and obliging us to sympathize with persons quite different from ourselves—whoever we may be. But archetypal field method currently lacks a defensible rationale. The lone fieldworker seeking to understand transient phenomena through personal experience slides all too easily from claims based on rigorous documentation to those resting on pretensions to superior (implicitly moral) individual judgment; this is a difficult position to sustain in the academy, particularly if, as is increasingly the case, the anthropologist reports not on the remote exotic but on the nearly familiar. In order to translate its mission into contemporary terms, anthropology will have to move even more self-consciously than it has already done toward new modes of representation, without abandoning the interpretative perspective that makes its very existence as a specialized enterprise worthwhile.

NOTES

1. I do not mean to suggest that there is a single discipline called "anthropology" that is practiced in identical fashion everywhere in the world. No matter which academic specialty one considers, one finds significant variations in its practice from one national context to another. Indeed, close inspection of any field in any country reveals idiosyncratic local traditions, so that one may stress the peculiarities of Chicago sociology, say, or Berlin physics, or Cambridge mathematics. But these local variations may be understood as dialects rather than languages, and, in fact, language communities offer our most reliable guide to coherent disciplinary populations. I write here, therefore, of Anglophone anthropology, with emphasis on its characteristic mode of sociocultural analysis.

Once one grants the family resemblance that links all variants of Anglophone anthropology, however, one is obliged to attend to a distinct genetic strain expressed in its American population. The beginnings of organized anthropology in nineteenth-century America indicate a strong line of filiation to the natural history sciences. But the German-born and -trained Franz Boas and his students came to dominate the field in the early twentieth century, and their work displayed contrary tendencies. From his training in natural science, Boas learned that inquiries should be directed toward establishing general laws. But during his student days, Boas also learned that idiosyncratic, historically specific manifestations of the human spirit might defy scientific generalization—a view that arguably loomed larger in his analysis as his career progressed. One can also identify a humanistic impulse in the British variant of Anglophone anthropology, but it is less strong than in the American variant. See, for example, Bunzl forthcoming.

2. It is worth noting that popular writing in the natural history sciences may still contain elements reminiscent of the writing of a century ago—personal details of investigators and the tribulations of their journeys that would be out of place in serious scholarship. See, for example, Sereno 1995.

3. Unquestionably, nineteenth-century naturalists conceived enterprises such as geology and zoology as distinct and founded specialized societies in which to pursue them as such. But any given individual was likely to pursue a range of interests within natural history—with the predictable result that scholarship in these fields betrayed authors' diverse enthusiasms.

4. Boas's fieldwork in Baffinland, unlike Haddon's in Oceania, led him to repudiate his original assumptions, however. As Boas's sometime collaborator Alexander Lesser observed, Boas found in Baffinland that "Eskimo behavior could not be explained by geographical environment except in trivial and shallow ways and that Eskimos often did things not because of geographical conditions but in spite of them" (Lesser 1968: 101). By contrast, Haddon did not repudiate the association he saw between cultural and geographical variation, but the students trained by Haddon and his associates in the 1898 Cambridge anthropological expedition to Torres Strait were to do so. See Kuklick 1996.

5. Pound is not best remembered today as an ecologist. He shortly transmuted his interest in plant sociology into a concern with the social basis of law and became a leader of legal opinion as dean of the Harvard Law School from 1916 to 1936. See Kalman 1986: 45–46.

6. I am indebted to Robert Kohler for this observation.

7. Perhaps the most conspicuous exception to this generalization is Alfred Russel Wallace. But Wallace might well have not become known as the codiscoverer of the theory of natural selection with Darwin had Darwin not effectively agreed to share credit with him. On Wallace's background and fieldwork career, see Camerini 1996.

8. When scholars become collectors today, they enjoy far more autonomy than nineteenth-century collectors did. They sell their services only on the condition that their employers recognize that the collector alone can determine which objects are worthy of acquisition; they cultivate this judgment through formal training and sustained practice. The acquisition of artifacts in the field is still likely to be seen as distasteful, low-status activity, although nowadays collectors address implicitly sympathetic audiences when they describe their unease in their role, presenting the moral compromises they have been obliged to make due to complex and unanticipated factors. See Price and Price 1992.

9. It is worth noting that during this period the fieldworkers who were supplying armchair anthropologists with data began to protest against the use made of their work. Consider the views of Lorimer Fison, who worked in Fiji as a missionary and educator, and his anthropological collaborator, A. W. Howitt. As Fison complained to L. H. Morgan in 1879, the arguments of a man such as John Lubbock could not be taken seriously, since his works could "be compiled by anybody who could afford to give an ordinary clerk a pound a week to make extracts from works on Savage Tribes in any good library." Moreover, he evidently considered himself exploited by armchair theorists; as he wrote to Morgan in 1880 after receiving an inquiry about his and Howitt's work from E. B. Tylor: "He seemed to consider that he has a heaven born right to the use of other people's brains and labors" (quoted in Stocking, ed., 1995: 25, 23).

THREE

Locating the Past

Mary Des Chene

I. HISTORY IN ANTHROPOLOGY

Anthropology has been a historical discipline for longer than it has been a field science. But the lineage of historical anthropology is not often claimed, composed as it is of now rather embarrassing ancestors, such as the socio-evolutionists, and of figures remembered for other achievements. Many earlier historical debates—like the great diffusionist controversy early in this century—are now abandoned. It would be an anticanonical history of anthropology that took not *The Nuer* (1940) but instead *The Sanusi of Cyrenaica* (1954) as Evans-Pritchard's master work. A history of history in anthropology properly would be a history of discomfiture, of turning away and then back again. From the grander questions of the nineteenth century—Where did *we* come from?—to the more circumscribed ones of modernist sensibility—How can things be *this* way?—anthropologists have packed and repacked their field kits, now stowing historical queries among the essential items, now jettisoning them as so much excess baggage.

Far from being revolutionary, then, current attention to history is, as such, central to disciplinary tradition. This is not to say, however, that we are merely reproducing the past, or not always so. The socioevolutionists' questions about the origins of social institutions are not our questions now, nor do we conceive of social change as a result of "culture *contact*," with the implication that previously impervious entities are suddenly in touch and with the overtone of contamination.

Indeed one could see the most recent turn to history as yet another effort to rid ourselves of two chronic legacies of earlier anthropologies: first, what Trouillot (1991) has called "the savage slot," a disciplinary inheritance he traces back to the Renaissance (cf. Fabian 1983: 147); second, and related, several common adjuncts of a commitment to holism—conceptions of societies as clearly bounded, overemphasis on integration and function- ality, and the valorization of personal experience as the means of knowing social worlds.

While virtually any topic that anthropologists pursue is now susceptible to historical treatment (and for this reason "historical anthropology" is not simple to characterize),[1] the theoretical motivations that have inspired his- torical anthropology are, arguably, responses to these legacies. There is a con- certed effort to depose the grand binarisms—the West versus the rest; prim- itive versus civilized; simple versus complex—to expunge them from our conceptual tool kit and, once understood not as tools for analysis but as his- torically constructed, efficacious elements of Western political projects (in- cluding social scientific ones), to subject these binarisms themselves to crit- ical historical analysis.[2] There is, perhaps most centrally, an attempt to theorize the relationships of the local to the global, leaving no place pris- tine, no society innocent of context or unimplicated in larger political processes. And there is a critique of the notion that the visible and the do- able are the sole legitimate objects of anthropological study. These recon- ceptions have entailed a move to historical explanation and, in many cases, have introduced historical social process and historical consciousness as sub- jects of anthropological study (cf. Comaroff and Comaroff 1992a; Geertz 1990; Rosaldo 1980, 1989a; Sahlins 1993).

During our most recent return to history, we have constructed a fairly confident narrative about how we turned away in the first place: function- alism is the main villain, structuralism an accessory after the fact. It may ap- pear anachronistic to invoke these paradigms, which are surely firmly situ- ated in the discipline's past. But as historical ethnographers say, the past informs the present. One may argue that we have thought our way out of functionalism—though this seems to me optimistic—and decided that structuralism does not define our thought, but it is far less clear that we have fundamentally altered our practices since the heyday of functionalism.

Stocking (1983, ed.,) has connected the institutionalization of fieldwork with a theoretical turn away from social evolutionism, a search for data "un- tainted" by evolutionary assumptions. In his reading, the institutionalization of fieldwork emerged quite directly from the early twentieth-century efforts at theoretical reorientation that eventually issued in functionalism. That ar- gument is persuasive, although I am inclined to a more dialectic view. It is striking that the emergence of the strongly presentist orientation of func- tionalism coincided quite closely with the institutionalization of fieldwork as the method, locus, and defining feature of anthropological work. Let me briefly outline three aspects of conceptions of "the field" and views about "fieldwork" that, arguably, influenced the development and endurance of ahistorical anthropology, of which I take functionalism and structuralism to be exemplary.

First, there is the matter of who has studied whom. Fieldwork premised on maximal cultural difference, exotic (and exoticized) locales, and the search for previously unstudied "field sites" made it likely that ethnographers would be neither culturally nor linguistically fluent upon arrival.[3] Many fieldwork accounts attest to an early reliance on tangible tasks, whether to gain linguistic competence while awaiting the epiphany of "rapport," or to fill idle, uncomfortable hours while others worked in more tangible fields. The early days of fieldwork are commonly reported to be filled with mapmaking, compiling word lists, collecting simple genealogies, and the like. Clifford (1988: 30–32) has remarked upon a pervasive privileging of the visual over the linguistic. We might equally note a privileging of the present over the past for the mundane reason that, however difficult to construe, the present is more accessible than the past. Faced with the overwhelming complexity of figuring out what might be going on at the moment, only those convinced that the key to comprehending that present lies in understanding antecedents will add to their burden the task of learning about the invisible past.

Second, both the tendency to do fieldwork in small communities and conceptualizations of "small-scale" societies as discrete, bounded objects of study surely made investigations into the past appear less significant. Lévi-Strauss's "cold" societies, Gluckman's structure-affirming rebellions, and a host of other formulations assured us that, while time may pass at the same rate everywhere, change is variably distributed among social formations and portions of the globe (cf. Pletsch 1981; Adas 1989). This belief had several effects, not least of which was to suggest to the aspiring fieldworker that, whenever research funds were acquired, visas in order, and porters arranged, "the field" would be ready and waiting. Anxiety over missing an infrequently held ritual is quite different from imagining that things change in fundamental respects—that "fieldwork" this year and the next are not interchangeable. Against this perspective, one may note a feature of anthropological discourse in nearly every period: that the ethnographer has arrived just prior to momentous changes and things will never be the same again. But this trope itself is premised on treating the past as a homogenous period and the present as its final iteration. The prevalence of this view across a range of theoretical orientations suggests that it rests precisely on awareness of change in the present, but assumes that change to be novel and unprecedented.

Third, views about history and historiography made the doing of historical research in the kind of locales to which anthropologists traditionally went—imagined as these sites variously were, as pristine, traditional, static, and so on—seem either impossible or unproductive. When historical evidence is equated with written documents, a person working in a nonliterate society will not pursue historical analysis. When a positivist view of historical knowledge prevails, oral materials look intrinsically unlikely to inform one about "what really happened."[4] And when field sites, and the societies they were taken to represent, appeared to be disconnected from—or at least little affected by—colonial contexts or incorporation within nation-states, many of the materials that have since looked like sources for historical ethnography appeared irrelevant to anthropological practice.

While we may now find "the field" a rather extraordinary ideological construct, it was originally a radical innovation, displacing the natural history expeditionary model (cf. Kuklick 1991; Stocking 1983), and this should not be overlooked. Current theoretical revision has produced no comparable innovation in practice. We now study not just homogeneity but also pluralism, not just the present but also the past, and our attention is focused not only on integration but also on permeable boundaries. Yet the model of a sojourn of at least nine months, and preferably more than a year, in a geographically defined field site remains standard disciplinary practice. There is a growing dissonance between research projects and research sites and methods. There is also an odd convergence with prefunctionalist anthropology; while we surely do not want to mount a Torres Straits Expedition II, it may again be time to become unmoored from "the field" that replaced such ventures.

These problems of what might be called the placement of practice are the subject of the remainder of this chapter. While I occasionally reflect on these problems as sources of skepticism in some quarters about recent ethnographic trends, my primary aim is to elucidate practical challenges of doing historical anthropology. Most discussions of the implications of historical study for anthropology have focused on theoretical and political questions.[5] What is said about innovations of practice has been overwhelmingly concerned with textual innovations in the production of ethnographies.[6] It is striking that, as we claim novelty for our projects both in conception and in result, we have had so little to say about that which intervenes—fieldwork.[7]

II. TOPOGRAPHIES OF THE FIELD

The Generic Field

"The field" pervades talk in departmental and conference corridors. We go there, return from there, and above all, we constantly make plans to go there. While in the field, we "do ethnography." The field unites us; however disparate our research foci and areal specialties, the field is the generic space within which we do what we do. And therefore, disciplinary convention has it, what we do is anthropology. This folk conception of a generic site of research, at once nowhere and everywhere—that is, anywhere an on-duty anthropologist happens to be—has consequences. Just as "the Other" is a designation that strips people of cultural and historical particularity, "the Field" strips places of their specificity; as the object and ground of anthropological practice, both "the Other" and "the Field" become ahistoricized conceptual entities, transformed by the ethnographic gaze.[8]

The generic field has thus been a unifying construct in the discipline.[9] It is perhaps in part because authors now detail their conceptions of their field sites in their ethnographies that the charter myth of a common destination has begun to come apart. As we read about the variety of ways in which different ethnographers define and arrange a place of work, and the variety of things they call fieldwork once they settle there, it becomes increasingly evident that "the field" is not so unitary a conception as the phrase implies. Studies that investigate the past make problematic the face-to-face localized encounter central to our conceptions of the generic and unifying "field." Since, quite literally, we can't go back, where is "the field"?[10]

The Situated Field

In practice, of course, anthropologists' field sites have been neither nowhere nor just anywhere. Within area studies circles, field sites are discussed in much more specific terms. Anyone setting out to do research does a great deal of pretheorizing of their field site, usually beginning at the broad level of a "culture area," a particular nation-state, perhaps a region, and finally a particular locale for fieldwork. We are trained to seek a fruitful fit between our theoretical concerns and a place that will illuminate them.[11] In order to reach one's intended field, one must display a good deal of prior knowledge about it, whether to funding agencies or orals committees. Indeed, the field is usually a rather heavily pretheorized somewhere. As Appadurai (1988a) has shown, virtually any field site in India has been pretheorized as a locus of hierarchy, influencing both topics of study and overall characterizations of social structure and process.

That "the field" might be anywhere is a fairly recent and still contested claim. Studying "at home," at least for initiatory fieldwork, is not considered by some to give a sufficient experience of difference. European field sites, to judge from the job market, are not quite as anthropological as "non-Western" ones. Many elements are evidently at work in these informal but far-reaching distinctions. Anthropological fieldwork has been premised on maximal cultural difference. The anthropologist has been assumed to be Western, so the field site must be non-Western.[12] Preferred sites have been small communities, based on the notion that both culture and social structure are most effectively observed (by anthropological methods) writ small.[13] Practice, happily, accords less and less with these prescriptions, as the tenets that made them appear to be common sense come under scrutiny and as the political-economy of the discipline is gradually altered.

The Historically Situated Field

Historical research raises another set of challenges to conceptions of the field, sometimes quite radically. Most disconcertingly, the field may not be a place at all, but a period of time or a series of events, the study of which will take a researcher to many places. Spatial contiguity is not essential to every kind of historical anthropological research. Yet even as we have revised our notion of possible fields, they have remained bounded locales. They may now be larger (cities as well as villages), Western as well as non-Western, provisional as well as permanent (see chapter 4), yet they remain bounded locales.[14] Indeed, it cuts to the heart of how anthropological fieldwork has been conceived to try to imagine work not premised on study in (if not necessarily of) a particular place.

Most historical anthropology, at least to date, is not so radical, however. As the Comaroffs have put it, "Historical anthropology . . . is dedicated to exploring the processes that make and transform particular worlds" (1992b: 31). They go on to assure us that "Insofar as global systems and epochal movements always root themselves somewhere in the quotidian, then, they are accessible to historical ethnography" (1992b: 39). Yet they also allow that "We remain heavily dependent on the observer's omniscient eye. And badly in need of a methodological apparatus to extend its range" (1992c: x).[15] We may yet try to study "global systems and epochal movements" in a way that is not rooted in the quotidian of particular locales, yet does not surrender all sense of local variability and human agency in the manner of world systems theory. But our contemporary practice of historical anthropology remains, for the most part, grounded. I concentrate here on the kind of "field" in which such historical research might be conducted.

From the point of view of a person doing historical research, "the field" may be neither a self-evident site nor a compelling metaphor for conceptualizing the terrain of study. Instead, the very task of defining a site or sites for research raises a number of questions. If one's work concerns events that have taken place in many locales, what renders one of these the primary site for research? If one's focus is on historical processes, what makes a geographically bounded residential unit the obvious object for study? If one's work concerns the lives of people who have more commonly been in motion than stationary—refugees, migrant workers, colonial district officers, academics—what makes the place where one happens to catch up with them in itself revelatory of that mobility and its meanings?

These are difficult questions. Answers will not be monolithic. Indeed, one positive outcome of historical research may be more attention to the methodological specificity of different topics of study: not "fieldwork" and its attendant tool kit, but a much wider range of research practices. I will look briefly at two propositions for defining a field that would be more amenable to historical ethnography. I then take up my own research as an example of some of the ways that traditional conceptions of the field are inadequate to historical study. I conclude this section not with any pat answers, but with some possibilities for quite a different conceptualization of historical anthropological projects, and the kind of fields and fieldwork these might entail.

Richard Fox argues for a "nearly new culture history." Not taking for granted that "Others," the given subject of anthropology, simply exist in field sites, "culture history pursues the question of who these others are and how they have come to be" (1991a: 95). He goes on to make an argument for how we should think of field sites and fieldwork if this is our project:

> Ethnography . . . finesses the question of where anthropologists should pitch their tents. It too often specifies a physical location—an inhabited jungle clearing, a village community, an urban barrio—in place of an intellectual position (cf. Fox 1972). Ethnography then has to claim authority on the basis of "having been there" and the special empathy it creates. Otherwise how could it justify its construction of "fieldwork" as meaning physical, rather than scholarly, placement? Culture history avoids these fictions about empathy; it need not take "fieldwork" to mean space instead of stance. (1991a: 96)

This seems to me to finesse the question in its own way. As Fox would undoubtedly agree, anthropologists have always included particular intellectual positions in their field kits, whether they have acknowledged it or not. That observation is never theory- or value-free seems well enough established, even though we have not necessarily learned how to cope with this fact. But fieldwork can never *only* mean stance, so long as we continue to interact with people, which seems a safe bet for the foreseeable future (cyborg anthropology aside). One cannot, then, simply set aside the question of physical location(s) and all the attendant methodological implications.

Another suggestion that seems to me more promising is what Marcus (1986) has dubbed "multi-locale ethnography." His concern is not with historical ethnography per se, nor is it with the places and practices of research. The problematic that he sets for himself is, however, relevant to both. Marcus asks, "What is holism once the line between the local worlds of subjects and the global world of systems becomes radically blurred?" (1986: 171). While he immediately turns this into a problem of text construction, one may fruitfully think about the kind of research practice that might produce the materials for that text.[16] A multilocale ethnography would, according to Marcus,

> try to represent multiple, blindly interdependent locales, each explored ethnographically and mutually linked by the intended and unintended consequences of activities within them. If the intent were merely to demonstrate random interdependencies by which everyone is unexpectedly connected to

everyone else in the modern world, if only you looked hard enough, this would be an absurd and pointless project. . . . Rather, the point . . . would be to start with some prior view of a system and to provide an ethnographic account of it, by showing the forms of local life that the system encompasses, and then leading to novel or revised views of the nature of the system itself, translating its abstract qualities into more fully human terms. (1986: 171)

He thinks of such ethnographies as studies of systems, still rooted in the quotidian, but stressing the interconnections among several locales. Marcus's imagined ethnographic text[17] would have to be based on practices quite different from those that have been or are currently extant in the discipline. What is of interest is the possibility of bringing into view historical connections simply not visible from the perch of the single fieldsite. Nor need this kind of approach be limited to studies focused on systems (his examples are markets, and capitalist modes of production, distribution, and consumption). It is not only market forces that migrate these days, but also those people affected by them. In addition, one might find the multilocale ethnography well suited to research whose central focus is a historically linked group of people, or an institution that has, over time, caused many people, from diverse locales, to traverse similar circuits.[18]

To see how multilocale research might produce new possibilities for historical anthropology, I turn to the limitations that conceptions of the field created for my own research when I studied the history of Nepali men's careers as Gurkha soldiers in the colonial Indian and British armies. Much of this research[19] concerned how the past informed the present: the effects of this labor on current economic and social arrangements, and the role of military experience in shaping men's views of their present circumstances. It thus made sense to carry out this work in a community that included many retired soldiers, and I purposely went to a large village heavily recruited for many years.

This bounded locale, while an obvious and *necessary* site for speaking to such men about their pasts,[20] was in no sense a *sufficient* vantage point from which to understand how past army careers informed the present. I made some effort to follow paths of migration, visiting urban sites to which some former soldiers had relocated. I interviewed former British officers while doing archival research in England. And I brought archival materials and published accounts of Gurkhas to Nepal, and translated and read them to former soldiers. All these were ways in which I worked to overcome limitations of the bounded field site when the object of study radiated in so many directions beyond it.

Yet it remains the case that while I was aware of post-army migration, both domestic and international, and of the fact that not all Gurkhas return to Nepal after retirement, I took place of origin, quite unthinkingly, to be a naturally primary site for research. What makes those who return home ethnographically prior to those who do not, other than that they are natives in their native place?[21] Time, money, and the constraints of visas made the village and points of migration within Nepal primary. But so too did my notion of "the field." While I thought, rather idly, that it would be ideal to work also in Malaysia, Hong Kong, Borneo, and Brunei, where many Nepali men had spent their army careers, it did not occur to me, for example, to ask one of them to accompany me on such a journey. Nor is it clear to me that the definitions of fieldwork that guide funding choices would countenance such a journey even now.

Since I first wrote the above paragraph, I have thought seriously about attempting just such a research trip. Some with whom I have discussed the idea have immediately seen the potentialities, while others smirked and implied that I was in search of a junket. One person memorably described such a project as a form of "beach ethnography." Yet even in my dissertation there are passages, like the following, that clearly show how multilocale work could have enriched my understanding:

> Gurungs have much experience of separation and they are skilled at keeping those who are gone palpably present. Threshing rice in a field where the year before one threshed with someone who is now absent evokes memories and stories that would not be recounted anywhere else. This relation of place and memory also informs the way that *lahures* [Gurkha soldiers] think about their time in the army. One of the tasks of spring is to cut bamboo for new baskets, mats and herding sheds. . . . Two Malaya *lahures* [men who served in the British Army in Malaya between 1948 and 1970] meeting on a forest path in the course of such a journey are as likely to converse in Malayan as in Gurung or Nepali. In the village Malayan occasionally functions as a secret language, a handy means for saying things like "Let's go drink some liquor at the hotel." . . . But in the forest it is a language connected with certain places and times. Conversations are simple—queries about where one is going, comments on the weather and the like. A mutual past is invoked and savored as two *lahures* pass in Malaya-like deep forest. It is when one leaves the paths and begins to hack one's way up steep tangled hillsides with a *khukri* [Nepali knife carried in the army] that tales about Malaya and Borneo are often told. It was during the course of this work that I heard about living for weeks in the deep jungle, sleeping two under a tarpaulin strung between the trees, on the wet jungle floor. I heard about eating out of "mess kits," in which the same container served as both pot and plate, and about going hungry when a fire could not be lit for security reasons or because supplies had run out. I heard about the varieties of snakes and spiders that inhabit the Malayan jungle, and about night "reconnaissance" missions, when one was as likely to encounter a tiger as a human enemy. I was told that this jungle, though I could imagine none denser, was like a well-trodden path compared to those in Borneo. Though they did not say so there in the jungle—because they did not need to—this was what *lahures* thought I should know if I wanted to know about their lives in the army. In the village they said, you must know about how we ate, how we slept, but

they found it difficult to tell me. In the jungle, as we sweated to cut bamboo together or to climb a steep hillside, the telling had resonance. Just as harsh terrain traversed in the course of difficult labor recalled times of hardship, easier paths taken in the course of lighter work inspired more light-hearted instruction. Walking single-file on forest paths my *lahure* friends delighted in vanishing into the woods. Silence would descend until a well-thrown stone would make me glance in the wrong direction. A chuckle might point me in the right direction, but the hidden *lahure* would invariably emerge from another direction, having silently circled around me. Direct questions about the skills that made them such good soldiers, in the British estimation, usually evoked a laugh or *"kuni"* (who knows?) in response, but when time and place were right, they delighted in showing me those skills. (Des Chene 1991: 348–350)

What might it add to my understanding to walk with former Gurkhas in the jungles of Malaysia or Borneo? Clearly, one cannot return to the "Malaya Emergency" in which so many of these men fought. But one could return to the site where a man killed Chinese guerillas. Talking about it there rather than (or in addition to) talking in his distant home would inevitably evoke different kinds of memories. When we do oral history of events in living memory, such potential is vast if we can get beyond our limited ideas of what constitutes the field and, equally, what constitutes the lives and memories of those who live in it.[22]

Arjun Appadurai (1988b) has given us the vivid image of the "incarcerated native." He used this image to point both to our conceptualization of bounded locales and static societies, and to the fact that while we arrive, by choice, to study, those who live "there" can only flee, resist, or comply. There is another aspect to this: ethnographers must learn to cope—both analytically and pragmatically—with the fact that many of those from whom they learn may be more "mobile"[23] than themselves. Research confined to a bounded locale when the topic of study is not geographically confined and when that locale is but one dwelling place of those about whom one hopes to learn is comparable in its problems to treating a freeze-frame image of a particular present as a generalizable portrait.

When one also wants to travel through time, "trying to look back and look sideways at the same time" as Geertz (1990: 323) has put it, this becomes a serious problem indeed. There are tangible institutional constraints on multilocale ethnographic projects that might do more than take many snapshots in a series of places. Some grants are defined by geographical area and do not accommodate research that transgresses the boundaries of "culture areas." Funds are, in any case, a scarce commodity. So, too, is time for research, whether leave time from teaching or the slot allotted to "fieldwork" in graduate programs. The scholarly challenges are equally daunting. A multilocale ethnography might require the learning not of one "field language," but of a number of languages. And while we can and should question what "areal competence" is taken to mean in anthropology, a multilocale ethnography would also entail acquiring knowledge about many places and their historical contexts.

The result I can imagine that would be quite radically different from current practice would be less emphasis on a measured "progress" from one research project to a new one. Rather, we might engage in more extended study. Quite literally, we might spend more time researching "one" topic,[24] even if this were extended over many periods of research—or, otherwise conceived, over breaks in research. Such research would be less fixed by and fixated on a priori definitions of locale, and more amenable to following cultural phenomena and political processes across both time and space.

Archives as Field Sites

Among the places anthropologists now go, when they go to the field, is the archive. Of all the transgressions that one generation is wont to perform when carrying on the traditions of previous ones, this has been greeted with perhaps the greatest discomfiture.[25] Are we to become historians? Armchair anthropologists once again? Across the aisle in the archives, historians sometimes cast a curious glance at these new arrivals as well. Situated between these gazes, anthropologists who go to archives have had to think about their claim to such places as legitimate field sites.

This is not to say that anthropologists have not previously looked at documents that they themselves did not write. Documents found "in the field" are treated as a somewhat different category than those deposited elsewhere. Preferably musty, casually brought out of baskets or satchels, "indigenous documents," especially in predominantly nonliterate field sites, sometimes have been treated as rare finds and great sources of cultural information. Records of land tenure, local censuses, and the like have also been possible sources of information—though until recently they have been mined more for factual information than examined as artifacts that could chart, for example, state interventions over time.

So it is not just reading notes that one did not write and that do not describe the (ethnographic) present that has caused unease. It is when an anthropologist who ostensibly studies India sits in an archive in England, one who studies Brazil is found in Portugal, an Indonesianist works in the Netherlands, that heads begin to shake. My examples, of course, point to likely sources of documents for colonial periods.[26] Many consider the study of such archival materials to be at best supplementary to, never constitutive of, fieldwork. Thus, the archive is more like a library than like a "field." While my own projects have sought to bring together archival materials, the results of oral historical research, and ethnographic research on the present, I would argue that there are eminently anthropological projects that might be conducted wholly in the archives.

The first line of defense against criticism of the archive as field site has been to assure skeptics that we take an anthropological attitude toward the documents we peruse. To study archives themselves—as cultural phenomena —would, of course, be an acceptably anthropological enterprise (cf. Cohn 1987 [1962]). It is doing fieldwork *in* archives that is suspect. But if one is studying the past, there are several ways in which it is bad faith or naiveté to claim that the past is intrinsically more "present" in material traces in a physical locale than in documents written at the time by actors with whom one cannot now speak. And there are several ways in which it is legitimate to say that one can (re)construct, in a process as painstaking as fieldwork in more traditional fields, knowledge about social worlds now past by treating both documents and their authors as interlocutors. The Comaroffs make the argument well:

> A historical ethnography, then, must begin by constructing its own archive. It cannot content itself with established canons of documentary evidence, because these are themselves part of the culture of global modernism—as much the subject as the means of inquiry. . . . Moreover, we have to operate with a working theory not merely of the social world, but also of the role of inscriptions of various kinds in the making of ideology and argument. . . . Our methods should tell us something of the way in which personal acts become social facts. . . . If texts are to be more than literary topoi, scattered shards from which we presume worlds, they have to be anchored in the processes of their production, in the orbits of connection and influence that give them life and force. (1992b: 34)

As one who pioneered this path advised me before I first set out "to the archives," archival work is an ethnographic enterprise. One must discover structural principles of organization, and who speaks to whom and in what register. The condensation of archival material into notes is an interpretive task akin to that of writing fieldnotes, and when notes of either sort are then elaborated into prose, the work is much the same.[27] But in the nature of the knowledge upon which one's interpretations rest, there remain crucial differences.

A good historian is sometimes said to have made the documents "speak." But the metaphor of conversation with the past should not be carried too far. A better metaphor would be that of "overhearing": it is from conversations among engaged and positioned subjects that one conjures answers to one's queries. The materials of the archives are a lacunary deposit from records of the past. Of what is missing, one only sometimes knows that it is missing at all.[28] One may "ask new questions" of the documents, or discover a document that answers one's query. But one cannot ask that the archives fill silences or that they comment on the fact of silence itself.

Imagine an ethnography based entirely on what one overheard in confidential conversations. Add to this that one overheard, say, only one-fifth of those conversations. Add further that those conversations concerned events and places that one had never experienced or seen. A second-order ethnography of this sort would hardly satisfy disciplinary expectations, even as they are currently being revised, yet they are conditions commonly confronted by archival researchers.

But the archives also contain extraordinary possibilities. My research on Gurkhas has ranged across 180 years. Even the hardiest of fieldworkers do not live so long. Imagining I had been "present" over this period of time, fieldwork still would not have been clearly superior to archival research. The work would require simultaneous access to an impossible array of subjects: governor-generals and countercolonial organizers, soldiers on opposite sides of battle lines. Allowing such transhistorical and omniscient observation is both the great power and the great illusion of the archives.

Ethnographers have sometimes entertained the illusion of achieving such a vantage point, especially when studying "small-scale" societies. But every ethnographer is, of course, positioned in multiple ways, not just in relation to texts, but also in relation to persons within a social field. A document cannot change itself as it encounters different readers, however astute its rhetoric.[29] One cannot say the same of those with whom ethnographers speak. Thus, the idea that face-to-face fieldwork is somehow a direct route to full(er) knowledge of either past or present is unconvincing. The ethnographer in the archives and in "the field" is not, in this sense, in such different kinds of research sites after all.

Though ethnography has the advantage of proceeding through dialogue and potentially addressing any question, eliciting rather than merely searching for answers, precisely this aspect of ethnographic practice has raised the most difficult questions about what sort of knowledge its results represent. One can argue that fieldwork is as fragmentary as some archival work may be, and that it is as amenable to the crafting of a partial portrait, both in the sense of incompleteness and in the sense of being shaped by our predilections. It is useful for us to be cognizant of the sometimes different epistemological challenges that archival research and field research present. But it becomes increasingly clear as we cast an ethnographic eye toward the past that to continue to valorize the face-to-face encounter will impoverish our accounts. It will be far more useful to attend to the relation between our research questions and the possible sources that will illuminate them, and to follow these wherever they may lead us and in whatever medium they may turn out to exist.

III. DISPLACING ANTHROPOLOGY

While we may have rejected the functionalist view of bounded cultural entities and harmoniously integrated social systems, the geographically defined field site held to be appropriate to the study of such entities and systems remains our dominant model. Indeed, we generally take it to be one of the strengths of anthropological research that we study in depth and attend to the minutiae of daily practice. Such research seems to require a well-defined "somewhere."[30] This is one source of unease, one that I find misguided, about recent ethnographic experimentation, and particularly about efforts to theorize transnational phenomena. Where is the field, or as I have heard it put more than once, Where's the ethnography? which amounts to the same question for those who worry. The addition of archives to our roster of possible field sites, the study of such nonlocalized phenomena as electronic communication, studies based wholly in the past, and a host of other shifts in our projects seem to be greeted by some as further gloomy evidence of the splintering or the decline of the discipline.

Yet, ironically, it is also an old and central disciplinary claim that anthropology ultimately illuminates much more than its traditional out-of-the-way fieldwork locales.[31] Anthropologists have always striven to move "beyond" the field, but only in theory. From efforts to discover the story of human evolution in the Australian Outback to claims about the nature of adolescence based on observations in Samoa, we have argued from the beginning that our task is not merely a description of the particular. Questions of generality and typicality have vexed anthropological theorizing from the inception of fieldwork and they are perhaps why the generic "field," a formulation that made it easier to avoid these questions, has undergone little scrutiny. We have, somewhat paradoxically, touted lengthy stays in clearly defined locales as the source of authority for our accounts,[32] and hastened to say—I quote Clifford Geertz here—"The locus of study is not the object of study. Anthropologists don't study villages (tribes, towns, neighborhoods . . .); they study in villages" (1973b: 22).

Study of events that occurred in the past and in many locales complicates this happy picture. Teasing the general out of the particular no longer appears necessarily to be best accomplished by pitching one's tent in one central location. Too many events that explain that center, however small or apparently remote, happen elsewhere. More literal movement "beyond the field"—to multiple and disparate sites of research, and to locales that did not previously count as "the field"—ought to be seen as holding great promise, not as threatening the heart of the ethnographic enterprise. Moving around (or not) as necessary and seeking traces of the past are two of many ways we might be able to achieve a less extractive kind of research, to study villages (towns, neighborhoods . . .), not just study in them, while still (or rather thereby) illuminating larger patterns and processes (or, as the current jargon has it, global flows). Making conceptual connections between place x and theory y is insufficient. It is by making historical connections between places that we can both make theoretical advances and better learn about the people and social phenomena we study. Historical research may thus lead us to take the present of the peoples and places we study more seriously.

There are, broadly speaking, two apparently divergent trends in historical ethnography.[33] Some recount the minutiae of social life in real time (e.g., Rosaldo 1980), while others concentrate on large-scale systems over long time periods (e.g., Mintz 1985). In the first case, rather than concatenating many observations of discrete events into a typical one, or many individuals into a social type, historical ethnographies often describe particular individuals and specific occurrences, taken not as representative of something else, but as subjects of analysis in themselves. One worry about this trend is that by hewing closely to the particular, one loses analytic power; ethnographies will resemble the map that Lewis Carroll imagined (when rolled out, it covered the entire terrain it represented). But good work of this kind has no such result. Rather, precisely by recounting particulars and paying attention both to intentions and unplanned contingencies—to the small details of which even the grandest events are composed—it provides powerful tools for explaining social processes.

In the other kind of historical ethnography, one may encounter few individuals, and hear scant detail about happenings in particular locales. Rather, such studies are often populated by systems and institutions—markets, political apparatuses, economies—and specific events are often of a large-scale kind—a revolution, colonization. One worry about this trend is that it is not ethnographic, failing to render intimate portraits of a small group of people and their place of residence. Another, more serious concern is that it runs roughshod over the intricate variations knowable only through close study of particular cases, and thus its general claims are not well grounded. Yet good work of this kind can bring into view the cumulative and widely ramifying effects of the activities of many people in many places, effects not readily discernible from any single location in either time or space.

It seems clear to me that we should want both kinds of accounts, and that together, they can teach us more than either separately. They depend, of course, on very different kinds of "fieldwork." It seems as foolish to argue that only one kind of ethnography is desirable as it is to argue that only one kind of "field" can or should be the site for anthropological research. The world is far too large and complex to hold sacred the connected, smallish plot of land known as "the field" as the only vantage point from which to observe it, and still to hold out hope of having much to say about it.

When "the field" need no longer consist of a geographically bounded locale, new horizons open up.[34] By attending to the invisible past, we may discover new topographies, ones specific to a field of study rather than dictated by disciplinary culture area maps. Historicized topographies can show us unsuspected connections—between sites previously treated as rather remote

and the nation-states of which they are a part, and between our own histories and those of people we study.[35] Altering our research practices, including the ways we conceptualize locales for study and understand such connections, is one step on the path to a more coeval treatment of other places
and other people. Timelessness and immobility have been two core components of the ideas—which still have some hold on the discipline—of the
"simple" society, the "traditional" society, or, more recently, the "developing"
society. Breaking with our fixed notions of the field will help us purge these
vestiges of social evolutionism. Historical research illuminates the many links
between places we have thought of as "the field" and those that we have not
imagined in this way. In the course of discovering such connections, I hope
that we will not just add more "field sites" to the anthropological map, but
instead fundamentally rethink the relations among places, projects, and
sources of knowledge.

NOTES

I presented an earlier version of this chapter at the 1993 meeting of the American Anthropological Association in a session of the same title as this book. I thank
Akhil Gupta and James Ferguson for inviting me to contribute to both the AAA session and the book. In 1984, Renato Rosaldo asked me how I thought the then fairly
recent resurgence of interest in history would alter the anthropological landscape.
Like a good historian, I have waited until I could look back to formulate a (partial)
reply, but I thank him for putting the question in my mind. The research in Nepal
and England that occasioned these reflections has been funded by the Social Science Research Council, the American Council of Learned Societies, and faculty research grants from the University of British Columbia and Bryn Mawr College.

1. Historical anthropology is not amenable to summation for several reasons. It
has no discrete subject matter, though some topics, such as nationalism and capitalism, have been more thoroughly "historicized" than others. It is thus better thought
of, as it has developed, as an orientation rather than as a "subdiscipline." Yet this too
is unsatisfactory, for many kinds of history—social, cultural, structural, Marxist, *An-
nales*, and others—have become intertwined with many strands of anthropology. Indeed, it sometimes appears that enduring arguments between, broadly speaking, ma-
terialist and idealist orientations in anthropology are now being rehearsed in a
historical idiom.

2. The literature on colonialism is the most prominent exemplar of a critique of
Western political projects in this vein. On social scientific essentializations of "the
Other" see, for example, Adas 1989; Appadurai 1988a, 1988b; Clifford 1988; Fabian
1983; Pletsch 1981; Said 1989; Trouillot 1991.

3. I set aside here instances in which one ethnographer works over many years
in one locale on the grounds that this has been more the exception than the norm.
Also, while we may speak about working in a place "for twenty years," this often refers
to one long (i.e., one- to two-year) research period and a number of short return
trips, sometimes with many years intervening. Among those who did carry out ex-

tensive work in a single locale in the past, why this *longue durée* vantage did not necessarily inspire historical accounts might be worth exploring. Besides theoretical orientations that led people away from historical investigations, one might want to consider the disciplinary requirement to study *new* topics, to move on and to "build" upon
previous work. Ironically this may, in itself, have worked against the development,
over time, of historical understanding.

4. Even Jan Vansina's important work *Oral Tradition* (1965) is characterized by a
preoccupation with how to extract true historical accounts from unreliable "witnesses." Cf. Vansina's partial reformulation of his views in *Oral Tradition as History*
(1985).

5. See, for example, Comaroff and Comaroff 1992a; Roseberry 1989; Thomas
1989b.

6. This should be distinguished as another kind of critique, not necessarily focused on historical study, though especially concerned of late with relations between
the local and the global. An important early statement is Marcus and Cushman 1982
(cf. Clifford and Marcus 1986; Geertz 1988). Behar and Gordon (1995) add to this
literature an examination of textual innovation in feminist anthropology. It is striking that historical ethnographies, which have been of necessity innovative in their
representational strategies, have not received much attention in literature on ethnographic writing. One exception is Geertz 1990 and the response by Rosaldo 1990.

7. From *Writing Culture* (Clifford and Marcus 1986) through *Recapturing Anthropology* (Fox 1991) to *Rereading Cultural Anthropology* (Marcus 1993), one sees this emphasis on theoretical reorientations and textual innovations. *Decolonizing Anthropology* (Harrison, ed., 1991) has more to say about practice, primarily the ethical
and political dimensions of encounters and depictions. *Fieldnotes* (Sanjek 1990) focuses on the writing done "in the field" but is concerned to characterize the production and use of "fieldnotes," not to rethink "fieldwork" in relation to contemporary problems.

8. Several audience members at the AAA session in which this chapter was initially presented described a dilemma arising quite directly from this habit of transforming places into fields. Doing research at home produced uncertainty: When was
their neighborhood "the field," and when was it (or could it ever be) simply their
neighborhood? They also raised the issue of closure: since "the field" was not a place
they would leave at the conclusion of research, research could not be concluded by
leaving, and it constantly erupted into what has traditionally been the discrete space
of "writing up."

9. Just as "the field" has served as a unifying construct in informal anthropological talk, so too has "the village" (one wonders if urban anthropologists use "the neighborhood" to the same effect).

10. A "field site" that meets with special skepticism is the archive, discussed in the
section "Archives as Field Sites." Studies that take on nonlocalized phenomena similarly raise challenges to the model of in situ observation. See, for example, Tunstall
1995.

11. There is good sense in this up to a point. One would not do well to study the
impact of the Internet in a place without electricity. But there is often a more troubling implication of a typology of societies in this dictum. The notion that some parts
of the globe are more "historical" than others is a case in point.

12. That this has not always been and is increasingly not the case does not change the implied norms of disciplinary practice. The contradictory experiences of foreign and minority graduate students in North American anthropology programs emphasize current disciplinary confusion over the relations between cultural identity and the possibility of conceiving of a place as a field site. The following is anecdotal, but telling. Several people have told me that they were forbidden or actively discouraged from doing dissertation research in their own countries, in Africa and Asia, places considered eminently suitable as anthropological field sites for nonnative researchers. On the other hand, foreign and minority students are frequently expected to study their "own" communities (I place "own" in quotation marks, for I include here Asian Americans expected to seek a field site in Asia, African Americans expected to do research in Africa, and so on). While the former case, however problematic, can charitably be seen as unthinkable adherence to a logic of observation-by-contrast, the latter case can only be understood as political. It is not merely a matter of Anglo-Americans imagining they have no culture (Rosaldo 1988) and therefore cannot be a suitable subject of study. Rather, one must conclude with Fabian that it is part of "a sustained effort to maintain a certain type of relation between the West and its Other" (1983: 149). Apparently, Others studying other Others is particularly disorienting vis-à-vis disciplinary conventions.

13. See Gilsenan 1991 for an informative account of his efforts to conceptualize an urban space as a field site when available models were studies of small rural sites. He speaks of searching for his "village" in the city.

14. Having two field sites for comparative purposes has long been a possibility. This strategy emphasizes the laboratory view of the field and attempts to create a situation in which some elements are varied, others held constant. It is clearly premised on the bounded locale, and far conceptually from the idea of historically connected multiple sites, which I discuss shortly in "The Historically Situated Field."

15. Asad (1994: 67) rightly criticizes the easy movement from observation of the present to observation of the past: "'The eye,' now transposed onto an imaginary plane, is able to inhabit freely the categories of time and space (like any good story teller and listener). In other words, the 'ethnographic gaze' is taken to be the source of a knowledge because it is rooted in the researcher's ability to observe, then to imagine a meaningful world around what is witnessed and finally to present a verbal image *corresponding* to that partly-imagined, partly-witnessed world. Existing texts are admitted to be important for the ethnographic researcher, but they play a supplementary role; it is the directly visible and locatable field that remains the privileged foundation. However, in the Comaroffs' presentation, the precise connection of that empiricist foundation to the extended world of the ethnographer's imagination is obscure because the historian—who can have no such privileged foundation—is also said to depend on 'the ethnographic gaze.' Yet the historian's 'field' is not, like the ethnographer's, a visual ground on which people live but a conceptual space within which she interacts with texts. The obscurity may be resolved if by 'the ethnographic gaze' we take the Comaroffs to mean the construction of a discursive universe inhabited by representative types."

16. By moving quickly to "text construction as the crucible for integrating the micro into the macro" (1986: 170), Marcus turns attention away from the question

of what an ethnographer places in that crucible: From where and how are the elements of such an ethnographic text collected? Marcus, of course, is only one influential exemplar of the turn to "experiments" with ethnographic representation as the most promising answer to epistemological and political dilemmas. But if the ingredients are not new, and the processes by which they are collected remain the same, can the product—ethnographies—be more than, at best, apparently novel, or at worst actively deceptive? Cf. Fardon 1990 for an insightful essay on the limits of textual experimentation to address the political and epistemological shortcomings of anthropology.

17. Marcus could find no exemplar of the multilocale ethnography, instead citing some novels and journalism as the nearest approximations. One might now propose Ghosh 1992 as an exercise in historical ethnography, very different in style from what Marcus envisioned, but achieving some of the effects he advocated.

18. In the case of historically linked groups of people, such ethnographic practice is already beginning to be carried out. Ethnographies of migrant workers, for example, now often include study both in places of origin and sites of migratory labor. An example of an institutional focus might be, for example, a study of a military organization.

19. I speak here of the "ethnographic" portion of my research as opposed to archival research on the institutional arrangements of the colonial army and British conceptions of their "native" soldiers. However, this division of the ethnographic and the archival can itself be brought into question. See the section "Archives as Field Sites."

20. Strictly speaking such a large village was *not* a necessary site. This is true only when one has a notion of a critical mass, or a quorum, necessary for anthropological work to proceed. That is to say, I expect that army life may have made just as much of a difference in the lives of Nepali men who now live where there are few or no other former soldiers as it has for those who live among many retired soldiers. A concern for representativeness (though not for typicality) thus conditioned my choice of the latter kind of research site. In itself, this produces a particular kind of understanding of the effects of soldiery, one dependent on where I situated myself.

21. To be fair to my past, I also initially planned research in Dehra Dun, India, a place where many former Gurkhas who did not return to Nepal now live. Difficulties of funding and worries about time and another country's visa requirements pushed this off my ethnographic map. It remains an imagined future field.

22. There are, of course, financial as well as conceptual barriers to such research, but whatever the pragmatic difficulties, they do not change the methodological potentialities.

23. Mobility, of course, need not signify privilege. Much movement is of necessity —migrant labor and the movement of refugees are two prominent examples of movement occasioned by political-economic conditions. Gurkhas carefully distinguish between "ghumna jāne" (wandering, or what tourists in Nepal do), and "kām mā jāne," or travel undertaken in the course of work.

24. The idea of "one" topic should be construed broadly here, in the sense that, say, Kenneth Burke's or Roland Barthes's oeuvre could be said to constitute an extended meditation on one theme. Given the emphasis here on historical research, perhaps E. P. Thompson's work on English history is a more apposite example.

25. The generational characterization is not altogether appropriate; the divide is most fundamentally an epistemological one. Such breaks do, however, tend to have a relation to periods of training.

26. There would, for many projects, also be relevant archives in India, Brazil, and Indonesia. Local archives, situated in the largest sense in "the field," are somewhat more accepted as field sites.

27. These tasks are not, however, identical. See the articles in Sanjek 1990 on the ways in which fieldnotes may occasion memories of things never written down, and on the use of "headnotes." These are also possible sources of postfield revision (cf. Fabian 1983).

28. This does not necessarily distinguish archival research from ethnographic research, but it is a stronger condition for archival work.

29. It is the social field of documents' authors that one must attempt to establish. But again, while the constraints differ, the problem is not fundamentally different when one studies contemporary social fields.

30. While I have concentrated here on field sites and some of the limitations of prior conceptualizations for historical work, I think that when one moves to research *practices*, the turn to serious historical analysis of cultural phenomena may cause one to take a closer look at the wisdom of past generations. While I will not pursue this issue here, some of the more synoptic approaches of the Boasians in which they viewed archaeological evidence, oral textual traditions, architecture, material culture studies, and so on as potentially illuminating for studies of cultural phenomena may now be rediscovered. This is not to say that historical anthropologists are engaged in a salvage anthropology, seeking a glimpse of a purer cultural past as were many of the Boasians, but some aspects of their methodological tool kit may prove appropriate to theoretical questions currently being pursued.

31. Any given place is, of course, only "out-of-the-way" in relation to some other specific reference point. Embedded ideas of periphery and center, West and non-West, assessments of global or national economic or strategic significance, and many other calculations are involved in anthropological characterizations of field sites as "remote." These notions have not been sufficiently scrutinized either.

32. As a Kwakiutl man once pointedly reminded me during a workshop on the politics of social science research, lengthy stays have sometimes simply given us sufficient time to become deeply mistaken.

33. The dichotomy presented here is but one among many possible characterizations of the kinds of historical ethnography.

34. Cf. Des Chene 1996 for a related argument about paying attention to the writings of those we have commonly attended to only as oral "informants" and to "indigenous" social analysis.

35. This formulation does not depend on any particular definition of "we" and "they," other than a researcher and a people who are subjects of research.

FOUR

News and Culture: Transitory Phenomena and the Fieldwork Tradition

Liisa H. Malkki

INTRODUCTION

A great deal of recent work in anthropology and elsewhere has emphasized the historical fragility and contingency of links between people and places, histories and nation-states, "identities" and "cultures." It has become evident that we as scholars must not only allow for but expect, and take very seriously, the transitory, deterritorialized, unfixed, processual character of much of what we study. In a suggestive essay, "Explaining the Present: Theoretical Dilemmas in Processual Anthropology," Sally Falk Moore observes that the fieldworker must ask not only "How was the present produced?" but also

> What is the present producing? What part of the activity being observed will be durable, and what will disappear? The structural-functional assumption that a society is best studied as if it were a system replicating itself has long been abandoned. The identification of change-in-the-making is one of the present objects of analysis. The normality of continuity is not assumed. Sameness being repeated is seen as the product of effort. (Moore 1987: 727)

This is a theoretical moment, then, in which it is possible to foreground not just historical structures but accidents of history, not just functioning systems but emergency measures. In some sense, these remarks would seem to state the obvious. But it is one thing to realize and accept something as a general theoretical insight and quite another to allow it really to transform our actually existing practices of ethnographic field research. How to create interconnections between theoretical understandings about the anthropological object and anthropological modes of knowledge, on the one hand, and fieldwork as a practical matter of craft and of politics, on the other, is, of course, one of the animating questions in this book as a whole.

Recognizing the methodological dilemmas that these conceptual trans-formations produce, Moore makes a powerful case for a processual anthro-pology, an intellectual practice that would foreground dimensions of time and indeterminacy; the coexistence of both repetition and innovation, both fixity and rupture; and processes and transformations whose outcomes and directions are not as predictable as they sometimes seem to be. In a similar spirit, this chapter is an attempt to take methodological account of the un-certainties and indeterminacies of history (Moore 1975, 1993b). Its central questions are these: In the face of long traditions of studying cultures as more or less stable, durable processes of order-making that retain and reproduce their constitutive patterns over time, what do we do with fleeting, transitory phenomena that are not produced by any particular cultural grammar? What should be the status of the material that has conventionally been cleaned off a finished ethnography—the freak occurrence, the anomaly, the un-representative figure, the nonrepeating pattern, the impermanent and un-remarked cultural form?

The transitory phenomena I am trying to identify are not readily analyzed in relation to "systems of meaning," "codes," or "canons." Moore's discus-sion of the concept of the event is clarifying here; she begins by quoting a well-known passage from Sahlins: "An event is not just a happening in the world: it is a *relation* between a certain happening and a given symbolic sys-tem. Meaning is realized . . . only as events of speech and action. *Event is the empirical form of system.*"[1] She then outlines her vision of an important theo-retical shift:

> One could say that in the past 25 years there has been a shift in attention from structure to event. But an event today is not simply an instantiation of an ex-isting structure in the manner of the Saussurean distinction between *langue* and *parole*. An event is not necessarily best understood as the exemplification of an extant symbolic or social order. Events may equally be evidence of the ongoing dismantling of structures or of attempts to create new ones. Events may show a multiplicity of social contestations and the voicing of competing cultural claims. Events may reveal substantial areas of normative indeterminacy. (Moore 1987: 729)

The transitory phenomena and accidentally shared experiences that I will explore here in relation to the anthropological fieldwork tradition are, pre-cisely, phenomena that are not instantiations of stable systems or structures, or even antistructural in Turner's familiar sense (Turner 1969; cf. van Velsen 1979; Jongmans and Gutkind 1967; Moore and Myerhoff 1975). This makes them difficult to localize as objects of field research. Dominant anthropo-logical tradition is not well equipped to work with such material, but, as I will suggest, methodological ideas can be gleaned from surprising quarters.

THE REFUGEE CAMP AS A FIELD SITE: "NATIVES"
IN AN "UNNATURAL" SETTING

I have been led to these more general questions about the concept of "the field" by a choice of field site I made several years ago. A key part of my research took place in a refugee camp named Mishamo Refugee Settlement in a sparsely settled region of western Tanzania. This ethnically exclusive camp housed some 35,000 Hutu refugees who had fled the mass killings of 1972 in Burundi. I have written about the 1972 refugees (as well as subsequent political violence in the region) at length elsewhere (Malkki 1995a, 1996). But since the 1972 refugees fled Burundi, the lives of millions of people in Rwanda, Burundi, and their neighboring countries have been radically transformed by massive violence and population displacements.

In the mid-1980s, refugee camps still looked like an exceptional and aberrant form of human settlement in east and central Africa, even though large refugee settlements were numerous. (The Tanzanian government, in particular, had long been generous in its asylum policies.) But now, the significance of refugee camps as a contemporary form of human settlement is inescapable in this region of Africa. Millions of people live in camps and other areas designated as transitional, temporary, or ad hoc.

That life—and fieldwork—in a refugee camp would involve indeterminacy and radical impermanence can be no great surprise to most people. These social realities might in fact be cited as a valid reason to conduct ethnographic fieldwork elsewhere. Indeed, when I was first planning the research project in western Tanzania, I did have conversations with colleagues about the camp as a place for fieldwork. To most (including my doctoral committee at the time), it must be said, the camp seemed a good place to explore the questions in which I was interested. But to others, it seemed an odd site precisely because of its impermanence as a form of human settlement.[2] One senior Africanist, noting his puzzlement, wondered aloud if it would even be possible to conduct real anthropological fieldwork in a refugee camp. He said of the refugees: "Hmm . . . I *suppose* you could treat them as a tribe." But this leap was dubious for him; for a refugee camp was not "a traditional African society," and the refugees were really not "a tribe" (cf. Kopytoff 1987; Vail 1989). His key concern in evaluating the suitability of a refugee camp as a field site seemed to be: Is this the site of "a society" or "a culture"?

Anthropologists went to "the field," in the classical scheme of things, in order to learn something about "the native point of view," about the culture of "a people," about people's lives in their "natural settings." Often they went to collect languages and cultural forms in an effort to salvage them from the pulverizing effects of Western imperial expansion and industrial capitalism. Sometimes the work of rescue and preservation was motivated simply by taxidermic logics; at other times it was part of complicated political struggles over history, power, and knowledge production.

Refugees are people who have been driven out of their homes; they are physically disconnected from the place that most people (many anthropologists included) would consider their natural setting, their cultural home, their indigenous region, perhaps even their origin. And as most studies of refugees will reveal at a glance, refugees in a camp are not treated by scholars or policy scientists as people in their "natural setting." Refugee status tends automatically to be treated as an unnatural, exceptional, spiritually risky, and unhealthy state of being (Malkki 1992, 1995b; cf. Appadurai 1988b).

A related problem in terms of the expectations of classical fieldwork is that a refugee camp is thought to present an extreme, and/or unique situation. Sometimes, when I present papers on the styles of national imagination, or on the interrelations between historical memory and violence among the Burundians exiled in Tanzania, I am reminded by someone in the audience that, "Well, these are rather extreme and unusual conditions, after all." Or, "Well, yes, this is all very interesting, but, after all, these were very unique circumstances." In many cases, the presumed uniqueness of the circumstances implies a diminished scholarly weight for the evidence. For the evidence is deemed to have been produced *not* in the normal course of social life, but in an anomalous, fleeting, uncharacteristic moment in the life of the culture and of the people—a freak occurrence in the big picture. It cannot be *representative*. So, the refugee camp is a suspect site for the study of, say, "a Hutu Culture."

This presumption of disqualifying uniqueness holds within it yet another mark against the refugee camp as a suitable site, one already mentioned in passing. Nobody expects a refugee camp to be in place indefinitely, ever accessible to the anthropologist's restudies. The whole point of a refugee camp is that it is not intended as a permanent human settlement, but as an emergency measure—a temporary humanitarian arrangement—for people who do not belong there, and who are expected to move on when it becomes possible to do so. It is perfectly reasonable to expect that in a refugee camp, the people, their everyday routines, their social relationships, political processes, and, indeed, the entire social context might well have disappeared or been transformed virtually beyond recognition in a matter of a few months or years. This wreaks havoc on the expectation of the replicability of field studies.[3]

ANTHROPOLOGY: THE SCIENCE OF THE ORDINARY?

Whatever their actual training or place of work, anthropologists today know that the dominant traditions of their discipline have been heavily oriented toward identifying and classifying patterns of culture, holistic principles of social organization, customary practices, oral traditions, bodies of law, systems of rules and prohibitions—in short, phenomena that are understood to have withstood the test of time. In our fieldwork, as well as our writing, we have long been oriented to look for the repetitive, the persistent, the normative—durable forms, (cf. Moore 1987, 1993b). This foregrounding of stable and repetitive patterns is, in fact, built into what are often seen as the *virtues* of the fieldwork method. We say fieldwork involves conducting "long-term" participatory research in a "community" or "society" and observing people's "ordinary," "everyday" routines and practices.

This methodological orientation has produced extremely valuable insights and understandings and will doubtless continue to do so. But it is worth noticing that these terms (the ordinary, the everyday, the routine, the long-term) carry a charge of expectations: it is expected that the people studied are not just a group of strangers thrown together haphazardly by accidental circumstances but form a more permanent, stable, and usually localized "*community*" or social world. Even when the collectivity has not been defined in cultural or ethnic terms, we tend to try to identify some parameters for the community form. It might be a neighborhood, a set of regulars at the YWCA or YMCA, the staff of a hospital, members of a club, inhabitants of an old-age home—something that would seem to promise some degree of stability over time. Where obvious ethnological parameters are absent, we tend to look for institutional or bureaucratic ones (cf. Hannerz 1980; Jongmans and Gutkind 1967; Epstein 1979). A community suggests not just boundedness, but stability and regularity. In all this, there is an expectation of the relative social, structural solidity of the object or site of study.

Moreover, what is most characteristically "anthropological" in the study of such communities is a focus on observable, face-to-face regularities; hence, "everyday life" is observed over the "long term." And associated with this valuation of the stable and the ordinary is a tendency to see formative power in the institutions of community and (especially) family, as it is broadly understood. Paul Gilroy has perceptively noted that one key mode of reductively conceptualizing culture is to think of it as something reproduced primarily and naturally within families:

> The term culture has expanded to displace any overt reference to "race" in the older, biological sense of the term. Culture is reductively conceived and is always primarily and "naturally" reproduced in families. The nation is, in turn, conceived as a neat, symmetrical accumulation of family units and the supposedly homogeneous culture—secured in part by sustained exposure to national history in the classroom—culminates in the experience of a unified and continuous national identity. (Gilroy 1990: 114)

Gilroy is right. People readily think of communities as extended families, and of the transmission of culture as a domestic, intergenerational process.[4] This is, of course, an old anthropological habit also. Note, for instance, that in her preface (1989: xi) to Ruth Benedict's *Patterns of Culture,* Margaret Mead writes that we use the term *culture* "for the systematic body of learned behavior which is transmitted from parents to children." Moore (1993b: 366) gives much more recent examples of this same model of transmission from an anthropology textbook published in 1987 and a 1985 social science encyclopedia entry on "culture." This vision of culture as a matter of generational and familial transmission has, of course, been thoroughly popularized and generalized as well. Examples of it pop up everywhere—in family lore, as in the commodification of "ethnicness." For instance, an advertisement for the Pier 1 Imports chain of retail stores in the United States promises invitingly:

> The history behind our ethnic decor is as colorful as the merchandise itself. For example, the craftsmanship and artistry found on our Indian brass and metal is the result of centuries-old skill that's been passed from generation to generation.

Even when we conceive of societies as structures of domination and highlight conflict and exploitation, it is still the durable, reproduced structures and institutions of social life that tend to occupy center stage. It is obviously not inherently "wrong" to look at durable forms or structures—and it would be nonsense to argue that durable structures and practices do not exist. The point is, simply, that the analytical centering of durable structures (or, at least, structures we *think of* as durable) moves other phenomena out of view—transitory, nonrepetitive, anomalous phenomena.[5] As a result, it becomes harder to see, analytically, how durable structures and transitory phenomena might (or might not) come into contact. This orientation of perspective has deeply influenced the anthropological style of imagining cultural community in "the field."

One resulting zone of exclusion consists of those relationships, experiences, and social constellations that are *not* familial, communal, or "representative" of a culture region. An example of what I have in mind is what might be provisionally named *accidental communities of memory*. A community of memory does not refer here to a local or national community, but rather to a less explicit and often more biographical, microhistorical, unevenly emerging sense of accidental sharings of memory and transitory experience. Barbara Myerhoff's development of the concept of "accidental communitas" has been helpful in naming what I am attempting to formulate, although I use the concept slightly differently. Her example of accidental communitas is Woodstock. In Woodstock, there is a sense of public culture, of a public event that marks and periodizes people. This is very useful in trying to conceptualize social generations in nonfamilial terms; people who share the sensibility of an era might be thought of as forming a historical generation of people (cf. Warren forthcoming).[6] But the communities of memory I am thinking about do not *necessarily* take such public, socially visible, narrativizable, or ritualized forms.

Examples of such accidental communities of memory might be: people who have experienced war together, whether as civilians or as combatants;[7] people who have lived in a refugee or internment camp together for a certain period; people who were bombed in Hiroshima or Nagasaki; people who all fled a particular revolution; people who are stricken by a particular illness; or people who worked together on a particular humanitarian or development project. In these examples, the intent is to suggest that it is the communities that are accidental, not the happenings. There is indeterminacy here not because these or other historical occurrences are haphazard, but because they bring together people who might not otherwise, in the ordinary course of their lives, have met.

People who have experienced such things together carry something in common—something that deposits in them *traces* that can have a peculiar resistance to appropriation by others who were not there. These momentary, out-of-the-ordinary periods of shared history can produce (more or less silent) communities of memory that neither correspond to any ethnologically recognizable community, nor form with any inevitability. They might not even be articulated as communities, not even by those who were "there." For those "who were there" usually get drawn back into other, more publicly consecrated collectivities like families and nations. They get normalized "back where they belong." In the face of these other, recognized, nameable communities, the communities of memory that form through accidents of life and hazards of history can be fragile and easily disembodied.

Accidental communities of memory in people's lives are perhaps especially fragile in the hands of anthropologists. The very processes of producing ethnographic knowledge seem to dissipate and destroy them. The anthropological convention of focusing on the first kind of community (families, cultures, nations, ethnic groups, neighborhoods, institutions, etc.) can make invisible or trivial those formative, consequential events that are accidental, fleeting, and anomalous. The first kind of community has been named and classified as worthy of "preservation" and protection, legislation and control, of innumerable interventions; the second often does not become nameable at all. But the transitory is not necessarily weak or fleeting in its *effects*. The picture is more complex (cf. Moore 1994).

The importance of these accidental, shared contexts is not only that people carry traces of them in their heads. This is not just a matter of memory or simply a psychological process. These memories—even when not very much narrativized—can powerfully shape what comes after. Who one is, what one's principles, loyalties, desires, longings, and beliefs are—all this can sometimes be powerfully formed and transformed in transitory circumstances shared by persons who might be strangers.

It might be said that these kinds of accidental communities leave traces and enjoy afterlives. But, again, these are not just biographical afterlives.

These can also be structural, social, political afterlives. I think that these are what I actually studied in Mishamo refugee camp: traces and afterlives. I found not "a Hutu culture" in the process of transmission from parents to children, but traces of the history and violence that had occurred far from the camp, long ago.

NEWS

If those conjunctures I have been trying to characterize—extraordinary, transitory, perhaps accidental circumstances that bring together persons in unexpected but consequential groupings—are not "cultural" enough for the anthropologists, they are often newsworthy enough for journalists. Journalists (so we nonjournalists like to think, at any rate) swoop in, "cover" all manner of extraordinary and unique circumstances, and leave with "a story" without any necessary expectation that they will "follow up." Their movements are dictated by "Events." They deal in "news," we deal in "culture," and news and culture seem to repel each other like oil and water—not least because they generally operate in such different temporal registers.

Most anthropologists might not worry overly about the incommensurabilities between journalistic and anthropological modes of knowledge; after all, "journalism" has seen heavy use in the discrediting of shallow or unserious anthropological field research. There are many good and obvious reasons for such scholarly disdain. But if it is true that, when a crisis hits, the journalists arrive just as the anthropologist is leaving, and if it is further true that we, as anthropologists, find ourselves working in less and less stable and peaceful sites (Nordstrom and Robben 1995), then it could prove worthwhile to think about ways of addressing the distance between news and culture. It no longer seems unproblematic or wise (if it ever was) to assume that anthropological modes of knowledge are naturally or properly superior to journalistic modes of knowledge, or that anthropology obviously, automatically produces more profound kinds of understanding.[8] Most relevantly, it seems important to acknowledge the largely unremarked connections that exist between the two sorts of work.[9]

I came to these thoughts about journalism in the course of research on questions of violence, political memory, and mass displacement in east and central Africa, as outlined above. Long since returned from "the field" and living in California, I found myself in circumstances where revisiting the regions around Rwanda and Burundi became difficult due to multiple political tragedies that heightened their political sensitivity (and due, also, to my changed personal circumstances). To get information about events there, I read (and carefully filed) every news account I could find, and I systematically watched television news for informative sound bites. (As a result of long months of watching, I came to think that most television news can aptly be characterized as "newszak," as a BBC World executive recently characterized CNN's rolling news.)[10] Other channels of information—personal letters, long-distance telephone calls, and reports commissioned by various international agencies—were often more useful and informative, but not as regular or economical as daily or weekly newspapers and news magazines. I could not help but realize how strongly I had to rely on journalistic modes of knowing. In time, I came to appreciate the profound differences in the quality of different journalistic sources on central Africa. I learned to have great regard for some bylines and to track others in outrage as they officiously, ignorantly recycled colonial rhetorics about Africa and "tribal hatreds" (Malkki 1996). I became very aware that, whatever my reactions to the range of news coverage on Rwanda and Burundi, "the news" was a dimension I could not do without, and that it had a significant effect in forming my views and questions about historical processes in the region.

Setting up a binary contrast between anthropological and journalistic modes of knowledge production, even provisionally, unduly homogenizes and simplifies both kinds of practice. There are, of course, vast differences among journalists, just as there are among anthropologists—and, on the other hand, the differences between particular anthropologists and particular journalists might be very slight. Yet again, among the best journalists, there are those like James Agee and Walker Evans (1976 [1939]) who have much to teach anthropologists.[11] It would be useful to mount a careful exploration of the actual differences and also (perhaps especially) the similarities between the intellectual, occupational, social practices that the terms *anthropology* and *journalism* name.

"A FORM OF A CARING VIGILANCE"

Dick Hebdige suggested in a recent talk (1993) that we need "a new kind of political imagination." He suggested that "we have need of a different, more open critique of objects," and that it might therefore be useful to think less in terms of ethnographic "description" than of "witnessing." Being a witness implies both a specific positioning and a responsibility of testimony, "*a form of a caring vigilance*" (Hebdige 1993).

The classic fieldworker has "field data"; the witness has testimony. To testify as a witness does not mean speaking *for* someone else; it is one's own testimony. I would like to suggest that Hebdige's concept of being a witness and of producing testimony that is a form of caring vigilance might help to negotiate the distance between news and culture. It is this mode of knowing that is better able, I would argue, to intelligently see accidental and "unnatural" communities—and to move the impermanent and the transitory, and also the nonfamilial, toward centrer-stage. This would seem to be a workable strategy for avoiding the reproduction of older models of studying "peoples," "communities," "ways of life," "systems," and of seeing instead what Gramsci in a famous passage called "traces": "'Knowing thyself' [is] a product of the historical process to date which has deposited in you an infinity of traces, without leaving an inventory."[12]

The notions of testimony and witnessing have, of course, complex histories, histories that might make their use in a new context misleading or even troublesome. Human rights work and many forms of political activism, religious evangelical work (Harding 1987), law, and police work are some of the most obvious places where these concepts are in use.[13]

There has been a good deal of work done on the testimonial or *testimonio* as a narrative form and political weapon, especially in Latin America (Sommer 1988; Salazar 1991; Harlow 1987; Scheper-Hughes 1992; McClintock 1991, 1995). The testimonial is "a life told to a journalist or anthropologist for political reasons" (McClintock 1991: 223), and its defining feature is that it has "an implied and often explicit 'plural subject,' rather than the singular subject we associate with traditional autobiography."[14] A very well-known testimonial is *I . . . Rigoberta Menchu* (Burgos-Debray 1984). The testimonial is not, of course, immune to the dangers of ethnologizing and holism that have so beset anthropology, nor to problems of romanticization. As Salazar (1991: 93) has noted, "In the 'Third World,' women's autobiographical texts have become an integral part of the intellectual, ideological, political, and even armed struggle waged by oppressed and silenced people against the powers of repressive states and hegemonic groups. However, the attempt to place some of these testimonies and autobiographies into larger contexts (both material and textual) is not without its problems. In Western intellectual circles, for instance, there is a tendency to romanticize these voices and to conceive of the subjects of the testimonials unproblematically" (cf. Scott 1994).

Witnessing, of course, may also refer to acting as a legal witness before a judicial tribunal in a court of law. But it is not only in the courtroom (the final stage of a prosecution) that we encounter the witness. Police work also depends on witnesses and testimony, and, in fact, offers a number of striking parallels to anthropological fieldwork. There is "a field" in police work as well as "field units"; there are police informants and police investigators; there are clues, evidence, and privileged information. The police often have a fine-grained, close knowledge of the neighborhoods within their jurisdiction. In this, they are like anthropologists. Yet, their will to knowledge and the effects of their knowledge production are generally quite different from those of anthropologists.

Examining the similarities and differences between police work and anthropology invites anthropologists to consider themselves in relation to two models: the anthropologist as investigator and the anthropologist as witness. As I have argued elsewhere (Malkki 1995a: 51), many factors push the anthropologist to try to assume the location of the detective or investigator.[15] (Funding agencies like the National Science Foundation, for example, ask applicants to name principal and coprincipal investigators, and graduate students are all too aware of the need to sound "official" in framing their research problems.) Anthropologists also routinely look for clues, follow hunches, assemble evidence, and work with cases.

But more than that, one sometimes gets deeply caught up in the practice of probing or digging for ever more information and of pursuing hidden, secret, or restricted knowledge in the (sometimes unexamined) belief that the hidden is more fundamental than the things that are more accessible to study—that unearthing secrets yields a "key" or a "code" to unlocking important mysteries about "a culture." But as Roberto Kant de Lima has pointed out, there is no reason to suppose that pursuing the hidden in itself guarantees that one is going to find out the most important things—or that one is being a good anthropologist. Against the logic of the investigation, then, there may be a greater wisdom in refraining from the maximal accumulation of "data" and the extraction of truth for its own sake.[16]

The anthropologist as witness is differently located. Here, the injunction to know "everything" and to find the key to unlock mysteries is not a central (or sometimes even a meaningful) activity. Trying to be an attentive listener, recognizing the situatedness of one's intellectual work (Haraway 1991), and affirming one's own connection to the ideas, processes, and people one is studying are more important in this kind of practice.

But it is not my purpose here to argue that being a witness is the only defensible mode of anthropological knowledge production, or that conducting an investigation is entirely unnecessary or "bad." (The very common habit of sorting things into good and bad is the least subtle and most naive aspect of the enterprise of criticism today.) A great deal of intellectually and politically important work has been done precisely under the model of the investigation. These two models represent different modalities of ethnographic authority. It is not essential to do away with the investigation in order to affirm the value of a methodological and political positioning as a witness. And to pursue a caring vigilance, to be a witness, is not to lose concern for questions of evidence or explanation.

OBJECTIVITY AND HONESTY: TOWARD A SITUATED EMPIRICISM

A recent study that explores the zones between anthropology and journalism is Mark Pedelty's *War Stories* (1995), a careful ethnography of the Salvadoran Foreign Press Corps Association (SPECA), the press corps that covered El Salvador during the 1980s. Pedelty's study examines the wide range of reporting on El Salvador. He traces the work of the best journalists to have written on El Salvador—journalists like Raymond Bonner, who was effectively terminated by the *New York Times* for his efforts. He also traces the work of the many "stringers" (freelancers) who feed much of the news to high-profile "parachuters" ("journalists who fly in for short periods to cover major events and crises" [Pedelty 1995: 20] and who do not necessarily understand very much at all about the social fields to which they have been assigned). Pedelty shows what happens to all these journalists' writings and careers in corporate systems of news making. His study ends with an uncompromising account of the problems with actual practices of news making, and—in an exploratory and constructive spirit—with an offer of alternatives to actually existing practices of journalism. Pedelty is an anthropologist; he might have been expected to offer anthropology as a remedy for the limitations of journalism. Anthropologists, after all, pay a great deal of attention to issues like social, political, and historical context; they do not content themselves with interviewing U.S. State Department officials (who, it turns out, are none other than the "well-placed Western diplomatic sources" one always reads about in the newspaper [Pedelty 1995]); they take time over their work; they routinely spend years learning field languages so as to be able to understand what is said to them. But Pedelty does not offer up anthropology as a cure for what ails journalism. What he does offer is what he learned from listening to Salvadoran and other journalists from different countries whom he came to know during his fieldwork. These are lessons that are, I think, valuable for the foregoing discussion of the contrast between the logic of the investigation and the logic of testimony, and for the methodological rethinking of both anthropological and journalistic practices. Especially in the United States, writes Pedelty,

> the dominant means of communication are rationalized in an obfuscational idiom of neutrality, independence, and objectivity. The journalistic ideal of objectivity began developing in the last century. Objective journalism did not become the dominant mode, however, until well into this century (Smith 1980: 61). In addition to providing a hedge against tendentious reporting, the objective code also guided the incipient mass media in their production of news sufficiently "acceptable to all its members and clients" (Schudson 1978: 4). Objectivity was partially a marketing tool. The positivistic pretenses of U.S. news media have created a set of irresolvable contradictions for working journalists. While the rules of objective journalism prohibit reporters from making subjective interpretations, their task *demands* it. A "fact," itself a cultural construct, can only be communicated through placement in a system of meaning shared by reporter and reader. (Pedelty 1995: 7)

For most Americans, Pedelty observes (1995: 8), "'ideology' is considered the antithesis of 'objectivity'"; but faith in objectivity "has itself become an ideology" in the sense that the discursive and social performance of objectivity (by officials of the United States Embassy, by journalists, government officials) helps both to mask relations of domination and oppression and to legitimate the existing order of things. Being asked to be "objective" in this context is like being asked to be "realistic," that is to "grow up" and stop being naively "idealistic." "*Objectivity asks us to accept the world 'as it is.'* . . . Incorporated into this network of knowledge production, we cede much of our creative social power to those with the greatest means to produce 'objective' truths and the greatest interest in maintaining them (Gitlin 1980: 6–7)," (Pedelty 1995: 8).

The ideal of objectivity is linked to institutional and political pressures to conform that are widely recognized in the world of journalism. A journalist working for a prominent wire service observed matter-of-factly that it has become nearly impossible to go against the current in reporting, and that the current is generated in the U.S. State Department and by national governments everywhere. To report phenomena and processes that go against the current will "get you labelled a kook, or get you fired." And in a recent article outlining the accelerating competition among major networks for a share of the international news business, the operating policy of Chris Cramer (former BBC News and Current Affairs head and new vice president and managing director of CNN International) was detailed as follows: "His game plan at the BBC was codenamed 'FIFO'—fit in, or fuck off" (Culf 1996: 23). A key part of fitting in is the competent performance of objectivity.

Pedelty gives an interesting account of a conversation he had with a Latin American journalist employed by an alternative international news service. They were discussing the "fundamental principle of North American journalism," objective journalism, and the journalist commented:

> It is a principle [objectivity] that I do not respect. . . . To me, total objectivity
> is a lie. . . . The most important thing is that you are honest . . . that you play
> with your cards on the table. (Pedelty 1995: 220)

This reporter considered that "the principles of objective journalism force the U.S. press to act in a 'dishonest' manner. Calixto [the journalist] was particularly critical of his North American colleagues' use of the 'Western Diplomat' attribution, stating, 'They lose credibility that way'" (Pedelty 1995: 220). Another journalist, Maria, made the very same contrast between objectivity and honesty: "Objectivity simply does not exist," argued Maria. "It is a very abstract concept. What exists is a profession, like any other, within which one can operate with honesty" (Pedelty 1995: 226).

> As in Calixto's case, Maria believes honesty should be the fundamental ethic
> of journalism. Maria places the ethic of honest journalism between two types
> of communication she considers fundamentally dishonest: objective journal-
> ism and propaganda. The greatest falsehood of objectivity is its disingenuous
> claim to unbiased and unmitigated truths. Objective journalists deny their sub-
> jectivities, rather than acknowledge and critically challenge them. They reduce
> complexities, rather than explain them. They evade contradiction, rather than

letting the reader in on the inevitable doubts and difficulties encountered in any act of discovery. "The reader should know that the reporter never has all of the information or all of the truth," said Maria. "The reporter must always offer an element of doubt." The principles of objective journalism compel reporters to forge a false sense of certainty, an overly simplified and concretized view of reality which chokes curiosity and inhibits critical thought. Propaganda, on the other hand, is more self-consciously dishonest. Authors of propaganda purposely disseminate false positions and facts in order to support what they consider "higher" truths. Objective and propagandistic reporters deny, and thus abuse their power of authorship. (Pedelty 1995: 227)[17]

In the context of El Salvador, it must have been particularly striking to see so many North American journalists proceeding—in the name of objectivity and impartiality—as if there were no connection between them, the government of the United States, and the running of the war they were covering. Doubtless, journalists in other parts of the world work in such zones of make-believe daily. The more general point I drew from these journalists' thoughts, however, was the necessity of acknowledging and seeking connection in the course of one's work, whether it is anthropology or journalism —of being open to the production of testimony when that seems appropriate. This does not mean that "truths" and "lies" are indistinguishable, or that "anything goes." This is not an abandonment of empiricism. It is another empiricism, one that calls objectivity into question, not in the name of relativism, but in the name of the kind of honesty that the journalists above had in mind.

CONCLUSION

The thoughts ventured here on news and culture, journalism and anthropological field research, are very provisional and exploratory in spirit. Beginning to look at journalistic practices has been suggestive for the methodological rethinking of anthropological fieldwork as a practice that might address in a more sophisticated way phenomena that are transitory and fleeting, anomalous and "unrepresentative."

I think here of two instances of a community of memory—or perhaps better, a community of imagination—instances that conventional anthropological practices of field research might never produce as objects of scholarly attention. In one instance, I was visiting a political leader named Gahutu Rémi in his compound in the refugee camp of Mishamo in Tanzania (my one and only visit to his household). He had one round mud house devoted to books—agronomy books, religious texts, dictionaries, and some novels (among them, I noted, a copy of Stendhal's *Le rouge et le noir, The Red and the Black*). I should have had a longer, more careful conversation with him about his books—Stendhal and the other authors with whom he had communed—

instead of seeing him so closely in relation to his geographical and "cultural" context. Reflecting on this missed conversation in hindsight, I learned something of methodological value.

The other instance dates from the Persian Gulf War. When Baghdad was bombed, books were found in the rubble of a man's house. One of them was a well-read, dedicated copy of *The Catcher in the Rye.* The remnants of this home library were reported as a human interest story in the daily North American press coverage of the war.

These books that belonged to people who have both long since died have stayed on in my thoughts and now present themselves as images of what anthropology's fieldwork has so often missed. They speak to the existence of accidental communities of memory, but also to communities of imagination (cf. Appadurai 1991) that have always tended to reach, willy-nilly, over and through categorical identities and pure locations, beyond families and national communities. Like people one might meet through accidents of history, they offer something important, a connection of value.

NOTES

I would like to thank for their comments all the participants in the conference that led to this book, most particularly Akhil Gupta, Jim Ferguson, and Joanne Passaro. Thanks also to Eric Kaldor and Erica Bornstein for thoughtful suggestions, and especially to Roberto Kant de Lima, without whose thoughts on police and the nature of anthropological investigations I would not have thought out important dimensions of this chapter. I would also like to thank all the people who offered valuable commentary on this work at the October 1996 colloquium organized by the Department of European Ethnology, University of Lund, Sweden, and most particularly Orvar Löfgren, Jonathan Friedman, Jonas Frykman, Per-Markku Ristilammi, and Steven Sampson. In Sweden, I also learned a great deal from conversations with Ulf Hannerz, who has just published the first of his ethnographic research on foreign correspondents (Hannerz 1996).

1. Sahlins (1985: 153), cited in Moore (1987: 729). Last emphasis is mine.

2. To others, the camp as field site suggested that I was not going to study indigenous cultural forms or local social history, but, rather, the "culture" of organizations, the refugee agencies.

3. Of course, a village might disappear just as thoroughly as a refugee camp (as in the razing of whole villages by the military in Guatemala), but its potential transitoriness does not confront the anthropologist as a key dimension to be factored into research plans.

4. Elsewhere I have suggested that this model of intergenerational, familial transmission of culture is particularly apparent in many studies of refugees where refugee women have a different, more pronounced status as "culture carriers" than do refugee men. Women are the ones who are thought to carry culture in conditions of displacement, suggesting that the mother-child bond is key in the ways in which social

scientists themselves think about the reproduction of culture, community, and identity (1995).

5. As Moore says (1993b: 366), "A 'current history' view of fieldwork must reject the durability test."

6. Kay Warren's forthcoming work, which traces how different generations of Mayan families in Guatemala conceptualize political activism and struggle, is very suggestive in the present context. It offers important insights into the question of historical and political generations, and invites us to consider both the theoretical and the methodological challenges of recognizing how much is *not* (or cannot be) shared or "transmitted" or reproduced across generations. She notes (in a draft manuscript of the essay): "The irony of an 'across generations' framing of the inquiry is that it forces anthropologists to double back on our conventional methodology for ethnographic production. Our analytical work brings institutions and events into focus, yet much of our field data come through personal and biographical channels. Writing becomes the process of effacing the personal encounter of fieldwork to achieve the appearance of a higher level of abstraction" (Warren forthcoming: 1–2).

7. Militaries everywhere seem to understand these communities of memory with strangers better than most. Veterans often share things among each other that are peculiarly resistant to narration and normalization.

8. The problems in journalistic practices of knowledge production are all too apparent, and many (including journalists) have written about this. See, e.g., Herman and Chomsky (1988); Gitlin (1980); Christians, Ferré, and Fackler (1993); Mankekar (1978); Gans (1980); Said (1981); Hallin (1986); Schiller (1981, 1989); Roach (1993).

9. Stuart Hall is an interesting figure here because he is a careful scholar who has succeeded in combining news and culture. He writes about current problems, like police repression and Margaret Thatcher, but is not a journalist.

10. Culf (1996: 23) offers an illuminating but discouraging picture about the international news business.

11. I would like to thank Sue Felleman and Teresa Caldeira for referring me to James Agee and Walker Evans.

12. Gramsci, cited in Gilroy (1990).

13. The term *witnessing* can of course also have prominent religious connotations, as in Nancy Scheper-Hughes's work (1992).

14. Doris Sommer (1988), cited in McClintock (1991: 223).

15. Cf. Carlo Ginzburg on "the inquisitor as anthropologist"(1992: 156–164).

16. Roberto Kant de Lima, personal communication, cited in Malkki (1995a: 51). I began to think about the connections between fieldwork and police work in the course of conversations with Roberto Kant de Lima, who has done ethnographic work among police in Brazil and the United States.

17. See also Pedelty's use of Bourdieu's characterization of objectivism (1977: 96). Pietilä (1995) has examined the relationships between objectivism and the use of visual images on television news.

FIVE

African Studies
as American Institution

Deborah Amory

INTRODUCTION

This chapter about African studies, race, and questions of identity has grown out of my own experiences in Africa and the academy. It began over ten years ago, when I first became involved in African studies. I noticed then what seemed to be a racial division of labor between African studies and Afro-American studies. Put in the crudest terms, white people did African studies, while black people did Afro-Am. The original question then was, Why this division of labor?

My own experiences as a researcher and teacher of African studies have provided various answers to that question. These experiences have been marked by certain dramatic shifts in consciousness as I have come to more complicated understandings of this "field" known as African studies. I have also been inspired in this struggle to understand one's relationship to one's field of study by seeing new historiographies of Africa emerge and by witnessing and participating in various struggles within the African Studies Association (ASA) over power and knowledge. In the context of a furious debate occasioned by a senior scholar's assertion of discrimination against white men in the field of African studies (Curtin 1995; see also *ASA News* 1995), I read Jan Vansina's *Living with Africa* (1994). In that lively and humble account of one man's life and work, Vansina argues, "There can be no such thing as a definitive historiography [of Africa]. Rather, many historiographies are possible. The glorious disorder generated by the vicissitudes of a researcher's life, in which all the themes are constantly brewing together, nicely illustrates this point" (1994: x).

In this chapter I recount two very different historiographies of African studies and then ask *why* they are so different. I argue that professional African studies *in the U.S.* was founded and continues to operate within certain parameters set out by American racism. This fact accounts for the racial division of labor noted above. But I also want to attend to the complex ways that people negotiate within racist structures and other institutionalized forms of inequality. By focusing on the politics of identity and location, I hope to escape the structuralist dichotomies of Self/Other, white/black, American/African—as if these oppositions could ever be mutually exclusive. Instead, I think it is important to emphasize how the lives and work of Africanists, Africans, researchers, and researched provide much more complex understandings of the workings of power and difference.

Over the past ten years, I visited Kenya as tourist, businesswoman, and academic researcher; slowly, I have come to understand how racial, gender, sexual, and class identities influence one's understandings of and experiences in Africa. From a naive romanticization of Africa as a place where race didn't matter to a bitter recognition of the inescapability of the legacies of colonial rule, I have come to realize that my understanding of African life is fundamentally shaped by my identity as a young white American woman. I will recount some of that story in the conclusion, "Wandering through African Fields," to illustrate the multiple ways we are positioned (in terms of race, class, gender, and national identity) in the field and to provide a sort of supporting counterpoint to the historiographies presented below.

DOMINANT DISCOURSES: SELF VERSUS OTHER

Much has been written about Africa as the eroticized, dark "Other" of a Western masculinist civilization and humanity. From literary studies (Gates 1985) to the field of primatology (Haraway 1989) to international AIDS prevention work (Patton 1992), there seems no doubt about it: Africa represents primeval Otherness for the West. Mudimbe (1988) argues convincingly that this Africa was invented by anthropology and colonialism and later answered by African inventions of the self, from the Negritude movement to African nationalist movements, culminating in independence during the 1960s. Trinh (1989) documents the role of anthropology in racializing and sexualizing "Third World" Others more generally. For the purposes of this discussion, I would like to ask how American race relations have played a role in this process of constituting Africa as Other to a white Western Self, and what effect this process has had on the fields of African studies and anthropology.

To get at some of the ways that American race relations have been institutionalized within the field of African studies, I will describe part of the history of the African Studies Association, one of the largest national associations in the United States for the study of Africa. This history demonstrates that the "field" of African studies has historically been constituted through the dialectic of an assumed white Self and black Other, notwithstanding that the Self is not always white, nor the Other always black.[1] This latter point is an important one, and I will return to it later.

The history of the ASA also highlights important sites of contestation and struggle that mark the process whereby dominant ideologies get materialized into institutional practice. In particular, the 1969 meetings of the ASA in Montreal focused on the racial and political tensions among those in North America who study Africa. I understand this event both as allegory and as evidence of structural problems within the ASA and the field of African studies that are still apparent today.[2] Indeed, the 1995 meetings in Orlando, Florida, featured similar discussions but in somewhat different tones and with different outcomes than the meetings in Montreal.

By focusing on one particular site of struggle, I aim to provide one example of the complex ways in which we are all situated with regard to the study of Africa. It is time to move beyond a simplistic Self/Other dichotomy to understand the complex ways in which we are all positioned—by race, gender, sexuality, class, and nationality—within an interconnected world (see Gilroy 1993; Mohanty 1991). While I emphasize how the basic tenets of fieldwork and questions of objectivity and authenticity authorize only certain kinds of scholarship, I also want to highlight how individuals and groups negotiate resistant alternatives to dominant structures of inequality.

HISTORY OF THE ASA

The African Studies Association was founded in the late 1950s, in the wake of other area studies programs that proliferated in the United States after World War II and with the onset of the Cold War. As with other area studies programs, policy imperatives have historically helped to define African studies. Most clearly, these links are seen in the involvement of individual Africanists in policy matters, and in continuing struggles over the allocation of money for the study of Africa.[3]

The 1969 ASA meetings in Montreal reflected and enacted broader social tensions between black and white, "First" and "Third" world, and also revealed various alliances among those positions. During the plenary session, a group of African and African American activists interrupted the presentation to take the stage and present a list of demands to the association. These demands included that "the study of African life be undertaken from a Pan-Africanist perspective," and that changes be made in "the ideological and structural bases of the organization," including equal representation for blacks on the governing board, changes in the membership criteria, and the establishment of a biracial committee to oversee the allocation of funds for research and publications (*African Studies Newsletter* 1969: 1–2).

The story of how these demands were rejected by the ASA leadership is somewhat long and complicated. In the end, the president of the ASA, on the advice of the association's lawyer, rejected the demands on procedural grounds, even though the predominantly white membership supported them. (This is a fascinating story in and of itself.) The refusal to enact these demands resulted in a painful split between the ASA and the African Heritage Studies Association (AHSA), a group subsequently formed by the African and African American activists who had presented the demands.

Many of the people (black and white) I have spoken to who were present in Montreal were so traumatized by the events that they stopped attending the ASA for many years. Charges leveled at the ASA included not only institutionalized racism and neocolonialism, but CIA involvement in the institution's affairs.[4] Leaving aside the validity of the accusations, I want to ask some more general questions about the event. What social relations of power were being so hotly disputed in Montreal, and what did they have to do with the production of knowledge? Why have American race relations been so easily grafted onto this particular academic field? What kind of "field" has been created in the process?

The social relations being contested in Montreal relied on (and re-created) a fundamental division between Self and Other that reasserted the power imbalance at work in that binary opposition. I base this argument on the fact of who and what was refused by the ASA leadership. "Who" included a coalition of African American and African activists, a historically powerful coalition that helped to forge an oppositional African identity to the primitive "Other" of colonialism and early anthropology (Mudimbe 1988: 77, 88). The long history of connections between African American and African intellectuals and activists led to the Pan-Africanist movement of the 1940s and 1950s and the development of militant nationalisms on both continents (see Gilroy 1993). The elite governing the ASA refused the demands of this coalition, even as a significant majority of the membership supported them.

The ASA leadership also refused the activists' demands for a Pan-Africanist study of Africa. This fact would seem to indicate that the study and theorizing of links between Africa and the Americas appeared dangerous, something I would refer to as a fear of Afrocentricity.[5] It is important to note, as Diawara argues (1993), that the broader social context of white supremacism in the United States provides the setting for this struggle. The militant nationalism of some forms of Afrocentrism has historically constituted a powerful answer to exclusionary practices and representations like the ones at work in Montreal.[6]

ORIGIN STORIES

In fact, the unbending dichotomy between black Africa and the white Western world is reproduced through various professional academic practices, and as such represents another example of what Mitchell (1990) terms the "everyday metaphors of power." The development of anthropology and African studies and the history of their professionalization highlight the ways in which racism, as a fundamental aspect of race relations in the United States, has structured the theoretical and practical terms of research about Africa. In order to prove my point, I will start with a discussion of origin stories both as representation and enactment of unequal power relations within the academy and American society at large.

Origin stories, as tales of origination and authenticity, serve as authorizing discourses that position those of us living in the present with reference to others in the past. Apical ancestors, as we say in anthropology, act as primary points of reference and typically embody certain essential characteristics (both physical and metaphysical) of those who follow. In contexts where race constitutes a fundamental aspect of social relations (as in the United States, for example), these ancestors serve as reference points for fundamentally racial genealogies.

Historically, heated debates in both African studies and anthropology have focused on the factual validity of oral histories and oral traditions, the form that origin stories typically take in "nonliterate" societies. In the present case, I invoke not only oral histories but also written evidence cited either at the margins or the heart of scholarly articles, as authors establish their intellectual ancestry by the authorities they cite. Besides intellectual debts, more material relations are also acknowledged by the seemingly perfunctory citing of agencies and fellowships that have funded relevant research. These practices indicate both the existence and power of scholarly genealogies.

The classic story of African studies in the United States begins with Melville Jean Herskovits, the "universally recognized dean of African studies in the United States" (Greenberg 1963: 3; see also McCall 1967; Southall 1983). Herskovits was one of the first American anthropologists to focus attention on the Caribbean and Africa as opposed to Native America (McCall 1967: 26). He is also considered the founder of African diasporic studies because his work was fundamentally concerned with tracing links between Africa and the New World and theorizing the African American process of "acculturation" (for example, see Scott 1991).[7]

A student of Franz Boas, Herskovits completed a library dissertation and received his Ph.D. from Columbia in 1923, publishing a paper in 1930 that applied the concept of "culture area" to Africa for the first time (Herskovits 1930). Subsequently, he made several field trips to both the Caribbean and Africa, and his work remained for a long time the only primary research completed by an American on Africa (see McCall 1967; Dike 1963). Moreover, Herskovits inspired an entire generation of students, encouraging their intellectual interests in Africa and securing their funding for research. Not incidentally, he was also active in professional associations, editing *American Anthropologist* from 1949 to 1952 and serving as a member of the Executive

Council of the International African Institute. He founded one of the first African studies centers, at Northwestern University, and helped to found and was elected first president of the ASA. Thus Herskovits's contribution to African and diasporic studies consisted of both intellectual and professional achievements; he played a key role in establishing the institutional structures that have come to define the field of African studies.

Clearly, Herskovits was the undisputed dean of professional African studies in the United States. I emphasize *professional* because his intellectual contributions gained prominence precisely as he consolidated material support for the discipline, much as Malinowski did in England. Yet alternative origin stories also exist and it is to these marginalized histories that I will now turn.

A recent issue of *Critique of Anthropology* (1992) is devoted to recovering the work of W. E. B. Du Bois and placing it at the center of the history of anthropology (see Harrison and Nonini, eds., 1992). Although Du Bois was trained as a historian at Harvard, receiving his Ph.D. in 1896, he combined a variety of methodologies and theoretical approaches to produce a vast body of work on Africa and Africans, as well as Africans in the diaspora. His contributions ranged across the disciplines of history, philosophy, sociology, and anthropology, and he was considered one of the leading intellectuals of his day (see, for example, Du Bois 1896, [1899] 1967, [1903] 1961, [1915] 1970, [1935] 1964, [1939] 1970).

Nonetheless, Du Bois's contributions to anthropology have largely been overlooked, even as he inspired a continuing tradition of African American scholarship. As Harrison argues, "Du Bois the historian and sociologist certainly deserves to be unveiled in the genealogy of African-Americanist anthropology" (1992: 241). Skinner (1983) also highlights how the erasure of Du Bois's and his students' work from the history of anthropology may be seen as a direct result of racism in the academy. Harrison argues that this fact has affected "the very character of anthropological discourse and practice" (1992: 254; see also Harrison 1988).

Du Bois, in fact, participated in a tradition of black scholarship on Africa, slavery, and the Americas that precedes the work of white Americans by over a century. As Skinner(1983) points out, African Americans wrote treatises on Africa as responses to slavery in the 1700s, and by the 1850s had organized the Niger Valley Exploring Party, a project designed both to resettle blacks in Africa and conduct scientific research. Based on this trip, Dr. Martin Delany produced the earliest African ethnography written by an American.[8] In 1895, the Steward Missionary Foundation for Africa at the Gammon Theological Seminary in Atlanta, Georgia, convened the Gammon Congress. This first congress on Africa held in the New World was organized to educate African Americans about Africa; a few white scholars attended, but the presenters and audience were predominantly black. In 1897, W. E. B. Du Bois,

Alexander Crummel, Paul L. Dunbar, John W. Cromwell, Francis Grimké, and others founded the American Negro Academy; in 1915, Dr. Carter G. Woodson founded the Association for the Study of Negro Life and History (see Skinner 1983).

Others (including Elliott Skinner, Faye V. Harrison, and Paul Gilroy) have documented the impressive array of scholarly publications produced and organizations founded by African Americans for the study of Africa and the diaspora. It seems more than mere accident that this entire tradition of scholarship is rarely referred to in "mainstream" anthropology or African studies. Nonetheless, a generation of African American anthropologists trace their intellectual descent through Du Bois, including Irene Diggs, Allison Davis, and St. Clair Drake (see Harrison 1992).[9] Indeed, Du Bois and Herskovits seem to serve as apical ancestors for two very different anthropological lineages. To put it bluntly, these two traditions represent the black and the white versions of African studies and even anthropology. Clearly, the division mirrors the crudest aspects of legalized segregation during the first half of this century, as well as contemporary relations of power in the United States. And we Africanists are not unaware of the situation; every account that describes the history of African studies mentions the long-standing tension between white scholars and black scholars (and scholarship) with regard to Africa and the diaspora. McCall (1967: 24) states, "The association of 'Afro-American' studies with Africanist anthropology is a constantly revived idea in the United States, but it always appears to some purists as an uneasy combination" (see also Southhall 1983: 72–73). In the following section, I argue that notions of objectivity and authenticity constitute key points around which this widespread "uneasiness" revolves, and note some of the ways this "discomfort" has been translated into discriminatory practices.

ON OBJECTIVITY, AUTHENTICITY, FIELDWORK, AND RACE

Black scholarship and the emerging fields of anthropology and African studies did not evolve in absolute isolation from one another. Harrison argues that early black scholars such as Du Bois were "vigilant *consumers* of professional anthropology" who read and critiqued the pseudoscientific theories of racial superiority; "this Black antithesis later converged with Boasianism, which coincided with and validated ideas that Black leaders already had" (Harrison 1992: 240, citing Drake 1980). These concerns were also apparent in Herskovits's work, although his concept of "acculturation" was later critiqued for overemphasizing the assimilation of blacks in the New World.

During the early part of this century, the question of black scholars' objectivity with regard to their work on Africa and the diaspora had important ramifications both within anthropology and among black scholars. Skinner describes the popularization of studies about Africa and the Caribbean among African Americans (1983: 14–16). By the 1920s, a strong lay tradition of writings about Africa had emerged, but within the broader context of American racism, this tradition posed a dilemma for black intellectuals. If they critiqued these writings, they could be seen as colluding with white society; more often, they simply remained silent, which meant that the lay tradition was not subjected to the same intellectual scrutiny that applied to other forms of scholarship (Skinner 1983: 15).

Additionally, Skinner argues that whites thought the lay tradition was the only work on Africa being conducted by African Americans, and dismissed it on a number of grounds:

> The passion with which laypersons defended Africa often offended the whites who felt that an ethically neutral scholarly enterprise should not be the subject of emotions. The white scholars failed to realize that as a politically powerful group they could hardly have been objective about Africa because, consciously or unconsciously, they had a position to defend. Few black scholars, however, believed that scholarship was impartial. Nevertheless, the problem for the black scholar was that the academically and politically dominant whites were the judges of what was scholarly and was propagandistic. (Skinner 1983: 16)

In this way, the tradition of activist scholarship exemplified by men such as Du Bois and Drake could easily be discounted within professional anthropology.

Perhaps the point is that an emphasis on the importance of objectivity to scientific research served as a double-edged sword. On the one hand, it was essential to establishing anthropology as a modern social science and, through the Boasian tradition, to discrediting pseudoscientific theories of racism. Yet it also served to block the recognition of black scholars' achievements in the field of African studies. For some time now, critiques of "objectivity" as a false construct that obscures the positionality of the alleged "objective" observer have been accepted in anthropology and the social sciences more generally.[10] Yet the effect of this notion of "objectivity" on theory and practice in anthropology has not been fully documented.

In anthropology, where fieldwork came to constitute the discipline's defining methodology, one traveled some distance to work and study among other people, "the natives." In this classic mode, which Gupta and Ferguson (chapter 1) describe as the archetype of fieldwork , one could not study one's "own" people. Rather, the geographic distance afforded by travel served to reinforce, both literally and metaphorically, the assumed objectivity of the outsider.

Given concerns about objectivity within professional anthropology, white Americans were initially authorized to study Africa, while African Americans were not. Thus, Herskovits counseled St. Clair Drake *not* to conduct fieldwork in Africa for his dissertation, because he would not be able to be "objective." In fact, it seems common knowledge that Herskovits regularly advised his African American graduate students not to study in Africa. While

Herskovits clearly supported his black graduate students (including both Africans and African Americans) in many ways, this support was constrained by its broader historical context. Drake, of course, conducted his dissertation fieldwork in England (an ironic play on colonized/colonizer and Self/Other dichotomies) on his way to becoming an eminent anthropologist and African American scholar.[11] The fact that white Americans, and not black Americans, were thought to possess "objectivity" in relation to Africa reflects the construction of race relations in the United States, where white constitutes the unmarked category (see Frankenberg 1993b). It also reflects some seemingly nonsensical assumptions about what race is, how identity is constituted, and who one's "own" people are.

Given the importance of "objectivity to professional African studies, it seems doubly ironic that American race relations have been so easily grafted onto Africa. Due to the transatlantic slave trade, Africa is often invoked as the defining historical and bodily moment in the constitution of black identity in the Americas. Here again, the social construction of race rests on certain instrumental uses of history and geography.[12] Social constructions of phenotypic difference often rely on mythic homelands, geographic places that serve as the original (and sometimes imaginary) points for the creation of difference. As Gilroy (1993) notes, black intellectuals have historically articulated the complexity of their positions with regard to both Africa and Western nation-states in a number of ways. In the context of U.S. race relations and as an effect of racism, however, this complex positionality is reduced to the binary opposition of black versus white.

Thus, in anthropology, a discipline devoted to the study of culture, race seems to have constituted a basic criterion determining where one could conduct fieldwork.[13] While African Americans obviously shared some important components of mainstream American culture with white Americans, not to mention the geographic space of North America, it was the real and symbolic "kinship" of African Americans and Africans that ultimately proved most important in the establishment of anthropology and African studies as disciplines. This fact highlights how Africa looms especially large for *both* blacks and whites in our national collective unconscious.

In discussions, colleagues have also suggested to me that following the split in Montreal, Africans effectively replaced African Americans within the membership of the ASA.[14] Recent scholarship in African studies, encouraged by the development of radical social history in the 1960s, emphasizes the inclusion of African "voices." Within the context of a structural dichotomy between an assumed white Self and the African Other, authenticity has become a basis for scientific validity, complementing objectivity as an opposite and equally essential form of truth. But as Kath Weston points out (chapter 9), the problem with being cast as the "native expert" is that one always remains the "native," and never simply the "expert."

The end result of the challenges to African studies in Montreal was the continuing constitution of African studies as a peculiar institution, a particular field of study. Although Herskovits clearly considers Africa and African peoples in the diaspora to constitute an integral whole, the professionalization of African studies by the 1950s deemphasized these ties. In Montreal, the white elite's refusal of activists' demands also contributed significantly to the intellectual division of labor I noted at the outset. African studies came to focus on Africa as a literal geographic space, to be studied largely apart from transnational movements of people, capital, and thought.[15]

Today, African studies literally refers to (and is restricted to) the continent of Africa. This "field" became the province of white elite scholars and (later) Africans, while Afro-American studies, a more symbolic field of diaspora and transnational processes and longings, became the province of African Americans. Perhaps it is no coincidence that a related effect of the racial division of labor between African studies and Afro-American studies is that these relatively marginal programs have to compete for scarce resources within the university. Struggles for funding and recognition reinforce the division and opposition between the two and their respective theoretical and political agendas.

LOOKING TOWARD THE FUTURE

Woven through dominant ideologies and institutional practices that position the white Western Self against the black African Other lie other strands of practice and history that highlight the complexities of our locations both within the academy and with reference to Africa, and the possibilities for constructive alliances across various differences. African American scholars in the Du Boisian tradition have in fact conducted fieldwork in Africa, making important contributions to anthropology and African studies. Also, the majority of the predominantly white membership of the ASA supported the activists' demands in Montreal. White women experience the sometimes jarring dislocations of gender identity that fieldwork entails, along with the privileges of whiteness. In moving beyond the twin authorizing discourses of objectivity and authenticity, and the monolithic dualism of black versus white, we need to understand how partial knowledges are produced from specific locations (Haraway 1988). It is precisely our consciousness of shifting locations in an interconnected world that can help us understand the complexities of our contemporary context (see Alarcón 1990; Anzaldúa 1987; Gilroy 1993; Mohanty 1991; Rosaldo 1989a).

We need to complicate our origin stories in order to revitalize contemporary African studies and anthropology. Different historiographies of African studies need to be written, and white American anthropologists need to recognize how American race relations have fundamentally shaped our professional worlds along with everything else. We are all positioned by various crosscutting systems of difference that are transformed into inequality, including race (the one most white Americans miss), but also including gender, sexual orientation, and class. We need to recognize these facts in our scholarship and simultaneously work to combat their effects within the profession, in the Du Boisian activist-scholar tradition.

The future I hope for African studies would attend to the historical construction of "the field" of African studies and the implications of different historiographies for future work. As recent studies of transnational and diasporic processes have demonstrated, the illusion of isolation for almost any geographic area affects how we conceptualize everything from "culture" to economic change. The "field" of African studies needs to be imagined much more broadly and more inclusively if African studies and anthropology are to repudiate the roles they have played in institutionalizing racism. Indeed, black scholars have already begun this important work. Manthia Diawara (1993) details various tensions and traditions within black cultural studies, arguing that a newer strand of culture theory and critique in the United States explores the complex ways Africans in the diaspora are multiply positioned by discourses and structures of inequality.

WANDERING THROUGH AFRICAN FIELDS

As I noted in the introduction, my own experiences in Africa have motivated me to understand the complex history of African studies. I first visited east Africa as a young tourist in 1981, and had one of those transformative experiences that white Africanists talk about when they say they simply "fell in love" with Africa. Although I originally traveled to Kenya for the express purpose of going on safari and "seeing the animals before they all die," I left deeply impressed by the human beauty of the place. I had discovered, I thought, a place where black people were resplendent and magnanimous in their power. For the first time, I lived as a visible racial minority, the oftentimes lone white figure in a sea of black faces. The kindness and generosity that individual Kenyans extended to me proved, I thought, that race *didn't* matter; here it was quality of the soul and not the color of the skin that counted most. In many ways, I felt that I had finally found a "home" worth the longing.

Subsequently, during college, I returned to Africa to study Swahili. Believing that race didn't matter, I tried to blend in with the scenery (otherwise known as "going native"). I wore *kangas* (the local women's cloth worn as a wrap), spoke Swahili, and talked only to Africans, disdaining the European tourist. I was happy spending my days only with women, respecting the local imperatives toward sexual segregation. And I was encouraged in this project by friends in Mombasa and Malindi who laughingly complimented me, saying, "Now, you are a *true* Swahili." The complex ironies of that joke were lost on me at the time.

After college, I returned to Kenya with a business partner; we bought jewelry and crafts there, and then I sold them in the United States. My business partner is a big, balding, white man who looks something like the stereotype of a colonial official. We made a good entrepreneurial pair as he played the tough guy and I played the sweet young girl. One night, in our hotel in Nairobi, the bartender started asking us questions. It turned out that he hoped to confirm certain rumors swirling around us: that I was born in Tanzania (I spoke Swahili better than Kenyan whites, and so must be from Tanzania), that my friend had met me on a previous safari, we had fallen in love, and he had whisked me off to the United States, where I had finished by schooling. We were home on holiday, according to gossip, for a visit with my parents. Quickly realizing that denying this unlikely (to me) scenario only made matters worse, my friend and I started to joke about the impending visit with the folks on the farm.

But the incident started me thinking, as I found myself inserted into local narratives about race, class, and gender identity. I was being positioned as a Tanzanian white woman in a very logical way. My proficiency in standard Swahili set me apart from the majority of white Kenyans, who speak a readily identifiable form of Swahili called "Kisetla" (the language of the settler, in other words). Many Kenyans who have contact with foreigners through tourism dream of escaping the poverty of Kenya through the largesse of a European benefactor. In the case of young women, this typically means becoming attached to an older man. One Kenyan who worked in the sex trade on the coast, in fact, moved to Germany with a man she met in Kenya, but was forced to return when he died unexpectedly. In this type of a context (the hotel workers being familiar with both tourists and dreams of escape), my liaison with an older man positioned me with reference to these local imaginings of transnational alliances, both liberating and exploitative.

In 1988, I returned to east Africa with a group of American teachers on a study tour of Kenya and Tanzania (Zanzibar), and my conviction that race didn't matter in Kenya finally crumbled. When I arrived at the Hilton Hotel's swank little pizzeria, accompanied by an African colleague, I was assumed to be alone. Only the African American teachers in our group were harassed on the street by police, who regularly tried to clear the downtown tourist district of Kenyans at night. And I learned something of the extreme racism and outright hatred shared by Kenyans of African and South Asian descent. I began to see the legacies of colonial rule everywhere around me; white skin still (oftentimes literally) bought power and privilege in a manner eerily reminiscent of the United States.

Traveling with this group of teachers also taught me how much American race relations informed different Americans' experience of Africa. Our group of twelve teachers, six black and six white, split right down the racial middle during our eight-week stay in east Africa. The white (and predominantly middle-class) teachers tended to experience the discomforts of "Third World" travel as an entertaining camping experience. The more "rustic" the hotel, the better; large bugs, dirty toilets, and electrical outages made the trip more authentic, more exotic. The black teachers, particularly those who had worked their way out of poor or working-class and urban childhoods, preferred clean, modern lodgings; the dirt and poverty around them served as painful reminders of life in the United States.

Each group, as well, articulated particular claims to understanding the "real" Africa. For some of the black teachers, the trip was about coming "home" to Africa, and at times they were welcomed as long-lost brothers and sisters by the Kenyans we met. For others, their experientially based understandings of poverty and race became the foundation of their claims to deeper knowledge. Some of the white teachers disparaged their black colleagues' attitudes as elitist ("What's wrong with a little dirt?" the white teachers said) or simply imaginary ("Well, slaves were never brought to the Americas from Kenya"). Instead, the white teachers argued for the authenticity of their own experience because they spent more time among "the people," visiting in homes and traveling to distant villages instead of sitting in luxury hotels. They also claimed a more "objective" understanding of the African past than these other Americans whose (fictive) kinship to contemporary Africans distorted the "truth."

These examples demonstrate how racial, gender, and class identities serve as markers that are used to position anthropologists in a variety of ways in "the field." My understanding of the events I witnessed in Africa was being refracted through my own identity, even as I was positioned within local discourses and social relations. Moreover, as I have learned more complicated histories concerning the study of Africa, I have been astonished to discover how faithfully the experiences of contemporary Americans in Africa reenact and reinscribe the dichotomies of black/white, authentic/objective, Self/Other that have historically structured the field of African studies. I recount my own experience because it has demonstrated to me the absolute partiality of my own understandings of Africa as a white American. The recounting, itself, has another goal as well: to challenge those same overbearing dichotomies. As we all pause on the brink of the twenty-first century to reconsider the goals and accomplishments of African studies, we still need to write more complex historiographies of Africa, historiographies that will be crucially important to complicating and enriching our understandings of Africa, ourselves, and the "field" of African studies.

NOTES

This project has evolved over several years through discussions with a number of colleagues. While I take full responsibility for the views presented here, I would also like to thank: Ann Biersteker, Jacqueline Nassy Brown, Mildred Dickemann, Paulla Ebron, James L. Gibbs, Jr., Akhil Gupta, Donald Moore, Laura Nelson, and Amy Stambach.

1. Given how many different racial and ethnic groups have been longtime U.S. residents and active participants in U.S. history, it seems amazing that U.S. race relations are described in dominant discourse as "black versus white." This black/white opposition mirrors the Self/Other opposition in simplicity and inaccuracy.

2. See also Zeleza for a humorous and ironic parody of what African studies is all about. The article ends by invoking the memory of Montreal, and the comment, "So much had changed, so little had changed" (1993: 22).

3. These struggles have included whether or not to accept defense money for the study of African languages, with African linguists in the ASA historically refusing to accept money toward this end from the Department of Defense. More generally, the history of African studies in the United States can be traced with reference to governmental funding sources, as Guyer demonstrates (1996).

4. Colleagues have described *Africa Retort*, a parody of the journal *Africa Report*, which was published following the events in Montreal and hinted at links between the ASA and the CIA.

5. By *Afrocentricity*, I do not mean any particular version of Afrocentrism, but the theorization of real and imagined connections between the African continent and peoples in the diaspora. See also Skinner (1983) regarding white fears of Afrocentricity; Gilroy (1993); and White (1990) for critical considerations of Afrocentricity.

6. See Diawara (1993) for a discussion of different strands of black studies in the United Kingdom and the United States, including the influences of black nationalism.

7. While Apter (1991) notes that Herskovits was not the first to study Africa's heritage in the New World (he mentions Du Bois, Woodson, Jean Prince-Mars of Haiti, Fernando Ortiz of Cuba, and contemporaries of Herskovits like Zora Neale Hurston and Brazilian ethnologists), his article focuses on a critique and reformulation of Herskovits's notion of "syncretism" in the diaspora. Alternatively, Gilroy's *The Black Atlantic* (1993) clearly positions itself with reference to the tradition of black scholarship in general and Du Bois's notion of "double consciousness" in particular.

8. See Gilroy (1993: 19–29) regarding Delany. Gilroy describes the Niger Valley Exploring Party as "the first scientific expedition to Africa from the Western hemisphere" (1993: 20).

9. Interestingly enough, Allison Davis is the first American anthropologist to be pictured on a postage stamp (*Anthropology Newsletter*, April 1994).

10. These critiques may be traced both to Said's work on Orientalism (1979) and to feminist critiques of epistemology (see, for example, Haraway 1988). Drawing on Said's work, Southall (1983) argues passionately for the importance of African scholars' contributions to African studies, highlighting the links between broader sociopolitical imbalances of power and scholarly production: "The essential charge of

African scholars of anthropology and African studies generally, or of Middle Eastern scholars and Orientalism, is that such Western scholarship has been carried out within the context of a power relation which Westerners either deny or belittle as irrelevant to the lofty objectivity of pure scholarship. . . . [In this context,] objectivity is another name for Western ethnocentrism and monopoly of the right to interpret other cultures to the world" (1983: 74).

11. Skinner notes how Drake had to volunteer to teach at the University of Liberia in the early 1950s, because of the difficulties of winning funding for research in Africa by black scholars (1983: 17).

12. Patton makes this point when she notes that the management of colonial peoples included important temporal (history) and spatial (geography) components (1992: 224).

13. Thanks to Laura Nelson for this insight. At the same time, as Sally Falk Moore has recently argued, Africa has served as perhaps the most important site for the production of anthropological knowledge (1993). I would simply highlight the irony of this fact, given the history of American anthropology's relationship to Africa.

14. Skinner (1983) makes this point as well. Southall also can be read as an articulate plea for the inclusion of Africans as legitimate researchers in African studies (1983). Interestingly enough, he makes no mention of the dilemmas faced by African American scholars.

15. Other evidence suggesting the literalization of "the field" in African studies includes a recent review of articles in the ASA flagship journal, *African Studies Review*. Based on an examination of the journal's last ten years, Sanders notes a trend toward emphasizing regional case studies over general thematic treatments or interdisciplinary work, the opposite of what is happening in other disciplinary journals (1993: 119). Not surprisingly, the review also concludes by pointing out the "noticeable" absence of published papers concerning women in Africa or feminist scholarship, again in contrast to other journals (Sanders 1993: 124).

SIX

The Waxing and Waning of "Subfields" in North American Sociocultural Anthropology

Jane F. Collier

Applicants to the graduate program in anthropology at Stanford University are asked to "indicate one to five topical interests" from a list that includes three of the four recognized "fields"—archaeology, linguistics, and biological anthropology—and a host of "topics" within sociocultural anthropology that range from the currently trendy (such as nationalism, sexualities, and media studies) to the possibly passé (such as folklore or psychological anthropology). The AAA *Guide to Departments of Anthropology* issued yearly by the American Anthropological Association, which requires faculty members to identify their specialties, reveals a similarly large variety of topical labels, not only within sociocultural anthropology but within other fields as well. Nevertheless, I think most North American anthropologists would recognize some topical labels as identifying widely acknowledged subfields (or subdisciplines), while others identify contested aspirants, and still others reflect recent specializations or the idiosyncratic interests of those who claim them.

In this chapter I offer some observations about the development, heyday, and decline of recognized subfield divisions within sociocultural anthropology in the United States, focusing on three interrelated factors that I believe influenced their trajectories: theoretical shifts within the discipline, the academic job market for anthropologists, and the national political and cultural context. My story links the fate of subfields to the aspirations and experiences of three academic generations, although—as should be obvious—neither the generations nor the history of subfields falls into neatly bounded units. Anthropologists of each generation advocate diverse theoretical approaches, whereas recognized subfields, such as economic anthropology, retain their adherents even though such topical specializations have been supplemented by other kinds of groupings. Nor do the three generations I discuss correspond to the development, heyday, and decline of subfields.

Rather, I attribute both the development and heyday of subfields to the academic generation that came of age in the 1940s and 1950s. Subsequent generations challenged the hegemony of subfields, but in different ways. Those who came of age in the 1960s and 1970s tended to advocate a return to holism, while the most recent generation, those coming of age in the 1980s and 1990s, are challenging the "master narratives" of holism but are not advocating a return to subfields.

I write as someone who belongs, more or less, to the middle generation and who participated in a topical subfield that never quite made it to accepted status: the anthropology of law. This would-be subfield flourished for a brief period in the 1960s and early 1970s but never achieved the recognition and independence of more established ones, such as psychological, economic, or political anthropology. But because the anthropology of law acquired, at least for a while, most of the trappings of a subfield, a brief look at its history can provide insights into the processes that shaped the trajectories of sociocultural subfields in general. I will thus begin by telling the story of this subfield, before discussing the trajectories of subfields within the discipline.

THE ANTHROPOLOGY OF LAW: A CASE STUDY

Laura Nader proposed the anthropology of law as a subfield in the mid-1960s at two conferences she organized, sponsored by the Wenner-Gren Foundation. The first, held in April 1964 at the Center for Advanced Study in the Behavioral Sciences at Stanford, California, was a "preliminary working conference" on the "ethnography of law" that brought together "a small group of anthropologists" from North America "to discuss their work in law and current trends in which *this field* is and should be developing" (Nader, ed., 1965: v; emphasis added). The second conference, held in Austria in December 1966, gathered an international group of scholars to continue the discussions (Nader, ed., 1969).

Nader's use of the word "field" suggests that the anthropology of law already existed at the time she was writing. It did. Joan Vincent, for example, observed that "legal anthropology became a strong contender for separate status within the discipline between 1940 and 1953, and Hoebel's 1954 textbook on primitive law marked its success" (Vincent 1990: 307). But Nader was proposing a different project from these studies. She observed that earlier works, "for the most part, utilized the case method and were essentially descriptive" (Nader, ed., 1965: 3). Nader, in contrast, proposed a comparative project.

Before World War II, most anthropological studies of "law" had attempted to portray the legal systems of particular peoples. These studies were about "primitive" (i.e., colonized) peoples and were often funded by, or intended to influence, colonial administrators. The anthropologists who wrote them (e.g., Barton 1919; Malinowski 1926; Schapera 1938; Rattray 1929; Hoebel 1940; Llewellyn and Hoebel 1941) usually hoped to convince colonial authorities that the "natives" had "laws" (or at least authoritative norms) that should be respected, even if such laws indicated a lower stage on the evolutionary scale than the developed legal systems of Western nations. After the war, most anthropologists turned from finding norms to describing the processes—judicial and political—that produced authoritative decisions (e.g., Gluckman 1955; Bohannan 1957; Gulliver 1963). This shift from norms to procedures may have been influenced by at least two factors: legal realists' definition of law as what the courts would decide, and postwar processes of decolonization. Analyses of how judges or notables reached decisions—whether intended or not by those who wrote them—usually portrayed the group studied as capable of governing themselves.

While Nader praised earlier studies for their high quality, she faulted them for having contributed little to theoretical developments in anthropology. "It must be confessed," she wrote, "that the anthropological study of law has not to date affected, in any grand way at least, the theory and methodology of the anthropological discipline, in the way that studies of kinship and language have, for example" (ed., 1965: 3). She implicitly blamed this failure on authors' lack of comparative work. Although authors of descriptive studies had commonly compared their findings to the findings of others, they had usually done so in order to argue for a particular definition of law, evolutionary scheme, or theoretical approach. Nader, in contrast, wanted to develop "an anthropological understanding of law in its various manifestations" (ed., 1965: 3). She hoped to understand how and why "law" varied, rather than how "societies" did. In her own work, she sought generalizations by comparing different groups within the same "society" (1964) and similar groups (such as village communities) in different "societies" (1965; Nader and Metzger 1963). At the time she organized her two conferences on law, for example, she also organized the Berkeley Village Law Project, sending graduate students to study disputing processes in villages around the world (Nader and Todd 1978).

When proposing a subfield of legal anthropology, Nader introduced her project with this observation:

> Since World War II there has been in anthropology a proliferation of various subdisciplines—such as the anthropology of religion, political anthropology, the anthropology of law—that will presumably merge into problem areas in the next decade; in the meantime we have developed these narrower fields in order to make some systematic progress in data accumulation and theory building. (Nader, ed., 1969: 1)

Several factors contributed to the proliferation of subdisciplines after World War II. One was undoubtedly the desire to encourage the "systematic progress in data accumulation and theory building" mentioned by Nader. "Science" enjoyed high prestige after World War II, and comparison was central to it. Shortly before the war, for example, Radcliffe-Brown had written:

> The task of social anthropology, as a natural science of human society, is the systematic investigation of the nature of social institutions. The method of natural science rests always on the comparison of observed phenomena, and the aim of such comparison is by a careful examination of diversities to discover underlying uniformities. Applied to human societies the comparative method used as an instrument for inductive inference will enable us to discover the universal, essential, characters which belong to all human societies, past, present, and future. (1940: xi)

The development of "narrower fields" in North American anthropology reflected Radcliffe-Brown's vision of "science," as scholars separated out "social institutions" for cross-cultural analysis. Nader participated in this project when she suggested that "dispute processes would offer a good starting place for comparison . . . because the modes of settlement are limited in number." And she described the goal of comparison as "understanding the conditions that defined the presence and use of specific dispute-resolving procedures" (Nader 1978: x).

Another factor contributing to the proliferation of subdisciplines was probably the increase in academic jobs for anthropologists after World War II.[1] As the U.S. economy boomed in the 1950s, the social sciences expanded, leading to the splitting apart of sociology-anthropology departments, the founding of new departments of anthropology, and the expansion of existing ones. An increase in jobs would encourage the development of anthropological subfields for at least three reasons. First, departments hoping to hire new faculty members would understandably argue that they needed specialists in topics not covered by existing faculty—if only because university administrators were unlikely to fund new positions if they imagined that faculty members would merely replicate themselves. Similarly, job-seekers had good reason to stress their topical and areal specializations as a way of arguing that they could add new courses to the offerings of departments they hoped would hire them. Second, an increasing demand for topical specialists would stimulate graduate programs to require specialized knowledge from graduate students.[2] And, third, a need to examine graduate students in specific topics would encourage anthropology faculties to develop subfields by defining core texts, writing authorized histories, and identifying bodies of specialists competent to judge a student's performance.

When Laura Nader proposed the subfield of legal anthropology, for example, she outlined a history of the subject, complete with core texts:

> Despite the fact that many of our pioneering ancestors were lawyers by training (Morgan, Maine, Bachofen, McLennen, and more lately Redfield), inter-

est in the anthropology of law has, until recently, had a gradual growth. Between the classic monographs of the nineteenth century (Maine 1861; and Fustel de Coulanges 1864) and the next milestones in the anthropological study
of law (Barton 1919; Gutmann 1926; Malinowski 1926; Hogbin 1934; and
Schapera 1938) several decades elapsed during which the majority of works
on law in preliterate societies were written by colonial administrators, missionaries, and the like rather than by anthropologists (see Nader, Koch, and
Cox 1964 [1966]). Studies of *primitive law* developed from collections of normative rules ("laws") to observations on the actual application of such rules.
(Nader, ed., 1965: 3; emphasis added)

Nader cited more works, ending with one published in 1963, the year before the conference. In subsequent paragraphs, she further defined the field
by setting out the "main themes and questions about law that have concerned
anthropologists" (ed., 1965: 3).[3]

Nader's use of the term "primitive law" suggests that she and those who
attended her conferences did not contest the common definition of anthropology as concerned with the study of "primitive" peoples. But Nader
and her collaborators did not want to confine the anthropology of law to
studying "primitives." Rather, she wanted the subfield to deal with lawlike
behaviors wherever they occurred, including disputing processes in so-
called developed or modern societies that were commonly ignored by legal
specialists. Nader proposed to distinguish anthropological studies of law not
only from studies of other social processes done by anthropologists, such as
analyses of kinship, religion, or politics, but also from studies of "law" done
by scholars in other academic disciplines, such as sociology, political science,
and, especially, law.

Although the anthropologists who attended Nader's first conference appear to have emphasized shared interests, those who attended the second
international conference "disagreed on both personal and intellectual levels," resulting in what Nader describes as a "turbulent" event (1969: viii). A
basic disagreement concerned whether or not the concepts developed by
Western legal scholars for understanding "law" in societies with written
codes and established courts could be applied by anthropologists to understand lawlike behaviors in non-Western societies. Similar debates over
the applicability of Western concepts seem to have occurred in all the topical subfields that achieved more or less recognized status. Given anthropology's mandate to study "primitive" manifestations of institutions whose
"modern" or "developed" forms were studied by other disciplines, anthropological subfields could hardly avoid debates over whether or not the concepts and methods developed to study "modern" society could be applied
to studying "primitives" (or "primitive survivals" within developed societies).
The most famous of these debates is, of course, that between the formalists
and substantivists in economic anthropology; the formalists argued that the

concepts of neoclassical economics could be applied everywhere, while substantivists argued that they applied only to groups who participated in capitalist markets.

Participants at Laura Nader's second conference also disagreed over whether or not anthropologists interested in studying lawlike behaviors should attend law school as well as study anthropology. Similar debates occurred in other subfields. Economic anthropologists, for example, argued over whether or not students needed training in neoclassical economics, while psychological anthropologists debated whether or not students should learn to administer and interpret psychological tests.

Although the anthropology of law acquired attributes of more successful subfields, such as core texts, a history, and central debates, it never achieved the status of a recognized subdiscipline. Vincent, for example, observed that "between 1954 and 1973, legal anthropology emerged as a distinctive subfield, respected by lawyers but neglected, for the most part, by anthropologists" (1990: 375). I attribute its decline within anthropology to three factors. First, it was founded too late. Because the anthropology of law was not proposed until the mid-1960s, most of the students who specialized in it did not receive their degrees until after 1970, when the academic job market for anthropologists was closing down. As a result, many never obtained academic positions. Second, the 1970s marked the reemergence of holistic approaches, as predicted by Laura Nader when she observed that subdisciplines would probably merge into broader problem areas in the next decade. Vincent, for example, suggested that "critical reviews" of Lloyd Fallers's *Law Without Precedent: Legal Ideas in Action in the Courts of Colonial Busoga* (University of Chicago Press, 1969) marked "an end-of-the-era shift from the study of 'legal ideas in action' to 'people in action using legal ideas'" (1990: 377). Within anthropology, the study of law merged into the broader problem area of understanding inequalities in power and privilege. Finally, the development of an interdisciplinary field of sociolegal studies in the United States, marked by the foundation of the Law and Society Association in 1964, contributed to the decline of legal anthropology by drawing anthropologists interested in law into sociolegal debates rather than anthropological ones, and into studying American communities rather than going abroad (Nader, personal communication).[4]

GENERATIONAL EXPERIENCES AND SUBFIELD TRAJECTORIES

When I began to study sociocultural anthropology as an undergraduate at Harvard-Radcliffe in the late 1950s, I perceived the field to be divided into area studies and theoretical topics. And within theoretical topics, the field was divided into various specialties, enshrined in courses. At the core were kinship and primitive religion. Arrayed around the core were psychological anthropology (or culture and personality), economic anthropology, and political anthropology. Looking back, I can see that these courses reflected the subject matters of surrounding social science disciplines. The central place accorded to kinship and religion reflects the cofounding of anthropology and sociology. Kinship and religion were the topics Durkheim investigated when trying to understand how "modern" society came to be. Psychological anthropology, which also occupied a cenral place in the Harvard anthropology department (and in the interdisciplinary department of social relations), reflected, I think, not only the close ties that Boas's students had formed with psychologists and the importance accorded to psychological processes in Talcott Parsons's systemic theory of society, but also the wide popularity enjoyed by Freudian and pop psychological theories in the United States. Economic and political anthropology seemed less developed at the time, but appeared to be rapidly coalescing into subfields.

Looking back, I can also see that these "theoretical topics" suggested a layer-cake vision of human society, with topics closest to "nature" on the bottom (psychological anthropology and kinship), through "society" (economic and political anthropology), to the frosting of "culture" (religion) on the top. This ordering reflected the imagined relationship among departments in liberal arts colleges or in schools of humanities and sciences, with the "natural" sciences on the bottom (closest to the "facts" of "nature" and to "truth"), the social sciences in the middle (where "facts" were contaminated with "values"), and the humanities as frosting on the cake of knowledge. This ordering also reflected the relative prestige (and funding) of departments, with the "hard" sciences on the "bottom" enjoying the most prestige and funding, up through the social sciences from "hardest" to "softest," with the "soft" humanities at the top surviving on the lesser funds accorded to subjects that might enrich human life, but were hardly necessary for human survival or "advancement." A similar layer-cake ordering also prevailed among social science departments, with psychology and economics on the bottom as closest to "nature" and most "scientific," followed by political science and sociology, with anthropology and history on the top, as the social sciences most contaminated by humanistic values and concerned with variations rather than universal truths.[5]

The "theoretical topics" enshrined in anthropology courses reflected not only a layer-cake vision of society, but also Malinowski's conception of functionalism.[6] Although I was taught that Radcliffe-Brown's social structural version of functionalism had triumphed over and replaced Malinowski's individualistic and biologistic functionalism, Malinowski appears to have won out, at least in North American anthropology of the 1950s and 1960s. During Radcliffe-Brown's stay in Chicago, he managed to introduce a version of structural functionalism to compete with Boasian cultural anthropology, which, by the 1930s, was dominated by "culture and personality" studies. But by the late 1950s, when I encountered American sociocultural anthropology, Radcliffe-Brown's emphasis on the needs of social structures had been replaced by assumptions about the needs of individual, biological humans.

Each of the core topics explored variations on how individual needs were filled. Psychological anthropology tended to focus on the causes and consequences of different patterns of child rearing, based on the implicit assumption that children everywhere needed to be loved, fed, weaned, toilet trained, and taught adult tasks. Kinship, at least in its dominant versions, explored different ways of organizing mating and marriage, based on the idea that babies everywhere needed socially recognized fathers. Economic anthropology analyzed the production and distribution of goods necessary for survival. Political anthropology rested on the Hobbesian assumption that competitive humans required a sovereign to prevent the war of each against all. And a dominant strain of primitive religion reflected Malinowski's view that religious beliefs allayed individuals' existential anxieties about the unpredictable world.

I can think of at least two reasons why Malinowski's individualistic version of functionalism triumphed over Radcliffe-Brown's structural version in the United States. One was undoubtedly the political climate. As the Cold War developed in the 1950s, evolutionary theories became identified with Marxism and their proponents were subtly shunned or actively persecuted. Although Radcliffe-Brown was neither an evolutionist nor a Marxist, his structural vision of functionalism led him to create typologies of societies that could easily be upended into evolutionary progressions (for example, the typology of political structures proposed by Fortes and Evans-Pritchard in *African Political Systems*). While Radcliffe-Brown agreed with Malinowski that "the task of social anthropology is the systematic investigation of the nature of social institutions," he argued that such institutions could not be understood apart from the social structures they functioned to maintain. As a result, social structures had to be classified. Because "we cannot hope to pass directly from empirical observations to a knowledge of general sociological laws or principles," he argued, "the immense diversity of forms of human society must first be reduced to order by some sort of classification" (1940: xi).

The deep strain of methodological individualism in North American social thought[7] also must have contributed to the triumph of Malinowski's version of functionalism. This strain is reflected in the array of social science departments in American universities. The two most prestigious disciplines —psychology and economics—treat behavior as resulting from the actions of individuals motivated by personal need or desire, whether rational or irrational, conscious or unconscious. As sociocultural anthropology tacitly assumed the task of studying "primitive" or "non-Western" versions of the social institutions whose "developed" and "modern" forms were monopolized by more prestigious and well-funded social science departments, anthropologists could hardly avoid being influenced by their methods and assumptions.

The first and most successful topical subfields developed by postwar anthropologists were those focusing on institutions studied by other social science departments: sociology, psychology, economics, and political science. Not only did such disciplines provide readily available models, but colleagues in those departments often turned to anthropologists for insights about human universals or about how "primitive" institutions differed from the "developed" ones they studied. Moreover, the growth of area studies after World War II (see chapter 5), may have stimulated anthropologists to develop topical subfields focusing on institutions dominated by other disciplines as a way of discovering what anthropology—as opposed to psychology, sociology, political science, economics, or history—could contribute to the understanding of particular world regions.

The subfields of sociocultural anthropology that developed after the first wave tended to explore topics monopolized by professional schools. I know that the anthropology of law was proposed in the mid-1960s, and I suspect that the anthropologies of medicine and education emerged around the same time. Schools of law, medicine, and education, however, differ from traditional social science disciplines in at least two ways. First, professional schools train practitioners; they teach students how to do something, not how to study it. As a result, their concepts and tools are less easily adapted to the requirements of anthropological research than are the tools of academic social science disciplines. Second, professional school faculty members tend to put teaching ahead of research, to follow different academic schedules, and—at least in schools of law and medicine—to receive considerably higher salaries than anthropologists, creating problems for colleagueship and collaboration on research projects.

Later subfields also differed from those that coalesced earlier, in that the later ones had little time to develop before 1970, when job openings in academic anthropology began to decline. Not only did students trained in the newer specialties have difficulty finding academic jobs where they could train new generations of students, but the decline in jobs fostered the merging of subfields when departments with open positions—particularly small departments—started to advertise for candidates who could bridge subfields or teach more than one of them.

At the same time, several anthropologists reacted to the apparent splintering of the discipline by calling for a return to holistic analysis. Young anthropologists, particularly those who came of age in the 1960s and 1970s during the civil rights movement, antiwar protests, and the feminist movement, were more interested in understanding the organization and perpetuation of social inequality than in studying how "primitives" raised children, exchanged goods, chose leaders, or worshiped gods. They criticized the functionalist assumptions underlying subfield divisions for implicitly endorsing the status quo, while also criticizing functionalism for its inability to account for social change and its lack of attention to history. They turned to European social and political thought, particularly the structural Marxism of Althusser, which was brought into anthropology through the works of Meillassoux, Godelier, and others. The young anthropologists also participated in the development of political economy, based on theories of underdevelopment (Gunder Frank 1967) and world systems (Wallerstein 1976). Symbolic anthropology, fortified by French structuralism and the European hermeneutic tradition, also flourished in the 1970s, as younger anthropologists avoided functionalist assumptions (and constricting subfield divisions) by treating all human behavior—rather than just religion—as culturally mediated.[8]

Laura Nader, as noted earlier, had already anticipated the decline and possible disappearance of subfields. Although she was instrumental in proposing the anthropology of law, and in training students in the topic, she never joined the Association of Political and Legal Anthropologists. She viewed the proliferation of subfields as a passing phase, and she was right. In 1981, Comaroff and Roberts suggested that the anthropology of law be abolished. They argued that conflicts should be studied not to analyze how they were handled, but to understand the wider sociocultural systems that shaped both conflicts and their methods of resolution.

Ironically, subfields began to merge and decline as active, cohesive groups in the 1980s—about the same time they became enshrined as membership groups in the American Anthropological Association, which was reorganized in 1983. Subfields have not disappeared, but today most seem reduced to "topical interests" of the kind reflected in the *AAA Guide* and the checklist sent to graduate school applicants. The old topical subfields that analyzed "primitive" manifestations of institutions monopolized by other social science disciplines and professional schools have been supplemented by groupings based on many different principles. Some, such as the Society for Cultural Anthropology or the revitalized American Ethnological Society, reflect the attempts of anthropologists who came of age in the 1960s to promote holistic visions. Other groupings reflect possibilities for nonacademic employment, such as the National Association of Practicing Anthropologists or the Council for Museum Anthropology. Still others are based on regional interests, whether of residence (the Northeastern Anthropological Association) or of specialization (the Society for the Anthropology of Europe). And affinity groups have emerged, some of which reflect their members' positions within the academic discipline (such as associations for senior and student anthropologists), while others reflect a convergence between members' personal characteristics and their focus of study (such as the Association of Feminist Anthropologists, most of whose members are women who study gender).

Given the proliferation of groupings within the American Anthropological Association, it is not surprising that most AAA members belong to more than one subgroup.

The recent emergence of affinity groups combining members' characteristics and their focus of study may reflect the current theoretical interest in relations between an author's "position" or "location" and the author's portrayal of the people studied. In the mid-1980s, anthropologists influenced by literary theorists explored the textual construction of anthropological authority (e.g., Clifford and Marcus 1986), while scholars belonging to groups previously studied by white Anglo anthropologists questioned the accuracy of such anthropologists' accounts and the ethnographer-informant relationships on which they were based. As the possibility of "objectivity," in the sense of lacking a standpoint, is increasingly called into question, anthropologists, particularly younger ones, have become interested in identifying— and identifying with—the positions from which they can make claims to knowledge (Haraway 1988). Information about the personal characteristics that led anthropologists to choose particular topics (and field sites) is becoming something to acknowledge and explore, whereas it previously circulated as backstage gossip.

In 1987, for example, ARGOH (the Anthropology Research Group on Homosexuality) changed its name to SOLGA (the Society of Lesbian and Gay Anthropologists) (Kutsche 1993). This name change reflects not just the success of nationwide movements for gay and lesbian liberation. It also reflects a theoretical move from "objectivity" to "engagement." Whereas the ARGOH name identified the "Others" being studied (i.e., "homosexuals"), the SOLGA designation signals the desire of members to explore the position they write from when studying people "like" themselves, when invoking "queer theory," or when studying others with whom aspects of their experience may or may not overlap. "A location," as noted by Gupta and Ferguson (chapter 1), "is not just something one ascriptively *has* (white middle-class male, Asian American woman, etc.)—it is something one strategically *works* at" (their emphasis). Affinity groups, such as SOLGA, radically call into question the boundary between "Self" and "Other" that was central to the "scientific, comparative" anthropology of the 1950s and that produced such subfields as the anthropology of law.

As suggested throughout this chapter, however, major changes in the kinds of groups that anthropologists form reflect shifts not only in theoretical approaches, but also in the academic job market and in political forces beyond the academy. Jobs continue to be scarce. The 1990s have not produced the increase in academic jobs for anthropologists that were predicted on the basis of population statistics. Instead, the long recession and associated cutbacks in university budgets have kept the job market tight. The one growth area seems to be in positions for "minority" scholars, fueled by student demands, faculty affirmative action policies, and university efforts to develop "multicultural" programs. This apparent demand for "minority" scholars has led to a privileging of information about a job candidate's ethnic group, race, sex, and sexual orientation.

This privileging of supposedly "personal characteristics," however, comes into conflict with the widely prevalent rhetoric of meritocracy. Despite the fact that "there is no neutral grid" through which judgments about "merit" can be made (chapter 1), the powerful roots of meritocracy in "capitalist ideology and the competitive conditions of academic production" put both hiring committees and job candidates into contradictory positions. Because hiring committees must take a candidate's personal characteristics into account if they are to avoid past discriminatory practices that penalized women and members of minority groups, they frequently consult the membership lists of affinity groups that imply their members' personal characteristics, such as the associations of black, feminist, and lesbian and gay anthropologists. Such lists are thus performing the often unintended and perhaps undesired functions of supplementing the information contained in personal names as ways of inferring, suggesting, and sometimes hiding the personal characteristics of job candidates. On the other hand, anthropologists seeking academic positions are often reluctant to disclose their personal characteristics. Not only do candidates want to be judged on their achievements, as encouraged by the rhetoric of meritocracy, but minority candidates also know that if they obtain a coveted job, unsympathetic others are likely to accuse them of having been hired "just because" they are female, black, gay, and so on.

Global processes are also helping to erode the boundary between the anthropologist's "Self" and the "Others" she or he studies. Mass movements of capital have brought "foreign" scholars to the United States, even as the lack of academic jobs in overdeveloped countries has sent "Westerners" abroad. At the same time, mass migrations of working people from poorer to richer regions of the world, combined with spreading poverty in developed nations as governments cut back on social spending, have brought "marginalized" peoples to the streets and parks surrounding American universities. North American anthropologists, of course, never needed to travel very far in order to find "Others" who spoke different languages or followed different customs. But such people once were studied mainly by sociologists interested in "poverty" or the "assimilation" of cultural minorities, rather than by anthropologists searching for "living cultures." Today, however, when the globalization of communication technologies, combined with the rise of ethnic nationalism, has exposed the hybrid nature of all "living cultures," people who once seemed on the way to becoming "cultureless" have instead been recast as active innovators, crafting usable identities from available cultural fragments. As a result, natives crafting identities seem to be engaged in the same project as anthropologists working at "locations." Both are trying to construct a place from which to speak and act in a shared world.

The globalization of communication technologies has also blurred the distinction between the anthropologist's "home" and "field site." Not only do many anthropologists now work at "home," but even anthropologists who thought they studied "faraway" places have found that their "informants" no longer stay put. Informants now communicate with anthropologists by telephone, fax, and E-mail, and they show up on the anthropologist's doorstep expecting—and usually receiving—the hospitality they once extended. At the same time, the globalization of the media ensures that anthropologists and their "informants" tend to see the same television programs, listen to the same music, read the same news stories, and so forth. Moreover, the people anthropologists study increasingly identify themselves by the same terms as anthropologists, such as by citizenship and political party affiliation. In the 1960s, for example, the Mayan Indians of Zinacantan, Chiapas, Mexico, tended to identify their political groups by the names of their current leaders; today, they identify them by the names of national political parties. And spokespeople for the 1994 Zapatista rebellion in Chiapas stress the links between their movement and the movements of indigenous peoples elsewhere in the Americas and the world.

In this chapter, I have traced the development and decline of anthropological subfields linked to subjects studied by other social science disciplines, suggesting that such subfields as psychological, economic, and political anthropology were constructed primarily by anthropologists who established their careers during the economic boom years following the end of World War II. When the social sciences in the United States were expanding in both personnel and global reach, anthropologists, working with colleagues in cognate disciplines, hoped to make "systematic progress in data accumulation and theory building" (Nader, ed., 1969: 1) in order to assess what anthropology could contribute to psychology, economics, political science, and area studies. Subsequent generations challenged these subdivisions, however, first advocating a return to holism in order to understand the persistence of racial, ethnic, and gender inequalities, and later questioning the possibility of objective reporting, based as it was on an imagined distinction between neutral observer and culturally embedded observed. By the 1990s, the old subfield divisions had been largely replaced by a more fluid and diverse set of topical labels, reflecting the ongoing struggle of anthropologists to define themselves and their interests in ways that will encourage dialogue among scholars (and activists) sharing similar concerns.

NOTES

This chapter has benefited from the comments of Deb Amory, Don Brenneis, George Collier, Sally Merry, Laura Nader, David Schneider, and others who attended the conference on "Anthropology and 'the Field': Boundaries, Areas, and Grounds in the Constitution of a Discipline."

1. Stocking also stresses the importance of jobs. He observes, for example, that the Society for Applied Anthropology, while founded before World War II, experienced a "tremendous upsurge" during the war years as anthropologists found jobs in government (1976: 35).

2. I do not know when graduate programs switched from requiring students to demonstrate expertise in general sociocultural anthropology to requiring them to pass exams in special topics, such as religion, kinship, or economic anthropology. But I imagine this change took place in the 1950s and 1960s.

3. Although others had written, or were writing, histories of anthropological studies of law (e.g., Bohannan 1964), I believe that Nader's history differs from those written by others in that she was not merely summarizing the state of knowledge about "law," but attempting to carve out a subfield for future research.

4. Don Brenneis (personal communication) has also suggested that because the anthropology of law was based on using the extended case method, it may have declined as journal editors, faced with increasing submissions, began rejecting articles containing long narrative passages.

5. A layer-cake ordering also prevailed within science departments, with physics on the bottom as closest to "truth," followed by chemistry, and topped off by biology.

6. This insight comes from Sylvia Yanagisako, with whom I taught a course on the history of anthropological theory.

7. I trace methodological individualism to the ideas expressed in this republic's founding documents. The founding "fathers" acted and wrote as if society were indeed the result of contracts negotiated between individual, self-interested "men." The assumption that social institutions reflect the cumulative choices of the individual humans who enact them continues to be enshrined in myriad practices of daily life, from voting in kindergarten, to signing job contracts, to voting in national elections.

8. My understanding of theoretical developments in the 1970s and early 1980s differs slightly from that of Sherry Ortner (1984). She treats both symbolic anthropology and structuralism as movements of the 1960s, superseded by Marxism in the 1970s, whereas I experienced a flowering and expansion of symbolic anthropology in the 1970s, led by such anthropologists as Sherry Ortner and Michelle Rosaldo (see also Sahlins 1976).

SEVEN

Anthropology and the Cultural Study of Science: From Citadels to String Figures

Emily Martin

Recently, anthropologists have begun to make startling new contributions to the study of Western science and culture, contributions that have depended on altering certain central features of the traditional concept of "fieldwork" and "the field." At first, most of us contemplating the anthropological study of Western science did so with considerable trepidation. For one thing, the field of social and cultural studies of science was already thickly dotted with the flags of explorers from other disciplines: history, sociology, cultural studies, philosophy, ethnomethodology, and so on, many selectively wielding some of the analytic categories and practical techniques of anthropology. In a recent review, Sharon Traweek counts at a minimum twenty academic disciplines engaged in the study of science, medicine, and technology (Traweek 1993).

To these one would want to add the critical work of Third World scholars such as J. P. Singh Uberoi, who, in *The Other Mind of Europe*, questions whether certain conceptions of knowledge might have arisen from different thinkers, such as Paracelsus or Leibniz, as instantiated in Goethe's writings, rather than Newton and Copernicus (Uberoi 1984). One would also want to add the writings of the Third World Network, whose declaration "Modern Science in Crisis: A Third World Response" begins, "There is a growing awareness that there is something intrinsically wrong with the very nature of contemporary science and technology. . . . Reductionism, the dominant method of modern science, is leading, on the one hand in physics, towards meaninglessness, and on the other, in biology, towards 'Social Darwinism' and eugenics. There is something in the very metaphysics of modern science and technology, the way of knowing and of doing, of this dominant mode of thought and inquiry, that is leading us towards destruction" (Third World Network 1993: 484–485).

In the face of all this work, some of us found it hard to imagine what room there could be for even more inquiries. In addition, as anthropologists we occupied a problematic position from which to scrutinize, rather than just apply, Western science. Science has long been an intrinsic part of the discipline of anthropology: for example, anthropology produced ethnoscience, in which the Others had the "ethno" and we had the "science." Anthropology liked to straddle the divide between the humanities and the sciences and claim some of both for its own. The "science" of linguistics could help us map the cognitive terrain of Philippine plant categories or African knowledge systems. All the natural sciences could be brought to bear on prehistoric remains, helping physical anthropologists understand the emergence of humans as a species. Thus, anthropologists in effect produced cultural accounts in which the tools of natural science had an essential, and uncriticized, place.

In spite of these complications, my own desire to study Western science was spurred on by three main factors. First, I had the sense that there was something profoundly (and tantalizingly) elusive about the study of Western science. It seemed to entail one of those impossible conundrums, like trying to push a bus in which you are riding, or trying, like the fish in Marx's example, to see the invisible water in which one swims. If science is the ground of nature, and the ground of my thought about it, how can I think about science outside itself? This elusiveness was brought home to me in a paper written by Gyorgy Markus, "Why Is There No Hermeneutics of Natural Sciences?" (Markus 1987). Here, he traces the extreme narrowness of the problems that contemporary science addresses to a deep transformation in the nineteenth century that caused science and scientists to belong to a separate profession. Scientific research communities became separated from the rest of society and the questions they considered ceased to have broad cultural significance. This was a sharp discontinuity from the seventeenth and eighteenth centuries, when science was embedded in society, recognized as widely influencing and being influenced by other discourses such as philosophy (1987: 16–17).

In a lecture given by Clifford Geertz on the possibility of a hermeneutic treatment of the natural sciences, he summarized the implications of Markus's article in this way: the view of nature now held by science (with some exceptions) no longer claims to be a worldview in the interpretivist sense. Instead, it claims to reveal reality. In spite of and because of this, Geertz urged his listeners to appropriate science as meaningful social action; to see science as "a particular story of how things stand," a story constructed in a particular historical setting. He questioned what had come to be taken for granted as "truth" in the sciences: objectivity as a standpoint, nature as an object, and materiality as reality.

Perhaps these sentiments were what led Geertz to frame group investigation at the Institute for Advanced Study during 1992 to 1993 around the theme "the social and cultural study of science," and to invite one or two anthropologists, as well as sociologists, historians, and philosophers. Perhaps these sentiments also led to his dismay when the group of us who were invited to be in residence failed utterly to create a working atmosphere, but instead acrimoniously bickered until the unpleasantness forced us to divide into two groups. The two camps were not distinguished by gender, age, nationality, or discipline, but seemingly only by willingness or reluctance to give up the scientific point of view as a privileged one. The subgroup that was willing to try giving it up was only able to do so by meeting bimonthly for informal seminars at Geertz's house. So, as I say, finding a way to study science culturally can prove elusive, at least in some settings.

The second factor that impelled my interest was a desire to look at science simultaneously as a "particular story of how things stand" and as an important part of the institutions that are exerting particularly brutal forms of power worldwide at the end of the twentieth century. The activities of multinational corporations have led to the increasing concentration and mobility of capital, which often lead to greater misery for the poor, as well as concomitant restructuring of the organization of work, both inside corporations and factories and in the spread of "home work." Technological developments entail vast alterations in how information is stored and retrieved, and the extent to which biological research focuses on genetics. In tandem there has been dramatic change in how both scientists and the person on the street conceptualize the components of the human body and the determinants of its health, the occurrence of virulent forms of racism, and an intense new biological essentialism.

The third factor that fueled my interest was my sense that, in spite of the number of disciplines already represented among those studying science culturally, cultural anthropology might have something important and even unique to add. I will discuss below some of the contributions anthropology has made to social studies of science, arguing that it has done so mostly by using a broad anthropological concept of culture together with quite traditional anthropological research techniques, such as participant observation. Simultaneously, the study of Western science has acted back on the discipline of anthropology itself, provoking debate about what the nature of fieldwork must be to encompass phenomena like science.

The anthropological study of Western science as a cultural phenomenon is a paradigm case of the kind of research this book seeks to highlight: research in which older frameworks of time and space have become less pertinent; research that "cannot be neatly contained within a 'field site,' a geographical/cultural space of otherness" (Gupta and Ferguson 1994). In the following, I want to consider a range of cases within the anthropology of science to explore how various studies are or are not contained within a "field site," and the range of consequences that can be associated with transgressing the boundaries or stretching the limits of the "field." I have grouped my discussion under three rubrics: citadels, rhizomes, and string figures.

CITADELS

I begin with some studies of science that, though nontraditional in their subject matter, are nonetheless quite contained within their field site. The natural sciences of the present day are heir to processes that have left most nonscientists thinking that scientists are set apart from the rest of history and society, as it were, in a citadel on a hill. Scientists claim to discover reality, not to construct it or to be themselves constructed. In Sharon Traweek's terms, they are "cultures of no culture." In a challenge to the veracity of this view, some anthropologists have begun to depict the (in fact) very rich and complex cultures of the natural sciences, ensconced within their citadels apart and above the rest of society. Sharon Traweek has described some of the fundamental presuppositions about time, space, matter, and persons that give the world of a high-energy physicist meaning; she has shown how those fundamental presuppositions take one form in the United States and another, quite different form in Japan, emphatically demonstrating their historically contingent nature (1988, 1992). In showing us that the world within this citadel has a culture in spite of itself, Traweek does an invaluable thing. Occasionally, she peeks over the wall from inside the citadel and wonders with the physicists what ordinary people outside are thinking about them—why, for example, the U.S. government is declining to fund the Texas supercollider. But the very position that allows her to capture so richly and movingly the cultural world of physics means that she, like the physicists, rarely actually ventures outside the walls. Her participant observation in their world entails participation in their isolation: as they see it, and as Traweek the ethnographer experiences it through sharing their world, they are outside society, encased (now that Traweek has shown it to us) in a culture of their own, but one that has little to do with anything outside it. The walls of the citadel (seen from this perspective) are left intact.[1]

Traweek's groundbreaking work opens up intriguing new questions: What would happen if another ethnographer wandered around outside the citadel walls and tried to find out why people do or do not support the supercollider? What if he or she tried to find out why Stephen Hawking's *A Brief History of Time* (1988) and the video based on it have become best-sellers? Now that we have the benefit of Traweek's work, the way is cleared to connect the lab in which the high-energy physicist tinkers with his machines and the living room in which a family watches Stephen Hawking talk about the universe, thus calling into question the solidity of the citadel walls.

There is another major approach to the walls of the citadel, taken by

Bruno Latour. In a series of studies beginning with a collaborative ethnography of a biology research lab, Latour makes the walls between the practices involved in science and parts of the rest of society permeable. We see how the "making of facts," and the resources necessary to construct them, depend on gathering allies in many places. Scientists must travel into government agencies, manufacturing concerns, press offices, and publishing houses, all the while communicating intensively, to build up support for the facts they wish to establish.

> They travel inside narrow and fragile networks, resembling the galleries termites build to link their nests to their feeding sites. Inside these networks, they make traces of all sorts circulate better by increasing their mobility, their speed, their reliability, their ability to combine with one another. (Latour 1987: 160–161)

Science in Action, Latour's book, bursts the bounds of the citadel walls, but I would claim that this gain comes at too high a price. The Latourian scientist who bursts upon the scene is an accumulating, aggressive individual born of capitalism, forming his networks and gathering his allies everywhere, resembling all too closely a Western businessman. We may wonder whether all scientists have, or ever had, such a monadic, agonistic, competitive approach to the world (Birke 1986). In particular, we might wonder whether some women scientists (for a host of reasons more excluded from playing these games than men) may have lived their scientific lives very differently, and garnered a measure of success in spite of it (Keller 1983). We might wonder whether the growth of such science as high-energy physics, where research is conducted by large collaborating groups with cooperative links to other such groups, would mitigate any tendency toward individual competition (Traweek 1988: 149, 153; Knorr Cetina 1992).

Another approach to the citadel walls has been taken by scholars like Rayna Rapp and Deborah Heath. They act as acute observers of the landscape who notice what should have been obvious to us all along, that many powerful collectives and interested groups dot the landscape all around the castle. Not only are they there, but they interact with the world inside the castle of science frequently and in powerful ways.[2] It is as if we thought of science as a medieval walled town, and it turns out it is more like a bustling center of nineteenth-century commerce, porous in every direction. Rapp describes how genetic counselors (they are not research scientists, but professionals whose specific job is to translate between the science of genetics and the public) communicate the meaning and implications of genetics and genetic testing to pregnant women. The women they translate science to are not passive recipients. "Knowledge" does not just travel one way. Rapp's vivid material makes plain the complexity of fitting new knowledge to diverse lives: a working-class, single mother chose to keep a fetus with XXY sex chromosomes (Klinefelter's syndrome), declaring him at the age of four "normal as far as I am concerned . . . and if anything happens later, I'll be there for him, as long as he's normal looking." On the other hand, a professional couple chose to abort a fetus with Klinefelter's, saying, "If he can't grow up to have a shot at becoming the President, we don't want him" (Rapp 1988: 152).

Positioning herself in a similar way to Rapp, Deborah Heath has done ethnographic work on the interface between a genetics lab and people with Marfan syndrome, a connective tissue disorder caused by a genetic abnormality, the one which probably affected Abraham Lincoln. In this interface zone she finds the National Marfan Foundation, the U.S. lay organization for affected individuals and their advocates, holding meetings attended by genetics researchers as well as people affected by Marfan. Here, the interface between the world of science and the public becomes membrane-thin. Researchers are "hurt" when people with Marfan do not like to look at an electron micrograph of the molecule altered by the genetic abnormality that affects them; when the researchers showed a slide of the hugely magnified molecule, someone in the audience hissed as if it were a villain.

Sometimes this close contact between the inside and outside of science can be emotional. One researcher became angry at Marfan patients after a National Marfan Foundation Conference. She was unsettled, saying, "The patients really think that I'm responsible to them [for finding a cure]." This expectation clashed with her belief that "pure science should follow its own course," even while she acknowledged that with a little readjustment she could push her research in directions that might provide more therapeutic findings (Heath forthcoming).

RHIZOMES

The next approach I will consider neither peers over the walls of science, nor shows us how porous and leaky they are. This approach asks whether the layout and design of the castle itself, and the logic of the actions of the scientists within it, might not be deeply embedded in the same countryside as the hamlets and villages surrounding it. This approach seeks to link the knowledge in the citadel, and its manner of production, with processes and events outside, processes that may be distant or spatially discontinuous from it.

Two images have been especially provocative to me as I have begun to think about this problem, both devised outside anthropology proper. The first comes from Katherine Hayles's work on the pervasive tendency to think about the world in terms of complex nonlinear systems. She sees this tendency as having arisen in culture in many domains at once, both in nonlinear dynamics and in post-structuralist literature, for example. She captures the nature of possible linkages between these domains with the image of a rising archipelago:

> Suppose an island breaks through the surface of the water, then another and another, until the sea is dotted with islands. Each has its own ecology, terrain, and morphology. One can recognize these distinctions and at the same time wonder whether they are all part of an emerging mountain range, connected both through substrata they share and through the larger forces that brought them into being. (Hayles 1990: 3)

The image of an archipelago has the merit of suggesting that visions of the world that "rise up," seeming salient or passionately interesting in science, might be part of the same processes by which those visions seem equally gripping in very different contexts outside science. But its detriment as an image is that it is too solid, too monolithic and—possibly—slowly moving. It can also be taken to imply that a substratum or deep structure underlies everything.

Another image that avoids these shortcomings comes from Deleuze—the image of the rhizome.

> A rhizome as a subterranean stem is absolutely different from roots and radicles. Bulbs and tubers are rhizomes. Rats are rhizomes. Burrows are too, in all of their functions of shelter, supply, movement, evasion, and breakout. The rhizome itself assumes very diverse forms, from ramified surface extension in all directions to concretion into bulbs and tubers. . . . Any point of a rhizome can be connected to anything other, and must be. This is very different from the tree or root, which plots a point, fixes an order. (Deleuze 1993: 29)

On the one hand, a rhizome finds it easy to make connections in many directions, and, on the other, a rhizome is not perturbed by having its connections severed.

> A rhizome may be broken, shattered at a given spot, but it will start up again on one of its old lines, or on new lines. You can never get rid of ants because they form an animal rhizome that can rebound time and again after most of it has been destroyed. (Deleuze 1993: 32)

Rhizomic things "evolve by subterranean stems and flows, along river valleys or train tracks; [they] spread like a patch of oil" (30). This image might do well to capture the kind of discontinuous, fractured, and nonlinear relationships between science and the rest of culture—for example, that between primatology and movies about primates—that Donna Haraway has given us:

> The women and men who have contributed to primate studies have carried with them the marks of their own histories and cultures. These marks are written into the texts of the lives of monkeys and apes, but often in subtle and unexpected ways. . . . Monkeys and apes—and the people who construct scientific and popular knowledge about them—are part of cultures in contention. (Haraway 1989: 2)

None of the people I have thus far mentioned in the archipelago-rhizome mode are anthropologists by disciplinary training, and therefore none has done fieldwork in the anthropological sense. Are there ways of studying ethnographically the discontinuous, nonlinear, fractured ways that might link the citadel to the rest of the world? My own recent work is an effort to do just that. And as an indication of how difficult it may be to gain legitimacy, when I described the range of sites at which my research was taking place (an immunology lab, various clinical HIV settings, AIDS activist volunteer organizations, several urban neighborhoods, corporate workplaces), one of my science studies colleagues, Karin Knorr Cetina, was horrified. Coming from a tradition of studying science in great detail inside the laboratory, she asked me, "Don't you know how to stay put?" But with the image of a rhizome in mind, anthropologists of science need not be confined. Some people can peer over the castle walls; some can look through the holes in its walls. And others can trace the convoluted, discontinuous linkages between what grows inside the castle walls and what grows outside.

Ethnographic inquiry into the "ramified surface extensions" of processes or phenomena would be as likely to trace connections between propensities or disinclinations in the "public" and what is thought a desirable project in science, as to trace connections in the other direction. In my own research, for example, I found that many biological researchers operate with a mechanistic view of the body—the body is divided up into compartments, arranged hierarchically under the head of ruling organs like the brain, clearly separated from the outside environment. Cause and effect are linear. In contrast, many nonscientists are operating with a very different notion of how the body works and how it relates to its environment. Often, the body is seen as a complexly interacting system embedded in other complex systems, all in constant change. No one part is always in charge. Change is nonlinear in the sense that small initial perturbations can lead to massive alterations in end results (Martin 1994).

One woman we interviewed, whose pseudonym is Vera Michaels, rejected the image of the immune system on the cover of *Time* (shown as a boxing match inside a man's body between the vicious virus and the T cell), because, as she said, "It depicts such violence going on in our bodies." She insisted that such violence is "not in there." She claimed her own representation would be "less dramatic":

> My visualization would be much more like a piece of almost tides or
>   something . . . the forces, you know, the ebbs and flows.
>
> [Could you draw anything like that?]
>
> I could. I don't think anybody would perceive it as a portrayal of the battle
>   within.

[What is it that ebbs and flows?]

The two forces, I mean, the forces . . . imbalance and balance.

As she spoke, she drew two graceful lines in the shape of rolling ocean swells, labeling it "the waves" and capturing her picture of the body in turbulent, constant change.

Often, people we interviewed for this study talked at great length about the impossibility of separating such an ever-changing body from its environment—health is affected by diet, water, air, mood, stress, relationships, the past, colors, work, and so on. Often, people turn to alternative medicine —acupuncture, homeopathy, chiropractic, herbs, natural foods—to address these concerns.

A recent study published in *The New England Journal of Medicine* showed the extent to which Americans use alternative therapies: "Extrapolation to the U.S. population suggests that in 1990 Americans made an estimated 425 million visits to providers of unconventional therapy. This number exceeds the number of visits to all U.S. primary care physicians (388 million). Expenditures associated with use of unconventional therapy in 1990 amounted to approximately $13.7 billion, three quarters of which ($10.3 billion) was paid out of pocket. This figure is comparable to the $12.8 billion spent out of pocket annually for all hospitalizations in the United States" (Eisenberg et al. 1993: 246).

Inside the citadel of science, there is a group of scientists who are focusing on the links between the immune system and the world outside the body, much as alternative medicine treats the body in its life environment. They are claiming that the immune system is a self-organizing network, a complex system of the sort Vera Michaels evoked. But today these scientists are considered "unconventional" and their views controversial. If this currently controversial view of the immune system were eventually to prevail within science (and there are many signs that it will), surely we would want to incorporate in any account of that development that such a view of health and the body was already at large in the general population. Developments in science would be participating in broader cultural developments, not simply reflecting them, but not necessarily leading them either. They might be rising on another island of the same archipelago or participating in the proliferation of one part of a rhizome in another place.

STRING FIGURES

As Max Black said long ago, metaphors both enlighten and blind at the same time. I would not want anyone to take away the impression that there is an actual thing out there in the world (or the ground or the field) that is the equivalent of the archipelago or the rhizome of knowledge. We are not looking for a thing; we are seeking to understand processes by which things, persons, concepts, and events become invested with meaning. Perhaps especially under conditions that pertain in late capitalism, one of the most useful metaphors of all is one that consists almost only of process—the string figures used in the game of cat's cradle, as evoked by Donna Haraway.

> The cat's cradle figures can be passed back and forth on the hands of several players, who add new moves in the building of complex patterns. Cat's cradle invites a sense of collective work, of one person not being able to make all the patterns alone. . . . It is not always possible to repeat interesting patterns, and figuring out what happened to result in intriguing patterns is an embodied analytical skill. (Haraway forthcoming)

In Donna Haraway's terms, in the anthropological study of science, we would be playing a kind of cat's cradle, a serious game "about complex, collaborative practices for making and passing on culturally interesting patterns" (Haraway forthcoming). Understanding how diverse, fragmented cultures are formed is one significant task for ethnography. We have moved from a landscape around a citadel on a hill to a game of string figures, because the "space" in which science and culture contend is too discontinuous, fractured, convoluted, and constantly changing for a map of any landscape to be useful. To traverse such a space, we need an image of process that allows strange bedfellows, odd combinations, discontinuous junctures: people with Marfan making geneticists feel guilty; the general public abandoning the nineteenth-century mechanistic, linear view of the body before most of the biological sciences have; a conception of health based on the immune system that only became generally accepted in the sciences in the 1970s and that has already reached general currency on the streets by the early 1990s.

String Figures in Action

The merit of the string figure image is that it embodies both discontinuity and connection simultaneously. I can hand my string figure over to you and go my own way, but which string patterns are then possible for you to make depends on all the figures produced by previous players. My fieldwork was filled with experiences that seemed to need this kind of description. One of the most striking occurred as I entered the terrain of business management.[3] Having grown interested in how health concerns are being handled in U.S. workplaces, I found my research leading me away from the domains of research immunology, HIV clinics, and urban neighborhoods where I began. Karen-Sue Taussig (one of the graduate students with whom I collaborated in the research) and I learned of a new kind of experiential training method in which workers and management would climb sheer walls and slender tall poles, cross high wires, and jump off cliffs on zip wires. We were invited to attend a daylong experience run by the training company, Vesta (a fictitious name), for the employees of Rockford Company (also a fictitious name), a multinational corporation in the top 10 of the Fortune 500. Twenty-two thousand Rockford employees were going through three days of workshops, as well as high- and low-ropes courses at a rural site on a large bay on the East Coast.

Protected by sophisticated mountain-climbing ropes and harnesses, teams of men and women workers and managers of all ages and physiques (as well as Karen-Sue and I) climbed forty-foot towers and leapt off into space on a zipline, climbed vertical forty-foot walls and rappelled down again, climbed a twenty-five-foot telephone pole that wobbled, stood up on a twelve-inch platform at the top that swiveled, turned around 180 degrees, and again leapt off into space. (This last is privately called the "pamper pole" by the experiential learning staff because people so often defecate in their pants while trying to stand up on it.)

According to the corporation, this was called "empowered learning." It is necessary because according to a Rockford Company brochure, "We are facing an unprecedented challenge. The world is changing faster than ever before. Our markets are becoming more complex; our products are changing; and we are facing global competition on a scale never before imagined." The brochure continues, "Our survival in the 90's depends upon our ability to change our ways of doing things." Success in the 1990s, "going over the wall," will require "letting go of old patterns and behaviors . . . taking a leap through difficult transitions and working hard at new beginnings"; "looking forward to change as a challenge, taking risks and innovating." Emphasis is on a qualitative break with the way one was in the past; like a caterpillar who transforms into a different kind of being, a butterfly, people are to be transformed.

The bodily experiences of fear and excitement deliberately aroused on the zipline and the pole are meant to serve as models for what workers will feel in unpredictable work situations. A participant said, "If we could capture the type of energy we experienced on the tower, at work, there'd be no limit to what we could do." We were told the ropes and walls and poles are also meant to scramble the characteristics usually associated with males and females. Men can feel fear on the high-ropes course, and learn to express their vulnerability; women can feel brave, and learn to see their ability to lead. Men and women can learn to appreciate these unaccustomed capacities in each other. In fact, during our participation in these events, men—even large muscular ones—quite often gave obvious verbal and emotional evidence that they were terrified of heights and confessed, amid much social support from the group, to this vulnerability afterward. (Talk we overheard among the men about having to go clean out their pants was only barely joking.) Women sometimes also showed their fear and confessed it, but they would receive much more praise from trainers and group members for stoicism, bravery, and physical exertion. In addition to gender barriers, the events are also meant to break down hierarchical barriers between management and labor. Groups that go through the exercises together are usually composed of both management and labor, and a boss might well be depending on his secretary or assembly-line worker to belay him with a rope when he jumps off a tower, and vice versa.

As a participant in the high-ropes course, I saw the experience as emblematic of a spectacular shift in what it takes to be a successful worker today. Although some of the towers that supported the activity were made of huge, solidly constructed frames, some of the apparatus was deliberately left loose and wobbly. Many exercises involved walking across a high wire. Not only did I experience the fear of having no visible support at a great height, but on those wobbly poles, wires, or platforms, I found the fear of being unmoored in space almost intolerable. The exercises combined the vertigo of standing on the edge of a high cliff with the stomach-dropping feeling that the edge of the cliff itself was beginning to crumble. I was literally moving from one position of instability to another.

In this terrified condition, each of us was to jump off into space, only to be caught by our harness (belayed by a coworker). There we were allowed to hang (very comfortably I can report) for a little while, swinging gently not too far from the ground. The harness completely and securely supported one's whole torso, so that one's reaction was to slump like a baby in a backpack. As other people jumped before me and relaxed into this passive, inert posture, I wondered why they did that. After I jumped and later saw a photograph of myself hanging in the harness, I realized I had done exactly the same thing.

Physically, the experience models the nature of the new workers that corporations desire: individuals—men and women—able to risk the unknown and tolerate fear, willing to explore unknown territories while adrift in space, but simultaneously able to accept their dependence on the help and support of their coworkers. The isomorphism between the bodily experience of this training and the results desired is entirely deliberate: as trainers often say, we were there to "experience the metaphor."

An executive of Rockford Company was very aware of the magnitude of change his employees were being asked to make. Evoking some of the qualities of the passive worker and machinelike organization familiar from the 1940s and 1950s, he said, "We made people the way they are! We can't just throw them away like old worn out machinery!! . . . We have treated people in the industrial environment as if they had no brain. Now they are becoming whole people, and that is rewarding." These new "whole people" are to be active in their willingness to tolerate risk and danger, as well as the insecurity of being literally ungrounded, but passive in their willingness to depend on the work group. Like the shifting poles, platforms, ropes, and wires, the nature of the person itself is to shift and to be able to tolerate continuing shifts.

When I was participating in these events, I had little idea at first whether they would shed any light at all on other parts of my research concerning the immune system. I had explained my research to the executives and trainers as an ethnographic study of concepts of health and the body in a scientific lab and urban neighborhoods—without mentioning the immune system specifically. I practically fainted with astonishment (this is an example of experiencing discontinuity and connection simultaneously) when I discovered that trainers elect to use the image of the immune system to convey the kind of flexible, innovative change they desire. While visiting Vesta headquarters in the southwest, I had a long interview with Mark Sandler (a pseudonym), the CEO of the company and the person who develops Vesta's training materials. He asked me to tell him more about my research interests. I discussed my research in an immunology lab. He exclaimed, "That is the very image I use because it works so perfectly to communicate what we want." What he meant to communicate was the image of a flexible and innovative body poised to respond in a continuously changing environment while constantly communicating with other such bodies. Sandler enlisted my help in sending him more material about the immune system to incorporate into his training materials; he wanted particularly apt and up-to-date scientific descriptions of how the immune system works.

His practice was to use the immune system as a metaphor to convey to workers or managers he was training what kind of a corporate and individual body they must strive for to survive in today's global marketplace. The corporate body must be one in which, exactly like the immune system, there is constant innovation and change, continual adaptation to a changing environment. Individuals (like the parts of the immune system) must have a great deal of flexibility, flexibility which will allow them to bend and adapt to constant change. They must even be able to adapt to dramatic overall state changes if the corporation no longer needs them at all.

The magnitude of the contemporary shift in body imagery we have begun to glimpse in the above descriptions is happening in connection with major shifts in the nature of work and the organization of the workplace. As I mentioned earlier, there is a major shift under way in the forces of production that began in the 1970s. This shift, associated with late capitalism, and often termed flexible specialization, has been called "the signature of a new economic epoch" (Borgmann 1992: 75).[4] The "flexibility" in this new shape of the economy refers to both labor and products: labor markets become more variable over time as workers move in and out of the work force more rapidly; the process of labor itself varies, too, as workers may take on managerial tasks and managers may spend time on the assembly floor, as dictated by changing production conditions. Products also become more flexible: design processes grow more versatile and technology can more rapidly adapt to the needs of production. "Specialization" refers to the custom marketing of goods produced cheaply in small batches for particular customers ("tailor-made" production) and the consequent end of mass production and standardized products (Smith 1991: 139).

The acceleration in the pace of product innovation and the exploration of highly specialized and small-scale market niches spawn new organizational forms, such as the "just-in-time" inventory-flows delivery system, which cuts down radically on stocks required to keep production flow going (Harvey 1989: 156). Laborers experience a speedup in the processes of labor and an intensification in the retraining that is constantly required. New technologies in production reduce turnover time dramatically, entailing similar accelerations in exchange and consumption. Time and space compression occur, as time horizons of decision making shrink and instantaneous communications and cheaper transport costs allow decisions to be effected over a global space (Harvey 1989: 147). Space is annihilated through the speedup of time. Multinational capital operates in a globally integrated environment: ideally, capital flows unimpeded across all borders, all points are connected by instantaneous communications, and products are made as needed for the momentary and continuously changing market.[5]

The people we met in my fieldwork have become involved in these processes in complex ways, as residents of neighborhoods in Baltimore, scientists in biology labs, and CEOs of major corporations experience the wrenching consequences of the increasing concentration of capital, both nationally and globally, and the decline of former manufacturing systems. In a variety of ways, experiences of continuous, linear lines along which one could cross a Cartesian time-space grid are vanishing.

Writing about ecological theories of nature, Donald Worster comments:

> Nature, many have begun to believe, is *fundamentally* erratic, discontinuous, and unpredictable. . . . Constant innovation, constant change, constant adjustment have become the normal experience in this culture. We have so far forgotten that life can be otherwise that we have come to accept as natural much of the chaos, uncertainty, and disintegration we find in our institutions and communities. We find it difficult nowadays to believe in any form of stability.
> (Worster 1993: 167, 179)

Both the scientist "seeing" the nature of the healthy body, and the manager "seeing" the nature of the ideal worker are trying in different ways to make sense of how they experience profoundly global processes. To have been "disciplined" by my colleague's shock about breaching the boundary of the laboratory walls would have meant missing how the particular string figure of the immune system was passed along. Perhaps herein lies one of the most compelling reasons that anthropological fieldwork—of science or anything else—can no longer be contained within any single location.

FINAL REMARKS

I do not intend to champion any one of the images I have discussed as best for all purposes for all time. Like the various tools in a toolbox, each may have different uses. The spatial image of the citadel on a landscape illuminates some of the ways science is regarded, and regards itself, even though the image's simplicity misses many things. Unlike rhizomes and string figures, it does not bring the temporal aspect of processes to the fore; unlike rhizomes or archipelagos, it lacks depths in which hidden or unknown things may take place.

Both rhizomes and string figures are inextricably spatiotemporal, and therefore are perhaps particularly well suited for an age like the present when "space is being annihilated by time." Both also convey an element of discontinuity: the rhizome can break away from its origin stalk and still produce a complete form; string figures appear to shift suddenly from one form like "cup and saucer" to another like "cat's whiskers."

Similarly, in the late capitalist world, information is spatially unmoored, able to travel across the globe at the speed of light. Powerful images, given life by corporate advertising and media industries of many kinds, also operate across spatially discontinuous realms. Objects and people seem to be in constant motion as well, composed of parts with different origins; computers and cars contain parts with a different country of origin stamped on each; people move from job to job, people whose concept of the body allows them to add prosthetic or cybernetic body parts as the need arises.

To return to my example, there is no necessary spatially contiguous, structural linkage between the corporate trainer I described and contemporary immunology. The links, even if they could be discovered, might turn out to be ephemeral, accidental, transient. The CEO of the training company might have learned about the current understanding of the immune system from any number of media—print or film—as easily as from his own allergy clinic or from the process of deciding whether to vaccinate his own children.

In the end, what enables anthropologists to contribute new insights to the study of Western science may be the anthropological notion of culture, which tries to understand any part of a culture in the broadest context that can be practically managed, while remaining committed to participatory fieldwork. So Sharon Traweek looks to fundamental cultural conceptions of time and space to illuminate what her physicist-informants say, and Rayna Rapp and Deborah Heath look to many contexts outside research science, from conversations with a new mother to lectures at a lay foundation's conference, to hear how knowledge of the health or illness of the body is produced.

Although the impetus for contextualizing what one studies as deeply as possible has an old and venerable tradition in anthropology, the contexts in which this fieldwork on science is being done are not like we imagined the field sites of our forebear to be: these field "sites" are not primarily spatial. Or rather, they include many different spaces that are discontinuous from each other. For this reason, we need new images to guide our thinking about how to define an appropriate context to produce understanding. The images I discuss here are only the beginning.

NOTES

Versions of this chapter were given at New York University and the City University Graduate Center and subsequently published as Martin 1996. Thanks are due for the many instructive comments I received on those occasions and to Sarah Franklin for getting me to write on this topic in the first place.

1. This description is somewhat overdrawn for the sake of the point that follows. Rather than intending any criticism of Traweek's work, I mean to convey admiration for her great skill as a fieldworker in such a difficult setting. It is apparent from all her work that *she* realizes physicists are actually deeply embedded in society.

2. In another domain, but with similarly powerful findings, David Hess has examined the boundaries created and defended by parapsychologists and New Agers in relation to their scientific skeptics in the United States (Hess 1993). In her commentary on a draft of this paper, Joan Fujimura pointed out to me that scientists are not the only ones who construct walls. Parapsychologists may deliberately construct walls in order to protect the domain of the paranormal for investigation; people who doubt the value of scientific research may construct walls to keep scientists out, as some African Americans have done with respect to sickle-cell anemia.

3. Some discussion about this research appears in another context in Martin 1994.

4. This term was first used in Piore and Sabel 1984.

5. See Piore and Sabel 1984 for a different analysis of the relationship between the global division of labor and flexible specialization.

EIGHT

"You Can't Take the Subway to the Field!": "Village" Epistemologies in the Global Village

Joanne Passaro

KNOWLEDGE AND DANGER

Whenever anthropologists learned that I had done fieldwork among home-less people in New York City, the question most commonly asked was whether—or how frequently—I slept out on the streets. The disappointment that invariably followed my emphatic "No, never" seemed to lay bare im-portant assumptions about ethnographic knowledge. I knew that some grad-uate students at the time were indeed sleeping in the streets, but I did not know any postdoctoral anthropologists who were. This difference raised in-teresting questions about how subjecting oneself to physical danger might still be part of a rite-of-passage aspect of fieldwork: even if we can no longer romanticize exotic "natives," we can nonetheless continue to romanticize the "young" ethnographer and his/her ethnographic project.

But what of the epistemology this view privileges? What claims to authority are made and legitimated in jeopardizing the physical or social well-being of the ethnographer and/or her informant? Is "better" knowledge that which is produced/secured at great risk? Such an evaluative stance, persistent if rarely articulated, is a holdover from the colonial mentality that once de-lighted in harrowing ethnographic accounts of the conquests of physical landscapes and of native reticence, when wresting "secrets" from remote "na-tives" was the *raison d'être* of the endeavor.

This vision of the anthropological project provided, in the early days of this century, justification for the creation of departments of anthropology and delimited the borders between anthropology and sociology (Stocking 1992a). Now, at the close of the century, it continues to legitimate those bor-ders in the face of social and political challenges from within and without. At a time when a number of departments of anthropology have been down-sized, closed, or merged, it may seem expedient to support a stance that maintains a uniquely anthropological project. But by holding onto comfortable "truths," we are obscuring analyses of what does in fact distinguish the various social sciences in the United States, and what kinds of knowledge we as anthropologists can and do produce, and how.[1]

To restate the problem, although explicit reference to primitive natives has generally disappeared from anthropological discourse, conceptions of "the field" that constituted and defined those natives persist. The world as viewed by anthropology is still broken up into "areas" and "sites" sanctioned for study, peopled with those who might no longer be exotic but who are still coherent Peoples (Dominguez 1989) and necessary Others. Because "the field" functions as the master symbol of the discipline, even when nontraditional field sites are admitted into the canon of anthropology, we nonetheless continue to inflect them with a host of assumptions generated by a colonial worldview. This has been the experience of a number of anthropologists attending the conferences on which this book is based. Kath Weston, for instance, has had to challenge assumptions about "primitives"—and thus about "appropriate" objects of analysis—in her work on queers, and she and Paulla Ebron (1994) have discussed the ways in which the researcher herself is read against aspects of her identity that are "marked," i.e., "non-universal." These experiences, as well as my own and those of others in this book, indicate that the process of taking anthropology out of "the field"—the geographically distant and exotic lands of Others—is far easier than taking "the field," i.e., colonial thinking, out of anthropology.

In this chapter I would like to call attention to some of the questions related to notions of the field and "real" fieldwork that were raised in my field experiences among homeless people in New York. I will begin by briefly going backward, to an earlier study I conducted in the so-called Mediterranean. In doing so, I hope to explore some of the issues that are ignored, finessed, or subsumed by archetypical and totalizing conceptualizations of "the field." In particular I will focus on some of the epistemological and methodological conflicts raised by my choices of nontraditional sites for field research: Paris and New York City.

"THE FIELD" AS PRISON-HOUSE, OR "THE MEDITERRANEAN"

The delineation of a culture area presupposes the specific kinds of Otherness to be found there. In my own work, I first encountered the frustrating teleology of this formulation in 1987, when I decided to do fieldwork among lesbian and feminist activists in France. A few of these women had participated in the breakup of the *Questions Feministes* collective, and some had described the central issue as how to define the category "woman" and whether or not "lesbians" were within it. When I began to write funding proposals, I was met with two responses: the questioning of Paris as a legitimate field site for an anthropologist, and the related argument that since I was interested in gender issues in France, the area I would be working in was not western Europe but the Mediterranean.

This was the Mediterranean of honor and shame, the behemoth whose contours were defined by Fernand Braudel (1972 [1949]) in his classic history. Braudel's Mediterranean was an ecological unit, while the Mediterranean literature in anthropology that began with the work of Pitt-Rivers (1961) and Campbell (1964) posited it as a cultural area defined by the presence of codes of honor and shame in hierarchical gender relations. In colonial anthropology, the Mediterranean was the dark "primitive" to Europe's pale "modern." Two central assertions—the existence of a unified Mediterranean and the existence of codes of honor and shame that delimited it— provided the ontological and epistemological foundations for a whole field of inquiry that then could set itself the task of "discovering" and "documenting" its very conditions of possibility.

This honor-and-shame-bound Mediterranean was one of isolated, atomistic, face-to-face communities, and by the mid-1980s it seemed practically and theoretically impossible to keep this concept of the Mediterranean afloat in the face of numerous challenges (national, feminist, and postmodern, to name a few). As early as 1980, Michael Herzfeld argued that "honor" and "shame" were imprecise glosses of native categories and that "massive generalizations" obscured the nature of particular phenomena (1980: 349), but nonetheless many researchers persisted in calling themselves "Mediterraneanists" and in asserting the region's unity. As late as 1985, for instance, David Gilmore was still looking to legitimate a conceptualization of the area as a unique cultural whole, but the argument he came up with, that "the Mediterranean cultures . . . conflate sex with gender"(1985: 4), did not, for obvious reasons, serve his cause.

The perpetuation of the notion of culture areas as coherent wholes is a vestige of what Rosaldo (1989a) has called "imperialist nostalgia"; as such, it cuts to the heart of a discipline built upon unequal and colonial encounters (Asad, ed., 1973).[2] While this nostalgia might well be politically and theoretically untenable, it does have practical advantages. Piña-Cabral (1989), for instance, has argued that the impetus for continuing to deploy a unified and romanticized Mediterranean came primarily from U.S. academics, with some collaboration from southern Europeans who had an ambiguous relationship to their "Europeanness" (1989: 400). He argued:

> Within the highly competitive and specialized world of American academia, this concern with the identity of the Mediterranean must . . . be understood as a reflection of the strategic options of anthropologists who . . . find that there is a payoff in being labelled Mediteraneanist. . . . (Piña-Cabral 1989: 401)

Piña-Cabral argues that notions of honor and shame and a unified Mediterranean were not as useful for anthropological comparison as they were for the legitimation of disciplinary authority and the maintenance of uniquely "anthropological" areas of expertise. Thus while for Braudel the delineation of the Mediterranean involved a conscious choice of structuralism ("to draw a boundary around anything is to define, analyse, and reconstruct it, in this case select, indeed adopt, a philosophy of history" [1972: 18]), for anthropologists in the 1970s and 1980s the choice was less about heuristics than about maintaining professional niches.

Piña-Cabral's argument is particularly illuminating in its emphasis on the central but undertheorized role that funding concerns play as the disciplinary—and disciplining—arbiters of what counts as anthropological knowledge.[3] It also implies what others (e.g., Moore 1994) have since asserted—that the delineation of the anthropological project as a necessarily comparative one privileges the construction of a particular kind of knowledge—based on "comparable facts"—which by necessity flattens and diminishes complexities and ephemeralities that might not fit into existing categories and modes of comparison. Thus, in the process of asserting the uniqueness of Mediterranean culture, much cultural difference—as well as similarity—was lost in the terms of analysis.

For my own project, begun in Paris in 1987, the Mediterranean culture area was irrelevant. I know many other researchers have found themselves in the same boat—facing canonized literatures and received truths that have little to do with, or actually undermine, the project at hand. But I have come to think that something in addition to funding imperatives and job security is at work here.

The anthropological project that became hegemonic in various struggles over professional and disciplinary authority was, significantly, one which limited our perceptions of the transformative potential of human action: in the "Mediterranean," as in many other "culture areas," the social rules and their centrality were assumed, leaving the ethnographer to chart their usually imperfect application "on the ground." Human agency was reduced to mere reaction and accommodation to preexisting social laws. This is what Haraway (1988) calls the God Trick of objectivity, which limits the parameters of our knowledge to what we already "know."[4]

This common "effect" of culture areas is, I think, an important element in their persistence. The loss of primitive atomism and various totalizing systems of determinism have left anthropology bereft of readily apprehensible and "manageable" objects of analysis, and Rosaldo's imperialist nostalgia might not mourn the death of "the primitive" as much as the epistemologically, methodologically, and politically controllable and overdetermined units of analysis that "primitives" represented. Efforts to retain methodological and epistemological control via the overpowering foundationalism of culture areas give the appearance of clarity even as they take it away:[5]

agency is typically assigned to elites, we "discover" coherent bodies of knowledge that recreate what we already assume, and we reinscribe the politics of
the status quo.[6] The heuristic of culture areas is, in important ways, a comfortable antiheuristic.

But again, these problems are not limited to either "the Mediterranean"
or "culture areas," as I learned in my research among homeless people in
New York.

"YOU CAN'T TAKE THE SUBWAY TO 'THE FIELD!'"

By 1990, when I was preparing to begin my dissertation research, I imagined
that if I worked in a nonsanctioned field site, the potential agency of my informants might not already be "determined" out of existence. This turned
out not to be the case, as I discuss in a number of ways in the sections that
follow.

Some of the first problems I encountered are indicated in the title of this
section, which follows the rhetorical practice of authenticating the ethnography that follows by introducing it in the words of an informant, preferably
in the "native dialect." In this case, though, the native was an academic I met
as we walked to a New York University conference on "home," and his dialect
was social theory. We had both just gotten off a downtown subway, and we noticed each other as we struggled over the unwieldy schedule of the day's events.
He was presenting a paper, he said. I was an anthropologist doing fieldwork,
I said. "You can't take the subway to the field!"[7] he protested, only half-joking.
"What kind of fieldwork can you do in such an uncontrolled environment?"

This last question hits the postcolonial ethnographic nail on the head. I
was asked it, or told it, in many guises—"Did you focus in on a more manageable subgroup, like a homeless women's shelter?"; "That family shelter[8]
sounds fascinating. Why not stay there and do an ethnography of it?"; "No
grant proposal that does not specify a workable field site will be funded."
This last piece of advice was repeated often, and although it is a commonplace that the gap between one's proposed research and the eventual project
is often huge, the disciplinary imperative was to delimit a "laboratory"/field
site (see Kuklick chapter 2) before getting caught up in the "chaos" of New
York. After having confronted the Mediterranean, though, I wanted the
boundary issue to be an empirical one, not one I had to delimit in advance—
I did not want to turn a single homeless shelter into an epistemologically
controlled unit like a "Mediterranean" village. Admittedly, New York City was
and is chaotic, uncontrolled, and unmanageable, but, then, so is all of postmodern space in a globalized world (Jameson 1991). To finesse the theoretical and methodological challenges of postmodernism by creating a
"homeless village" seemed besides the point of social inquiry, even if I would
be doing so "only" for a grant proposal. Because my field site was readily ac-

cessible, and because of Duke graduate school policies that supported student research, I had an option: I could apply to my own university for funding for a summer of exploratory fieldwork. But many of my peers, within Duke and without, did not and do not have this option, and grant proposals are written, and "fields" and "units of analysis" are delimited, from distant armchairs.

During the years of my research, issues of methodological control were often raised within a framework of nostalgia, particularly when they were about the existence of homeless "subcultures": Did they exist? Was I looking in the right places? What about the encampments and subway tunnels? Groups of homeless people did sometimes organize into relatively stable communities of various kinds, but none of these seemed to be the "subcultures" I was asked about. I often felt that my various disciplinary interrogators would be happiest if I discovered some sort of secret communication system among homeless people like the codes of hoboes earlier in the century. In this case, the subcultural, exotic status of the homeless could be inscribed, and with luck I might never have to step into the chaotic present at all.

This problem—the imperative of coherence in the face of transition and instability—is similar to that confronted by Liisa Malkki (chapter 4). Malkki argues that the epistemology and the methodology of "the fieldwork tradition" aim at the construction of unitary, "permanent" knowledge and are poorly equipped to theorize or indeed accept the "permanence" of ephemeral phenomena and fragmentary understandings. In my own work, because I chose a field site such as New York, the chaos I was warned against occupied the same position as Malkki's "transitory phenomena"—both were anathema to the construction of traditional anthropological knowledge.

THE EPISTEMOLOGY OF "DISTANCE"

For my subway informant, the site problem of New York had a corollary— the "distance" problem. By "taking the subway to the field," I interpreted him to mean not only that metropolitan New York was an inappropriate field site, but that it was especially inappropriate for *me*. The social distance I was traveling, he thought, was not great enough; I might be too close to "see well." But to other people, assumptions about the degree of "Otherness" necessary between the ethnographer and her informants made my choice of studying homelessness at least partially redeeming: "This is a much better idea than studying lesbians!" one anthropologist enthusiastically informed me, assuming that I was less Other to some group called "lesbians" than to "the homeless."

In both cases, the assumption was that an epistemology of "Otherness" was the best route to "objectivity," that as an outsider I would be without the ideological filters or stakes in the outcome of my study that an insider would have. But at this point at the close of the century, we already know that "objectivity" is not a function of "distance"; that "Otherness" is not a geographical given but a theoretical stance; and that we do indeed have a stake in our work. In fact, I felt far less "Other" to the homeless people I worked with than to lesbians in Paris, despite the fact that I was a nonhomeless lesbian. But though these distances, and my own or my informants' ability to manipulate or mitigate them, became an important aspect of my work, for most people the essential question was whether by doing fieldwork in the United States I was "distant enough" to produce adequate ethnographic knowledge. Whether I was "close enough" was never an issue.

In addition, taking the subway to the field also meant that travel to and from the field was a daily occurrence, not the romantic combination of long plane, jeep, and footpath treks that provided the enthnographer time to enter into a "new world." But I did not enter and reenter the field every day—the New York I lived, worked, and played in was all "the field," whether I was at the opera, eating Ukrainian food in the East Village, or at a homeless shelter.

Daily life in the city required that I, like any New Yorker, navigate many complex series of encounters and negotiate often enormous social differences. One example makes this clear, and adds a twist to the "distance" problem. In the spring of 1991, literary agent Charlotte Sheedy introduced me to Lane Montgomery, a screenwriter who was working on a script about homelessness. Lane had assumed that I was in school in New York, and when she heard that I was at Duke she asked, "Oh, do you know Angie?" I thought Lane was referring to one of her daughters, but the "Angie" in question turned out to be the late Ambassador Angier Biddle Duke, whom I had never met and under usual circumstances would never be in the position to meet. A few weeks later, though, I did meet Ambassador Duke for breakfast at his home at River House. We had a long and lively conversation about mutual interests and experiences in Central America and Eastern Europe, and at the end of the meal, Ambassador Duke invited me to return to his home later that afternoon, "for cocktails with Shevardnadze."

I had various research activities planned for that day, so I walked the sixty or so blocks south from River House both to dissipate my disbelief and to get some of those tasks done. At that time I was studying the ways homeless people were being hustled off expensive shopping streets, so I canvassed the avenues talking to police, store owners, and homeless vendors and panhandlers. I then tried to arrange a follow-up interview with Jean, a homeless woman who traveled into New York every day from Jersey City to panhandle.

The thoughts and feelings I had about Jean were typical of my reactions to homeless people—there but for a couple of breaks go I. Like Jean, I had come from a working-class family; like Jean, I had often been marginally employed before returning to undergraduate school; like Jean, I had gone back to college because of the need to earn a living wage. But unlike Jean, I was going to meet the Soviet politician Eduard Shevardnadze in three hours.

It is typically assumed that I had to negotiate chasms of social difference in working with homeless people, but while those differences existed, they were not as dramatic as my encounters with the other extreme were. For instance, in preparing for my return to Ambassador Duke's home that day, I realized that the neat-but-casual clothes I had worn for breakfast were both the best clothes I had and also totally inappropriate for cocktails. After an hour of panic, I placed an emergency call to Charlotte Sheedy, eventually borrowing a handpainted blazer and a flowing black skirt for the event. I felt odd in someone else's skin, a point driven home in the elevator at River House when another guest admired the jacket and asked who had designed it. In contrast, I never had to borrow clothes, or even "dress down," to work among homeless people. Nonetheless, I do not conceptualize my visits to Ambassador Duke's apartment as "leaving the field"—that such extremes of privilege and devastation coexist in such close quarters in New York City is not coincidence, and elites were as much a part of my analysis as homeless people were. But again, as in my research in France, the assumptions about to whom I felt and was "Other" were way off the mark.

"OTHER" VOICES: SACRED OR PROFANE?

The assumption that homeless people were my "Others" typically went hand-in-hand with a related judgment—that homeless people were, at least, an appropriate anthropological object because they were "marginal." But some people assumed that "the homeless" were sacred in their marginality, while to others they were profaned by it. Both positions severely limited understandings of the agency and subjectivity of homeless people.

In conceptualizing "the homeless"—or, as in Weston's case (chapter 9), "queers"—as "primitive" or marginal, we are not setting "them" up in relation to ourselves in the same way as anthropologists once did to "primitives," who were conceptualized as our evolutionary ancestors. "The homeless" do not represent "us" before Gutenberg, but rather "us" after Willie Horton. They are the rejects of *internal* colonialism, peripheralized because of their positions within our race, class, and gender systems of domination and subordination. This lack of "distance" makes them doubly suspect—the position of homelessness in U.S. society stigmatizes not only homeless men and women themselves, but also their words.

During the first year of my fieldwork, when I discussed my research or presented aspects of it in talks, I was sometimes angrily challenged by students and by anthropologists: "How can you believe what they're telling you?"[9]

"Their stories will just be self-serving, blaming everyone but themselves." Upon questioning my questioners, I found that while the statements of homeless people might be seen as suspect, those of other marginal or subaltern groups were not considered similarly tainted. I sometimes compared the "stories" of homeless people to *testimonios* like that of Rigoberta Menchu, and asked my audiences whether the latter were perceived to have a different epistemological status. The example of Rigoberta brought various fault lines to the fore: not all subaltern voices are equally challenged—particularly suspect are the voices of those who live within the borders of our internal colonial system, and most especially, those of black men.

Thus, while working among "marginal" people within the U.S. might have given me a tenuous toehold on ethnograpic terra firma, it also reinscribed a Geertzian notion of the anthropologist-as-interpreter, since some "natives" could not be trusted to speak for themselves. Again, this fallback position was a comforting one, in that it justified and legitimated the anthropological enterprise.

But on the other hand, and usually from the opposite political perspective, many homeless advocates and homelessness theorists fell into a similar epistemological trap. Most advocates of the homeless and most of the representations of homeless people in media and in the literature go to great lengths to avoid the victim-blaming approaches that characterized earlier "culture of poverty" models. Theorizing about homelessness is generally confined to macroeconomic analyses of changes in global capitalism and the massive defunding of housing programs under Reaganomics. But concern about blaming homeless people simultaneously silences homeless people; most theorists do not give them agency for fear that they might be, somehow, "to blame." In most analyses, homeless people are usually still "victims," though "blameless."[10]

Whether or not I felt that homeless people were "victims," it did not seem methodologically useful to characterize them that way, as appeared to be the route proposed by Marcus and Fischer (1986). With that approach, I would be too afraid to ask questions of homeless people for fear that I would oppress them. In contrast, while conducting fieldwork in New York, I found what Nancy Scheper-Hughes (1992) so movingly describes in her research on Brazil—that most of the homeless people I met were happy to talk, to be listened to, to feel that their lives and experiences were important. And as I began to listen to the stories of homeless people, I heard what many advocates feared all along—that many homeless people "chose" to become homeless.

This "choice" was certainly narrowly constrained: for women it was often a matter of deciding whether to keep suffering domestic abuse, while for some men who felt that their roles as breadwinners were unbearably restrictive and unrewarding, the only alternative to nuclear families was the streets.[11] Again, these choices were restricted, most particularly, by global, local, and personal economies; many other people could flee domestic violence or restrictive gender roles and yet avoid homelessness. But by listening to homeless people, I heard not only the expected critique of global capitalism, but also a trenchant and urgent critique of the nuclear family imperative.

Had I not had the luxury of exploratory fieldwork, which freed me of the necessity of defining a project and selecting units of analyses based on existing literatures, I am not sure if I would have seen this aspect of homelessness. Once I heard a number of homeless men and women describe their experiences within nuclear families, I decided to look for patterns and similarities in the lives of other homeless people. It was only then that I felt ready to bound a "field," select units of analysis, and write grant proposals.

THE DIALECTIC OF PARTICIPATION AND OBSERVATION

While it did not seem epistemologically sensible for me to delimit a field site in advance of arriving in the field, it was possible for me to do so because I had chosen to work in the United States, had already decided on homelessness in New York as the focus of my study, and was eligible for student loans. Nonetheless, once I returned to New York in September 1990 after two months of exploratory research, the old question still remained: "But what will you do when you step off the boat?"[12]

The traditional anthropological methodology, participant observation, is largely unelaborated, but I found that by conceptualizing participation and observation as elements in dialectical tension, I had a rich heuristic, one that necessitated attention to multiple perspectives in order to produce adequate social description and analysis. I knew that I wanted to explore homeless people's experiences within nuclear families, but I did not want to skew my understanding by making those experiences my only point of entry into the lives of homeless people. I decided to choose sites that would afford me positionalities at varying points along a participant-observer continuum.[13]

I volunteered in a city-run family emergency shelter, working and talking with mostly women and children clients as well as city workers; I joined meetings, demonstrations, and social activities with the men from Homeward Bound, the only shelter/self-help group run by homeless people themselves; I worked with a group of lawyers and law students at a weekly welfare rights clinic run at a large downtown soup kitchen; I volunteered at the Interfaith Assembly on Homelessness and Housing, a nonprofit advocacy and aid organization; and I interned, researched, and wrote articles for *City Limits*, a progressive magazine that served as a watchdog for housing and community issues in city and state government. These sites were not the only postions I interacted or observed from, and I did not spend equal amounts of time in them all. They were, however, the scaffolding around which I built the rest of my activities—interviewing panhandlers, joining or watching demonstrations, discussing books and going to films and plays with homeless people, playing cards, spending days in the Forty-second Street library, and sitting in Central Park or one of the numerous other parks where homeless people congregated.

Once I had determined these sites and some research strategies, I did not apply for many grants; as anyone working in the United States knows, few funding sources consider our work "real" anthropology. But I was lucky, and I did get a grant, though not from a traditional source within the discipline. The Aspen Institute had just begun, in 1991, to offer substantial funding for U.S. research, and I was awarded a generous grant from within their Non-Profit Sector Research Fund.

But I paid heavily for that first year of what Anna Tsing referred to as "freedom from 'discipline.'"[14] I had to face the personal and professional insecurity of beginning fieldwork without a grant, and I had to take out a $15,000 student loan. While I never have regretted the intellectual aspects of that decision, I often have rued the financial ones, and I suspect that I will have plenty of company. Given the complicity of social science granting agencies in keeping traditional notions—like culture areas, coherence, and "the Mediterranean"—afloat, challenges to old views of ethnographic authority will continue to be costly in the face of the often invisible powers that determine what anthropology is and should be.

More troubling to me—now that I am out of graduate school, finished with the book based on my dissertation research, and comfortably settled in my first job—is that career advancement and age seem to mitigate against continued challenges to disciplinary traditions. I am no longer eligible for student loans—will I mortgage what I own to finance another year or two of fieldwork instead of crafting an armchair proposal? I doubt it. The disciplinary and institutional norming processes that confront graduate students affect all of us at all stages of our careers and research. For though the requirements of grant proposals might be one part of the problem, the requirements of publication are, as Dan Bradburd has suggested, another. Bradburd argues that despite the fact that much of what most ethnographers experience, observe, and collect while doing fieldwork does not match or confirm what is "already known," the process of writing those experiences up for committee approval or publication—like the initial process of applying for funding—is an institutionally norming and disciplining one.[15] Since theorizations and generalizations—and not the messiness of everyday life—are what is considered fundable, publishable, and indeed—by most of us—valuable, much of what does not fit into received categories or already elaborated theory often winds up on the cutting room floor.

RETHINKING THE FAMILY, RACE, AND GENDER

I have been arguing that disciplinary imperatives, funding requirements, and the received truths of existing literatures all combine to overdirect our research along avenues of what we already know, expect, or assume. But the problems are not merely external to us as researchers; I learned during exploratory fieldwork that my own positionalities and politics were equally double-edged, leading me to some problems and blinding me to others.

Before even setting foot in New York, I assumed that whatever kind of project I developed, I would probably work with homeless women. Their problems, I thought, were more serious than men's problems, for in addition to all the other dangers of the street, women faced the constant threat of rape or other physical assault. When I arrived in New York, I noticed far more men on the streets than women, but even the dramatic differences in numbers did not, at first, alert to me the existence of a noteworthy problem. It was only when daily observations at a variety of sites repeatedly indicated significant differences along lines of gender (and race, though that was expected) that I even thought to pose my first question.

On Sundays I worked with a team of lawyers and law students at a welfare rights project at the St. Francis Xavier soup kitchen. From our vantage point on a dais at the entrance to the service area, I counted the people in line; each week, about 1,200 homeless people came for supper, and each week no less than 90 percent of those people were African American men. When I asked Father John Bucki and Sister Mary Galeone, the parish administrators, where the women were, Sister Mary was surprised: "I've been here five years and I never thought about it! They must be over in Queens and in Brooklyn in the Tier Twos for families [transitional housing—emergency shelters are Tier One housing]. But it's true, we hardly ever see women, except in the first seating [for elderly and handicapped people in the neighborhood who are not homeless]. I guess they don't need us."

Sister Mary was right; homeless women do not need emergency services like soup kitchens for long. As I investigated this fact, I learned that beliefs about the differential social value of people of various genders, races, and family statuses were central to the *persistence*—as opposed to the occurrence—of homelessness among men in general, and black men in particular. One of the obvious ways that these beliefs have become instantiated is in the operation of the welfare state.

Welfare is, and has been since the inception of the welfare state, maternalist and protectionist, designed to protect women and children (see, e.g., Skocpol 1992; Wach 1993; Koven and Michel 1993; L. Gordon 1990). In this country, so-called mother's pensions were built into the Social Security Act in 1935. In Title IV of that act, Aid to Dependent Children, a program was established that would pay cash benefits to mothers, primarily widows, who were deprived of their husbands' support (Trattner 1979). This program was expanded in the mid-1960s in response to protests organized by the National Organization of Women against the exclusion of divorced and unmarried mothers (Sklar 1993). The program is now known as AFDC, Aid to Families with Dependent Children.

Today, AFDC is the only federally mandated welfare program. Initially, the redefinition of "family" in the 1960s was a feminist breakthrough: for the first time in U.S. history, social welfare programs were designed so that women and their children could survive without husbands, and without getting married.

But in the last decade, AFDC has been at the center of much of the welfare debates. Feminist welfare critics, particularly Linda Gordon (see most recently Gordon 1990, 1994a), have argued that "welfare is a women's issue" (Gordon 1994b: 311), meaning that maternalist welfare policies are designed to keep women dependent and in need of paternal and patronizing Uncle Sam. Gordon is right, but viewed from the perspective of homelessness, her arguments must be recast. Although women are patronized, they can and do strategize and capitalize on their available options in order to survive. And although Gordon and Nancy Fraser write in a footnote that the grim realities of welfare are "as bad or worse" for men (Fraser and Gordon 1994: 323 n. 12), they and other feminists generally ignore this fact. Poor and homeless men are treated far worse, both by law and custom, and often have nothing to strategize with. In arguing that welfare is a women's issue, Gordon assumes that men would not get such treatment. She is right, for in most states men get no treatment at all.

At the time of my fieldwork, only twelve states offered welfare to single, childless adults. New York was, and so far remains, one of them. But according to a recent U.S. Department of Housing and Urban Development report,

> Even in New York, where virtually all sheltered families receive welfare benefits, it is noteworthy that, at most, 10 percent of all single individuals receive them.[16]

Most of the homeless people with children are women; as "families" (defined as such by both de jure policy and de facto sentiment), these women and their children are frequently able to go all the way through the system—from emergency shelter, to Tier II transitional housing, and then, finally, to an apartment. It is practically impossible for a "single" (i.e., childless) man to get the support and concern that women do; the celebration of the nuclear family and the ideologies surrounding gender converge to make the homeless man an object of scorn rather than of empathy. In New York City it is next to impossible for a man to survive without a woman, or, more to the point, without fathering children. Men accurately perceive their position at the absolute bottom of every priority list, and many eventually move to start new families so that they, too, might benefit from being seen as a "family member."

This picture was complicated by the fact that I was learning that many homeless men and women point to the nuclear family as a problem relevant to their homelessness—women who are fleeing from domestic violence and abuse, and men who feel that their positions as breadwinners rip them off, that "love lasts only as long as the paycheck." Although "the family" is frequently identified as a problem in these ways, it is nonetheless posited as the only solution to homelessness. Mothers, and less often fathers—"family members"—are the only adults who will be able to escape homelessness, for as "family members" they are valued above childless adults. And as I learned to my horror, this situation insures that efforts to protect women and children by according them a special status will backfire; as long as having children is the only way to survive, childless men and women will bear them, recreating the very same unit—the nuclear family—that was the problem in the first place.

In short, though many different classifications of people might become homeless at any given time, not all of them will remain homeless or will have the same choices. The interaction of naturalized ideologies of race and gender difference produces a system of formal and informal practices that insure, in general, that most homeless women of all races will be housed. As "mothers" or potential mothers, they are thought to deserve special treatment and protection (generally from men). Homeless men, and especially African American men, are seen as "dangerous" and "aggressive," and they are left to the streets.

It is probable that I would not have "seen" this phenomenon so clearly had I specified sites and units of analysis before setting foot in New York. On the one hand, the situation is completely obvious, as any foray into the streets of Manhattan makes immediately palpable. But on the other hand, the blinders put in place by the literature—combined with disciplinary imperatives to delineate "the problem" before arriving, and my own feminist politics—might well have started me so far along in another direction that reorienting myself would have been difficult, if not impossible. I would have certainly learned, and "seen," other things, but in so doing, I might have ignored a great deal of unremarked and "invisible" human suffering.

ANTHROPOLOGY AND ITS OBJECTS

Ironically, given my complaints about the imperatives of unitary objects of analysis, the people who *remain* homeless in New York are, in important ways, "a people"—African Americans, and, more precisely, African American men. And these men do occupy a bounded "field"—the streets, subways, and park benches of the city—a field as spatially "incarcerating" (Appadurai

1988b) as the other space to which large numbers of African American men are increasingly consigned—prison. Homelessness is both place-based and race-based identity; there is, as in the "Mediterranean" and in other of our analytic constructs, an isomorphism of space and race (and, in this case, gender).

The point of reconfiguring anthropology is, for me, not merely a question of how to do better social science. The challenge to represent and understand the world around us more adequately, to see beyond the epistemologies of received categories of collective identity and the assumptions about anthropology and fieldwork that continue to reinscribe various "Others" of internal and external colonialism, is part of a struggle to understand how we might best participate in ethnographic practices of liberation. The racial and ethnic hatreds escalating across the globe, and the not unrelated phenomenon of homelessness and the increasingly desperate situations of the people I worked with, underscore for me the urgency of redefining the anthropological project.

The units and categories we use, or challenge, as anthropologists are aspects of the pervasive and naturalized systems of domination and subordination that interpellate "us" as well as our "objects." An anthropology of liberation would seem to require, above all, continual challenges to our own objectifying practices, practices which, intentionally or not, cut down to "manageable" size the multiple, interconnected, overdetermined, and enormously complex subjectivities of the people we study.

I have tried to suggest in this chapter that one of the reasons we still study in epistemological "villages," or try to, is a practical one: we need, somehow, to define projects that we can actually "do." Defining localities in a globalized, deterritorialized world is not obvious, and the critical practice required to keep convenient and fictive villages of collective identities at bay is overwhelming. As my own work among homeless people and Liisa Malkki's work among refugees (chapter 4) so painfully remind us, postmodern power is often maintained by simultaneously creating and fragmenting, inscribing and erasing, collective identities. Unless anthropology can adopt units and strategies of analysis capable of "seeing" and understanding unstable, hybridized, and nonholistic experiences, we will fail at our object of adequate social analysis, and we will remain part of the postcolonial problem we helped create.

NOTES

I would like to thank the participants of the "Anthropology and 'the Field'" conference for their comments and suggestions, especially Jim Ferguson, Liisa Malkki, Kath Weston, Akhil Gupta, Jane Collier, Talal Asad, and George Stocking. I would also like to thank Claudia Koonz, Carol A. Smith, and Daniel Bradburd for their readings of other versions of this chapter.

1. For a provocative analysis of the ways in which "being there" and "staying there"—i.e., the combination of cumulative, singular, and serendipitous encounters that shape ethnographic representation—produce a uniquely *anthropological* understanding distinct from other genres of writing and inquiry, see *Being There: Fieldwork and Understanding* by Daniel Bradburd.

2. This is not to say, however, that anthropology was or is the only discipline with an interest in preserving notions of coherence and cultural unity.

3. Conversations with Don Brenneis at the conference were extremely helpful and illuminating on this point. See also Brenneis 1994.

4. Pierre Bourdieu (1977) and many others in various fields (e.g., the kinship literature) have made similar points.

5. One response to colonial anthropology does not fare much better in this regard. While colonial anthropology reproduced people without history, postmodern critiques of anthropology, both internal and external, focus instead on texts without history (Vincent 1991). In so doing, they not only create straw "readers," but often do away with readers entirely, constructing an eerie ethnographic present peopled only with texts.

6. Donna Haraway has argued similarly about foundationalism and its twin: "Relativism is the perfect mirror twin of totalization in the ideologies of objectivity; both deny the stakes in location, embodiment, and partial perspective; both make it impossible to see well" (1991: 191).

7. See chapter 9 for a similar protest: "Fieldwork with gay people is not fieldwork."

8. Advice about creating "manageable" units of analysis referred far more often to homeless "women" and "families" as potentially manageable entities than to "men." At the end of this chapter I discuss some implications of this rather alarming discourse.

9. Ruth Frankenberg (1993a) encountered a similar challenge in somewhat different circumstances.

10. Two recent exceptions are D. Wagner (1993) and Jencks (1994).

11. I discuss these experiences and feelings briefly at the end of this chapter and at length in *The Unequal Homeless: Men on the Streets, Women in their Place* (1996).

12. This question was reported to me by Virginia Dominguez as the standard response to highly theoretical but methodologically underdeveloped graduate student proposals at the University of Chicago while she was a student there.

13. Emily Martin discusses a similar metholodological strategy in other terms in chapter 7.

14. This phrase came in remarks made by Anna Tsing at the conference "Anthropology and 'the Field,'" sponsored by Stanford University and the University of California, Santa Cruz, in February 1994.

15. Personal communication with Dan Bradburd.

16. U.S. Department of Housing and Urban Development, Office of Policy Development and Research, Division of Policy Studies, *A Report on Homeless Assistance Policy and Practice in the Nation's Five Largest Cities* (1989), p. 56.

NINE

The Virtual Anthropologist

Kath Weston

What walks like an ethnographer, talks like an ethnographer, packs a tape recorder, jots incessant notes, publishes, travels to conferences and applies for jobs just like an ethnographer, even begs and blunders and cajoles like an ethnographer, but is not and never can be a "real" ethnographer? Welcome to the netherworld of virtual anthropology, the state to which the field methodically consigns its "un-fit," a mode of inhabiting the discipline that substitutes ceaseless interrogation for all the comforts of home. How can you expect to teach based upon this sort of fieldwork? Why didn't you study genuine families? Real women and real men? Authentic (pure, isolated, acceptable) natives? How can you have any perspective as an "insider"? Do you really call this anthropology?

The virtual anthropologist is the colleague produced as the Native Ethnographer.[1] Fixed as the one who sets out to study "her own," she attracts, disturbs, disorders. She may have acquitted herself with highest honors during her professional training. She may have spent long hours in the field, carefully researching a topic central to the intellectual history of the discipline. If she is lucky, she will carry with her a pedigree from an outstanding graduate program. (Being advantageously positioned in terms of class hierarchies helps.) If she is very smart and very, very lucky, she may eventually secure a position at a top-ranked university (although precisely because she has been rendered virtual she is less likely to garner such accolades). In short, she may have gone through all the motions expected to bring about professional legitimacy, and, with it, access to what resources the profession has to offer (salary, students, coastal residence, travel, grants). Yet her work will remain suspect, subject to inspection on the grounds of authenticity rather than intellectual argument or acumen.

Too often described as a marginal figure, unfairly exiled to the periphery of the discipline, the virtual anthropologist actually moves through the professional landscape as a creature of another order. She is irredeemably Other, but not as the result of anything so blatant as an operation of exclusion based upon race, sex, class, ethnicity, nationality, or sexuality ("We don't hire/serve/need [epithet of choice] here"). Instead, oppression operates obliquely to incarcerate her within a hybrid category. It is as the Native Ethnographer that the virtual anthropologist finds her work judged less than legitimate, always one step removed from "the real stuff."

CURIOUSER AND CURIOUSER:
THE CASE OF QUEER ETHNOGRAPHY

Back in graduate school, when I first decided to study lesbians and gay men in the United States, the faculty members who mentored me pronounced the project "academic suicide." I found it hard to disagree. Before I could proceed, I had to reconcile myself to the possibility (probability?) that I would never get a job in "my field." (At least, I thought, I would get a book out of it: a way to present my research to a wider public.) One glance at the gloomy employment picture for ethnographers who had studied "homosexuality" reinforced this assessment. Almost none of them held appointments in anthropology, if they had jobs at all.

Is it simply that people were more likely to bow down before that spectral figure, homophobia, back in the early 1980s? I don't think so. Graduate students still write to me, torn between the desire to run off with their first love, queer studies, and the advice of elders to accept the more sensible arranged marriage with "another culture" that would move them securely into "mainstream" anthropology. While job prospects may have improved ever so slightly, the structural circumstances that undercut the legitimacy of queer researchers who study queer topics remain. Anthropology's colonial heritage has formed a field that disciplines its natives in a society that nativizes its queers.

The points at which I have been and continue to be produced as a Native Ethnographer tend to be points of evaluation. These are the sites at which the discipline fields its ethnographers: not just job interviews, but conference presentations, book reviews, skewed readings of published research, and the many small interactions that mint that coin of the academic realm, national reputation (reputation as what?). Comments on such occasions range from the generic dismissal ("Fieldwork with gay people is not fieldwork") to the more refined art of the backhanded compliment ("When I saw the title for your talk, I thought it would be a really flaky topic, but you've just transformed my whole notion of kinship"). More often, those reactions remain unspoken, coiled back into the reception of essays like this. Which is your first inclination as a reader: to reduce the essay to a protest against the discrimination aimed at certain "kinds" of people or to read it for its theoretical contribution to debates on identity, subjectivity, and ethnographic writing?

Reactions to the threat posed by the hybridity of the Native Ethnographer may be couched as expressions of concern: "Some people (not me, of course, I'm your friend) think that if we were to offer you a job here, you would become an advocate." (Don't we all advocate for something?) Then there is the repetitive deployment of that thoroughly neutral category, "fit," as in, "We love your work, but you just wouldn't fit into this department." (Ever wondered why?)

For a change of pace, inventive sorts resort to the thinly veiled objection on methodological grounds: "Lesbians and gay men are too small a segment of society for your results to be meaningful." (As opposed to research on that multitude, the Yanomami?) "Well, there aren't many x left, but when you study the x you are studying an entire social system." (Even Marx, who aspired to a systems analysis, sought a point of entry—alienation, commodity fetishism—that offered a unique line of sight into the whole.) "But why bother with queer theory? It's just a passing fad." (Like the Sapir-Whorf hypothesis? Or game theory? How about that onetime razor's edge of anthropological analysis, structuralism?) Every bit as disconcerting as the historical and political ignorance embedded in such a litany is the utter lack of irony with which otherwise astute colleagues pose these questions.

My dance with professional death would have been humorous if it weren't so costly. Anyone who brings the wrong color or area of competence to her work is familiar with the pressures of having to do more and better than peers to get ahead. But it's difficult to describe the unsettling experience of watching your job history recast as a cautionary tale for the benefit of graduate students still in training. Or the sense of moving through the world more ghost than legend in one's own time. Or the slow and painful realization that the portable inquisition is likely to follow you even if you someday manage to secure a "good" position. Not that the vagaries of the job market make it easy for most applicants to land the job of their dreams (cf. Nelson [1995], Roseberry [1996]). Still, in my case, there was the telltale specificity of the grounds for incredulity and dismissal: Explain why you call this anthropology.

Mistakenly concluding that my subjection to reality checks in an interrogative key was the consequence of conducting research on a stigmatized topic, mentors devised tactics to mitigate the effects of a risky focus of study. Arranged in chronological order, their advice went something like this: As long as you do theory, everything will be okay. Write your way out. Just finish your dissertation. Just get your degree. Once you sign a book contract, things will start to change. Just wait until the book is in press. Wait until the book comes out in print. Wait until people have time to read the book. Maybe that second book manuscript will turn the tide. Perhaps if you broadened your geographic area a bit (say, from lesbians and gay men in the United States to Western Civilization)?

What these routinized strategies for establishing professional credentials failed to take into account are the processes that can render an anthropologist virtual. For that peculiar anthropological subject/object, the Native Ethnographer, career strategies that rely solely on meritocracy or a move to the disciplinary center necessarily prove inadequate.[2] To the degree that queerness is read not only through your research but through your body, hybridity becomes impossible to ignore.

GOING ETHNOGRAPHER

If one is not born an anthropologist, neither is one born a native. Natives are produced as the object of study that ethnographers make for themselves (Appadurai 1988b; Fabian 1983). Coming of age "there" rather than "here" is generally enough to qualify you for this anthropological makeover. Expatriates, of course, need not apply: suitable candidates must be able to lay claim to the ethnicities and nationalities assigned to their place of origin. In Europe and the United States (anthropology's "here"), attribution of native status becomes a bit more complicated. Assignees tend to occupy a sociohistorical location that makes them suitable for exoticization. Darker skin and deviance are always a plus.

With their self-absorption, sexual obsession, love of pageantry, celebration of the body, and party-going nature (please!), queers could have been sent over from central casting to play the savages within. Stereotypes all, but stereotypes that are remarkably continuous with the construction of the primitive in the annals of anthropology.[3] Much as accusations of idleness placed European beggars in a structurally analogous position to those certifiable savages, the "Hottentots" (Coetzee 1985), so the facile reduction of fieldwork among lesbians and gay men to "an extended vacation" evokes the frivolous, childlike behavior in which barbarians everywhere wallow.

Of course, lesbians and gay men do not offer the "best" natives for study. In representation, if not in action, they appear too modern, too urban, too here and now, too wealthy, too white.[4] Below the perceptual horizon are queers with rural origins, immigrant status, empty pocketbooks, racial identities at variance with the Anglo. Ironically, the gay movement's problematic tendency to draw analogies between sexual and racial identity—as though all gays were white and people of color could not be gay—has encouraged even white queers who study queers to be taken as "insider" ethnographers in a way that heterosexual white anthropologists studying their "own" communities are not.[5]

Unlike "primitive" or "savage," the term *native* has made something of a comeback in recent years. This particular return of the repressed has occurred after a pluralist fashion that takes little notice of the power relations that produce different types of nativity. (I'm a native, you're a native, we're a native, too.) But each nativizing move can only be understood in its specificity. As the century turns the corner, queers are constructed not just as natives tethered to the symbolics of residence or birth, but as natives-cum-savages. Like primitives, who got such a bad rep after ethnologists decided they had not evolved to the point of practicing monogamous marriage, queers have been saddled with a sexuality that is popularly believed to evade the strictures of social control. For lesbians and gay men of color, these representations become overdetermined, given the racist legacy that primitivizes and hypersexualizes everyone but the Anglo.

As postmodern-day savages, queers have only a few, mostly unsavory, choices: they can be lazy or restless, noble, self-indulgent, or cruel. The articulate presence of these domestic but not domesticated natives is doubly disturbing because it disrupts the homogeneity of "home," that imagined space of sameness and security that shadows "the field."[6] To the degree that the queer who studies queers has been nativized, she joins a long line of African American, American Indian, South Asian Indian, Mexican, and Brazilian anthropologists trained in "American" universities.[7] Like it or not, she is bound to incite professional insecurities about a changing world in which natives not only read the ethnographies that purport to explain them, but also threaten to show up in a graduate program near you.

So it is not surprising that the aspiring anthropologist who is known to be "that way" finds herself reduced to her sexuality with the presumption that queer nativity is a prior attribute she brought with her into higher education. Forget for a moment the complexities of history and circumstance that undercut the utopian vision of a perfect native. Ignore the possibility that our anthropologist may not interpret her sexuality in terms of identity categories and identity politics. Table every theory you know that tells you identities do not produce transparent, shared experiences waiting to be expressed. Set aside the differences of race and religion and class and nationality that guarantee she will never be the consummate "insider" familiar with every nuance of a bounded community. Never mind that her own discipline is implicated in constructing the (queer) native as an internally homogeneous category. When she embarks upon a career in anthropology, she is likely to be seen as native first, ethnographer second.

Now bring the set-asides in the preceding paragraph back into focus. The complications they introduce into one-dimensional portraits of "the ethnographer" or "the native" describe precisely what is at stake when I characterize the Native Ethnographer as a hybrid.

Hybridity is a term that has lost in precision what it has gained in popularity as it has found its way into discussions of multiculturalism.[8] Although many writers have begun to use "hybrid" and "mixed" interchangeably, hybridity technically describes a process that compounds rather than mixes attributions of identity. If you want to understand the conflicts, suspicion, and general volatility of social relations that surround the lucky incumbent of the Native Ethnographer position, this distinction becomes indispensable.

Think back to that mystical moment in chemistry class when the instructor explained the difference between mixtures and compounds.[9] A mixture is something like a teaspoon of salt stirred together with a spoonful of pepper. Given lots of time, good eyes, and a slightly maniacal bent, a person can sort a mixture back into its original components, placing the pepper, grain by grain, in one pile, and the salt in another. A compound is another matter altogether. Compounds also combine disparate elements, but they join those elements through a chemical reaction that transforms the whole into something different from either of its constituent parts. Water is a compound of oxygen and hydrogen. Put the two together in certain proportions under particular conditions and you will find a liquid where you might expect a gas. Trying to divide water into its elements mechanically, molecule by molecule, drop by drop, would be a fool's errand. Assuming that you understand the properties of water because you once inhaled "pure" oxygen could lead to early death by drowning.

So hybridity is not the sum of an additive relationship that "mixes" two intact terms (Native + Ethnographer). A person cannot understand what it means to be positioned as a Native Ethnographer by reading an essay or two on representations of savagery and then brushing up on the latest in interview techniques. Attempting to grasp each term in isolation is as fruitless as trying to spot the elements of hydrogen and oxygen in your morning cup of coffee. If you come up with anything at all, it is likely to be your own reflection.[10]

But if hybridity is not an additive relationship, neither is it the joining of two terms by a Lacanian slash (Native/Ethnographer). The slash is really nothing more than a variant of the mixture model that problematizes the relationship between the terms. A Native/Ethnographer would be someone who moves, more or less uneasily, between two fixed positions or "worlds" (professional by morning, queer by night). But no two identities attributed to the same body are that separable, that discrete. Nobody checks identities at the door. Whether or not the Native Ethnographer embraces the categories that define her, she is not a split subject, but a hybrid who collapses the subject/object distinction (more on this in a moment).

To continue the science analogy, if there is a chemical reaction that creates the Native Ethnographer as a particular sort of hybrid, it is the act of studying a "people" defined as one's own.[11] Or more accurately, it is the performance of this research activity in the context of the same set of social relations that produces inanities like the characterization of "insider" fieldwork as one long party. (I don't know what kind of parties you go to, but spin the bottle looks pretty good next to 350 days of fieldnotes.) All of this is a social product. Studying "one's own" is no more a matter of natural affinity than nativity is the consequence of birth.

Whether someone becomes nativized—much less primitivized—depends upon matters of history and power that extend well beyond the academy. (To repeat: darker skin and deviance are always a plus.) The mere act of surveying someone with an anthropological (or sociological, or historiographic) gaze is not enough to transform her into a native or credit her with membership in "a people." Veterans who study warfare are not nativized in the same way as queers who study sexuality, and the work of these veterans is much less likely to be read off their bodies.[12]

Because our youthful hero has been produced as a virtual anthropologist only in relationship to her object of study, her ethnography will be perpetually interpreted through her (now increasingly essentialized) nativity. "Evidence" of her sexuality pops up in her work in unexpected places, like Elvis at a road rally or Our Lady of Sorrows in Vegas. And this double-edged process does not require ignorance or ill will to wreak the havoc it does.

Through it all, the Native Ethnographer grapples with the instability of the terms that represent her. Colleagues who misrecognize hybridity as an additive relationship find themselves disturbed by the native's apparent ability to morph the anthropologist.[13] Imagining that the two parts coexist side by side within her, they ask questions that are the equivalent of trying to separate a compound by mechanical means. Their insistence on establishing a standard for "real" fieldwork and "real" anthropology attempts to ferret out the native in the anthropologist like the pepper in the salt. Surely somewhere there must be an advocate hiding behind the professional mask, the savage in ethnographer's clothing. Meanwhile, the anthropologist who finds herself mired in nativity in the eyes of colleagues can attempt to extricate herself by "going ethnographer": emphasizing observation over participation, or insisting on the authenticity of her research ("I did fieldwork, too, you know").

Although these offensive and defensive moves may seem opposed in the high-stakes game of authentication, they share an insistence on the importance—indeed, the possibility—of separating the ethnographer from the native. But the two terms cannot be neatly distinguished once the discipline has brought them into a relationship of hybridity. As a compound state, hybridity represents something more complex than an "intersection" of separate axes of identity. The operations that transform the whole into something qualitatively different from the sum of its parts makes it impossible to tease out the various ways in which research area and nativization combine to provide a basis for discrimination.

Was it studying the United States or the way you stood with your hands in your pockets (too butch) that led the interviewer to pose that hostile question about "real fieldwork"? Funny, another guy asked the same thing when the job specified a geographic focus on the United States, so maybe it's not geographic area after all. But if it wasn't area and it wasn't the hands in the pockets (still not sure about that one), maybe it was because you couldn't put to rest those lingering fears that, if appointed, you would become a crusader for "your people."

There are plenty of grounds these days for charging someone with a failure to perform "real anthropology." Studies of Europe or the United States, studies that traverse national borders, studies "up" instead of "down," studies of "one's own," studies that refuse to exoticize the stigmatized: all have been dismissed, at one time or another, as less than legit. But there is a pattern and a specificity to the occasions on which anthropologists have rallied to the real. In periods of disciplinary complacency as well as the current era of budget cuts and postcolonial reflection, the anthropologist known as the Native Ethnographer has repeatedly been taken to task for passing herself off as the genuine article and falling short of authentic practice.

When Native Ethnographers attempt to prove themselves real in the face of the inevitable interrogation, they face the old duck dilemma: however convincingly they may walk and talk, quack and squawk, as they perform the time-honored rituals of professional legitimation, they will look like an ethnographer before they will be taken as (a real) one. As hybrids, they are continuously produced in the cyberspace of the virtual. As hybrids, they compound subject with object. As hybrids, they become at once hypervisible and invisible, painfully obtrusive and just as readily overlooked.

In the course of professionalization, Native Ethnographers emerge from graduate programs that promise to transform the benighted Them (natives) into the all-knowing Us (anthropologists). On the job market, Native Ethnographers labor under the suspicion that greets shape-shifters, those unpredictable creatures who threaten to show up as Us today, Them tomorrow. The very presence in the discipline of queers who study queers could complicate this dichotomy between Us and Them in useful ways. But in the absence of the thoroughgoing reevaluation of the anthropological project that an understanding of hybridity entails, the irresolvable question that faces the virtual anthropologist remains: How are *these* ethnographers to make their Other?

I, NATIVE

To be taken seriously as a scholar, it is not enough to author ethnographies: our aspiring anthropologist must establish herself as an authority. But as a hybrid, she will find that she cannot authorize herself through recourse to the same time-tested rhetorical strategies that other anthropologists have employed to create professional credibility. The instability of hybridity and the discomfort it inspires make it well-nigh impossible to speak or write from the subject position of "I, Native Ethnographer." Social relations inside and outside the profession pull her toward the poles of her assigned identity, denying her the option of representing herself as a complex, integrated, compound figure. Instead of writing as "I, Native Ethnographer"—or some equally compound subject position—she ends up positioned as *either* "I, Native," *or* "I, Ethnographer." The nuance of the two as they are bound up together is lost.

"Why not try objectivity?" you ask. This distancing device served well enough to secure the reputations of anthropologists in days gone by. Surveying her subjects with an omniscient gaze, the virtual anthropologist sometimes attempts to prove herself real by setting out to occupy the "I, Ethnographer" position with a vengeance. It's bad enough to study a fringe topic; why risk calling attention to an ethnicity shared with "informants" or committing a stigmatized sexual identity to print? Far better to play God. To remind the reader that society casts the Native Ethnographer as "one of them" would be to acknowledge that the author has helped create the universe she observes. Come to think of it, even gods have been known to spin a creation myth or two. Strictly empiricist anthropologists (good girls) don't.

Now this objectivist stance is not bad as a form of resistance to the ways that nativization reduces people to one-dimensional representatives of "their" putatively homogeneous society or community. But the author who writes as "I, Ethnographer" ignores at her peril the impact of her specific social positioning upon her research. And she pays a price when she bows to pressures to disembody herself in order to disavow nativity.

All right, then. Let's turn to the strategy of explicitly inserting oneself into the text, a gambit popularized by what has been dubbed the reflexive turn in anthropology. Writing under the ethnographic "I" means that the author must write *as* someone or something: a situated "self." What's in a pronoun? In reflexive writing, the narrator—as distinct from the author—generally situates herself in terms of identities that carry weight in Euro-American societies. Gender, ethnicity, class, nationality, and (once in a while) sexuality come to the fore.

Of course, reflexivity does not automatically confer credibility. (Witness a friend's reaction when she first leafed through my book on gay kinship ideologies, *Families We Choose* [Weston 1991]: "There certainly are a lot of 'I's' in your book! Is this supposed to be social science?") But reflexivity has the advantage of calling attention to differences that make a difference. If you set out to study a former colony from the former metropole, it just might affect how you are received. If your parents once numbered themselves among the colonized, your reception may shift accordingly. If people "in the field" code you as a woman with money to spend, that assessment can affect your research in ways that bear examination. If you have never done drag but the person you're interviewing has, a "shared" gay identity may or may not affect the results you get on tape. But it is probably worth noting.

Reflexivity reminds the reader to view the circumstances of the anthropologist in relation to the circumstances of the people studied. It also highlights the ways in which the ethnographer's hand, however light, shapes the presentation of data from the field. Still, so much attention to identities can foster a dangerously reassuring belief in equality ("We're all 'I's' here") in situations where serious disparities prevail. All the pious calls for dialogue and mutual respect between the ethnographer and her subjects cannot change the fact that socially structured inequalities do not dissolve under the influence of acknowledgment and understanding. Reflexivity is not, in itself, an equalizing act.

Here lies the danger that reflexivity poses for the Native Ethnographer. To the extent that she uses identity categories to describe herself in her scholarship, she will most likely be read as speaking from the "I, Native" rather than the "I, Native Ethnographer" position. *Her* use of "I" splits the hybridity of the Native Ethnographer by giving nativity pride of place over professional standing. This nativization is the effect not of authorial intent but of power relations in the wider society. Even as I sit at my desk calling attention to the ways that nativization writes people out of the discipline, I am aware that the use of the first person in this chapter may end up reinforcing a tendency to view my work through the narrowing lens of an ascribed lesbian identity.[14] Why else would I be sent manuscripts for review on anything to do with queers (lesbians and ecology, anyone?), but so little material on the theoretical questions about ideology and identity that inform my research?

For the anthropologist who gets nativized as lesbian, gay, or bisexual, "coming out" when she writes up her data can create more problems than it resolves. By and large, the critique associated with reflexivity has addressed power relations between anthropologists and their "informants."[15] But what about the power differentials embedded in relationships with professional "peers"? Which do you think would be harder: to reveal your positioning as a middle-class heterosexual white male, or as some deeper shade of queer? The price of methodological responsibility is higher for people positioned lower. Or, as Lady Macbeth might have said about much of the reflexive soul-searching to date, "What need we fear who knows it, when none can call our power to account?"

When the Native Ethnographer writes about how constructions of her gender or ethnicity or sexuality affected her research, she may provide insights that are crucial for interpreting her results, but she also subjects herself to an insidious sort of surveillance. Although sexualities need not be inscribed *on* bodies (no, Ethel, you can't always know one when you see one), the publications the virtual anthropologist produces will begin to be read *through* her body. Now thoroughly ensconced in nativity, she is likely to be credited with the "instant rapport" that is but one of the illusory attributes of the insider: zap and cook, stir and eat, point and shoot, speak and be in accord, listen and understand. Culturally marked aspects of her identity flag "like" identities among her research subjects, while attributes that place her within the magic circle of domination encourage other aspects of her work to be overlooked.

Since the publication of *Families We Choose*, I have been intrigued by the patterned ways in which it is read and not read. As part of my research for the volume, I conducted a year of fieldwork in San Francisco, getting to know a wide range of gay men, lesbians, bisexuals, "don't-categorize-me's," and even the occasional heterosexual. The parameters of my field research are clearly laid out in the book, both in my words and in the voices of people I interviewed. Yet readers often transform *Families We Choose* into a lesbian text, turning me into a researcher who studies lesbians (what else?) and effectively erasing 50 percent of an interview sample composed of equal numbers of lesbians and gay men. Meanwhile, the racial diversity of the sample goes unremarked, despite its rarity amid the largely white social science studies of homosexuality. Each of these characterizations of the book filters my research through my placement in fields of identity and fields of power. *Families We Choose* is the product of a hybrid "I" who has been nativized in particular ways within and without the text: as a white (unmarked), lesbian (most certainly marked) scholar.

When the politics of reflexivity engage with the complex representation that is the Native Ethnographer, they end up looking more retro than radical. As though stigmatization and skewed readings were not enough, the forced retreat to an "I, Native" subject position embroils the writer in an inhospitable economy of disclosure and revelation. Leaving aside for the moment the associations of moral culpability attached to the confessional form, the concept of coming out of the closet implies the existence of a coherent, prefabricated identity waiting to be expressed for the pleasure of the viewing audience. Yet historical and cross-cultural research emphasizes the cultural specificity of the identity categories ("the" homosexual) that organize sexuality into a domain in Anglo-European societies (Weston 1993).

What is it, then, that can render even well-read scholars stupid in the face of identity politics? With a rudimentary knowledge of the literature on identity, how can they persist in asking such questions as "What was it like to work as an insider ethnographer?" (Inside what? An unbounded, heterogeneous population that can be neither counted nor defined?) Rhetorical questions, to be sure. The point is this: Coming out in print, however artfully executed, can too easily be misinterpreted as a public statement of the "truth" about a sexuality that is supposed to create automatic solidarity with at least some of the people encountered in the field.

Interestingly, the "coming out" passage in *Families We Choose* is barely that.

I read it now as a failed attempt to resist nativization without obscuring my implication in identity categories that affected my field research:

> "Are you a lesbian? Are you gay?" Every other day one of these questions greets my efforts to set up interviews over the telephone. Halfway through my field-work, I remark on this concern with the researcher's identity while addressing a course in anthropological field methods. "Do you think you could have done this study if you weren't a lesbian?" asks a student from the back of the class-room. "No doubt," I reply, "but then again, it wouldn't have been the same study." (Weston 1991: 13)

While this passage recounts a "real life" incident, I strategically selected that incident and crafted the passage with care. Students and potential research subjects supply the categories (lesbian, gay) that cast my sexuality in the mold of identity. No variant of "homosexual" passes my lips, although it could be argued that I tacitly assent to those categories with a response ("No doubt") that leaves their terms intact. To round things off, the setting—a methods class!—introduces an element of irony that beckons the reader to reflection.

What else might a close reading of this passage suggest? My departure from an identity politics that credentials certain people as "insiders" and insists that only "authentic" members of a group may speak.[16] My belief that power and positioning matter. My impatience with identity-based constructions of sexuality that cannot accommodate a range of intimacies and attractions.

Too subtle, perhaps? But what rhetorical devices besides the ethnographic "I" are available to the hybrid who cannot reconcile herself to the fate of having her professional persona endlessly recycled through nativity? After she has exhausted the possibilities of authorizing herself through strategies of objectivity and reflexivity, what's a virtual anthropologist to do when it comes to the thankless task of getting people to read her work through something besides persona and physique?

In a pinch, there's always reportage with an eyewitness twist. Nothing like building the implicit claim "I was there" (Sorry, pal, you weren't) into an ethnographic narrative to lay claim to special insights inaccessible to the general reader (cf. Clifford 1988; Geertz 1988). Of course, that claim depends upon maintaining a clear separation between there and here, a separation usually worked out by mapping categories of people onto place. Natives are the ones who are always there, always embodied, always open to scholarly in-spection. Ethnographers are the ones who go there ("the field") to study na-tives with every intention of returning here ("home"), whether "here" lies across the seas or in a co-op apartment on the other side of town (see Clif-ford 1988; see also chapter 1 of this book). The odd anthropologist out has been known to jump disciplinary ship by "going native," but that hardly counts as an option for the ethnographer already located as a native. Be-cause the virtual anthropologist's hybridity blurs the distinction between researcher and researched, she cannot create ethnographic authority by distancing herself in time or space from the people she studies. There is now, here is there, and we are them.[17]

Like an eagle caught far from its range, the Native Ethnographer's wings become tangled in the power lines that join two senses of "my people": the colonialist's "*my* people" and the activist's "my *people.*" It's hard to say which formulation is more problematic: the first with its hierarchy of racial and labor relations left intact, or the second with all the limitations of the nationalist vision of an imagined community that undergirds identity politics.[18] The virtual anthropologist once again finds herself in an untenable position, unwilling or unable to produce "*my* people" (the Other of anthropological inquiry), and incapable of extricating herself from the grip of the professionally dangerous perception that she should "naturally" call some nativized group "my *people.*" Understandably loath to exoticize that which she cannot leave behind, she is less likely than most of her colleagues to build professional credibility on the backs of "informants" through an orientalizing move.

If all else fails, then, our ever-resourceful anthropologist can attempt to make the best of nativization by taking a stand on native authority.[19] Barely articulated notions of informant expertise have been embedded all along in the process of making ethnographic writing credible. Natives are the ones with a corner on the academic market for (genuine) experience, the kind worth documenting and transcribing and playing the voyeur to. Natives are well known to have bodies and practical knowledge, the better to filter their nativity through. For the real anthropologist, in contrast, experiential authority and embodiment end with the "return from the field."

No visible work discipline attaches to the visceral, concrete labor of "writing up." When books and essays make the ethnographer's body visible, they depict its toils and deprivations in the field, seldom at the keyboard. Where, in experimental ethnography are the endless cups of tea or coffee, sore muscles, aching head, and stiff hands from hours bent over a keyboard? When did the work of producing a monograph count as real experience, or for that matter, manual as well as mental labor? With the demise of armchair anthropology, who ever heard of an anthropologist, reflexive or otherwise, establishing credibility by proclaiming "I was there . . . for years . . . in my study"?[20]

If the labor of writing disappears for the ethnographer, the arduousness of research tends to fade from view for the native who "goes to the field." Working in a country or community portrayed as one's own becomes "not work," much as teaching a language is assumed to require no training for people labeled "native speakers." This ethnographic variant of natural rhythm (note the racialized and sexualized subtext) casts the virtual anthropologist once again as instant insider, accepted with open arms into the ethnographic utopia of a homogeneous community. Her experience as a native— the only experience about which she can speak authoritatively from the "I, Native" position—is taken to be familiar and complete, yielding knowledge acquired with little or no effort.[21]

Savaged again, and to what avail? Disappointingly, native authority doesn't get the virtual anthropologist very far. In a scholarly world that places a premium on explanation, the meaning of experience must remain opaque to the native in order to be revealed by that privileged interpreter, the social scientist. Being university trained, the virtual anthropologist can always pull the old hat trick (today native, tomorrow ethnographer; now you see the native, now you don't). But she will be hard put to write from the Native Ethnographer position, much less to work through its contradictions.

So the virtual anthropologist goes through her long- or short-lived career constantly being pulled toward one or the other of the poles of her hybridity. Try as she might, she will not be able to produce a fully legitimized account of her field research. Why can't she authorize herself in the same way as the real anthropologist? Because most of the rhetorical strategies that establish ethnographic authority are predicated upon a separation of object from subject. And the prescribed cure for this mind/body split—reflexivity —does not free the author from the trap. Even the most celebrated of experimental ethnographies end up reinstating a division between you and I, native and ethnographer, Other and Self, often at the very moment they "allow" people from the field to speak.[22]

There is, of course, one final (though limited) strategy familiar to informants everywhere who have exercised their perfect native authority with witty abandon. Whether ad-libbing "traditional" songs and stories, or making jokes at the anthropologist's expense that are received in all seriousness and duly recorded for publication, natives have always participated in an improvisatory construction of what is "empirically" available for study, including their own nativity (Limón 1991; Paredes 1978; Rosaldo 1989a; Sarris 1991). Instead of letting parody pass as realism, the Native Ethnographer can be "true" to the hybridity forced upon her by creating parodies—rather like this essay—that are marked as such. Anthropologists may be nativized or virtualized, hybridized or realized. But camp is camp is camp.[23]

The problem with the Native Ethnographer, though, is that she won't stay put: the slippery rascal keeps sliding over from the object (Native) into the subject (Ethnographer) position. Hybridity is disconcerting precisely to the degree that it collapses the subject/object distinctions that work to insulate "us" from "them." Because the categories that nativize her combine with professional identity to yield a hybrid compound, she encounters a double bind when it comes time to write. To produce anthropology at all, she must treat the components of her hybridity as merely additive (Native + Ethnographer) or split (Native/Ethnographer) by writing from only one subject position at a time, unless hybridity itself becomes the focus of the piece. And each time her work submits to this double bind, as it must, it surrenders the intricate operations of hybridity to the oversimplifications of nativity or objectivity.

Just in case legions of readers inspired by the density of the last paragraph find themselves moved to set out on a quest for a better formula for ethnographic writing, let me add that this is a case where rhetoric is not enough. In the end, ethnographic authority is more than "affected" by race or gender or sexuality or a host of other identities (cf. D. Gordon 1990). Those identities filter through both hybridity and a subject/object divide produced in social arenas apart from the text. Through it all, the legitimacy of the generic, unmarked anthropologist is read into reality by the very power relations that read the virtual anthropologist out.

PERIPHERAL RE-VISION

Although being read out of "real" anthropology increases the chances that the Native Ethnographer will be marginalized within her discipline, the two processes are actually distinct. Not that there has been any noticeable expansion of appointments for queers who study queers in anthropology departments at top-ten universities. But virtuality does not assign the Native Ethnographer a particular position—be it center or margin—in the metaphorical space of the field. Instead, virtuality consigns her to the unnerving experience of moving through the professional landscape as something just short of genuine, regardless of where she plants her professional feet. It's about becoming not-real, though not quite imitation either, in ways that make her unmappable.[24]

Marginality models import the geopolitics of empire into the cyberspace of academic politics. Bemidji State becomes to the University of Michigan what the imperial outpost is to the metropolis (cf. Ashcroft, Griffiths, and Tiffin 1989; hooks 1984; Spivak 1990). Prestigious departments occupy the symbolic center of the academic universe, and their centrality, far from insulating them behind ivory-tower walls, grants them a high degree of control over the resources necessary to do the kind of anthropology that confers professional credibility. Hierarchies of practice and place ensure that aspiring anthropologists who "don't make the grade" are shipped off to the colonies ("the margins"), where long hours, temporary status, lack of leave time, too many committees, too many classes, high student-teacher ratios, and research conducted on the fly make a ticket to the center more improbable with each passing megawork day.

Yet the virtual is not the marginal. Why else would the Native Ethnographer remain virtual, regardless of whether she occupies the center or periphery of the academic world? She cannot make herself "real" by changing the theoretical topic she studies or the institution she serves. A time-tested focus like politics, the latest in transnationalism, Stanford or Podunk U.— it's all the same when it comes to hybridity. The compound position from which the Native Ethnographer speaks leaves her somewhere between sub-ject and object, Us and Them, pedestrian reality and "here comes trouble."

In this sense, the process of hybridization that renders someone virtual is not equivalent to growing up on the wrong side of the tracks or enrolling in a school on the wrong side of the Mississippi. The upwardly mobile scholar who migrates from the periphery to an elite institution may work hard to maintain her marginality by writing on behalf of "her people" or remem-bering what it was like to come of age on the wrong side of town (hooks 1990).[25] But the virtual anthropologist who comes into the intellectual's equivalent of an inheritance needs no reminder. She remains virtual at the very moment she wins the all-expenses-paid trip to an institution at the heart of the discipline. Purveyors of digs and doubts will track her down, even in her endowed chair. The girl could be responding to questions at the press conference called to celebrate her receipt of a Macarthur award (dream on!), and she would be kidding herself if she believed it impossible for some joker to rise up out of the audience to say, "Your work's very interesting, very in-teresting indeed, but why do you call it anthropology?"

With a little luck, the virtual anthropologist *may* live to pursue her career as an "outsider within," in Patricia Hill Collins's (1990) sense of a person as-signed to a subordinate position in the belly of the beast.[26] Surely you've run across her: the lone member of the faculty allotted a windowless office, the one "inadvertently" dropped from the invitation list to departmental func-tions, or the one relentlessly included on the invitation list to departmental functions (where she can expect to have the pleasure of being shown off as the embodiment of her colleagues' liberality and goodwill). But the virtual anthropologist is just as likely to pass her days as the outsider without: job-less, piecing together academic appointments, crisscrossing the globe in her search for admission to the tenured elect, consigned to the academy's back of beyond, eventually giving up or giving out.

Excised or tokenized, the virtual anthropologist inherits much of the lone-liness associated with the outsider-within position, but little of its fixity. Her problems do not stem from being a dyke out of (her) place in academe, but from those seemingly unpredictable shifts from Native to Ethnographer and back again. What makes her virtual is neither a fixed identity (the house queer) nor a fixed location (at center or margins), but a compounding of identity with research that sets her in motion as a Native Ethnographer. At issue is not who she "is" or where she stands, but whether onlookers see her as a Native rising up out of the community she studies. If they do, the game's up: she'll be rendered virtual, going under to that telltale hybridity, another casualty of the kind of Othering that sends its targets ricocheting between subject positions.

No surprise, then, that virtuality does not yield to protests against exclusion from the center or efforts to jockey for a better position. Strategies of inclusion attempt to better the lot of the marginalized professional by confronting the forces of discrimination that have pushed her to the periphery. Strategies of critique rely upon the keen insight and creativity that some scholars believe accompany the view from the edge (see hooks 1990). Both tactics keep in place a territorial model for conceptualizing power relations. Both keep the long-suffering aspirant oriented to the field's metaphorical center, whether she adopts the stance that says, "Let me in!" or the voice that admonishes, "Let me tell you what's problematic about being in!"

A virtual anthropologist cannot pin her hopes on the search for a level playing field or a place in the sun, because these spatial metaphors keep intact the process of nativization that is her bane.[27] Natives in, natives out: the same pieces are shuffled around the board with nothing to challenge their construction. But the polymorphic character of the virtual anthropologist makes her a shape-shifter at center or margin. Our hero's heightened visibility *as* a Native Ethnographer is the very condition of her invisibility. Now you see her, now you don't, because when you do see her, you can view her only through the lens of hybridity.

Though the topic may be academic suicide, the implications of being rendered virtual do not stop at books left unwritten and derailed careers. Being read out of reality transports the nativized scholar who studies "her own" into a different dimension of meaning altogether. The Native Ethnographer, in the full glory of her hybridity, confronts the conventional definition of anthropology as the study of (the hu)man, or even the study of cultural differences, with the possibility that the field might be more appropriately conceptualized as a site for the *production* of difference. Unlike headhunters and firewalkers from days gone by, safely contained "over there" in "the field," the virtual anthropologist's location "within" the discipline threatens to expose her inquisitors' participation in the power relations that fuel the process of nativization.

In the libraries and in the halls, queers who study queers find themselves grouped with other Native Ethnographers whose bid for professional status entails being reduced to the categories (sexuality, ethnicity, what have you) that are supposed to organize their identities. It's easy to forget that these one-dimensional representations feed back into the communities ethnographers study. At a time when "natives" worldwide resort to quoting ethnographies to explain their "traditions" to the state and to themselves, the virtual anthropologist is the ghost in a disciplinary machine whose finest documentary efforts have doubled as exotica, intervention, and spectacle. If anybody can help anthropology retool, she's the one.

NOTES

An earlier version of this chapter was presented in 1995 at the colloquium series in the Department of Anthropology, Princeton University. The essay has benefited greatly from a series of conversations with Deb Amory, Jared Braiterman, Susan Cahn, Rebecca Etz, Kristin Koptiuch, Yasumi Kuriya, Thaïs Morgan, Geeta Patel, Suzanne Vaughan, participants in the 1994 Anthropology and "the Field" conference organized by Jim Ferguson and Akhil Gupta at Stanford University and the University of California, Santa Cruz, and participants in the 1994 Thinking, Writing, Teaching, and Creating Justice conference hosted by the Center for Advanced Feminist Studies at the University of Minnesota. Smadar Lavie read the manuscript and offered many thoughtful suggestions, not all of which could be incorporated here. Special thanks to VéVé Clark for the irreverent comments and heartfelt exchange that helped make this essay what it is today. Finally, my thanks to colleagues like Celia Alvarez, Jean Comaroff, John Comaroff, Tim Diamond, Smadar Lavie, Sylvia Yanagisako, and above all the late David Schneider, who have all challenged in productive ways the processes that can render someone virtual.

1. "Native" is a problematic term that keeps people in their place by essentializing their characters, bounding their communities, and otherwise subjecting them to the disciplinary legacies of racism that emerged from colonial rule (Bhabha 1994a; Narayan 1993). In this chapter, I capitalize Native Ethnographer to underscore the category's status as representation rather than birthmark.

2. Whether the production of the scholar who studies "her own" as a particular sort of hybrid obtains for fields like literature or sociology, I leave to colleagues from those disciplines to determine. In some respects, the Native Ethnographer is a subject position peculiar to anthropology, with its long history of participation in the colonial ventures that produced "the native" as an object of Euro-American subjugation. Yet the processes of nativization unleashed by colonialism proceed apace within the academy as well as the world at large. Scholars of color who work in "ethnic studies" have found themselves produced in analogous fashion for the viewing (dis)pleasure of colleagues. As a candidate for the top position on a university campus, Arturo Madrid (1992: 10) confronted the question, "Why does a one-dimensional person like you think he can be the president of a multidimensional institution like ours?" Lisa Duggan (1995) fielded similar insults from colleagues who wondered aloud how she, a "gay historian" (note the collapse of subject researcher into object research), could possibly be qualified to teach "generic" topics in American history. With regard to anthropology, Ruth Behar (1993: 299) eloquently conveys the effects of an identity politics that filters scholarship back through bodies whenever the bodies in question are marked as Other: "You mainly read women anthropologists for their critiques of androcentrism, and you mainly read anthropology or cultural criticism by people of color for their particular accounts of local places, or at best, as grist for your already grinding theoretical mill. You don't read either for 'high theory,' the sort of understandings that are supposed to be of such translocal importance that they can serve as grids for work anywhere. The more neutralizing the translation of local accents, the better. Ironic, isn't it? Can this be the discipline whose legitimacy is so wrapped up in foreign languages and worlds?"

3. This nativization of gay men and lesbians across race is quite evident in "The

Gay Agenda," a video produced by a right-wing group in California and widely distributed to libraries across the United States. The video intersperses footage from the annual San Francisco gay and lesbian pride parade with talking heads who are trotted on screen to present unfounded statistics about "cure" rates and sexual habits of homosexuals. Against a visual montage of gyrating bodies, naked body parts, and sexual innuendo, a narrator intones dire warnings about the out-of-control sexuality and insatiable hunger for political power lurking behind the mild-mannered facade of gay rights groups. These hypersexualized and hyperbiologized representations of queers draw upon a long and racist history of depicting imagined threats to civilization as "we" know it, from portrayals of African Americans during Reconstruction to characterizations of aliens in horror films (cf. Bukatman 1993: 262).

4. Anthropologists have tended to construct morally graded variants of the (ideal but vanishing) native along continua from good to bad, genuine to faux, traditional to modern, rural to urban, inner-city to suburban, living in pristine isolation to having been corrupted by the lures of Western civilization (see chapter 1). Because the ideal native is also the native considered most suitable for study, it is not so surprising that, despite the recent nativization of lesbians and gay men, there has been no rush of anthropologists to the gold fields of queer studies.

5. This is not to say that queers of color and white queers in the United States occupy the same position, even vis-à-vis queerness, as a result of nativization. Witness the anger and discomfort voiced by several members (most of them people of color) of the Society of Lesbian and Gay Anthropologists when the group sold T-shirts that read, "These natives can speak for themselves." In this instance the term *native* became a contested site, with distributors of the T-shirt arguing that they had *reappropriated* the term *native* and critics decrying what they regarded as an *appropriation* of ethnicity carried out by a predominantly white group (cf. Bustos-Aguilar 1995: 164–165). Bustos-Aguilar presents a thoughtful, impassioned critique of the ways in which white gay ethnographers have colluded in (not-yet-post-)colonial relations. His remarks are particularly scathing on the subject of the colonialist presumptions that continue to infuse research projects on same-sex eroticism and on the tendency for fieldwork "abroad" to edge over into sex tourism or surveillance.

6. Patel (1994) and Raiskin (1994) discuss how processes of nativization undercut the complexity of ambiguously sexed/raced/nationalized bodies by tethering people to fixed social locations. On the discomfort and ambivalence associated with the racialized and sexualized colonial stereotype that helps produce the native, see Bhabha (1994a, b). For a feminist critique of home as a locus of safety and familiarity, see Martin and Mohanty (1986) and M. B. Pratt (1991). Visweswaran (1994: 101–104) takes the feminist critique one step further with her concept of "homework." Homework is not a matter of conducting "fieldwork at home," but a rejection of fieldwork in favor of a method and a politics of location in which "home" marks the site(s) from which a person writes, studies, and speaks (see also the discussion of Visweswaran's work in Lavie and Swedenburg [1996]).

7. "Joins," that is, if colleagues have not already located her in this lineage by virtue of ethnicity, religion, and/or nationality (cf. Ashcroft, Griffiths, and Tiffin [1989]). For authors who write explicitly, though not always contentedly, from the position of "native anthropologist" or "insider ethnographer," see Abu-Lughod (1991), D. Jones (1970), Limón (1991), Narayan (1993), Sarris (1991, 1994), and Zavella (1993).

8. Gloria Anzaldúa (1987; "borderlands" and "*mestizaje*"), Homi Bhabha (1994a; hybridity as a product of colonial encounters), and Gerald Vizenor (1990; "cross-bloods") have laid much of the theoretical groundwork for discussions of identities that will neither stay pure nor stay put. For examples incorporating the concepts of hybridity and *mestizaje* into scholarly discussions of multiculturalism, see Lavie and Swedenburg (1996), Lowe (1991), Lugones (1994), and West (1993). Hale (1994: 18) explores the complex relationship between *mestizaje*, nationalist ideologies, and the state, as well as the contention that *mestizaje* represents a "new form of colonialism" for people who identify as *indígenas*. In the intellectual borderlands where academic and popular audiences meet and meld, Lisa Jones (1994) and Greg Tate (1992) have also challenged readers to grapple with the historical contingencies of raced categories. M. B. Pratt (1995) deftly conveys the slipperiness of terms like *woman, man,* and *lesbian sexuality.* Asad (1993), Crenshaw (1995), and Weston (1995) explore some of the material consequences of an identity politics that depends upon bounded, mutually exclusive categories like "sex" and "race" for its (in)effectiveness.

9. Nancy Hewitt (1992) has also used the distinction between mixtures and compounds to clarify matters of difference and identity in the United States. I am grateful to Rebecca Etz for calling this to my attention.

10. Narayan (1993) uses the term "hybridity" in her thought-provoking essay on the so-called native anthropologist, but in the sense of an additive rather than a compound relationship. In Narayan's account, hybridity brings two static, given social locations into a relationship, producing what I describe here as a mixture. Her discussion of "enactments of hybridity," which turn everybody into a hybrid with respect to something, includes a valuable exploration of the ways in which identities are selected and highlighted contextually. Yet this emphasis carries with it the danger of glossing over the power relations that historically have marked particular people as particular sorts of hybrids. I see hybridity as a process that, once contextually invoked, not only locates but also subordinates people by encouraging most things they do or say to be interpreted through the compound category taken to define their hybridity.

11. The operations of hybridity may also help explain the anecdotal evidence that people who simultaneously claim a queer identity and study queer communities have greater difficulty finding employment than individuals who do one or the other. See also Newton (1993b).

12. "Natives" may be construed as objects for study, but not all objects of study are construed as natives. Anderson's now classic work (1983) on nationalism and imagined communities explores the processes that affiliate certain identities (but not others) with membership in "a people." For more on the impact of the fantasy of primitivism on anthropological practice and popular imagination, see Kuper (1988).

13. In this sense, hybridity has the potential to disrupt processes of nativization that attempt to fix subjects and hold them steady. On morphing and shape-shifting, see Bukatman (1993) and Smith (1993). On hybridity as a "space" of productivity, see Muñoz (1995). But see also Young (1995), who cautions that the concept of hybridity can subtly reinforce (neo)colonialist fears of miscegenation and lend credence to efforts to police the boundaries of ostensibly pure (often racialized) categories. Awkward (1995) insightfully explores tensions between the instability of categories of gender or race (or class or sexuality), and the tendency to treat these categories of

difference as though they were set in stone. For some of the ways in which natural-
izing identity works to naturalize power, see Yanagisako and Delaney (1995).

14. I am grateful to Susan Cahn, always up for a good paradox, for helping me
articulate this point.

15. But see Newton (1993c), who has taken reflexive anthropology to task for its
failure to acknowledge that sexuality can be another arena in which ethnographers
wield power over people "in the field."

16. Coombe (1993) offers an excellent critique of simplistic mappings of "voice"
onto identity, standpoint, authenticity, or authority to speak on behalf of a group.

17. For further discussion of these authorizing devices, see Fabian (1983) on temporal distancing; Clifford (1988), Geertz (1988), and M. L. Pratt (1986) on geographic
distancing; and Appadurai (1988b) on the rhetorical mapping of people onto place
entailed in nativization. Lavie and Swedenburg (1996) discuss the breakdown of distinctions between "home" and "field," researcher and researched, in the wake of di-
asporas and resistance movements.

18. On the relationship between imagined communities and identity politics, see
Anderson (1983), Bhabha (1990), and Berlant and Freeman (1993).

19. Here again, however, the virtual anthropologist's extremely high level of education limits the legitimacy achievable with this tactic by rendering her a less than
ideal native.

20. On the topic of the "manual" work discipline attached to "mental" labor, I
am indebted to a series of discussions with Thaïs Morgan.

21. The point is not that social positioning and experience make no difference,
but rather that they are not transparent and do not lead to effortless understanding or instant rapport (Behar 1993; Sarris 1991, 1994; Scott 1992). Narayan (1993)
offers an excellent critique of the misleading implications of the term *insider
anthropologist*.

22. In Behar's *Translated Woman* (1993), for example, the author's "I" frames Esperanza's first-person account, effectively transforming Esperanza's "I" into a "you"
(similarly for Shostak [1981] with Nisa, Crapanzano [1980] with Tuhami, and a host
of others). The framing devices of authorship, introductions, and moments of reflexivity that have the power to interrupt the flow of a narrative undermine the apparent egalitarianism of first-person pronouns by smuggling in old dichotomies. The
resulting accounts, however innovative, end up consolidating "I, Native" and "I, Ethnographer" as mutually exclusive positions from which to speak and write. It's Self
and Other, Us and Them, anthropologist and informant all over again. For the virtual anthropologist, in contrast, recourse to the ethnographic "I" makes nativization,
exoticization, and stigmatization that much more likely to ensue. I am grateful to Geeta
Patel for clarifying and queering my thinking about the work of pronouns in a text.

23. See Newton (1979, 1993a) and Román (1993) for analyses of camp as a form
of intervention and resistance. Ross (1993) is more cautious, noting the link between
camp and capitalist forms of commodity fetishism.

24. On the distinction between the virtual, the simulated, and the imitative, see
Rheingold (1991) and Woolley (1992).

25. But see Bhabha's (1990: 292) guarded response to revisionist interpretations
that treat marginality as a potential site for resistance as well as victimization. Perhaps, he comments, scholars have been too quick to celebrate the virtues of exile.

26. Collins grounds her concept of "the outsider within" in African American women's work as slaves and domestic servants. She argues that the conditions of oppression responsible for locating black women's labor squarely in the domestic space of white families afford African American women a distinctive (and potentially subversive) perspective on white elites. More infiltrator than member, the outsider within occupies a vantage point that allows her to see things veiled from the privileged themselves.

27. Hybridization as a Native Ethnographer is a more complex operation than the exile that results from "discrimination," because hybridization is not an unmediated consequence of bearing the stigmata of nativity (cf. D'Emilio 1992). Neither do center/periphery models, with their concomitant strategies of inclusion and critique, disrupt the process of nativization. This is a case in which Lefebvre (1991) is right to reject the geometric bent in the scholarly imagination that turns everything into a "space."

TEN

Spatial Practices:
Fieldwork, Travel, and the Disciplining
of Anthropology

James Clifford

For George Stocking

The day after the Los Angeles earthquake of 1994, I watched a TV interview with an earth scientist. He said he had been "in the field" that morning looking for new fault lines. It was only after a minute or so of talk that I realized he had been flying around in a helicopter the whole time. Could this be fieldwork? I was intrigued by his invocation of the field, and somehow unsatisfied.

My dictionary begins its long list of definitions for "field" with one about open spaces and another that specifies cleared space. The eye is unimpeded, free to roam. In anthropology Marcel Griaule pioneered the use of aerial photography, a method continued, now and again, by others. But if overview, real or imagined, has long been part of fieldwork, there still seemed to be an oxymoronic bump in the earth scientist's airborne "field." Particularly in geology, indeed in all the sciences that value fieldwork, the practice of research "on the ground," observing minute particulars, has been a sine qua non. The French analogue, *terrain*, is unequivocal. Gentlemen-naturalists were supposed to have muddy boots. Fieldwork is earthbound—intimately involved in the natural and social landscape.

It was not always so. Henrika Kuklick (chapter 2) reminds us that the move toward professional field research in a range of disciplines, including anthropology, took place at a particular historical moment in the late nineteenth century. A presumption in favor of professional work that was downclose, empirical, and interactive was quickly naturalized. Fieldwork would put theory to the test; it would *ground* interpretation.

In this context, flying around in a helicopter seemed a bit abstract. Yet, on reflection, I had to allow the earth scientist his practice of going "into the field" while never setting foot there. In some crucial way, his use of the term qualified. What mattered was not simply the acquisition of fresh empirical data. A satellite photo could provide that. What made this fieldwork was the act of physically *going out* into a *cleared place of work.* "Going out" presupposes a spatial distinction between a home base and an exterior place of discovery. A cleared space of work assumes that one can keep out distracting influences. A field, by definition, is not overgrown. The earth scientist could not have done his helicopter "fieldwork" on a foggy day. An archaeologist cannot excavate a site properly if it is inhabited or built over. An anthropologist may feel it necessary to clear his or her field, at least conceptually, of tourists, missionaries, or government troops. Going out into a cleared place of work presupposes specific practices of displacement and focused, disciplined attention.

In this chapter I hope to clarify a crucial and ambivalent anthropological legacy: the role of travel, physical displacement, and temporary dwelling away from home in the constitution of fieldwork. I will discuss fieldwork and travel in three sections. The first sketches some recent developments in sociocultural anthropology, showing where classic research practices are under pressure. I suggest why fieldwork remains a central feature of disciplinary self-definition. The second section focuses on fieldwork as an embodied spatial practice, showing how, since the turn of the century, a disciplined professional body has been articulated along a changing border with literary and journalistic travel practices. In opposition to these purportedly superficial, subjective, and biased forms of knowledge, anthropological research was oriented toward the production of deep, *cultural* knowledge. I argue that the border is unstable, constantly renegotiated. The third section surveys current contestations of normative Euro-American travel histories that have long structured anthropology's research practices. Notions of community insides and outsides, homes and abroads, fields and metropoles, are increasingly challenged by postexotic, decolonizing trends. It is much less clear what counts, today, as acceptable fieldwork, the range of spatial practices "cleared" by the discipline.

I borrow the phrase "spatial practice" from Michel de Certeau's book *The Practice of Everyday Life* (1984). For de Certeau, "space" is never ontologically given. It is discursively mapped and corporeally practiced. An urban neighborhood, for example, may be laid out physically according to a street plan. But it is not a space until it is practiced by people's active occupation, their movements through and around it. In this perspective, there is nothing given about a "field." It must be worked, turned into a discrete social space, by embodied practices of interactive travel. I will have more to say, en route, about the expanded sense, and limitations, of the term *travel* as I use it. And I will be concerned, primarily, with norms and ideal-types. In chapter 1, Gupta and Ferguson argue that current practice potentially draws on a broad range of ethnographic activities, some of them unorthodox by modern standards. But they confirm that, since the 1920s, a recognizable norm has held sway in the academic centers of Euro-America.[1] Anthropological fieldwork has represented something specific among overlapping sociological and ethnographic methods: an especially deep, extended, and interactive research encounter. That, of course, is the ideal. In practice, criteria of "depth" in fieldwork (length of stay, mode of interaction, repeated visits, grasp of languages) have varied widely, as have actual research experiences.

This multiplicity of practices blurs any sharp, referential meaning for "fieldwork." What are we talking about when we invoke anthropological fieldwork? Before proceeding, I must linger a moment on this problem of definition. Elementary semantics distinguishes several ways meanings are sustained: roughly, by reference, concept, and use. I will draw primarily on the latter two, commonly qualified as "mentalist" (Akmajian et al. 1993: 198–201). Conceptual definitions use a prototype, often a visual image, to define a core against which variants are evaluated. A famous photograph of Malinowski's tent pitched in the midst of a Trobriand village has long served as a potent mental *image* of anthropological fieldwork. (Everyone "knows" it, but how many could describe the actual scene?) There have been other images: visions of personal interaction—for example, photos of Margaret Mead leaning intently toward a Balinese mother and baby. Moreover, as I have already suggested, the word "field" itself conjures up mental images of cleared space, cultivation, work, ground. When one speaks of working *in* the field, or *going* into the field, one draws on mental images of a distinct place with an inside and outside, reached by practices of physical movement.

These mental images focus and constrain definitions. For example, they make it strange to say that an anthropologist in his or her office talking on the phone is doing fieldwork—even if what is actually happening is the disciplined, interactive collection of ethnographic data. Images materialize concepts, producing a semantic field that seems sharp at the "center" and blurred at the "edges." The same function is served by more abstract concepts. A range of phenomena are gathered around prototypes; I will, in deference to Kuhn (1970: 187), speak of *exemplars.* Just as a robin is taken to be a more typical bird than a penguin, thus helping to define the concept "bird," so certain exemplary cases of fieldwork anchor heterogeneous experiences. "Exotic" fieldwork pursued over a continuous period of at least a year has, for some time now, set the norm against which other practices are judged. Given this exemplar, different practices of cross-cultural research seem less like "real" fieldwork (Weston chapter 9 of this book).

Real for whom? The meaning of an expression is ultimately determined by a language community. This *use* criterion opens space for a history and sociology of meanings. But it is complicated, in the present case, by the fact that those people recognized as anthropologists (the relevant community) are critically defined by having accepted and done something close (or close enough) to "real fieldwork." The boundaries of the relevant community have been (and are increasingly) constituted by struggles over the term's proper range of meanings. This complication is present, to some extent, in all community-use criteria for meaning, especially when "essentially-contested concepts" (Gallie 1964) are at stake. But in the case of anthropologists and "fieldwork," the loop of mutual constitution is unusually tight. The community does not simply use (define) the term "fieldwork"; it is materially used (defined) by its senses. A different range of meanings would make a different community of anthropologists, and vice versa. The sociopolitical stakes in these definitions—issues of inclusion and exclusion, center and periphery—need to be kept explicit.

DISCIPLINARY BORDERLANDS

Consider the project of Karen McCarthy Brown, who studied a vodou priest-ess in Brooklyn (and accompanied her on a visit to Haiti). Brown traveled into the field by car, or on the New York subway, from her home in Man-hattan. Her ethnography was less a practice of intensive dwelling (the "tent in the village") and more a matter of repeated visiting, collaborative work. Or perhaps what was involved was what Renato Rosaldo once called, in a dis-cussion of what makes anthropological ethnography distinctive, "deep hang-ing out."[2] Before working with Alourdes, the subject of her study, Brown had made research trips to Haiti. But when she visited Alourdes for the first time, she felt a new kind of displacement:

> Our nostrils filled with the smells of charcoal and roasting meat and our ears with overlapping episodes of salsa, reggae, and the bouncy monotony of what Haitians call jazz. Animated conversations could be heard in Haitian French Creole, Spanish, and more than one lyrical dialect of English. The street was a crazy quilt of shops: Chicka-Licka, the Ashanti Bazaar, a storefront Christian church with an improbably long and specific name, a Haitian restaurant, and Botanica Shango—one of the apothecaries of New World African religions of-fering fast-luck and get-rich-quick powders, High John the Conqueror root, and votive candles marked for the Seven African Powers. I was no more than a few miles from my home in lower Manhattan, but I felt as if I had taken a wrong turn, slipped through a crack between worlds, and emerged on the main street of a tropical city. (Brown 1991: 1)

Compare this "arrival scene" (Pratt 1986) with Malinowski's famous "Imagine yourself set down [on a Trobriand Island beach]" (Malinowski 1961). Both rhetorically construct a sharply different, tropical "place," a topos and topic for the work to follow. But Brown's contemporary version is pre-sented with a degree of irony: her tropical city in Brooklyn is sensuously real *and* imaginary—an "illusion," she goes on to call it, projected by an ethnog-raphic traveler in a complexly hybrid world-city. Hers is not a neighborhood (urban village) study. If it has a microcosmic locus, it is Alourdes's three-story row house in the shadow of the Brooklyn-Queens Expressway—home of the only Haitian family in a black North American neighborhood. Diasporic "Haiti," in this ethnography, is multiply located. Brown's ethnography is situated less by a discrete place, a field she enters and inhabits for a time, than by an interpersonal relationship—a mixture of observation, dialogue, apprenticeship, and friendship—with Alourdes. With this relationship as its center, a cultural world of individuals, places, memories, and practices is evoked. Brown frequents this world both in Alourdes's house, where ceremonies and socializing take place, and elsewhere. Brown's "field" is wherever she is with Alourdes. She returns, typically, to sleep, reflect, write up her notes, and lead her life at home in lower Manhattan.

Following established fieldwork practice, Brown's ethnography contains little detail about the everyday life in Manhattan interspersed with the visits to Brooklyn. Her field remains discrete, "out there." And while the relationship/culture under study cannot be neatly spatialized, a different place is visited intensively. There is a physical, interpersonal interaction with a distinct, often exotic, world, leading to an experience of initiation. While the spatial practice of dwelling, taking up residence in a community, is not observed, the ethnographer's movement "in" and "out," her coming and going, is systematic. One wonders what effects these proximities and distances have on the way Brown's research is conceived and represented. How, for example, does she pull back from her research relationship in order to write about it? This taking of distance has typically been conceived as a "departure" from the field, a place clearly removed from home (Crapanzano 1977). What difference does it make when one's "informant" routinely calls one at home to demand help with a ceremony, support in a crisis, a favor? Spatial practices of travel and temporal practices of writing have been crucial to the definition and representation of a *topic*—the translation of ongoing experience and entangled relationship into something distanced and representable (Clifford 1990). How did Brown negotiate this translation in a field whose boundaries were so fluid?

A similar but more extreme challenge for the definition of "real" fieldwork is raised by David Edwards in his article "Afghanistan, Ethnography, and the New World Order." Entering anthropology with hopes of returning to Afghanistan to conduct "a traditional sort of village study in some mountain community," Edwards confronted a war-torn, dispersed "field": "Since 1982, I have carried out fieldwork in a variety of places, including the city of Peshawar, Pakistan, and various refugee camps scattered around the Northwest Frontier Province. One summer, I also traveled inside Afghanistan to observe the operations of a group of *mujahadin*, and I have spent quite a bit of time among Afghan refugees in the Washington, D.C., area. Finally, I have been monitoring the activities of an Afghan computer newsgroup" (Edwards 1994: 345).

Multilocale ethnography (Marcus and Fischer 1986) is increasingly familiar; multilocale *fieldwork* is an oxymoron. How many sites can be studied intensively before criteria of "depth" are compromised?[3] Roger Rouse's fieldwork in two linked sites retains the notion of a single, albeit mobile, community (Rouse 1991). Karen McCarthy Brown stays within the "world" of an individual. But David Edwards's practice is more scattered. Indeed, when he begins to link his dispersed instances of "Afghan culture," he must rely on fairly weak thematic resonances and the common feeling of "ambiguity" they produce—at least for him. Whatever the borders of Edwards's "multiply-inflected" cultural object (Harding 1994), the range of spatial practices he adopts to encounter it is exemplary. He writes that he has "carried out fieldwork" in a city and refugee camps; he has "traveled" to observe the *mujahadin*; he has "spent quite a bit of time" (hanging out deeply?) with Afghans in Washington, D.C.; and he has been "monitoring" the exiled computer newsgroup. This last ethnographic activity is the least comfortable for Edwards (1994: 349). At the time of writing, he has only been "lurking," not posting his own messages. His research on the Internet is not yet interactive. But it is very informative. Edwards intensively listens in on a group of exiled Afghans—male, relatively affluent—worrying together about politics, religious practices, and the nature and boundaries of their community.

The experiences of Karen McCarthy Brown and David Edwards suggest some of the current pressures on anthropological fieldwork seen as a spatial practice of intensive dwelling. The "field" in sociocultural anthropology has been constituted by a "historically specific range of distances, boundaries, and modes of travel" (Clifford 1990: 64). These are changing, as the geography of distance and difference alters in postcolonial/neocolonial situations, as power relations of research are reconfigured, as new technologies of transport and communication are deployed, and as "natives" are recognized for their specific worldly experiences and histories of dwelling and traveling (Appadurai 1988b; Clifford 1992; Teaiwa 1993; Narayan 1993). What remains of classic anthropological practices in these new situations? How are the notions of travel, boundary, coresidence, interaction, inside and outside, which have defined the field and proper fieldwork, being challenged and reworked in contemporary anthropology?

Before taking up these questions, we need a clear sense of what dominant practices of the "field" are at issue, and what issues of disciplinary definition constrain current arguments. Fieldwork normally involves physically leaving "home" (however that is defined) to travel in and out of some distinctly *different* setting. Today, the setting can be Highland New Guinea, or it can be a neighborhood, house, office, hospital, church, or lab. It can be defined as a mobile society, that of long-distance truckers, for example—providing one spends long hours in the cab, talking (Agar 1985). Intensive, "deep" interaction is required, something canonically guaranteed by the spatial practice of extended, if temporary, dwelling in a community. Fieldwork can also involve repeated short visits, as in the American tradition of reservation ethnology. Teamwork and long-term research (Foster et al. 1979) have been variously practiced in different local and national traditions. But common to these practices, anthropological fieldwork requires that one do something more than pass through. One must do more than conduct interviews, make surveys, or compose journalistic reports. This requirement continues today, embodied in a flexible range of activities, from coresidence to various forms of collaboration and advocacy. The legacy of intensive fieldwork defines *anthropological* styles of research, styles critically important for disciplinary (self-) recognition.[4]

There are no natural or intrinsic disciplines. All knowledge is interdisciplinary. Thus, disciplines define and redefine themselves interactively and competitively. They do this by inventing traditions and canons, by consecrating methodological norms and research practices, by appropriating, translating, silencing, and holding at bay adjacent perspectives. Active processes of *disciplining* operate at various levels, defining "hot" and "cold" domains of the disciplinary culture, certain areas that change rapidly and others that are relatively invariant. They articulate, in tactically shifting ways, the solid core and the negotiable edge of a recognizable domain of knowledge and research practice. Institutionalization channels and slows, but cannot stop, these processes of redefinition, except at peril of sclerosis.

Consider the choices faced today by someone planning the syllabus for an introductory graduate proseminar in sociocultural anthropology.[5] Given a limited number of weeks, how important is it that novice anthropologists read Radcliffe-Brown? Robert Lowie? Would it be better to include Meyer Fortes or Kenneth Burke? Lévi-Strauss, surely . . . but why not also Simone de Beauvoir? Franz Boas, of course . . . and Frantz Fanon? Margaret Mead or Marx . . . or E. P. Thompson, or Zora Neale Hurston, or Michel Foucault? Melville Herskovits perhaps . . . and W. E. B. DuBois? St. Clair Drake? Work on photography and media? Kinship, once a disciplinary core, is now actively forgotten in some departments. Anthropological linguistics, still invoked as one of the canonical "four fields," is very unevenly covered. In some programs, one is more likely to read literary theory, colonial history, or cognitive science. . . . Synthetic notions of *man*, the "culture-bearing animal," that once stitched together a discipline now seem antiquated or perverse. Can the disciplinary center hold? In the introductory syllabus, a hybrid selection will eventually be made, attuned to local traditions and current demands, with recognizably "anthropological" authors at the center. (Sometimes the "pure" disciplinary lineage will be cordoned off in a history of anthropology course, required or not.) Anthropology reproduces itself while selectively engaging with relevant interlocutors: from social history, from cultural studies, from biology, from cognitive science, from minority and feminist scholarship, from colonial discourse critique, from semiotics and media studies, from literary and discourse analysis, from sociology, from psychology, from linguistics, from ecology, from political economy, from. . . .

Sociocultural anthropology has always been a fluid, relatively open discipline. It has prided itself on its ability to draw on, enrich, and synthesize other fields of study. Writing in 1964, Eric Wolf optimistically defined anthropology as a "discipline between disciplines" (Wolf 1964: x). But this openness poses recurring problems of self-definition. And partly because its theoretical purview has remained so broad and interdisciplinary, despite recurring attempts to cut it down to size, the discipline has focused on research practices as core, defining elements. Fieldwork has played—and continues to play—a central disciplining function. In the current conjuncture, the range of topics anthropology can study and the array of theoretical perspectives it can deploy are immense. In these areas the discipline is "hot," constantly changing, hybridizing. In the "colder" domain of acceptable fieldwork, change is also occurring but more slowly. In most anthropological milieus, "real" fieldwork continues to be actively defended against other ethnographic styles.

The exotic exemplar—coresidence for extended periods away from home, the "tent in the village"—retains considerable authority. But it has, in practice, been decentered. The various spatial practices it authorized, as well as the relevant criteria for evaluating "depth" and "intensity," have changed and continue to change. Contemporary political, cultural, and economic conditions bring new pressures and opportunities to anthropology. The range of possible venues for ethnographic study has expanded dramatically, and the discipline's potential membership is more diverse. Anthropology's geopolitical location (no longer so securely in the Euro-American "center") is challenged. In this context of change and contestation, academic anthropology struggles to reinvent its traditions in new circumstances. Like the changing societies it studies, the discipline sustains itself in blurred and policed borderlands, using strategies of hybridization and reauthentification, assimilation and exclusion.

Suggestive boundary problems emerge from David Edwards's awkward time on the Afghan Internet. What if someone studied the culture of computer hackers (a perfectly acceptable anthropology project in many, if not all, departments) and in the process never "interfaced" in the flesh with a single hacker. Would the months, even years, spent on the Net be fieldwork? The research might well pass both the length-of-stay and the "depth"/interactivity tests. (We know that some strange and intense conversations can occur over the Net.) And electronic travel is, after all, a kind of *dépaysement*. It could add up to intensive participant observation in a different community without one's ever physically leaving home. When I've asked anthropologists whether this could be fieldwork, they have generally responded "maybe," even, in one case, "of course." But when I press the point, asking whether they would supervise a Ph.D. dissertation based primarily on this kind of disembodied research, they hesitate or say no: it would not be currently acceptable fieldwork. Given the traditions of the discipline, a graduate student would be ill advised to follow such a course. We come up against the institutional-historical constraints that enforce the distinction between fieldwork and a broader range of ethnographic activities. Fieldwork in anthropology is sedimented with a disciplinary history, and it continues to function as a rite of passage and marker of professionalism.

A boundary that currently preoccupies sociocultural anthropology is that which separates it from a heterogeneous collection of academic practices often called "cultural studies."[6] This border renegotiates, in a new context, some of the long-established divisions and crossings of sociology and anthropology. Qualitative sociology, at least, has its own ethnographic traditions, increasingly relevant to a postexoticist anthropology.[7] But given fairly firm institutional identities, in the United States at least, the border with sociology seems less unruly than that with "cultural studies." This new site of border crossing and policing partly repeats an ongoing, fraught relationship with "textualism" or "lit crit." The move to "recapture" anthropology—manifested in dismissals of the collection *Writing Culture* (Clifford and Marcus 1986) and more recently, often incoherently, in sweeping rejections of "postmodern anthropology"—is by now routine in some quarters. But the border with cultural studies may be less manageable; for it is easier to maintain a clear separation when the disciplinary Other—literary-rhetorical theory or textualist semiotics—has no fieldwork component and at best an anecdotal, "ethnographic" approach to cultural phenomena. "Cultural studies," in its Birmingham tradition as well as in some of its sociological veins, possesses a developed ethnographic tradition much closer to anthropological fieldwork. The distinction "We do fieldwork, they do discourse analysis" is more difficult to sustain. Some anthropologists have turned to cultural studies ethnography for inspiration (Lave et al. 1992), and indeed there is much to learn from its increasingly complex articulations of class, gender, race, and sexuality. Moreover, what Paul Willis did with the working-class "lads" of *Learning to Labour* (1977)—hanging out with them at school, talking with parents, working alongside them on the shop floor—is comparable to good fieldwork. Its depth of social interaction was surely greater than, say, that achieved by Evans-Pritchard during his ten months with hostile and reluctant Nuer.

Many contemporary anthropological projects are difficult to distinguish from cultural studies work. For example, Susan Harding is writing an ethnography of Christian fundamentalism in the United States. She has done extensive participant observation in Lynchburg, Virginia, in and around Jerry Falwell's church. And of course the television ministry of Falwell and others

like him is very much her concern—her "field." Indeed, she is interested
not primarily in a spatially defined community but in what she calls the "discourse" of the new fundamentalisms.[8] She is concerned with TV programs,
sermons, novels, media of all kinds, as well as with conversations and everyday behavior. Harding's mixture of participant observation, cultural criticism,
and media and discourse analysis is characteristic of work in the current
ethnographic border zones. How "anthropological" is it? How different is
Susan Harding's frequenting of evangelicals in Lynchburg from Willis's or
Angela McRobbie's studies of youth cultures in Britain or the earlier work
of the Chicago School sociologists? There are certainly differences, but they
do not coalesce as a discrete method, and there is considerable overlap.

One important difference is Harding's insistence that a crucial portion
of her ethnographic work involves *living with* an evangelical Christian family. Indeed, she reports that this was when she felt she had really "entered
the field." Previously, she had stayed in a motel. One might think of this as
a classic articulation of fieldwork deployed in a new setting. In a sense it is.
But it is part of a potentially radical decentering. For there can be no question of calling the period of intensive coresidence in Lynchburg the essence
or core of the project to which the TV viewing and reading were ancillary.
In Harding's project, "fieldwork" was an important way of finding out how
the new fundamentalism was lived in everyday terms. And while it certainly
helped define her hybrid project as anthropological, it was not a privileged
site of interactive depth or initiation.

Harding's work is an example of research that draws on cultural studies,
discourse analysis, and gender and media studies, while maintaining crucial
anthropological features. It marks a current direction for the discipline, one
in which fieldwork remains a necessary but no longer privileged method.
Does this mean that the institutional border between anthropology, cultural
studies, and allied traditions is open? Far from it. Precisely because the crossings are so promiscuous and the overlaps so frequent, actions to reassert identity are mounted at strategic sites and moments. These include the initiatory process of graduate certification, and moments when people need to
be denied a job, funding, or authority. In the everyday disciplining that makes
anthropologists and not cultural studies scholars, the boundary is reasserted
routinely. Most publicly perhaps, when graduate students' "field" projects
are approved, the distinctive spatial practices that have defined anthropology tend to be reasserted—often in nonnegotiable ways.

The concept of the field and the disciplinary practices associated with it
constitute a central, ambiguous legacy for anthropology. Fieldwork has become a problem because of its positivist and colonialist historical associations
(the field as "laboratory," the field as place of "discovery" for privileged sojourners). It has also become more difficult to circumscribe, given the proliferation of ethnographic topics and the time-space compressions (Harvey

1989) characteristic of postmodern, postcolonial/neocolonial situations. What will anthropology make of this problem? Time will tell. Fieldwork, a research practice predicated on interactive depth and spatialized difference, is being "reworked" (Gupta and Ferguson's term in chapter 1), for it is one of the few relatively clear marks of disciplinary distinction left. But how wide can the range of sanctioned practices be? And how "decentered" (Gupta and Ferguson) can fieldwork become before it is just one of a range of ethnographic and historical methods that the discipline uses in concert with other disciplines?

Anthropology has always been more than fieldwork, but fieldwork has been something an anthropologist *should* have done, more or less well, at least once.[9] Will this change? Perhaps it should. Perhaps fieldwork will become merely a research tool rather than an essential disposition or professional marker. Time will tell. At present, however, fieldwork remains critically important—a disciplining process and an ambiguous legacy.

THE FIELDWORK HABITUS

The institutionalization of fieldwork in the late nineteenth and early twentieth centuries can be understood within a larger history of "travel." (I use the term in an expanded sense, of which I will say more in a moment.) Among Westerners traveling and dwelling abroad, the anthropological fieldworker was a latecomer. Explorers, missionaries, colonial officers, traders, colonists, and natural scientific researchers were well-established figures before the emergence of the on-the-ground anthropological professional. Prior to Boas, Malinowski, Mead, Firth, and their colleagues, the anthropological scholar usually remained at home, processing ethnographic information sent by "men on the spot" who were drawn from among the sojourners just mentioned. If metropolitan scholars ventured out, it was on survey and museum-collecting expeditions. Whatever exceptions there may have been to this pattern, interactive depth and coresidence were not yet professional requirements.

When intensive fieldwork began to be championed by the Boasians and Malinowskians, an effort was required to distinguish the kind of knowledge produced by this method from that acquired by other long-term residents in the areas studied. At least three "disciplinary Others" were held at arm's length: the missionary, the colonial officer, and the travel writer (journalist or literary exoticist). Much could be said about anthropology's fraught relations with these three professional alter egos whose purportedly amateur, interventionist, subjective accounts of indigenous life would be "killed by science," as Malinowski put it (1961: 11).[10] My focus, here, is limited to the border with literary and journalistic travel. As a methodological principle, I do not presuppose the discipline's self-definitions, whether positive ("we have special research practice and understanding of human culture") or negative ("we are *not* missionaries, colonial officers, or travel writers"). Rather, I assume that these definitions must be actively produced, negotiated, and renegotiated through changing historical relationships. It is often easier to say clearly what one is *not* than what one *is*. In the early years of modern anthropology, while the discipline was still establishing its distinctive research tradition and authoritative exemplars, negative definitions were critical. And in times of uncertain identity (such as the present), definition may be achieved most effectively by naming clear *outsides* rather than by attempting to reduce always diverse and hybrid *insides* to a stable unity. A more or less permanent process of disciplining at the edges sustains recognizable borders in entangled borderlands.

Anthropological research travelers have, of course, regularly depended on missionaries (for grammars, transportation, introductions, and in certain cases for a deeper translation of language and custom than can be acquired in a one- or two-year visit). The fieldworker's professional difference from the missionary, based on real discrepancies of agenda and attitude, has had to be asserted against equally real areas of overlap and dependency. So, too, with colonial (and neocolonial) regimes: ethnographers typically have asserted their aim to understand not govern, to collaborate not exploit. But they have navigated in the dominant society, often enjoying white skin privilege and a physical safety in the field guaranteed by a history of prior punitive expeditions and policing (Schneider 1995: 139). Scientific fieldwork separated itself from colonial regimes by claiming to be apolitical. This distinction is currently being questioned and renegotiated in the wake of anticolonial movements, which have tended not to recognize the distance from contexts of domination and privilege that anthropologists have claimed.

The travel writer's transient and literary approach, sharply rejected in the disciplining of fieldwork, has continued to tempt and contaminate the scientific practices of cultural description. Anthropologists are, typically, people who leave and write. Seen in a long historical perspective, fieldwork is a distinctive cluster of travel practices (largely but not exclusively Western). Travel and travel discourse should not be reduced to the relatively recent tradition of literary travel, a narrowed conception that emerged in the late nineteenth and early twentieth centuries. This notion of "travel" was articulated against an emerging ethnography (and other forms of "scientific" field research) on the one hand, and against tourism (a practice defined as incapable of producing serious knowledge) on the other. The spatial and textual practices of what might now be called "sophisticated travel"—a phrase taken from *New York Times* supplements catering to the "independent" traveler[11]—function within an elite, and highly differentiated, tourist sector defined by the statement "We are *not* tourists." (Jean-Didier Urbain in *L'idiot du voyage* [1991] has thoroughly analyzed this discursive formation. See also Buzzard 1993.)

The literary tradition of "sophisticated travel," whose disappearance has been lamented by critics such as Daniel Boorstin and Paul Fussell, is reinvented by a long list of contemporary writers—Paul Theroux, Shirley Hazzard, Bruce Chatwin, Jan Morris, and Ronald Wright, among others.[12]

"Travel," as I use it, is an inclusive term embracing a range of more or less voluntaristic practices of leaving "home" to go to some "other" place. The displacement takes place for the purpose of gain—material, spiritual, scientific. It involves obtaining knowledge or having an "experience" (exciting, edifying, pleasurable, estranging, broadening). The long history of travel that includes the spatial practices of "fieldwork" is predominantly Western-dominated, strongly male, and upper middle class. Good critical and historical work is now appearing in this comparative domain, paying attention to political, economic, and regional contexts, as well as to the determinations and subversions of gender, class, culture, race, and individual psychology (Hulme 1986; Porter 1991; Mills 1991; Pratt 1992).

Before the separation of genres associated with the emergence of modern fieldwork, travel and travel writing covered a broad spectrum. In eighteenth-century Europe, a *récit de voyage* or "travel book" might include exploration, adventure, natural science, espionage, commercial prospecting, evangelism, cosmology, philosophy, and ethnography. By the 1920s, however, the research practices and written reports of anthropologists had been much more clearly set apart. No longer scientific travelers or explorers, anthropologists were defined as fieldworkers, a change shared with other sciences (see chapter 2). The field was a distinctive cluster of academic research practices, traditions, and representational rules. But while competing practices and rhetorics were actively held at bay in the process, the newly cleared disciplinary space could never be entirely free of contamination. Its borders would have to be rebuilt, shifted, and reworked. Indeed, one way to understand the current "experimentalism" of ethnographic writing is as a renegotiation of the boundary with "travel writing," which was agonistically defined in the late nineteenth century.

"Literariness," held at a distance in the figure of the travel writer, has returned to ethnography in the form of strong claims about the prefiguration and rhetorical communication of "data." The facts do not speak for themselves; they are emplotted rather than collected, produced in worldly relationships rather than observed in controlled environments.[13] This growing awareness of the poetical and political contingency of fieldwork—an awareness forced on anthropologists by postwar anticolonial challenges to Euro-American centrality—is reflected in a more concrete textual sense of the ethnographer's location. Elements of the "literary" travel narrative that were excluded from ethnographies (or marginalized in their prefaces) now appear more prominently. These include the researcher's routes into and through "the field"; time in the capital city, registering the surrounding national/transnational context; technologies of transport (getting there as well as being there); and interactions with named, idiosyncratic individuals, rather than anonymous, representative informants.

In an earlier discussion, I have worked to decenter the field as a naturalized practice of *dwelling* by proposing a crosscutting metaphor—fieldwork as *travel encounters* (Clifford 1992). To decenter or interrupt fieldwork-as-dwelling is not to reject or refute it. Fieldwork has always been a mix of institutionalized practices of dwelling and traveling. But in the disciplinary idealization of "the field," spatial practices of moving to and from, in and out, passing through, have tended to be subsumed by those of dwelling (rapport, initiation, familiarity). This is changing. Ironically, now that much anthropological fieldwork is conducted (like Karen McCarthy Brown's) close to home, the materiality of travel in and out of the field becomes more apparent, indeed becomes constitutive of the object/site of study. Fieldwork in cities must distinguish itself from other forms of interclass, interracial travel and appreciation, marking a difference from established traditions of urban social work and liberal "slumming." The home of the research traveler exists in a politicized prior relation to that of the people under study (or, in contemporary parlance, the people "worked with"). These latter may themselves travel regularly to and from the home base of the researcher, if only for employment. (The "ethnographic," cross-cultural knowledge of a maid or service worker is considerable.) These parallel, sometimes intersecting, spatiopolitical relations have also been present in "exotic" anthropological research, particularly when colonial or neocolonial flows of armies, commodities, labor, or education materially link the poles of fieldwork travel. But images of distance, rather than of interconnection and contact, have tended to naturalize the field as an Other *place*. The socially established routes constitutive of field *relations* are harder to ignore when the research is conducted nearby or when airplanes and telephones compress space.

Fieldwork thus "takes place" in worldly, contingent relations of travel, not in controlled sites of research. Saying this does not simply dissolve the boundary between contemporary fieldwork and travel (or journalistic) work. There are important generic and institutional distinctions. The injunction to dwell intensively, to learn local languages, to produce a "deep" interpretation is a difference that makes a difference. But the border between the two relatively recent traditions of literary travel and academic fieldwork is being renegotiated. Indeed, the example offered above by David Edwards's multiple sites of encounter brings fieldwork (dangerously, some may feel) close to travel. This rapprochement takes a different form in Anna Tsing's innovative ethnography *In the Realm of the Diamond Queen* (1993). Tsing conducts fieldwork in a classic "exotic" site, the Meratus Mountains of South Kalimantan, Indonesia. While preserving disciplinary practices of intensive local interaction, her writing systematically crosses the border of ethnographic analysis and travel narration. Her account historicizes both her own and her subjects' practices of dwelling and traveling. She derived her knowledge from specific encounters between differently cosmopolitan, gendered individuals, not cultural types. (See, particularly, Part Two: "A Science of Travel.") Her field site in what she calls an "out of the way place" is never taken for granted as a natural or traditional environment. It is a contact space produced by local, national, and transnational forces of which her research travel is a part.

Edwards and Tsing exemplify exotic fieldwork at the edges of changing academic practice. In both, differently spatialized, we see the increased prominence of practices and tropes commonly associated with travel and travel writing.[14] These are currently visible in much anthropological ethnography, figuring different versions of the routed/rooted researcher, the "positioned subject" (Rosaldo 1989a: 7). Signs of the times include a trend toward use of the first-person singular pronoun in accounts of fieldwork, presented as stories rather than as observations and interpretations. Often the field journal (private and closer to the "subjective" accounts of travel writing) leaks into the "objective" field data. I am not describing a linear movement from collection to narration, objective to subjective, impersonal to personal, coresidence to travel encounter. It is a question not of a progression from ethnography to travel writing but rather of a shifting balance and a renegotiation of key *relations* that have constituted the two practices and discourses.

In tracking anthropology's changing relations with travel, we may find it useful to think of the "field" as a habitus rather than as a place, a cluster of *embodied* dispositions and practices. The work of feminist scholars has played a crucial role in specifying the social body of the ethnographer, while criticizing the limitations of androcentric "gender-neutral" work and opening up major new areas of understanding.[15] Similarly, anticolonial pressures, colonial discourse analysis, and critical race theory have decentered the predominantly Western, and white, traditional fieldworker. Seen in light of these interventions, the fieldwork habitus of the Malinowskian generation appears as the articulation of specific, disciplined practices.

This normative "body" was *not* that of a traveler. As it drew on older traditions of scientific travel, it did so in sharpened opposition to romantic, "literary," or subjective strands. The body legitimated by modern fieldwork was not a sensorium moving through extended space, across borders. It was not on an expedition or a survey. Rather, it was a body circulating and working (one might almost say "commuting") within a delimited space. The local map predominated over the tour or itinerary as a technology of physical location. Being there was more important than getting there (and leaving there). The fieldworker was a homebody abroad, not a cosmopolitan visitor. I am, of course, speaking broadly of disciplinary norms and textual figures, not of the actual historical experiences of field anthropologists. In varying degrees, these diverged from the norms while being constrained by them.

Emotions, a necessary part of the controlled empathy of participant observation, were not accorded primary expression. They could not be the chief source of public judgments about the communities under study. This was particularly true of negative assessments. The moral judgments and curses of the travel writer, based on social frustrations, physical discomforts, and prejudices, as well as on principled criticism, were excluded or downplayed. An understanding rapport and measured affection were favored. Expressions of overt enthusiasm and love were circumscribed. Anger, frustration, judgments on individuals, desire, and ambivalence went into private diaries. The scandal provoked, in some quarters, by the publication of Malinowski's intimate diary (1967) was related to the glimpse it gave of a less temperate, more race- and sex-conscious, subject/body in the field. Early public transgressions of the professional habitus include works by Leiris (1934, written as a field journal), Bowen (1954, in novel form), and Jean Briggs (1970, in which personal emotions perhaps for the first time were central to an ethnographic monograph).

If emotions tended to be marginalized, so, for the most part, did the researcher's experiences of gender, race, and sex. Gender, while occasionally featured (particularly in the "marked," female case), was not publicly recognized as constituting the research process in a systematic way. Margaret Mead, for example, did at times conduct research and write "as a woman," crossing defined women's and men's spheres, but her disciplinary persona was that of a scientifically authoritative cultural observer, of unmarked gender and by default "male." Her more "subjective," "soft" stylistic experiments and popular writings did not bring her credit within the disciplinary fraternity, where she adopted a more "objective," "hard" voice. Lutkehaus (1995) provides a contextual account of these historically gendered locations and Mead's shifting persona. Male researchers of Mead's generation did not conduct research "as men" among locally defined women and men. Many purportedly holistic "cultural" accounts were, in fact, based on intensive work with men only. Overall, the constraints and possibilities attached to the researcher's gender were not salient features of the field habitus.

The same went for race. Here, sociocultural anthropology's important theoretical and empirical critique of racialist essences doubtless influenced the professional habitus. "Race" was not the social/historical formation of contemporary critical race theorists (for example, Omi and Winant 1986; Gilroy 1987), but a biological essence whose "natural" determinations were contested by the contextual determinations of "culture." Anthropologists, the culture-bearing scholars, needed to decenter and cross over putatively essential racial lines. Their interactive and intensive understanding of cultural formations gave them a powerful tool against racial reductions. But in attacking a *natural* phenomenon, they did not confront race as a *historical* formation that located their subjects politically and that simultaneously constrained and empowered their own research (Harrison 1991: 3).[16] Occasionally, this positioning could be glimpsed—for example, in Evans-Pritchard's introduction to *The Nuer* (1940); but it was not part of the explicit body, the professional habitus, of the fieldworker.

By contrast, travel writers often noticed color and spoke from a racialized position. Of course, they were not necessarily critical of the relations involved —often quite the reverse! The point is not to celebrate a relatively greater awareness of race—and gender—in travel writing, but to show how, in contrast, the habitus of the ethnographer downplayed these historical determinations. However marked it was by gender, race, caste, or class privilege, ethnography needed to transcend such locations in order to articulate a deeper, *cultural* understanding. This articulation was based on powerful techniques, including at least the following: extended coresidence; systematic observation and recording of data; effective interlocution in at least one local language; a specific mix of alliance, complicity, friendship, respect, coercion, and ironic toleration leading to "rapport"; a hermeneutic attention to deep or implicit structures and meanings. These techniques were designed to produce (and often did produce, within the horizons I am trying to delimit) more contexual, less reductive understandings of local lifeways than did the passing observations of the traveler.

Some writers who could be classified as travelers stayed for extended periods abroad, spoke local languages, and had complex views of indigenous (as well as of creole/colonial) life. Some classified as ethnographers stayed relatively short times, spoke languages badly, and did not interact intensively. The range of actual social relations, communicative techniques, and spatial practices deployed between the poles of fieldwork and travel is a continuum, not a sharp border. There has been considerable overlap.[17] But in spite of, or rather because of, this border complexity, the discursive/institutional lines had to be clearly drawn. This need sustained pressures which, over time, gathered empirical experiences closer to the two poles. In this process, the "superficiality" of the traveler and travel writer was opposed to the "depth" of the fieldworker. But one might also say, provocatively, that the former's "promiscuity" was disciplined in favor of the "family values" often invoked in ethnographic prefaces: fieldwork as a process of getting along with others, of adoption, initiation, learning local norms—much as a child learns.

The habitus of modern fieldwork, defined against that of travel, has proscribed interactive modes long associated with travel experience. Perhaps the most absolute continuing taboo is on sexual liaisons. Fieldworkers could love but not desire the "objects" of their attention. On the continuum of possible relations, sexual entanglements were defined as dangerous, too close. Participant observation, a delicate management of distance and proximity, should not include entanglements in which the ability to maintain perspective might be lost. Sexual relations could not be avowed sources of research knowledge. Nor could going into trance or taking hallucinogens, though the taboo there has been somewhat less strict, a certain amount of "experimentation" sometimes being justifiable in the name of participant observation. Sexual experimentation was, however, out of bounds. A disciplined, participant-observer "went along" with indigenous life, selectively.

At its inception, though, the taboo on sex may have been less against "going native" or losing critical distance than against "going traveling," violating a professional habitus. In travel practices and texts, having sex, heterosexual and homosexual, with local people was common. Indeed in certain travel circuits, such as the nineteenth-century *voyage en Orient*, it was quasi-obligatory.[18] A popular writer such as Pierre Loti consecrated his authority, his access to the mysterious and feminized Other, through stories of sexual encounter. In fieldwork accounts, however, such stories have been virtually nonexistent. Only recently, and still rarely, has the taboo been broken (Rabinow 1977; Cesara 1982). Why should sharing beds be a less appropriate source of fieldwork knowledge than sharing food? There may, of course, be many practical reasons for sexual restraint in the field, just as certain places and activities may be off-limits to the tactful (and locally dependent) sojourner. But they are not off-limits in all places and at all times. Practical constraints, which vary widely, cannot account for the disciplinary taboo on sex in fieldwork.[19]

Enough has been said, perhaps, to make the central point: a disciplinary habitus has been sustained around the embodied activity of fieldwork: an ungendered, unraced, sexually inactive subject interacts intensively (on hermeneutic/scientific levels, at the very least) with interlocutors. If actual experiences in the field have diverged from the norm, if the taboos have sometimes been broken, and if the disciplinary habitus is now publicly contested, its normative power remains.

Another common travel practice before 1900, cross-dressing, was suppressed or channeled in the disciplining of modern fieldwork's professional "body." This is a far-reaching topic, and I must limit myself to preliminary remarks. Daniel Defert (1984) has written suggestively on the history of "clothing" in codes of European travel observation prior to the nineteenth century. A substantial, integral link was once assumed between the person and his or her outward appearance—*habitus*, in Defert's premodern usage.[20] In a deep sense it was understood that "clothes make the man" ("*L'habit fait le moine*"). Interpretations of *habitus*, not to be confused with *habits* (clothes) or with the later concept of culture, were a necessary part of travel interactions. This included the communicative manipulation of appearances—what might be

called, somewhat anachronistically, cultural cross-dressing. By the nineteenth century, in Defert's account, *habitus* had been reduced to *habits*, to
surface coverings and adornments; *costume* had emerged as a deformation
of the richer *coustume* (a term which combined the ideas of costume and
custom).

Clothes would become just one of many elements in a taxonomy of observations made by scientific travelers, components of an emerging *cultural*
explanation. Defert perceives this transition in Gérando's scientific advice
to travelers and explorers, published in 1800. Explorers have often merely
described the clothes of indigenous peoples, he wrote. You should go further and inquire why they may or may not be willing to give up their traditional clothing for ours, and how they conceive the origin of their customs
(Defert 1984: 39). Here, the interpretive grid of *habitus* is replaced (and made
to seem superficial) by a deeper conception of identity and difference. Travel
relations had long been organized by complex and highly codified protocols, "surface" semiotics and transactions. The interpretation and manipulation of clothing, gesture, and appearance were integral to these practices.
Seen as the outcome of this tradition, nineteenth-century cultural cross-dressing was more than just dress-up. A serious, communicative play with appearances and a site of crossover, it articulated a less absolute or essential
notion of difference than that instituted by relativist notions of culture with
their concepts of nativeness inscribed in language, tradition, place, ecology,
and—more or less implicitly—race. The experiences of a Richard Burton
or an Isabelle Eberhardt passing as "Orientals," and even the more blatantly
theatrical costuming of Flaubert in Egypt or Loti on shore leave, partake of
a complex tradition of travel practices held at arm's length by a moderniz-
ing ethnography.[21]

Seen from the perspective of fieldwork (intensive, interactive, based in
language learning), cross-dressing could appear only as superficial dress-up,
a kind of touristic slumming. In this view, the practices of an ethnographer
like Frank Hamilton Cushing, who adopted Zuni dress (and even, it has been
suggested, produced "authentic" indigenous artifacts), would be somewhat
embarrassing. His intensive, interactive research was not quite "modern fieldwork." A similar sense of embarrassment is experienced today by many viewers of Timothy Asche's film *A Man Called Bee*, devoted to Napoleon Chagnon's
research among the Yanomami. I am thinking particularly of the opening
shot, which zooms in slowly on a painted, scantily clad figure in a fighting
pose who turns out, finally, to be the anthropologist. Whatever the intent of
this opening, satiric or otherwise (it's not entirely clear), the impression remains that this is not a "professional" way to appear. A certain excess is reg-
istered, perhaps too easily written off as egotism. Liza Dalby's book *Geisha*
(1983), which includes photographs of the anthropologist being transformed through makeup and wearing full geisha attire, is more acceptable,

since the adoption of a geisha "habitus" (in Defert's older sense—a mode of being, manifested through clothes, gesture, and appearance) is a central issue in her participant observation and written ethnography. Yet the photographs of Dalby looking almost exactly like a "real" geisha break with established ethnographic conventions.

At another pole are the photographs published by Malinowski (in *Coral Gardens and Their Magic* [1935]) of himself in the field. He is dressed entirely in white, surrounded by black bodies, sharply distinguished by posture and attitude. This is a man insistently not about to "go native." Such a self-presentation is akin to the gestures of colonial Europeans who dressed formally for dinner in sweltering climates so as not to feel they were slipping "over the edge." (The miraculous starched collars of Conrad's accountant in *Heart of Darkness* are a paradigm case in colonial literature.) But ethnographers have not, typically, been so formal, and I would suggest that their fieldwork habitus was more of an intermediate formation, predicated on not theatrically standing out from local life (not asserting their difference or authority by wearing military uniforms, pith helmets, and the like), while remaining clearly marked by white skin, proximity to cameras, notepads, and other nonnative accoutrements.[22] Most professional fieldworkers did not try to disappear into the field by indulging in "superficial" travel practices of masquerade. Their embodied distinction suggested connections at deeper, hermeneutic levels, understandings forged through language, coresidence, and *cultural* knowledge.

More than a few telling glimpses of the anthropologist's habitus, overlapping and distinct from that of the traveler, are provided by Lévi-Strauss in *Tristes Tropiques* (1973). "In September 1950," he writes, "I happened to find myself in a Mogh village in the Chittagong hill tracts." After several days, he ascends to the local temple, whose gong has punctuated his days, along with the sound of "childish voices intoning the Burmese alphabet." All is innocence and order. "We had taken off our shoes to climb the hillock, and the fine, damp clay felt soft under our bare feet." At the entry to the simple, beautiful temple, built on stilts like the village houses, the visitors perform "prescribed ablutions," which after the climb through the mud seem "quite natural and devoid of any religious significance."

> A peaceful, barn-like atmosphere pervaded the place and there was a smell of hay in the air. The simple and spacious room which was like a hollowed-out haystack, the courteous behaviour of the two priests standing next to their beds with straw mattresses, the touching care with which they had brought together or made the instruments of worship—all these things helped to bring me closer than I had ever been before to my idea of what a shrine should be like. "You need not do what I am doing," my companion said to me as he prostrated himself on the ground four times before the altar, and I followed his advice. However, I did so less through self-consciousness than discretion: he knew that I did

not share his beliefs, and I would have been afraid of debasing the ritual gestures by letting him think I considered them as mere conventions: but for once,
I would have felt no embarrassment in performing them. Between this form of
religion and myself, there was no likelihood of misunderstanding. It was not a
question of bowing down in front of idols or of adoring a supposed supernat-
ural order, but only of paying homage to the decisive wisdom that a thinker, or
the society that created his legend, had evolved twenty-five centuries before and
to which my civilization could contribute only by confirming it. (1973: 410–411)

Going barefoot could hardly be a casual gesture for Lévi-Strauss: but here,
along with ritual cleansing prior to entering the shrine, it seems simply natural. Everything draws him into sympathy and participation. But he marks
a line at the physical act of prostration. The line expresses a specific *discretion*, that of a visitor who looks beyond "mere conventions" or going along
with appearances to a deeper level of respect based on historical knowledge
and cultural comprehension. The anthropologist's authentic bow to Bud-
dhism is a mental one.

Lévi-Strauss is tempted, retrospectively at least, to prostrate himself in the
hill temple. Another anthropologist might well have done so. My point in
noticing this line between physical and hermeneutic acts of connection is
not to claim that Lévi-Strauss draws it in a place typical of anthropologists. I
do want to suggest, however, that a similar line will be drawn somewhere,
sometime, in the maintenance of a professional fieldwork habitus. Lévi-
Strauss is clearly not one of those Western spiritual travelers who sojourn in
Buddhist temples, shaving their heads and wearing saffron robes. And in this
he represents the traditional ethnographic norm. One could, of course, imagine a Buddhist anthropologist becoming almost indistinguishable, in both
practice and appearance, from other adepts during a period of fieldwork in
a temple. And this would be a limit case for the discipline, to be treated with
suspicion in the absence of other clearly visible signs of professional *discretion* (etymologically: a separation).[23]

Today, in many locations, indigenous people, ethnographers, and tourists
all wear T-shirts and shorts. Elsewhere, distinctions of dress are more salient.
In highland Guatemala it may be a necessity of decorum, a sign of respect
or solidarity, to wear a long skirt or an embroidered shirt in public. But this
is hardly cross-dressing. Can, should, an anthropologist wear a turban,
yarmulke, *jallabeyya, huipil*, or veil? Local conventions vary. But whatever tactics are adopted, they are employed from a position of assumed *cultural* discretion. Moreover, as ethnographers work increasingly in their own societies,
the issues I have been discussing in an exoticist frame become confused, the
lines of separation less self-evident. Embodied professional practices of "the
field"—gendered, raced, sexualized locations and crossovers, forms of self-
presentation, and regulated patterns of access, departure, and return—are
renegotiated.

REROUTING THE FIELD

I have tried to identify some of the sedimented practices through and against which newly diverse ethnographic projects struggle for recognition within anthropology. Established practices come under pressure as the range of sites that can be treated ethnographically multiplies (the academic border with "cultural studies") and as differently positioned, politically invested scholars enter the field (the challenge of a "postcolonial anthropology"). The latter development has far-reaching implications for disciplinary reinvention. Fieldwork defined through spatial practices of travel and dwelling, through the disciplined, embodied interactions of participant observation, is being rerouted by "indigenous," "postcolonial," "diasporic," "border," "minority," "activist," and "community-based" scholars. The terms overlap, designating complex sites of identification, not discrete identities.

Kirin Narayan (1993) questions the opposition of native and nonnative, insider and outsider anthropologists. This binary, she argues, stems from a discredited, hierarchical colonial structure. Drawing on her own ethnography in different parts of India, where she feels varying degrees of affiliation and distance, Narayan shows how "native" researchers are complexly and multiply located vis-à-vis their work sites and interlocutors. Identifications crosscut, complement, and trouble each other. "Native" anthropologists—like all anthropologists, Narayan argues—"belong to several communities simultaneously (not least of all the community we were born into and the community of professional academics)" (Narayan 1993: 24). Once the structuring opposition between "native" and "outside" anthropologist is displaced, the relations of cultural inside and outside, home and away, same and different that have organized the spatial practices of fieldwork must be rethought. How does the disciplinary injunction that fieldwork involve some sort of *travel*—a practice of physical displacement that defines a site or object of intensive research—constrain the range of practices opened up by Narayan and others?

In Narayan's analysis, fieldwork begins and ends in displacement, enacted across constitutive borders—fraught, amorous edges. There is no simple, undivided, "native" position. Once this is recognized, however, the hybridity she embraces needs specification: What are its limits and conditions of movement? One can be more or less hybrid, native, or "diasporic" (a term that perhaps best captures Narayan's own complex locations) for determinate historical reasons. Indeed, the title of "native" or "indigenous" anthropologist might be retained to designate a person whose research travel leads out and back from a home base, "travel" understood as a detour through a university or other site that provides analytic or comparative perspective on the place of dwelling/research. Here, the usual spatialization of home and abroad would be reversed. Moreover, for many fieldworkers, neither the university nor the field provides a stable base; rather, both serve as juxtaposed sites in a mobile comparative project. A continuum, not an opposition, separates the explorations, detours, and returns of the indigenous or native scholar from those of the diasporic or postcolonial.[24] Thus, the requirement that anthropological fieldwork involve *some* kind of travel need not marginalize those formerly called "natives." The roots and routes, the varieties of "travel," need to be more broadly understood.

Recent work by Mary Helms (1988), David Scott (1989), Amitav Ghosh (1992), Epeli Hau'ofa et al. (1993), Teresia Teaiwa (1993), Ben Finney (1994), and Aihwa Ong (1995), among others, has reinforced a growing awareness of discrepant travel routes—traditions of movement and interconnection not definitively oriented by the "West" and an expanding cultural-economic world system. These routes follow "traditional" and "modern" paths, within and across contemporary transnational and interregional circuits. A recognition of these paths makes space for travel (and fieldwork) that does not originate in the metropoles of Euro-America or their outposts. If, as is likely, some form of travel or displacement remains a constituting element in professional fieldwork, reworking the "field" must mean multiplying the range of acceptable routes and practices.

An attention to the varieties of "travel" also helps clarify how, in the past, cleared spaces of scientific work have been constituted through the suppression of cosmopolitan experiences, especially those of the people under study. Generally speaking, the localization of "natives" meant that intensive interactive research was done in spatially delimited fields and not, for example, in hotels or capital cities, on ships, in mission schools or universities, in kitchens and factories, in refugee camps, in diasporic neighborhoods, on pilgrimage buses, or at a variety of cross-cultural sites of encounter.[25] As a Western travel practice, fieldwork was grounded by a historical vision, what Gayatri Spivak calls a "worlding," in which one section of humanity was restless and expansive, the rest rooted and immobile. Indigenous authorities were reduced to native informants. The marginalization of travel practices, those of researchers and hosts, contributed to a *domestication* of fieldwork, an ideal of interactive dwelling that, however temporary, could not be seen as merely passing through. That anthropology's interlocutors often saw things differently did not, until recently, disturb the discipline's self-image.[26]

Alternate forms of travel/fieldwork, whether indigenous or diasporic, grapple with many problems similar to those of conventional research: problems of strangeness, privilege, miscomprehension, stereotyping, and political negotiation of the encounter. Ghosh is especially trenchant on the potentially violent miscomprehensions and stereotypes integral to his research as a *doktor al Hindi* among Muslims. Epeli Hau'ofa speaks for an interconnected "Oceania," but he does so as a Tongan living in Fiji, a location not forgotten by his diverse Islander audiences. At the same time, the routes and encounters of ethnographers such as Ghosh or Hau'ofa are different from those of traditional fieldwork sojourners. Their cultural comparisons need not presuppose a Western, university home, a "central" site of theoretical accumulation. And while their research encounters may involve hierarchical relations, they need not presuppose "white" privilege. Their work may or may not crucially depend on colonial and neocolonial circuits of information, access, and power. For example, Hau'ofa publishes in Tonga and Fiji and wants to articulate an old/new "Oceania." In this he differs from Ghosh, who publishes, crucially though not exclusively, in the West. The language(s) the ethnography uses, the audiences it addresses, the circuits of academic and media prestige it appeals to, may be discrepant from, though seldom unconnected with, the communicative structures of global political economy. A case in point: *A New Oceania*, by Hau'ofa et al. (1993), was delivered to me by hand.[27] Published in Suva, the book would not have reached me through my normal reading networks. Can a work centered and routed like this one intervene in Euro-American anthropological contexts? What are the institutional barriers? The power to determine audiences, publications, and translations is very unevenly distributed, as Talal Asad has often reminded us (Asad 1986).

The oxymoronic term "indigenous anthropologist," coined at the beginning of the ongoing postcolonial/neocolonial recentering of the discipline, is no longer adequate to characterize a wide range of scholars studying in their home societies. Difficult issues arise. How exactly will "home" be defined? If, as I assume, no *inherent* authority can be accorded to "native" ethnographies and histories, what constitutes their *differential* authority? How do they supplement and criticize long-established perspectives? And under what conditions will local knowledge enunciated by locals be recognized as "anthropological knowledge"? What kinds of displacement, comparison, or taking of "distance" are required for family knowledge and folk history to be recognized as serious ethnography or cultural theory by the disciplinary center?

Anthropology potentially includes a cast of diverse dwellers and travelers whose displacement or travel in "fieldwork" differs from the traditional spatial practice of the field. The West itself becomes an object of study from variously distanced and entangled locations. Going "out" to the field now sometimes means going "back," the ethnography becoming a "notebook of a return to the native land." In the case of a diasporic scholar, the "return" may be to a place never known personally but to which she or he ambivalently, powerfully "belongs." *Returning* to a field will not be the same as *going out* to a field. Different subjective distances and affiliations are at stake.

A growing awareness of these differences has emerged within Euro-American anthropology during recent decades. In an important discussion, David Scott named some of the historical locations constraining an emergent "postcoloniality" in anthropology:

By raising in different ways the problem of "place" and the non-Western anthropologist, both Talal Asad (1982) and Arjun Appadurai (1988a) have suggested that to undermine the asymmetry in anthropological practice many
more such anthropologists should study Western societies. This, to be sure, is
a step in the right direction inasmuch as it subverts the pervasive notion that
the non-Western subject can speak only within the terms of his/ her own culture. Moreover, it privileges in some degree the possibility of tacking back and
forth between cultural spaces. At the same time, it would seem to fix and repeat the colonially established territorial boundaries within which the postcolonial is encouraged to move: center/ periphery—and typically, the center
of neocolonial governance and the periphery of origin. European and American anthropologists continue to go where they please, while the postcolonial
stays home or else goes West. One wonders whether there might not be a more
engaging problematic to be encountered where the postcolonial intellectual
from Papua New Guinea goes, not to Philadelphia but to Bombay or Kingston
or Accra. (Scott 1989: 80)

Escape from the polarizing historical force field of the "West" is no easy matter, as Scott's subsequent discussion of Ghosh makes clear. But Scott also argues that the cross-cultural "tacking" of anthropologists should not be reduced to movements between centers and peripheries in a world system.
Contemporary ethnography, including Scott's own from Jamaica via New
York to Sri Lanka, is necessarily "traveling in the West" (Ghosh, quoted by
Scott 1989: 82). It is also traveling in and against, through the West.

Ethnography is no longer a normative practice of outsiders visiting or
studying insiders but, in Narayan's words, of attending to "shifting identities
in relationship with the people and issues an anthropologist seeks to represent" (Narayan 1993: 30). How identities are negotiated relationally, in determined historical contexts, is thus a process constituting both the subjects
and objects of ethnography. Much emerging work now makes these complex
relational processes explicit. Paulla Ebron (1994, forthcoming), for example, conducts research on Mandinka praise-singers both in West Africa and
in the United States, where they find appreciative audiences. Her ethnography is multiply located and—as she clearly shows—entangled in the traveling culture circuits of world music and tourism. Ebron's ethnography also
works in tension with a history of dominant Western inventions of Africa—
she cites Mudimbe (1988)—and more or less romanticized African American projections formed in reaction to histories of racism. Ebron moves among
these intersecting contexts. "Africa" cannot be held "out there." It is an em-
powering and problematic part of her own African American tradition as
well as a relay—not an origin—in a continuing diasporic history of transits
and returns. This history implicates her academic ethnography, whose site
is the relational negotiation of "subjects in difference," a space where praise-
singers, tourists, and anthropologists claim and negotiate cultural meanings.
Her field includes the airports where these travelers cross.

"Indigenous," "postcolonial," "diasporic," or "minority" attachments are frequently at issue in the way anthropological "fields" are negotiated. Scholars such as Rosaldo (1989a), Kondo (1990), Behar (1993), and Limón (1994), to cite only a few, define the spatial practices of their fieldwork in terms of a politics of locations, of tactically shifting insides and outsides, affiliations and distances. Their anthropological "distance" is challenged, blurred, relationally reconstructed. Often, they express their complex situated knowledges by textual strategies in which the embodied, narrating, traveling scholar-theorist is prominent. But this choice should be seen as a critical intervention against disembodied, neutral authority, not as an emerging norm. There is no narrative form or way of writing inherently suited to a politics of location. Others working within and against a still predominantly Western anthropology may choose to adopt a more impersonal, demystifying, indeed objective rhetoric. David Scott and Talal Asad are strong examples. Their discourses are, nevertheless, openly that of politically committed, situated scholars, not neutral observers. A very wide range of rhetorics and narratives—personal and impersonal, objective and subjective, embodied and disembodied—are available to the located scholar-traveler. The only tactic excluded, as Donna Haraway has said, is the "God Trick" (Haraway 1988).

Most of the anthropologists cited in the previous section have done something *like* traditional fieldwork: studying "out" or "down." This has contributed to their survival, indeed success, within the academy, even as they work to criticize and open it up. The licensing function of having done "real" fieldwork—intensive and displaced from the university—remains strong. Indeed, ethnography that takes place within *diasporic* affiliations may be more easily accepted than research whose attachments, however ambivalent, are indigenous or *native*. (Recall that these locations fall on an overlapping continuum, not on either side of a binary opposition.) Diasporic (dis)locations have travel and distance built into them, usually including metropolitan spaces. Native (re)locations, while they include travel, are centered in a way that makes the metropole and the university peripheral. I have suggested that displacement, Scott's "tacking" between cultural spaces, remains a constitutive feature of anthropological fieldwork. Can this displacement be extended to include travel to and through the university? Can the university itself be seen as a kind of field site—a place of cultural juxtaposition, estrangement, rite of passage, transit, and learning? Mary John (1989) opens such a possibility in her prescient discussion of a compromised, emergent "anthropology in reverse" for postcolonial feminists: a coerced and desired travel in "the West," and an unstable coexistence of roles—anthropologist, and native informant. How does travel through the university reposition the "native" place where the anthropologist maintains connections of residence, kinship, or political affiliation that go beyond visiting, however intensive? Angie Chabram explores this repositioning in her provocative sketch of a Chicana/o "oppositional ethnography" (Chabram 1990). Here, "minority" and "native" trajectories may overlap: rooted in the "community" (however defined) and routed through academia.

When ethnography has primarily served the interests of community memory and mobilization and only secondarily the needs of comparative knowledge or science, it has tended to be relegated to the less prestigious categories of "applied anthropology," "oral history," "folklore," "political journalism," or "local history." But as fieldwork becomes differently rooted and routed in some of the ways I have been tracking, many scholars may take a renewed interest in applied research, oral history, and folklore, stripped now of their sometimes paternalistic traditions. The oral history/community mobilization work of the El Barrio Project at the New York Centro de Estudios Puertorriqueños is a frequently cited example (see Benmayor 1991; Gordon 1993). Dara Culhane Speck's *An Error in Judgement* (1987) carefully fuses community memory, historical scholarship, and current political advocacy. Esther Newton's subtle articulation of margins, as loyal lesbian participant-observer, outsider/insider in a predominantly gay male community, produces an exemplary fusion of local history and cultural criticism (Newton 1993a). Epeli Hau'ofa's research in Tonga is another case in point (as distinct from his exoticist work in Trinidad or his studies in Papua New Guinea, where he was a different kind of "Pacific" outsider). Returning to do research in his native Tonga, Hau'ofa writes in more than one language and style both to analyze and influence local responses to Westernization. He maintains a stylistic distinction between writing for the discipline, writing as political intervention, and writing as satiric fiction (Hau'ofa 1982). But the discourses are clearly connected in his view, and others might be more inclined than he to blur them.

To do "professional" anthropology, one must maintain connections with university centers and their circuits of publication and sociality. How close must these connections be? How central? When does one begin to lose disciplinary identity at the margins? These questions have always faced scholars working for governments, corporations, activist social organizations, and local communities. They continue to trouble, and discipline, the work of the differently located anthropologists I have been discussing. Moreover, the university itself is not a single site. Though it may have Western roots, it is hybridized and transculturated in non-Western places. Its ties to nation, to "development," to region, to post-, neo-, and anticolonial politics can make it a significantly different base of anthropological operations, as Hussein Fahim's pioneering collection *Indigenous Anthropology in Non-Western Countries* (1982) makes clear. In principle at least, universities are sites of comparative theory, of communication and critical argument among scholars. The ethnographic or ethnohistorical interpretations of non-university authorities are seldom recognized as fully scholarly discourse; rather, they tend to be seen as local, amateurish knowledge. In anthropology, the research that produces such knowledge, however intensive and interactive, is not fieldwork.

The disciplinary "Other" who perhaps most epitomizes the border at issue here is the figure of the *local historian*. This supposedly partisan chronicler and keeper of the community's records is even harder to integrate with conventional fieldwork than the emerging figures of the diasporic postcolonial, the oppositional minority scholar, or even the traveling native. Tainted by a presumed immobility and by assumptions of amateurism and boosterism, the local historian, like the activist or culture-worker, lacks the required professional "distance." As we have seen, this distance has been naturalized in spatial practices of the "field," a circumscribed place one enters and leaves. Movement in and out has been considered essential to the interpretive process, the management of depth and discretion, absorption and "the view from afar" (Lévi-Strauss 1985).

The disciplinary border that keeps locally based authorities in the position of informants is, however, being renegotiated. Where and how the boundary is redrawn—which spatial practices will be accommodated by the evolving tradition of anthropological fieldwork and which will be excluded—remains to be seen. But in this context it may be useful to ask how the legacy of fieldwork-as-travel helps to account for an issue raised during recent presidential sessions on diversity at the American Anthropological Association: the fact that North American minorities are entering the field in relatively small numbers. Anthropology has difficulty reconciling goals of analytic distance with the aspirations of organic intellectuals. Has the discipline adequately confronted the problem of doing sanctioned, "real" fieldwork in a community one wants *not* to leave? Departure, taking distance, has long been crucial to the spatial practice of fieldwork. How can the discipline make room for research that is importantly about return, reterritorialization, belonging —attachments that go beyond gaining rapport as a research strategy? Robert Alvarez (1994) provides a revealing discussion of these issues, showing how different kinds of community involvement in the course of research are valued and devalued by the discipline in ways that tend to reproduce a white hegemony.

The definition of "home" is fundamentally at issue here. In local/global situations where displacement appears increasingly to be the norm, how is collective dwelling sustained and reinvented? (See Bammer 1992.) Binary oppositions between home and abroad, staying and moving, need to be thoroughly questioned (Kaplan 1994). These oppositions have often been naturalized along lines of gender (female, domestic space versus male travel), class (the active, alienated bourgeoisie versus the stagnant, soulful poor), and race/culture (modern, rootless Westerners versus traditional, rooted "natives"). The fieldwork injunction to go elsewhere construes "home" as a site of origin, of sameness. Feminist theory and gay/lesbian studies have, perhaps most sharply, showed home to be a site of unrestful differences. Moreover, in the face of global forces that coerce displacement and travel, staying (or making) home can be a political act, a form of resistance. Home is not, in any event, a site of immobility. These few indications, of which much more could be said, should be enough to question anthropological assumptions of fieldwork as travel, going *out* in search of *difference*. To a degree these assumptions continue to apply in practices of "repatriated" fieldwork (Marcus and Fischer 1986) and of "studying up" (Nader 1972). The field remains *somewhere else*, albeit within one's own linguistic or national context.

An unsettling discussion of "home" with reference to anthropological practice is provided by Kamala Visweswaran (1994). She argues that feminist ethnography, part of an ongoing struggle to decolonize anthropology, needs to recognize the "failure" that is inevitably bound up with the project of cross-cultural translation in power-charged situations. Precisely at "those moments when a project is faced with its own impossibility" (98), ethnography can struggle for accountability, a sense of its own positioning. Building on Gayatri Spivak's formulation of every cultural/political subject's "sanctioned ignorances," Visweswaran argues that by openly confronting failure, feminist ethnography discovers both limits and possibilities. Among the latter are critical movements "homeward." In a section titled "Homework, Not Fieldwork," she develops a concept of ethnographic work not based on the home/field dichotomy. "Homework" is not defined as the opposite of exoticist fieldwork; it is not a matter of literally staying home or studying one's own community. "Home," for Visweswaran, is a person's location in determining discourses and institutions—cutting across locations of race, gender, class, sexuality, culture. "Homework" is a critical confrontation with the often invisible processes of learning (the French word *formation* is apt here) that shape us as subjects. Playing on the pedagogical senses of the term, Visweswaran proposes "homework" as a discipline of unlearning as much as of learning. "Home" is a locus of critical struggle that both empowers and limits the subject wherever she or he conducts formal research. By deconstructing the home/field opposition, Visweswaran clears space for unorthodox routings and rootings of ethnographic work.

In a related, but not identical vein, Gupta and Ferguson (chapter 1) urge an anthropology focused on *"shifting locations* rather than *bounded fields."* Theirs is a reformist rather than a deconstructive project. While rejecting the tradition of spatially restricted research, they preserve certain practices long associated with fieldwork. Anthropology still studies "Others" intensively and interactively. It provides, they remind us, one of the few Western academic sites where unfamiliar, marginalized, nonelite peoples are seriously attended to. Long-term immersion, interest in informal knowledge and embodied practices, an injunction to *listen* are all elements of the field-work tradition they value and hope to preserve. Moreover, Gupta and Ferguson's notion of shifting locations suggests that even when the ethnographer is positioned as an insider, a "native" in her or his community, some taking of distances and translating differences will be part of the research, analysis, and writing. No one can be an insider to all sectors of a community. How the shifting locations are managed, how affiliation, discretion, and critical perspective are sustained, have been and will remain matters of tactical improvisation as much as of formal methodology. Thus, whatever comes to be recognized as a reformed fieldwork will entail David Scott's "tacking between cultural spaces," though not necessarily or solely along colonial or neocolonial axes of center and periphery.

Moreover, the constitutive displacements need not be between "cultural" spaces, at least not as the term is conventionally defined in spatial terms. An ethnography focused on shifting locations would assume only that the borders negotiated and crossed were salient to a co-constructed project in a specific "contact zone" (Pratt 1992). This would mean not that the borders in question were invented or unreal, but only that they were not absolute and could be crosscut by other borders or affiliations also potentially relevant to the project. These other constitutive locations might become central in other historical and political conjunctures or in a differently focused project. One cannot represent "in depth" all salient differences and affinities. For example, a middle-class researcher studying among working people may find class to be a critical location, even if his or her research topic is explicitly focused elsewhere—say, on gender relations in secondary schools. In this case, race might or might not be a site of crucial difference or affinity.

A project will always "succeed" on certain axes and "fail" (in Visweswaran's constitutive sense) on others. Thus, we should not confuse a more or less conscious research strategy of shifting locations with *being located* (often antagonistically) in the ethnographic encounter. For an Indian Hindu working in Egypt, religion may be imposed as a prime differentiating factor, asserting its salience for a research project on agricultural techniques, in spite of the author's desires (Ghosh 1992). Moreover, the process need not be antagonistic. A student of his or her own community may be located firmly and lovingly as "family," thus putting real restrictions on what can be probed and revealed. A gay or lesbian ethnographer may be constrained to highlight or downplay sexual location, depending on the political context of research. Or an anthropologist from Peru may find himself or herself negotiating a national boundary when working in Mexico, but a racial one in the United States. The examples could be multiplied.

None of these locations is optional. They are imposed by historical and political circumstances. And because locations are multiple, conjunctural, and crosscutting, there can be no guarantee of shared perspective, experience, or solidarity. I build here on a nondismissive critique of identity politics that has been compellingly stated by June Jordan (1985) and developed by many others (for example, Reagon 1983; Mohanty 1987). In ethnography, what was previously understood in terms of *rapport*—a kind of achieved friendship, kinship, empathy—now appears as something closer to *alliance building*. The relevant question is less "What fundamentally unites or separates us?" and more "What can we do for each other in the present conjuncture?" What, from our similarities and differences, can we bend together, hook up, articulate? (See Hall 1986: 52–55; Haraway 1992: 306–315.) And when identification becomes too close, how can a disarticulation of agendas be managed, in the context of alliance, without resorting to claims to objective distance and tactics of definitive departure? (For a sensitive account of these issues in the context of lesbian ethnography, see Lewin 1995.)

A stress on shifting locations and tactical affiliations explicitly recognizes ethnography's political dimensions, dimensions that can be hidden by presumptions of scientific neutrality and human rapport. But "political" in what senses? There are no guaranteed or morally unassailable positions. In the present context—a shift from rapport to alliance, from representation to articulation—rigid prescriptions of advocacy have a tendency to emerge. An older politics of neutrality with its goal of ultimate disengagement may simply be reversed—a binary starkly evident in the juxtaposition of eloquent, opposing essays by Roy d'Andrade and Nancy Scheper-Hughes in a 1995 forum of *Current Anthropology*. The place for a politics of skepticism and critique (not to be confused with dispassion or neutrality), for engaged disloyalty, or for what Richard Handler (1985, quoting Sapir) calls "destructive analysis," seems endangered. An alliance model leaves little room for work in a politicized situation that pleases none of the contestants. I am not suggesting that such research is superior or more objective. It, too, is partial and located. And it should not be excluded from the range of situated research practices now contending for the name "anthropology."

These are just some of the dilemmas facing anthropological ethnography as its roots and routes, its different patterns of affiliation and displacement, are reworked in late twentieth-century contexts. What remains of *fieldwork*? What, if anything, is left of the injunction to travel, to get out of the house, to "enter the field," to dwell, to interact intensively in a (relatively) unfamiliar context? A research practice defined by "shifting locations," without the prescription of physical displacement and extended face-to-face encounter, could after all describe the work of a literary critic, attentive, as many are today, to the politics and cultural contexts of different textual readings. Or, once freed of the notion of a "field" as a spatialized site of research, could an anthropologist investigate the shifting locations of her or his own life? Could "homework" be autobiography?

Here we cross a blurred border that the discipline is struggling to define. Autobiography can, of course, be quite "sociological"; it can move systematically between personal experience and general concerns. A certain degree of autobiography is now widely accepted as relevant to self-critical projects of cultural analysis. But how much? Where is the line to be drawn? When is self-analysis dismissed as "mere" autobiography? (One sometimes hears rather modest amounts of personal revelation in ethnographies described as solipsism or "navel-gazing.") Writing an ethnography of one's subjective space as a kind of complex community, a site of shifting locations, could be defended as a valid contribution to anthropological work. It would not, I think, be widely recognized as fully or characteristically *anthropological* in the way that work in an externalized *field* still is. One could hardly count on being awarded a Ph.D. or finding a job in an anthropology department for autobiographical research. The legacy of the field in anthropology requires, at least, that "firsthand" research involve extended face-to-face interactions with members of a community. Practices of displacement and encounter still play a defining role. Without these, what are under discussion are not new versions of fieldwork but a range of quite different practices.

In this chapter, I have tried to show how definite spatial practices, patterns of dwelling and traveling, have constituted fieldwork in anthropology. I have argued that the disciplining of fieldwork, of its sites, routes, temporalities, and embodied practices, has been critical in maintaining the identity of sociocultural anthropology. Currently contested and under renegotiation, fieldwork remains a mark of disciplinary distinction. The most disputed elements of traditional fieldwork are, perhaps, its injunction to leave home and its inscription within relations of travel that have depended on colonial, race-, class-, and gender-based definitions of center and periphery, cosmopolitan and local. The linked requirement that anthropological fieldwork be intensive and interactive is less controversial, although criteria for measuring "depth" are more debatable than ever. Why not simply purge the discipline's exoticist travel legacy while sustaining its intensive and interactive styles of research? In a utopian mode one might argue for such a solution, and indeed things seem to be moving in this general direction. A radical course is urged by Deborah D'Amico-Samuels in an essay that anticipates many of the critiques previously referred to. She questions traditional spatial and methodological definitions of the "field," concluding rigorously: "The field is everywhere" (1991: 83). But if the field is everywhere, it is nowhere. We should not be surprised if institutional traditions and interests resist such radical dissolutions of fieldwork. Thus, some forms of travel, of disciplined displacement in and out of one's "community" (seldom a single place, in any event), will probably remain the norm. And this disciplinary "travel" will require at least a serious sojourn in the university. I conclude, provocatively, in this hazardous future tense.

Travel, redefined and broadened, will remain constitutive of fieldwork, at least in the near term. This will be necessary for institutional and material reasons. Anthropology must preserve not only its disciplinary identity but also its credibility with scientific institutions and funding sources. Given a shared genealogy with other natural science and social science research practices, it is no accident that the field has, at times, been called anthropology's "laboratory." Criteria of objectivity associated with a detached, outside perspective are strongly represented in the academic and government milieus that control resources. Thus, sociocultural anthropology will remain under pressure to certify the scientific credentials of an interactive, intersubjective methodology. Researchers will be constrained to take a certain "distance" from the communities they study. Of course, critical distance can be defended without appealing to ultimate grounds of authority in scientific objectivity. At issue is how distance is manifested in research practices. In the past, physically leaving the "field"—to "write up" research results in the presumably more critical, objective, or at least comparative environment of the university—was seen to be an important guarantee of academic independence. As we have seen, this spatialization of "inside" and "outside" locations no longer enjoys the credibility it once did. Will anthropology find ways to take seriously new forms of "field" research that diverge from earlier models of university-centered travel, spatial discontinuity, and ultimate disengagement?

As anthropology moves, haltingly, in postexoticist, postcolonial directions, a diversification of professional norms is under way. The process, accelerated by political and intellectual critiques, is reinforced by material constraints. In many contexts, given falling levels of funding, sociocultural fieldwork will increasingly have to be conducted "on the cheap." For graduate students, relatively expensive long-term sojourns abroad may be out of the question, and even a year of full-time research in a U.S. community can be too expensive. While traditional fieldwork will certainly maintain its prestige, the discipline may come to resemble more closely the "national" anthropologies of many European and non-Western countries, with short, repeated visits the norm and fully supported research years rare. It is important to recall that professional fieldwork in the Malinowskian mold depended materially on the mobilization of funding for a new "scientific" practice (Stocking 1992b). "Subway ethnography," like Karen McCarthy Brown's (discussed above), will be increasingly common. But even as visiting and "deep hanging out" replace extended coresidence and the tent-in-the-village model, legacies of exoticist fieldwork influence the professional habitus of the "field" —now conceived less as a discrete, other place than as a set of embodied research practices, as patterns of discretion, of professional distance, of coming and going.[28]

I have located fieldwork in a long, increasingly contested tradition of

Western travel practices. I have suggested, too, that other travel traditions and diasporic routes can help renovate methodologies of displacement, leading to metamorphoses of the "field." "Travel" denotes more or less voluntary practices of leaving familiar ground in search of difference, wisdom, power, adventure, an altered perspective. These experiences and desires cannot be limited to privileged male Westerners—although that elite has powerfuly defined the terms of travel orienting modern anthropology. Travel needs to be rethought in different traditions and historical predicaments. Moreover, when criticizing specific legacies of travel, one should not come to rest in an uncritical localism, the inverse of exoticism. There is truth in the cliche "travel broadens."[29] Of course, the experience offers no guaranteed results. But, often, getting away lets uncontrollable, unexpected things happen (Tsing 1994a). An anthropologist friend, Joan Larcom, once told me ruefully and gratefully: "Fieldwork gave me some experiences I didn't think I deserved." I remember thinking that a discipline requiring this of its adepts must be onto something. Is it possible to validate such experiences of displacement without reference to a mystified, professional "rite of passage"?

Sojourning somewhere else, learning a language, putting oneself in odd situations and trying to figure them out can be a good way to learn something new, simultaneously about oneself and about the people and places one visits. This commonplace truth has long encouraged people to engage with cultures beyond their own. It underlies what still seems most valuable in the linked/distinct traditions of travel and ethnography. Intensive fieldwork does not produce privileged or complete understandings. Nor does the cultural knowledge of indigenous authorities, of "insiders." We are differently situated as dwellers and travelers in our cleared "fields" of knowledge. Is this multiplicity of locations merely another symptom of postmodern fragmentation? Can it be collectively fashioned into something more substantial? Can anthropology be reinvented as a forum for variously routed fieldworks—a site where different contextual knowledges engage in critical dialogue and respectful polemic? Can anthropology foster a critique of cultural dominance that extends to its own protocols of research? The answer is unclear: powerful, newly flexible, centralizing forces remain. The legacies of the "field" are strong in the discipline and deeply, perhaps productively, ambiguous. I have focused on some defining spatial practices that must be turned to new ends if a multiply centered anthropology is to emerge.

NOTES

Thanks to the following people for critical readings: Judith Aissen, James Ferguson, Akhil Gupta, Susan Harding, Michelle Kisliuk, Ann Kingsolver, William Ladusaw, and David Schneider.

1. For the emergence of this fieldwork norm and its "magic," see George Stocking's classic account (Stocking 1992a: chapter 1). My discussion here is largely lim-

ited to Euro-American trends. I join Gupta and Ferguson (chapter 1 of this book) in admitting my "sanctioned ignorance" (Spivak 1988; John 1989) of many non-Western anthropological contexts and practices. And even within the contested but powerful disciplinary "center," my discussion is primarily focused on North America and, to some extent, England. If the issues raised extend beyond these contexts, they do so with reservations I am not yet able to discuss systematically.

2. Renato Rosaldo made this comment at the "Anthropology and 'the Field'" conference on 18 April 1994. The context was a comparison of ethnography by postexotic anthropologists and cultural studies scholars, a discussion of what, in the absence of extended coresidence, guarantees interactive "depth."

3. In his recent survey of emerging "multi-sited ethnography," George Marcus (1995: 100) confronts this question and argues that such ethnographies are "inevitably the product of knowledge bases of varying intensities and qualities." He adds: "It is perhaps anthropologists' appreciation of the difficulty of doing intensive ethnography at any site and the satisfaction that comes from such work in the past when it is done well that would give them pause when the ethnographer becomes mobile and still claims to have done good fieldwork." Overall, Marcus's important attempt to grasp an emergent phenomenon bypasses the question of *fieldwork.* He simply calls all the new mobile practices *ethnography,* a manifestly interdisciplinary orientation, albeit retaining certain recognizable anthropological features: upclose perspectives, cross-cultural translations, language learning, attention to everyday practices, and the like.

4. Criteria of adequate fieldwork have tended to be enforced through tacit consensus rather than explicit rules. A professional culture recognizes "good" ethnography and ethnographers in ways that can appear obscure, even arbitrary, to an outsider. I am not concerned, however, with distinguishing research of different quality or with showing how such distinctions function professionally. This would require a history and sociology of the discipline that I am not qualified to supply.

5. A single offering that would attempt to integrate current work in physical anthropology and archaeology is barely conceivable. Most departments sustain separate tracks with hopes—more or less serious—of cross-fertilization.

6. It is a fraught border that, in the United States at least, can take the form of turf wars. On the anthropological side, there has been recurrent grumbling about misuse of the culture concept and superficial ethnography. Moreover, some embattled anthropologists have been tempted to dismiss cultural studies as just more trendy "postmodernism." This reflex is currently visible in negative reactions to the new editorial policies of Barbara and Dennis Tedlock at the discipline's flagship journal *American Anthropologist.* A motion to censure the journal's "postmodern turn" was introduced (and defeated) at the American Anthropological Association's annual meeting. Expressing a more ambivalent sense of the fraught border, Dale Eickelman (quoted by the *Chronicle of Higher Education*) finds a recent "photo-studded article on the marketing of religious kitsch in Cairo [to be] something 'radically new' for the journal, work that 'recaptures some of the territory appropriated by cultural studies'" (Zalewski 1995: 16). Handler (1993) gives a judicious account of the cultural studies border, from the anthropological side.

7. One thinks of the Chicago School. More recently, one might mention Howard Becker's work (e.g., 1986) or work by Van Maanen (1988), Burawoy et al. (1991),

and Wellman (1995), all of which explicitly address anthropological debates about ethnographic authority. Anthropology has until relatively recently been distinguished from sociology by a research *object* (the primitive, the tribal, the rural, the subaltern—especially non-Western and premodern). Michèle Duchet (1984) has traced the emergence of anthropology's special object to eighteenth-century anthropology-sociology, which divided up the globe according to a series of familiar dichotomies: with/without history, archaic/modern, literate/nonliterate, distant/nearby. Each opposition has, by now, been empirically blurred, politically challenged, and theoretically deconstructed.

8. My comments here are based on conversations with Susan Harding. Indeed, her hybrid research practice was my starting point for reconsidering the "field" in anthropology. Publications from her work in progress include Harding 1987, 1990, and 1993.

9. As I send this chapter to press, I sadly note the death of my colleague David Schneider, who never tired of reminding me that fieldwork was not the sine qua non of anthropology. His general position, a critique of my work among others, has just appeared in *Schneider on Schneider* (1995: esp. chapter 10), a mordant, hilarious, intemperate book of interviews. Schneider argues that famous anthropologists are distinguished by ideas and theoretical innovations rather than by good fieldwork. Ethnography, as he sees it, is a process of generating reliable facts that tend to confirm preconceived ideas or are irrelevant to the work's final conclusions. Fieldwork is the empirical alibi for a questionable positivism. He dismisses claims that field research involves a distinctive or particularly valuable form of interactive learning. But under pressure from his interlocutor, Richard Handler, Schneider retreats from his more extreme points. For example, he accepts that good ethnography and theory are not strictly separable in the forging of reputations and recognizes that anthropologists do (misguidedly) place a special, defining emphasis on fieldwork. He also concedes that work in the field can produce new ideas and challenge presuppositions. He does not comment, however, on how approved ethnography functions in normative ways within the discipline. Schneider's characteristically vehement strictures are a corrective to the focus of this paper. And his final position seems to be that if fieldwork is indeed a distinctive mark of sociocultural anthropology, it should not be fetishized. I agree. I do not agree that anthropology is (read, should be) "the study of culture." That, too, is a problematic disciplinary life raft. I will miss David's loyal provocations and certainly do not claim the last word in this argument.

10. See also Lowie's *History of Ethnological Theory* (1937), which begins by sharply distinguishing anthropological ethnography from exoticist, "literary" travel. See Mary Louise Pratt's critique (1986) of this discursive move.

11. The "Sophisticated Traveler" supplements, which feature travel essays by well-known writers, are—along with the weekly Sunday travel section—major sources of advertisement revenue. An introduction by *New York Times* editors A. M. Rosenthal and Arthur Gelb to the first of a series of anthologies based on the supplements claims an equivalence between sensitive journalism and literary travel writing (Rosenthal and Gelb 1984).

12. Many "good" bookstores now consecrate the tourist/traveler distinction by maintaining well-stocked, *separate* sections for guidebooks and travel books.

13. Van Maanen (1988) provides a balanced account of new approaches to ethnographic writing and their consequences for fieldwork—anthropological and sociological. The title of his book, *Tales of the Field*, is indicative of my present theme: travelers, not scientists, tell tales.

14. Marcus (1995: 105–110) replaces the image of ethnographic dwelling with that of "following." Multisited ethnography ranges widely, and on routes that often cannot be prefigured.

15. The literature is now very extensive. Golde (1986), Moore (1988), Bell, Caplan, and Karim (1993), and Behar and Gordon (1995) indicate the current range of feminist agendas. The latter work appeared just as this chapter was being sent to press, and thus has been used sparingly.

16. An exception is the neglected work of Ruth Landes. Sally Cole's illuminating account (1995), which arrived too late to be integrated in this chapter, confirms, I think, Landes's general approach. Landes gave sustained attention to "race," resisting its subsumption under "culture." She gave prominence to issues of embodiment and sexuality in fieldwork, which she presented in relational, personal terms. She broke the disciplinary taboo on sexual liaisons in the field. *The City of Women* (1994 [1947]), her work on *candomblé* in Bahia, was dismissed by powerful gatekeepers, according to Cole, as a "travelogue" (tainted also by association with the devalued genres of journalism and folklore). The work of another casualty of professionalization, Zora Neale Hurston, was marginalized in similar ways, seen as too subjective, literary, or folkloric. Hurston's reception was (and still is) compounded by essentialist notions of racial identity that have construed her negatively as a limited native ethnographer and positively as a conduit for black cultural authenticity. Such receptions, academic and nonacademic, elide the different worlds and affiliations of race, gender, and class negotiated by her work on the rural South, the Harlem Renaissance, and Columbia University. The Hurston literature and debates are now quite extensive. Hernandez (1995) provides a valuable discussion.

17. Boon 1977 is a prescient historical exploration. Anthropologists are beginning to write self-consciously about and in this borderland (Crick 1985; Boon 1992; Dubois 1995).

18. On Flaubert's sexualized Orientalist travels see Behdad (1994). One might also mention Bali as a site for gay sex tourism before 1940.

19. One of the consequences, perhaps, of this taboo on physical sex has been to restrict discussion of the "erotics" of fieldwork. Newton (1993c) provides an antidote.

20. I have previously been using the term *habitus* in the generally recognized social-scientific sense made familiar by Bourdieu (1977). This notion sees the social inscribed in the body: a repertoire of practices rather than rules, a disposition to play the social game. It makes conceptions of social and cultural structure more processual: embodied and practiced. Unlike Defert's usage, it presupposes modern notions of society and culture. The older sense of habitus sees subjectivity as a matter of concrete, meaningful gestures, appearances, physical dispositions, and apparel without reference to these determining structures, which became hegemonic only in the late nineteenth century.

21. The case of Isabelle Eberhardt is complicated by the coincidence of gender and cultural cross-dressing. See Ali Behdad's acute discussion (1994).

22. In her gently reflexive ethnography *Storytellers, Saints, and Scoundrels* (1989), Kirin Narayan provides a photo of herself in the field. The focus of her research was the apartment of Swamiji, a Guru storyteller in India, and the photo shows several women seated on the apartment floor. None of them is Narayan, though were she seated among them, she would not with her sari and "Indian" features be easily distinguished from the other South Asian women. The caption reads: "Listening attentively from the women's side of the room. The bag and camera cover mark my presence." The accoutrements of her trade occupy the ethnographer's discrete place. Indeed, throughout the book, Narayan's tape recorder is an explicit topic of discussion for Swamiji and his followers.

23. Appearances are powerful. Dorrine Kondo (1986: 74) begins her important exploration of the processes of dissolution and reconstitution of the self in fieldwork encounters with a disturbing glimpse of her own image, reflected in a Tokyo butcher's display case as she shops for her Japanese "family." For an instant she is indistinguishable in every particular—clothes, body, gesture—from a typical young housewife, "a woman walking with a characteristically Japanese bend in the knees and sliding of the feet. Suddenly I clutched the handle of the stroller to steady myself as a wave of dizziness washed over me. . . . Fear that perhaps I would never emerge from this world into which I was immersed inserted itself into my mind and stubbornly refused to leave, until I resolved to move into a new apartment, to distance myself from my Japanese home and my Japanese existence." In the border-crossings of fieldwork, a holistic "experience" is mobilized, and at risk. Kondo argues that this embodied experience needs to be brought into explicit ethnographic representation.

24. On the nonidentical, imbricated, relationship of indigenous, diasporic, and postcolonial locations, see Clifford (1994).

25. I am, of course, referring to normative patterns and pressures. Much fieldwork has, in fact, been done outside the (metonymic) "village" or "field site." In anthropology, this is permitted, as long as the work is seen to be peripheral to a central site of intensive encounter. In other fieldwork traditions—for example, those of elicitation and transcription in linguistics—hotels and even universities can be primary "field" sites. Such practices have been actively discouraged in anthropology.

26. Thus, many anthropologists were stung—or bemused—by attacks such as Deloria's in *Custer Died for Your Sins* (1969). The predatory visitor he described, little better than a tourist, seemed a caricature. Anthropologists were being hostilely "located," roughly shaken out of a self-confirming persona.

27. Thanks to Teresia Teaiwa. For her own very complex "native" location, see joannemariebarker and Teaiwa (1994).

28. In the short run, notions of "real fieldwork," shaped by canonical exemplars, will continue to relegate emergent practices to what Weston (chapter 9) calls "virtual ethnography," not quite fieldwork. But the enforcing of fieldwork norms is uneven, and to a degree always has been. How hierarchies of practice in a diversified/fragmented discipline are sustained and reformed remains to be seen.

29. I hold to this even in the face of my colleague Chris Connery's *mots* on Paul Theroux: "Travel narrows!"

REFERENCES

Abu-Lughod, Lila
1991   Writing against Culture. In Recapturing Anthropology: Working in the Present. Richard G. Fox, ed. Pp. 137–162. Santa Fe, N.Mex.: School of American Research Press.
———, ed.
1993   Screening Politics in a World of Nations. Public Culture 5 (spring): 465–604.
Adas, Michael
1989   Machines as the Measure of Man: Science, Technology, and Ideologies of Western Dominance. Ithaca, N.Y.: Cornell University Press.
Adler, Judith
1988   (On youth travel). Annals of Tourism Research.
African Studies Newsletter
1969   2(6–7): (November–December). Entire issue.
Agar, Michael
1985   Independents Declared: The Dilemma of Independent Trucking. Washington D.C.: Smithsonian Institution Press.
Agee, James, and Walker Evans
1976[1939] Let Us Now Praise Famous Men. New York: Ballantine.
Akmajian, Adrian, et al.
1993   Linguistics: An Introduction to Language and Communication. Cambridge, Mass.: MIT Press.
Alarcón, Norma
1990   The Theoretical Subject(s) of This Bridge Called My Back and Anglo-American Feminism. In Making Face, Making Soul: Haciendo Caras. Gloria Anzaldúa, ed. Pp. 356–369. San Francisco: Spinsters /Aunt Lute.
Allen, R.
1995   Mali Adventure, from Timbuctu to Dogon Country. The New York Times Magazine, part 2 (17 September): 24–27, 36, 38.

Alvarez, Robert
 1994   Un Chilero en la Academia: Sifting, Shifting, and the Recruitment
             of Minorities in Anthropology. In Race. Steven Gregory and Roger
             Sanjek, eds. Pp. 257–269. New Brunswick, N.J.: Rutgers University
             Press.
American Anthropological Association
 1994   AAA Guide to Departments of Anthropology, 1994–1995. Arlington,
             Va.: American Anthropological Association.
 1995   AAA Guide to Departments of Anthropology, 1995–1996. Arlington,
             Va.: American Anthropological Association.
Anderson, Benedict
 1983   Imagined Communities: Reflections on the Origin and Spread of Na-
             tionalism. London: Verso.
Ang, Ien
 1985[1982] Watching Dallas: Soap Opera and the Melodramatic Imagination.
             Della Couling, trans. New York: Routledge.
Anzaldúa, Gloria
 1987   Borderlands/La Frontera: The New Mestiza. San Francisco: Spin-
             sters/Aunt Lute.
Appadurai, Arjun
 1988a   Introduction: Place and Voice in Anthropological Theory. Cultural
             Anthropology 3(1): 1, 16–20.
 1988b   Putting Hierarchy in Its Place. Cultural Anthropology 3(1): 36–49.
 1991   Global Ethnoscapes: Notes and Queries for a Transnational Anthro-
             pology. In Recapturing Anthropology: Working in the Present.
             Richard G. Fox, ed. Pp. 191–210. Santa Fe, N. Mex.: School of Amer-
             ican Research Press.
Apter, Andrew
 1991   Herskovits's Heritage: Rethinking Syncretism in the African Diaspora.
             Diaspora 1(3): 235–260.
Asad, Talal
 1982   A Comment on the Idea of a Non-Western Anthropology. In Indige-
             nous Anthropology in Non-Western Countries. Hussein Fahim, ed.
             Pp. 284–288. Durham, N.C.: Carolina Academic Press.
 1986   The Concept of Cultural Translation in British Social Anthropology.
             In Writing Culture: The Poetics and Politics of Ethnography. James
             Clifford and George Marcus, eds. Pp. 141–164. Berkeley: University
             of California Press.
 1993   Genealogies of Religion: Discipline and Reasons of Power in Chris-
             tianity and Islam. Baltimore: John Hopkins University Press.

 1994   Ethnographic Representation, Statistics, and Modern Power. Social
             Research 61(1): 55–88.
———, ed.
 1973   Anthropology and the Colonial Encounter. Atlantic Highlands, N.J.:
             Humanities Press.

ASA News
  1995   ASA Board of Directors Responds to Phillip Curtain Essay. (April–
              June): 10.
Ashcroft, Bill, Gareth Griffiths, and Helen Tiffin
  1989   The Empire Writes Back: Theory and Practice in Post-Colonial Lit-
              eratures. New York: Routledge.
Awkward, Michael
  1995   Negotiating Difference: Race, Gender, and the Politics of Position-
              ality. Chicago: University of Chicago Press.
Bammer, Angelika, ed.
  1992   The Question of "Home." New Formations 17.
Barton, Roy
  1919   Ifugao Law. University of California Publications in American Ar-
              chaeology and Ethnology 15(1): 1–186.
Bates, Robert H., V. Y. Mudimbe, and Jean O'Barr, eds.
  1993   Africa and the Disciplines. Chicago: University of Chicago Press.
Becker, Howard
  1986   Doing Things Together. Evanston, Ill.: Northwestern University
              Press.
Behar, Ruth
  1993   Translated Woman: Crossing the Border with Esperanza's Story.
              Boston: Beacon Press.
Behar, Ruth, and Deborah A. Gordon, eds.
  1995   Women Writing Culture. Berkeley: University of California Press.
Behdad, Ali
  1994   Belated Travelers: Orientalism in the Age of Colonial Dissolution.
              Durham N.C.: Duke University Press.
Bell, Diane, Pat Caplan, and Wazir Jahan Karim, eds.
  1993   Gendered Fields: Women, Men, and Ethnography. New York: Rout-
              ledge.
Bellah, Robert, Richard Madsen, William M. Sullivan, Ann Swidler, and Steven M.
              Tipton, eds.
  1985   Habits of the Heart: Individualism and Commitment in American
              Life. New York: Harper and Row.
Benmayor, Rina
  1991   Testimony, Action Research, and Empowerment: Puerto Rican
              Women and Popular Education. In Women's Words: The Feminist
              Practice of Oral History. Sherna Berger Gluck and Daphne Patai, eds.
              New York: Routledge.
Bennoune, Mafhoud
  1985   What Does It Mean to Be a Third World Anthropologist? Dialectical
              Anthropology 9(1–4): 357–364.
Berlant, Lauren, and Elizabeth Freeman
  1993   Queer Nationality. In Fear of a Queer Planet: Queer Politics and So-
              cial Theory. Michael Warner, ed. Pp. 193–229. Minneapolis: Univer-
              sity of Minnesota Press.

Bhabha, Homi K.
  1990   DissemiNation: Time, Narrative, and the Margins of the Modern Na-
              tion. In Nation and Narration. Homi K. Bhabha, ed. Pp. 291–322. New
              York: Routledge.

  1994a   Of Mimicry and Man. In The Location of Culture. Pp. 85–92. New
              York: Routledge.
  1994b   The Other Question: Difference, Discrimination, and the Discourse
              of Colonialism. In The Location of Culture. Pp. 66–84. New York:
              Routledge.
Birke, Linda
  1986   Women, Feminism, and Biology: The Feminist Challenge. New York:
              Methuen.
Bohannan, Paul
  1957   Justice and Judgment among the Tiv. London: Oxford University Press.
  1964   Anthropology and the Law. In Horizons of Anthropology. Sol Tax,
              ed. Pp. 191–199. Chicago: Aldine.
Boon, James
  1977   The Anthropological Romance of Bali, 1597–1972: Dynamic Per-
              spectives in Marriage and Caste, Politics and Religion. New York: Cam-
              bridge University Press.

  1992   Cosmopolitan Moments: Echoey Confessions of an Ethnographer
              Tourist. In Crossing Cultures: Essays in the Displacement of Western
              Civilization. Daniel Segal, ed. Pp. 226–253. Tucson and London: Uni-
              versity of Arizona Press.
Borgmann, Albert
  1992   Crossing the Postmodern Divide. Chicago: University of Chicago
              Press.
Bourdieu, Pierre
  1977   Outline of a Theory of Practice. Cambridge, England: Cambridge
              University Press.

  1984   Distinction: A Social Critique of the Judgment of Taste. Cambridge,
              Mass.: Harvard University Press.
Bourgois, Philippe
  1991   Confronting the Ethics of Ethnography: Lessons from Fieldwork in
              Central America. In Decolonizing Anthropology: Moving Further To-
              ward an Anthropology for Liberation. Faye V. Harrison, ed. Pp.
              110–126. Washington, D.C.: Association of Black Anthropologists,
              American Anthropological Association.
Bowen, Elenore Smith (pseud. of Laura Bohannan)
  1954   Return to Laughter. New York: Harper and Row.
Bradburd, Daniel
  1997   Being There: Fieldwork and Understanding. Washington, D.C.: The
              Smithsonian Institution Press.
Bradford, P. V., and H. Blume
  1992   Ota Benga: The Pygmy in the Zoo. New York: St. Martin's Press.

Braudel, Fernand
1972[1949] The Mediterranean. 2 vols. New York: Harper Colophon.
Brenneis, Donald
  1994   Discourse and Discipline at the National Research Council: A Bu-
              reaucratic Bildungsroman. Cultural Anthropology 9(1) 23–36.
Briggs, Jean
  1970   Never in Anger. Cambridge, Mass.: Harvard University Press.
British Association for the Advancement of Science (BAAS)
  1879   Report of the Forty-Ninth Meeting. London: John Murray.
Brody, J. E.
  1996   Gombe Chimps Archived in Video and CD-Rom. New York Times,
              Science Times (20 February): C1, C8.
Brown, Karen McCarthy
  1991   Mama Lola: A Vodou Priestess in Brooklyn. Berkeley: University of
              California Press.
Browne, J.
  1983   The Secular Ark. New Haven: Yale University Press.
Browne, M. W.
  1994   Clash on Fossil Sales Shadows a Trade Fair. New York Times (15 Feb-
              ruary): B5, B10.
Bukatman, Scott
  1993   Terminal Identity: The Virtual Subject in Postmodern Science Fic-
              tion. Durham, N.C.: Duke University Press.
Bunzl, M.
  Forth–   Franz Boas and the Humboldtian Tradition. In George W. Stocking,
  coming   ed. History of Anthropology 8. Madison: University of Wisconsin
              Press.
Burawoy, Michael, et al.
  1991   Ethnography Unbound: Power and Resistance in the Modern Me-
              tropolis. Berkeley: University of California Press.
Burgos-Debray, Elisabeth, ed.
  1984   I . . . Rigoberta Menchu: An Indian Woman in Guatemala. London:
              Verso.
Burton, Michael L., Carmella C. Moore, John W. M. Whiting, and A. Kimball Romney
  1996   Regions Based on Social Structure. Current Anthropology 37(1):
              87–123.
Bustos-Aguilar, Pedro
  1995   Mister Don't Touch the Banana: Notes on the Popularity of the Eth-
              nosexed Body South of the Border. Critique of Anthropology 15(2):
              149–170.
Buzzard, James
  1993   The Beaten Track: European Tourism, Literature, and the Ways to
              Culture, 1800–1918. Oxford: Oxford University Press.
Camerini, J. R.
  1996   Wallace in the Field. In Science in the Field. H. Kuklick and R.
              Kohler, eds. Osiris 11: 44–65.

Campbell, J. K.
    1964   Honour, Family, and Patronage. Oxford: Oxford University Press.
Cesara, Manda
    1982   Reflections of a Woman Anthropologist: No Hiding Place. New York: Academic Press.
Chabram, Angie
    1990   Chicana/o Studies as Oppositional Ethnography. Cultural Studies 4(3): 228–247.
Chakrabarty, Dipesh
    1992   Postcoloniality and the Artifice of History: Who Speaks for Indian Pasts? Representations (37): 1–26.
Christians, Clifford, John Ferre, and Mark Fackler
    1993   Good News: Social Ethics and the Press. New York: Oxford University Press.
Clifford, James
    1988   The Predicament of Culture: Twentieth-Century Ethnography, Literature, and Art. Cambridge, Mass.: Harvard University Press.
    1990   Notes on (Field) Notes. In Fieldnotes: The Makings of Anthropology. Roger Sanjek, ed. Pp. 47–69. Ithaca, N.Y.: Cornell University Press.
    1992   Traveling Cultures. In Cultural Studies. Lawrence Grossberg, Cary Nelson, and Paula A. Treichler, eds. Pp. 96–112. New York: Routledge.
    1994   Diasporas. Cultural Anthropology 9(3): 302–338.
Clifford, James, and George Marcus, eds.
    1986   Writing Culture: The Poetics and Politics of Ethnography. Berkeley: University of California Press.
Coetzee, John M.
    1985   Anthropology and the Hottentots. Semiotica 54(1–2): 87–95.
Cohn, Bernard
    1987[1962] An Anthropologist among the Historians. In An Anthropologist among the Historians and Other Essays. Pp. 1–17. Oxford: Oxford University Press.
Cole, Sally
    1995   Ruth Landes and the Early Anthropology of Race and Gender. In Women Writing Culture. Ruth Behar and Deborah A. Gordon, eds. Pp. 166–185. Berkeley: University of California Press.
Collins, Patricia Hill
    1990   Black Feminist Thought: Knowledge, Consciousness, and the Politics of Empowerment. New York: Routledge.
Comaroff, Jean, and John Comaroff
    1992a   Ethnography and the Historical Imagination. Boulder, Colo.: Westview Press.
    1992b   Ethnography and the Historical Imagination. In Ethnography and the Historical Imagination. Pp. 3–48. Boulder, Colo.: Westview Press.
    1992c   Preface. In Ethnography and the Historical Imagination. Boulder, Colo.: Westview Press.

Comaroff, John L., and Simon Roberts
  1981   Rules and Processes. Chicago: University of Chicago Press.
Conrad, Joseph
  1902   Heart of Darkness. Cambridge, Mass.: R. Bentley.
Coombe, Rosemary
  1993   The Properties of Culture and the Politics of Possessing Identity: Na-
              tive Claims in the Cultural Appropriation Controversy. Canadian Jour-
              nal of Law and Jurisprudence 6(2): 249–285.
Coombes, A. E.
  1994   Reinventing Africa. New Haven: Yale University Press.
Coronil, Fernando
  1995   Introduction to the Duke University Press Edition. In Cuban Coun-
              terpoint: Tobacco and Sugar, by Fernando Ortiz. Durham, N.C.: Duke
              University Press.
Correa, Mariza
  1991   Reports: An Interview with Roberto Cardoso de Oliveira. Current An-
              thropology 32 (June): 335–343.
Crapanzano, Vincent
  1977   The Writing of Ethnography. Dialectical Anthropology 2(1): 69–73.
  1980   Tuhami: Portrait of a Moroccan. Chicago: University of Chicago
              Press.
Crenshaw, Kimberlé
  1995   Mapping the Margins: Intersectionality, Identity Politics, and Violence
              against Women of Color. In After Identity: A Reader in Law and Cul-
              ture. Dan Danielsen and Karen Engle, eds. Pp. 332–354. New York:
              Routledge.
Crick, Malcolm
  1985   Tracing the Anthropological Self: Quizzical Reflections on Field
              Work, Tourism, and the Ludic. Social Analysis 17 (August): 71–92.
Culf, Andrew
  1996   Global Rush to be First with the News. Manchester Guardian Weekly
              (16 June): 23.
Curtin, Philip
  1995   Ghettoizing African History. Chronicle of Higher Education (3
              March).
Dalby, Liza
  1983   Geisha. Berkeley: University of California Press.
D'Amico-Samuels, Deborah
  1991   Undoing Fieldwork: Personal, Political, Theoretical and Method-
              ological Implications. In Decolonizing Anthropology: Moving Further
              toward an Anthropology for Liberation. Faye V. Harrison, ed. Pp.
              68–85. Washington, D.C.: Association of Black Anthropologists,
              American Anthropological Association.
D'Andrade, Roy
  1995   Moral Models in Anthropology. Current Anthropology 36(3): 399–
              408.

D'Emilio, John
    1992   Not a Simple Matter: Gay History and Gay Historians. In Making Trou-
                ble: Essays on Gay History, Politics, and the University. New York: Rout-
                ledge.
de Certeau, Michel
    1984   The Practice of Everyday Life. Berkeley: University of California Press.
de Lima, Roberto Kant
    1992   The Anthropology of the Academy: When We Are the Indians. Knowl-
                edge and Society: The Anthropology of Science and Technology (9):
                191–222.
Defert, Daniel
    1984   Un genre ethnographique profane au XVIe siècle: Les livres d'habits
                (Essai d'ethno-iconographie). In Histoires de l'anthropologie (XVIe–
                XIXe siècles). Britta Rupp-Eisenreich, ed. Pp. 25–42. Paris: Klinck-
                sieck.
Deleuze, Gilles
    1993   Rhizome versus Trees. In The Deleuze Reader. C. V. Boundas, ed. Pp.
                27–36. Minneapolis: University of Minnesota Press.
Deloria, Vine, Jr.
    1969   Custer Died for Your Sins. New York: Macmillan.
Des Chene, Mary
    1991   Relics of Empire: A Cultural History of the Gurkhas, 1815–1987. Ph.D.
                diss., Stanford University.
    1996   Ethnography in the *Janajati-Yug:* Lessons from Reading *Rodhi* and other
                Tamu Writings. Studies in Nepali History and Society 1(1): 97–161.
Diawara, Manthia
    1993   Black Studies, Cultural Studies, Performative Acts. In Race, Identity,
                and Representation in Education. Cameron McCarthy and Warren
                Crichlow, eds. Pp. 262–267. New York: Routledge.
Dickey, Sara
    1993   Cinema and the Urban Poor in South India. Cambridge, England:
                Cambridge University Press.
Dike, K. Onwuka
    1963   In Memoriam: Melville Jean Herskovits. African Studies Bulletin
                6(1): 1–3.
Distant, W. L.
    1912   Preface. The Zoologist, 4th ser., 16: iii–iv.
Dominguez, Virginia R.
    1989   People as Subject, People as Object. Madison: University of Wiscon-
                sin Press.
Dorst, John
    1987   Rereading Mules and Men: Toward the Death of the Ethnographer.
                Cultural Anthropology 2(3): 305–318.
Drake, St. Clair
    1966   Race Relations in a Time of Rapid Social Change. New York: National
                Federation of Settlements and Neighborhood Centers.
    1980   Anthropology and the Black Experience. Black Scholar 11(7): 2–31.

1987   Black Folk Here and There: An Essay in History and Anthropology.
            Vol. 1. Los Angeles: Center for Afro-American Studies, University of
            California.
1990   Black Folk Here and There: An Essay in History and Anthropology.
            Vol. 2. Los Angeles: Center for Afro-American Studies, University of
            California.
Drake, St. Clair, and Horace R. Cayton
1993[1945] Black Metropolis: A Study of Negro Life in a Northern City. Intro-
            duction by Richard Wright. Foreword by William Julius Wilson.
            Chicago: University of Chicago Press.
Du Bois, W. E. B.
1896   The Suppression of the African Slave Trade to the United States of
            America, 1638–1870. New York: Longmans, Green.
1961[1903] The Souls of Black Folk: Essays and Sketches. New York: Fawcett.
1964[1935] Black Reconstruction in America: An Essay Toward a History of the
            Part Which Black Folk Played in the Attempt to Reconstruct Democ-
            racy in America, 1860–1880. Cleveland, Ohio: Meridian Books.
1967[1899] The Philadelphia Negro: A Social Study: New York: Schocken.
1970[1915] The Negro. New York: Oxford University Press.
1970[1939] Black Folk Then and Now: An Essay in the History and Sociology of
            the Negro Race. New York: Octagon.
Dubois, Laurent
1995   "Man's Darkest Hours": Maleness, Travel, and Anthropology. In
            Women Writing Culture. Ruth Behar and Deborah A. Gordon, eds.
            Pp. 306–321. Berkeley: University of California Press.
Duchet, Michèle
1984   Le partage des savoirs: Discours historique et discours ethnologique.
            Paris: Editions La Découverte.
Duggan, Lisa
1995   The Discipline Problem: Queer Theory Meets Lesbian and Gay His-
            tory. GLQ: A Journal of Lesbian and Gay Studies 2(3): 179–191.
Dumont, Jean-Paul
1978   The Headman and I. Austin: University of Texas Press.
Ebron, Paulla
1994   Subjects in Difference: When And When We Enter. Paper presented
            at the conference, Anthropology and "the Field," Stanford Univer-
            sity and University of California, Santa Cruz, February.
Forth-   Traffic in Men. In Cultural Encounters: Gender at the Intersection
coming   of the Local and the Global in Africa. Maria Grosz-Ngate and Omari
            Kokoli, eds. London: Routledge.
Edwards, David
1994   Afghanistan, Ethnography, and the New World Order. Cultural An-
            thropology 9(3): 345–360.
Eisenberg, David M., et al.
1993   Unconventional Medicine in the United States: Prevalence, Costs,
            and Patterns of Use. The New England Journal of Medicine 328:
            246–252.

Enslin, Elizabeth
    1994   Beyond Writing: Feminist Practice and the Limitations of Ethnography. Cultural Anthropology 9(4): 537–568.

Epstein, A. L., ed.
    1979   The Craft of Social Anthropology. Oxford: Pergamon Press.

Escobar, Arturo
    1994   Encountering Development: The Making and Unmaking of the Third World. Princeton: Princeton University Press.

Evans-Pritchard, E. E.
    1940   The Nuer: A Description of the Modes of Livelihood and Political Institutions of a Nilotic People. Oxford: Clarendon Press.
    1954   The Sanusi of Cyrenaica. Oxford: Clarendon Press.

Fabian, Johannes
    1983   Time and the Other: How Anthropology Makes Its Object. New York: Columbia University Press.

Fahim, Hussein, ed.
    1982   Indigenous Anthropology in Non-Western Countries. Durham, N.C.: Carolina Academic Press.

Fardon, Richard, ed.
    1990   Localizing Strategies: The Regionalization of Ethnographic Accounts. Washington, D.C.: Smithsonian Institution Press.

Ferguson, James
    Forth-   Anthropology and Its Evil Twin: "Development" in the Constitution
    coming   of a Discipline. In Development Knowledge and the Social Sciences. Frederick Cooper and Randall Packard, eds. Berkeley: University of California Press.

Finn, F.
    1916   Preface. The Zoologist, 4th ser., 20: iii.

Finney, Ben
    1994   Voyage of Rediscovery: A Cultural Odyssey through Polynesia. Berkeley: University of California Press.

Foster, George, et al., eds.
    1979   Long-Term Field Research in Social Anthropology. New York: Academic Press.

Fox, Richard G.
    1972   Rationale and Romance in Urban Anthropology. Urban Anthropology 1: 205–233.
    1991a   For a Nearly New Culture History. In Recapturing Anthropology: Working in the Present. Richard G. Fox, ed. Pp. 93–114. Santa Fe, N.Mex.: School of American Research Press.
    1991b   Introduction: Working in the Present. In Recapturing Anthropology: Working in the Present. Richard G. Fox, ed. Pp. 1–16. Santa Fe, N.Mex.: School of American Research Press.

———, ed.
    1991   Recapturing Anthropology: Working in the Present. Santa Fe, N.Mex.: School of American Research Press.

Frankenberg, Ruth
  1993a   But How Did You Know They Were Telling You the Truth?
          Reflections on Fieldwork among the Whitefolk. Paper presented to
          the Anthropology and "the Field" panel at the annual American An-
          thropological Association meeting, Washington, D.C.
  1993b   White Women, Race Matters: The Social Construction of Whiteness.
          Minneapolis: University of Minnesota Press.
Fraser, Nancy, and Linda Gordon
  1994   A Genealogy of Dependency: Tracing a Keyword of the U.S. Welfare
          State. In Signs 19(3): 309–336.
Frazer, J. G.
  1932   Obituary. Canon John Roscoe. Nature 130: 917–919.
Fustel de Coulanges, N. D.
  1864   The Ancient City. New York: Doubleday.
Gallie, W. R.
  1964   Philosophy and the Historical Understanding. London: Chatto and
          Windus.
Gans, Herbert
  1980   Deciding What's News. New York: Vintage.
Garson, J. G., and C. H. Read, eds.
  1892   Notes and Queries on Anthropology. London: The Anthropological
          Institute.
Gates, Henry Louis, Jr., ed.
  1985   "Race," Writing, and Difference. Chicago: University of Chicago Press.
Geertz, Clifford
  1973a   The Interpretation of Cultures: Selected Essays. New York: Basic Books.
  1973b   Thick Description: Toward an Interpretive Theory of Culture. In The
          Interpretation of Cultures: Selected Essays. Pp. 3–30. New York: Ba-
          sic Books.
  1988   Works and Lives: The Anthropologist as Author. Stanford, Calif.: Stan-
          ford University Press.
  1990   History and Anthropology. New Literary History 21(2): 321–335.
  1995   After the Fact: Two Countries, Four Decades, One Anthropologist.
          Cambridge, Mass.: Harvard University Press.
Ghosh, Amitav
  1992   In an Antique Land. New York: Knopf.
  1994   The Global Reservation: Notes toward an Ethnography of Interna-
          tional Peacekeeping. Cultural Anthropology 9(3): 412–422.
Gilbert, S.
  1988   Cellular Politics: Just, Goldschmidt, Waddington, and the Attempt
          to Reconcile Embryology and Genetics. In The American Develop-
          ment of Biology. R. Rainger, K. R. Bensen, and J. Maienschein, eds.
          Pp. 307–351. Philadelphia: University of Pennsylvania Press.
Gilmore, David
  1985   Introduction. In Sex and Gender in Southern Europe. D. Gilmore
          and M. A. Gwynne, eds. Special issue of Anthropology 9(1–2): (May–

Gilmore, David (*continued*)
        December).
Gilroy, Paul
    1987   There Ain't No Black in the Union Jack: The Cultural Politics of Race
                and Nation. London: Hutchinson.
    1990   Nationalism, History, and Ethnic Absolutism. History Workshop Jour-
                nal 30: 114–120.
    1993   The Black Atlantic: Modernity and Double Consciousness. Cam-
                bridge, Mass.: Harvard University Press.
Gilsenan, Michael
    1991   Very Like a Camel: The Appearance of an Anthropologist's Middle
                East. In Localizing Strategies: The Regionalization of Ethnographic
                Accounts. Richard Fardon, ed. Pp. 222–239. Washington, D.C.: Smith-
                sonian Institution Press.
Ginzburg, Carlo
    1992   Clues, Myths, and the Historical Method. Baltimore: Johns Hopkins
                University Press.
Gitlin, Todd
    1980   The Whole World Is Watching: Mass Media in the Making and the
                Unmaking of the New Left. Berkeley: University of California Press.
Gluck, Sherna Berger, and Daphne Patai, eds.
    1991   Women's Words: The Feminist Practice of Oral History. New York:
                Routledge.
Gluckman, Max
    1955   The Judicial Process among the Barotse of Northern Rhodesia. Man-
                chester, England: Manchester University Press.
Goetzman, W. H.
    1967   Exploration and Empire. New York: Knopf.
Goldberger, Marvin L., Brendan A. Maher, and Pamela Ebert Flattau, eds.
    1995   Research Doctorate Programs in the United States: Continuity and
                Change. Washington, D.C.: National Academy Press.
Golde, Peggy, ed.
    1986   Women in the Field: Anthropological Experiences. Second Edition.
                Berkeley: University of California Press.
Goldschmidt, Walter R.
    1947   As You Sow. New York: Harcourt, Brace.
Gordon, Deborah A.
    1990   The Politics of Ethnographic Authority: Race and Writing in the
                Ethnography of Margaret Mead and Zora Neale Hurston. In Mod-
                ernist Anthropology. Marc Manganaro, ed. Pp. 145–162. Princeton:
                Princeton University Press.
    1993   Worlds of Consequence: Feminist Ethnography as Social Action. Cri-
                tique of Anthropology 13(4): 429–443. Special issue on Women Writ-
                ing Culture. Ruth Behar, ed.
Gordon, Edmund T.
    1991   Anthropology and Liberation. In Decolonizing Anthropology: Mov-
                ing Further toward an Anthropology for Liberation. Faye V. Harri-

son, ed. Pp. 149–167. Washington, D.C.: Association of Black Anthropologists, American Anthropological Association.

Gordon, Linda
1990   Woman's Body, Woman's Right. New York: Penguin.
1994a   Pitied but Not Entitled: Single Mothers and the History of Welfare, 1890–1935. New York: Free Press.
1994b   A Right to Live. Review of Brutal Need: Lawyers and the Welfare Rights Movement, 1960–1973, by Martha F. Davis. The Nation 258(9): 308–311 (March 7).

Gough, Kathleen
1967   Anthropology: Child of Imperialism. Monthly Review 19(11): 12–27.
1968   New Proposals for Anthropologists. Current Anthropology 9: 403–407.

Greenberg, Joseph H.
1963   In Memoriam: Melville Jean Herskovits. African Studies Bulletin 6(1): 3.

Greenhouse, Carol J.
1985   Anthropology at Home: Whose Home? Human Organization 44(3): 261–264.

Grimshaw, Anna, and Keith Hart
1991   C. L. R. James and "The Struggle for Happiness." Critique of Anthropology 11(2): 195–203.

Grove, R.
1993   Conserving Eden: The (European) East India Companies and their Environmental Policies on St. Helena, Mauritius and in Western India, 1660 to 1854. Comparative Studies in Society and History 35(2): 318–351.

Gulliver, Philip
1963   Social Control in an African Society. Boston: Boston University Press.

Gunder Frank, André
1967   Capitalism and Underdevelopment in Latin America. New York: Monthly Review Press.

Gupta, Akhil, and James Ferguson
1992   Beyond "Culture": Space, Identity, and the Politics of Difference. Cultural Anthropology 7(1): 6–23.
1994   Anthropology and the Field: Boundaries, Areas, and Grounds in the Constitution of a Discipline. Paper presented at the conference, Anthropology and "The Field," Stanford University and University of California, Santa Cruz, February.
1997   Culture, Power, Place: Ethnography at the End of an Era. In Culture, Power, Place: Explorations in Critical Anthropology. Akhil Gupta and James Ferguson, eds. Durham, N.C.: Duke University Press.
————, eds.
1997   Culture, Power, Place: Explorations in Critical Anthropology. Durham, N.C.: Duke University Press.

Gutmann, B.
1926   Das Recht der Dschagga. Munich: Beck

Guyer, Jane I.
    1996   African Studies in the United States: A Perspective. Atlanta, Ga.:
                African Association Studies Press.
Haddon, A. C.
    1890   Manners and Customs of the Torres Straits Islanders. Nature 42:
                637–642.
    1893   The Secular and Ceremonial Dances of Torres Straits. Archives In-
                ternationales d'Ethnographie 6: 131–162.
    1900   Studies in Anthropogeography of British New Guinea. The Geo-
                graphical Journal 16: 265–291, 414–441.
    1905   Presidential Address to Section H of the British Association for the
                Advancement of Science. In Report of the Seventy-Fifth Meeting. Pp.
                511–527. London: John Murray.
————, ed.
    1901, 1903 Reports of the Cambridge Anthropological Expedition to Torres
                Straits. Cambridge, England: Cambridge University Press.
Haila, Yrjö
    1992   Measuring Nature: Quantitative Data in Field Biology. In The Right
                Tools for the Job. A. E. Clarke and J. H. Fujimura, eds. Pp. 233–253.
                Princeton: Princeton University Press.
Hale, Charles R.
    1994   Between the Guevara and the Pachamama: Mestizos, Indians, and
                Identity Politics in the Anti-Quincentenary Campaign. Critique of An-
                thropology 14(1): 9–39.
Hall, Stuart
    1986   On Postmodernism and Articulation: An Interview with Stuart Hall.
                Journal of Communication Inquiry 10(2): 45–60.
Hallin, Daniel
    1986   The "Uncensored War": The Media and Vietnam. Berkeley: Univer-
                sity of California Press.
Halpern, Joel, and E. A. Hammel
    1969   Observations on the Intellectual History of Ethnology and Other So-
                cial Sciences in Yugoslavia. Comparative Studies in Society and His-
                tory 11(1): 17–26.
Handler, Richard
    1985   On Dialogue and Destructive Analysis: Problems in Narrating
                Nationalism and Ethnicity. Journal of Anthropological Research
                41(2): 171–182.
    1993   Anthropology is Dead! Long Live Anthropology! American Anthro-
                pologist 95(4): 991–999.
Handler, Richard, and Daniel Segal
    1990   Jane Austen and the Fiction of Culture. Tucson: University of Arizona
                Press.
Hannerz, Ulf
    1980   Exploring the City: Inquiries toward an Urban Anthropology. New
                York: Columbia University Press.

1986   Theory in Anthropology: Small is Beautiful? The Problem of Complex Cultures. Comparative Studies in Society and History 28(1): 362–367.

1996   Transnational Connections: Culture, People, Places. New York: Routledge.

Haraway, Donna

1988   Situated Knowledges: The Science Question in Feminism and the Privilege of Partial Perspective. Feminist Studies 14(4): 575–599.

1989   Primate Visions: Gender, Race, and Nature in the World of Modern Science. New York: Routledge.

1991   Simians, Cyborgs, and Women: The Reinvention of Nature. New York: Routledge.

1992   The Promises of Monsters: A Regenerative Politics for Inappropriate/d Others. In Cultural Studies. Lawrence Grossberg, Cary Nelson, and Paula A. Treichler, eds. Pp. 295–337. New York: Routledge.

Forth-   A Technoscience Fugue in Two Parts: Mice into Wormholes. In Cyborg
coming   Anthropology. Gary Downey, Joe Dumit, and Sharon Traweek, eds. Santa Fe, N.Mex.: School of American Research.

Harding, Susan

1987   Convicted by the Holy Spirit: The Rhetoric of Fundamental Baptist Conversion. American Ethnologist 14(1): 167–181.

1990   If I Should Die Before I Wake: Jerry Falwell's Pro-Life Gospel. In Uncertain Terms: Renegotiating Gender in American Culture. Faye Ginsburg and Anna Tsing, eds. Pp. 76–97. Boston: Beacon Press.

1993   Born-Again Telescandals. In Culture, Power, History. Nicholas Dirks, Geoffrey Eley, and Sherry Ortner, eds. Pp. 539–556. Princeton: Princeton University Press.

1994   Further Reflections. Cultural Anthropology 9(3): 276–278.

Harlow, Barbara

1987   Resistance Literature. New York: Methuen.

Harrison, Faye V.

1988   Introduction: An African Diaspora Perspective for Urban Anthropology. Urban Anthropology 17(23): 111–141.

1991   Anthropology as an Agent of Transformation: Introductory Comments and Queries. In Decolonizing Anthropology: Moving Further toward an Anthropology for Liberation. Faye V. Harrison, ed. Pp. 1–14. Washington, D.C.: Association of Black Anthropologists, American Anthropological Association.

1992   The Du Boisian Legacy in Anthropology. Critique of Anthropology 12(3): 239–260. Special issue on W. E. B. Du Bois and Anthropology. Faye V. Harrison and Donald Nonini, eds.

———, ed.

1991   Decolonizing Anthropology: Moving Further toward an Anthropology for Liberation. Washington, D.C.: Association of Black Anthropologists, American Anthropological Association.

Harrison, Faye V., and Donald Nonini, eds.
    1992   Introduction to W. E. B. Du Bois and Anthropology. Critique of An-
                thropology 12(3): 229–237.
Harvey, David
    1989   The Condition of Postmodernity: An Enquiry into the Origins of So-
                cial Change. Oxford: Basil Blackwell.
Haskell, T. L.
    1977   The Emergence of Professional Social Science. Bloomington: Indi-
                ana University Press.
Hastrup, Kirsten, and Peter Elsass
    1990   Anthropological Advocacy: A Contradiction in Terms? Current An-
                thropology 31 (June): 301–311.
Hastrup, Kirsten, and Karen Fog Olwig, eds.
    1996   Siting Culture. London: Routledge.
Hau'ofa, Epeli
    1982   Anthropology at Home: A South Pacific Islands Experience. In In-
                digenous Anthropology in Non-Western Countries. Hussein Fahim,
                ed. Pp. 213–222. Durham, N.C.: Carolina Academic Press.
Hau'ofa, Epeli, et al.
    1993   A New Oceania: Rediscovering Our Sea of Islands. Suva, Fiji: School
                of Social and Economic Development, The University of the South
                Pacific.
Hawking, Stephen
    1988   A Brief History of Time: From the Big Bang to Black Holes. New York:
                Bantam.
Hayles, N. Katherine
    1990   Chaos Bound: Orderly Disorder in Contemporary Literature and Sci-
                ence. Ithaca, N.Y.: Cornell University Press.
Heath, Deborah
    Forth-   Bodies, Antibodies, and Partial Connections. In Cyborg
    coming   Anthropology. Gary Downey, Joe Dumit, and Sharon Traweek, eds.
                Santa Fe, N.Mex.: School of American Research.
Hebdige, Dick
    1993   Going Global: Culture in the Nineties. Multimedia presentation to
                the Department of Anthropology Colloquium Series, University of
                California, Irvine, 16 March.
Heide, Margaret J.
    1995   Television Culture and Women's Lives: Thirtysomething and the Con-
                tradictions of Gender. Philadelphia: University of Pennsylvania Press.
Helms, Mary
    1988   Ulysses' Sail: An Ethnographic Odyssey of Power, Knowledge, and Ge-
                ographical Distance. Princeton: Princeton University Press.
Herman, Edward, and Noam Chomsky
    1988   Manufacturing Consent: The Political Economy of the Mass Media.
                New York: Pantheon Books.
Hernandez, Graciela
    1993   Multiple Mediations in Zora Neale Hurston's Mules and Men. Cri-

tique of Anthropology 13(4): 351–362. Special issue on Women Writing Culture. Ruth Behar, ed.

1995　　Multiple Subjectivities and Strategic Positionality: Zora Neale Hurston's Experimental Ethnographies. In Women Writing Culture. Ruth Behar and Deborah A. Gordon, eds. Pp. 148–165. Berkeley: University of California Press.

Herskovits, M. J.

1930　　The Culture Areas of Africa. Africa 3(1): 59–77.

Herzfeld, Michael

1980　　Honor and Shame: Problems in the Analysis of Moral Systems. Man 15: 339–351.

1987　　Anthropology through the Looking Glass: Critical Ethnography in the Margins of Europe. Cambridge, England: Cambridge University Press.

Hess, David J.

1993　　Science in the New Age: The Paranormal, Its Defenders and Debunkers, and American Culture. Madison: University of Wisconsin Press.

Hevly, B.

1996　　The Heroic Science of Glacier Motion. In Science in the Field. H. Kuklick and R. Kohler, eds. Osiris 11: 66–88.

Hewitt, Nancy A.

1992　　Compounding Differences. Feminist Studies 18(2): 313–326.

Hewitt de Alcantara, Cynthia

1984　　Anthropological Perspectives on Rural Mexico. London: Routledge and Kegan Paul.

Hoebel, E. Adamson

1940　　The Political Organization and Law-ways of the Comanche Indians. Memoir 54. Washington, D.C.: American Anthropological Association.

Hofer, Tamas

1968　　Anthropologists and Native Ethnographers in Central European Villages: Comparative Notes on the Professional Personality of Two Disciplines. Current Anthropology 9(4): 311–315.

Hogbin, Ian

1934　　Law and Order in Polynesia. London: Christophers.

hooks, bell

1984　　Feminist Theory: From Margin to Center. Boston: South End Press.

1990　　Choosing the Margin as a Space of Radical Openness. In Yearning: Race, Gender, and Cultural Politics. Pp. 145–153. Boston: South End Press.

Huizer, Gerri, and Bruce Mannheim (eds.)

1979　　The Politics of Anthropology. The Hague, Netherlands: Mouton.

Hulme, Peter

1986　　Colonial Encounters: Europe and the Native Caribbean, 1492–1797. London: Methuen.

Hurston, Zora Neale

1935　　Mules and Men. Philadelphia: Lippincott.

Hurston, Zora Neale (*continued*)
  1969[1942] Dust Tracks on a Road. New York: Arno Press.
  1978[1937] Their Eyes Were Watching God. Urbana: University of Illinois Press.
Hymes, Dell, ed.
  1972   Reinventing Anthropology. New York: Pantheon Books.
Jakubowska, Longina
  1993   Writing About Eastern Europe. In The Politics of Ethnographic
              Reading and Writing: Confrontations of Western and Indigenous
              Views. Henk Driessen, ed. Pp. 143–159. Fort Lauderdale, Fla.: Verlag
              Breitenback.
James, Cyril Lionel Robert
  1963[1938] The Black Jacobins: Toussaint L'Ouverture and the San Domingo Rev-
              olution. 2nd ed. New York: Vintage Books.
  1969   A History of Pan-African Revolt. 2nd ed. Washington, D.C.: Drum and
              Spear Press.
  1983[1963] Beyond a Boundary. New York: Pantheon Books.
Jameson, Fredric
  1991   Postmodernism, or, The Cultural Logic of Late Capitalism. Durham,
              N.C.: Duke University Press.
Jencks, Christopher
  1994   The Homeless. Cambridge, Mass.: Harvard University Press.
joannemariebarker, and Teresia Teaiwa
  1994   Native InFormation. Inscriptions 7: 16–41.
John, Mary
  1989   Postcolonial Feminists in the Western Intellectual Field: Anthropol-
              ogists and Native Informants. In Traveling Theorists, Traveling
              Theories: Inscriptions 5: 49–74. James Clifford and Vivek Dharesh-
              war, eds. Santa Cruz, Calif.: UCSC Center for Cultural Studies.
Jones, Delmos J.
  1970   Toward a Native Anthropology. Human Organization 29: 251–259.
Jones, Lisa
  1994   Bulletproof Diva: Tales of Race, Sex, and Hair. New York: Doubleday.
Jongmans, D. G., and P. C. W. Gutkind
  1967   Anthropologists in the Field. Assen, The Netherlands: Van Gorcum.
Jordan, June
  1985   Report from the Bahamas. In On Call: Political Essays. Pp. 39–49.
              Boston: South End Press.
Kalman, L.
  1986   Legal Realism at Yale, 1927–60. Chapel Hill: University of North Car-
              olina Press.
Kaplan, Caren
  1994   The Politics of Location as Transnational Feminist Practice. In Scat-
              tered Hegemonies: Postmodernity and Transnational Feminist Prac-
              tices. Inderpal Grewal and Caren Kaplan, eds. Pp. 137–151. Min-
              neapolis: University of Minnesota Press.
  1996   Questions of Travel: Postmodern Discourses of Displacement.
              Durham, N.C.: Duke University Press.

Keller, Evelyn Fox
1983   A Feeling for the Organism: The Life and Work of Barbara McClintock. New York: W H Freeman.
Knorr Cetina, Karin
1992   The Couch, the Cathedral, and the Laboratory: On the Relationship between Experiment and Laboratory in Science. In Science as Practice and Culture. A. Pickering, ed. Pp. 113–138. Chicago: University of Chicago Press.
Kondo, Dorinne
1986   Dissolution and Reconstitution of Self. Implications for Anthropological Epistemology. Cultural Anthropology 1(1): 74–88.
1990   Crafting Selves: Power, Gender, and Discourses of Identity in a Japanese Workplace. Chicago: University of Chicago Press.
Kopytoff, Igor, ed.
1987   The African Frontier: The Reproduction of Traditional African Societies. Bloomington: Indiana University Press.
Koven, Seth, and Sonya Michel
1993   Mothers of a New World. New York: Routledge.
Krieger, M.
1992   Doing Physics. Bloomington: Indiana University Press.
Kuhn, Thomas
1970   The Structure of Scientific Revolutions. 2nd ed., enlarged. Chicago: University of Chicago Press.
Kuklick, Henrika
1991   The Savage Within: The Social History of British Anthropology, 1885–1945. Cambridge, England.: Cambridge University Press.

1996   Islands in the Pacific: Darwinian Biogeography and British Anthropology. American Ethnologist 23: 611–638.
Kuper, Adam
1988   The Invention of Primitive Society: Transformations of an Illusion. New York: Routledge.
Kutsche, Paul
1993   One View of Our History from 1984 to 1987. SOLGA Newsletter 15 (Oct.): 2–27.
Lamphere, Louise, ed.
1992   Women, Anthropology, Tourism, and the Southwest. Frontiers 12(3): 5–150.
Landes, Ruth
1994[1947] The City of Women. New York: Macmillan; Reprint with a new introduction by Sally Cole, Albuquerque: University of New Mexico Press.
Larsen, A.
1993   Not Since Noah: The English Scientific Zoologist and the Craft of Collecting, 1800–1840. Ph.D. diss., Princeton University.
1995   Does a Bird in the Hand Equal a Bird in the Book? Paper presented at the annual meeting of the History of Science Society.

Latour, Bruno
　1987　　　Science in Action. Cambridge, Mass.: Harvard University Press.
Lave, Jean, Paul Duguid, Nadine Fernandez, and Eric Axel
　1992　　　Coming of Age in Birmingham. Annual Review of Anthropology 21: 257–282.
Lavie, Smadar, and Ted Swedenburg
　1996　　　Between and Among the Boundaries of Culture: Bridging Text and Lived Experience in the Third Timespace. Cultural Studies 10(1): 154–179.
Leach, Edmund R.
　1954　　　Political Systems of Highland Burma. Cambridge, Mass.: Harvard University Press.
Lefebvre, Henri
　1991　　　The Production of Space. Oxford: Basil Blackwell.
Leiris, Michel
　1934　　　L'Afrique fantôme. Paris: Gallimard.
Lesser, A.
　1968　　　International Encyclopedia of the Social Sciences. Vol. 2. David Sills, ed. S.v. Boaz, Franz. New York: Macmillan and The Free Press.
LeVine, R. A.
　1973　　　Culture, Behavior, and Personality. Chicago: Aldine.
Lévi-Strauss, Claude
　1973　　　Tristes Tropiques. New York: Athenaeum.
　1985　　　The View from Afar. New York: Basic Books.
Lewin, Ellen
　1995　　　Writing Lesbian Ethnography. In Women Writing Culture. Ruth Behar and Deborah A. Gordon, eds. Pp. 322–335. Berkeley: University of California Press.
Limón, José
　1991　　　Representation, Ethnicity, and the Precursory Ethnography: Notes of a Native Anthropologist. In Recapturing Anthropology: Working in the Present. Richard G. Fox, ed. Pp. 115–136. Santa Fe, N.Mex.: School of American Research Press.
　1994　　　Dancing with the Devil: Society and Cultural Poetics in Mexican-American South Texas. Madison: University of Wisconsin Press.
Llewellyn, K., and E. A. Hoebel
　1941　　　The Cheyenne Way. Norman: University of Oklahoma Press.
Löfgren, Orvar
　1995　　　The Nation as Home or Motel? On the Ethnography of Belonging. Presidential address to the Society for the Anthropology of Europe at the annual meeting of the American Anthropological Association, Washington, D.C. November.
Lorde, Audre
　1984　　　Sister Outsider: Essays and Speeches. Freedom, Calif.: Crossing Press.
Lowe, Lisa
　1991　　　Heterogeneity, Hybridity, Multiplicity: Marking Asian American Differences. Diaspora 1(1): 24–44.

Lowie, Robert
    1937   The History of Ethnological Theory. New York: Farrar and Rinehart.
Lubbock, J.
    1871   On the Development of Relationships. Journal of the Anthropological Institute 1: 1–26.
Lugones, Maria
    1994   Purity, Impurity, and Separation. Signs: Journal of Women in Culture and Society 19(2): 458–479.
Lutkehaus, Nancy
    1995   Margaret Mead and the "Rustling-of-the-Wind-in-the-Palm-Trees School" of Ethnographic Writing. In Women Writing Culture. Ruth Behar and Deborah A. Gordon, eds. Pp. 186–206. Berkeley: University of California Press.
Mackay, D.
    1993   The Burden of Terra Australis: Experiences of Real and Imagined Lands. In From Maps to Metaphors. R. Fisher and A. Johnston, eds. Pp. 263–289. Vancouver: University of British Columbia Press.
Madrid, Arturo
    1992   Missing People and Others Joining Together to Expand the Circle In Race, Class, and Gender. Margaret L. Andersen and Patricia Hill Collins, eds. Pp. 6–11. Belmont, Calif.: Wadsworth.
Maine, Sir Henry S.
    1861   Ancient Law. London: John Murray.
Malinowski, Bronislaw
    1926   Crime and Custom in Savage Society. London: Kegan, Paul, Trench, Trubner & Co.
    1935   Coral Gardens and Their Magic. Bloomington: Indiana University Press.
    1961   Argonauts of the Western Pacific. New York: Dutton.
    1967   A Diary in the Strict Sense of the Term. New York: Harcourt, Brace and World.
Malkki, Liisa
    1992   National Geographic: The Rooting of Peoples and the Territorialization of National Identity among Scholars and Refugees. Cultural Anthropology 7(1): 24–44.
    1995a   Purity and Exile: Violence, Memory, and National Cosmology among Hutu Refugees in Tanzania. Chicago: University of Chicago Press.
    1995b   Refugees and Exile: From "Refugee Studies" to the National Order of Things. Annual Review of Anthropology 24: 495–523.
    1996   Speechless Emissaries: Refugees, Humanitarianism, and Dehistoricization. Cultural Anthropology 11(3): 377–404.
Mallabarman, Adwaita
    1993[1956] A River Called Titash. Kalpana Bardhan, trans. Berkeley: University of California Press.
Mankekar, D. R.
    1978   One Way Free Flow: Neo-colonialism via News Media. Delhi: Indian Book Company.

Mankekar, Purnima

1993a   National Texts and Gendered Lives: An Ethnography of Television
Viewers in a North Indian City. American Ethnologist 20(3): 543–563.

1993b   Television Tales and a Woman's Rage: A Nationalist Recasting of Drau-
padi's "Disrobing." Public Culture 5: 469–492.

Marcus, George E.

1986   Contemporary Problems of Ethnography in the Modern World System. In Writing Culture: The Poetics and Politics of Ethnography.
James Clifford and George Marcus, eds. Pp. 165–193. Berkeley: University of California Press.

1995   Ethnography in/of the World System: The Emergence of Multi-sited
Ethnography. Annual Review of Anthropology 24: 95–117.

———, ed.

1993   Rereading Cultural Anthropology. Durham, N.C.: Duke University
Press.

Marcus, George E., and Dick Cushman

1982   Ethnographies as Text. Annual Review of Anthropology 11: 25–69.

Marcus, George E., and Michael M. J. Fischer

1986   Anthropology as Cultural Critique: An Experimental Moment in the
Human Sciences. Chicago: University of Chicago Press.

Markus, Gyorgy

1987   Why Is There No Hermeneutics of Natural Sciences? Some Preliminary Theses. Science in Context 1: 5–51.

Martin, Biddy, and Chandra Talpady Mohanty

1986   Feminist Politics: What's Home Got to Do with It? In Feminist Stud-
ies/Critical Studies. Teresa de Lauretis, ed. Pp. 191–212. Bloomington: Indiana University Press.

Martin, Emily

1994   Flexible Bodies: Tracking Immunity in America from the Days of Polio to the Age of AIDS. Boston: Beacon Press.

1996   Citadels, Rhizomes, and String Figures. In Technoscience and Cyber
Culture. S. Aronowitz, B. Martinsons, and M. Menser, eds. Pp. 97–109.
New York: Routledge.

Mason, B. S.

1994   An Archipelago in the Bay of Bengal. The New York Times (Sunday,
30 October). sec. 5 Travel: 6–7.

McCall, Daniel F.

1967   American Anthropology and Africa. African Studies Bulletin 10(2):
20–34.

McClintock, Anne

1991   "The Very House of Difference": Race, Gender, and the Politics of
South African Women's Narrative in Poppie Nongena. In The Bounds
of Race: Perspectives on Hegemony and Resistance. Dominick La-
Capra, ed. Pp. 196–230. Ithaca, N.Y.: Cornell University Press.

1995   Imperial Leather: Race, Gender, and Sexuality in the Colonial Contest. New York: Routledge.

McCook, S.

1996   "It may be the truth, but it is not evidence": Paul du Chaillu and the
          Construction of Authority in the Nineteenth Century Field Sciences.
          In Science in the Field. H. Kuklick and R. Kohler, eds. Osiris 11:
          177–200.

McGee, W. J.

1897   The Science of Humanity. American Anthropologist 10: 241–272.

Mead, Margaret

1989   Preface. In Patterns of Culture, by Ruth Benedict. Pp. xi–xiv. Boston:
          Houghton Mifflin.

Mehos, D.

n.d.   Nature Displayed: Science and Culture at the Amsterdam Zoo. Ph.D.
          diss., University of Pennsylvania.

Michaels, Eric

1994   Para-ethnography. In Bad Aboriginal Art and Other Essays. Pp.
          165–176. Minneapolis: University of Minnesota Press.

Mills, Sara

1991   Discourses of Difference: An Analysis of Women's Travel Writing and
          Colonialism. London: Routledge.

Mintz, Sidney

1970   Foreword. In Afro-American Anthropology: Contemporary Perspec-
          tives. Norman E. Whitten, Jr., and John F. Szwed, eds. New York: Free
          Press.

1985   Sweetness and Power: The Place of Sugar in Modern History. New
          York: Viking.

Mitchell, Timothy

1990   Everyday Metaphors of Power. Theory and Society 19: 545–577.

Mohanty, Chandra Talpade

1987   Feminist Encounters: Locating the Politics of Experience. Copyright
          1: 30–44.

1991   Introduction: Cartographies of Struggle. In Third World Women and
          the Politics of Feminism. Chandra Talpade Mohanty, Ann Russo, and
          Lourdes Torres, eds. Bloomington: Indiana University Press.

Moore, Henrietta

1988   Feminism and Anthropology. Minneapolis: University of Minnesota
          Press.

1994   A Passion for Difference: Essays in Anthropology and Gender. Bloom-
          ington: Indiana University Press.

Moore, Sally Falk

1975   Epilogue: Uncertainties in Situations, Indeterminacies in Culture. In
          Symbol and Politics in Communal Ideology: Cases and Questions.
          Sally Falk Moore and Barbara Myerhoff, eds. Pp. 210–239. Ithaca, N.Y.:
          Cornell University Press.

1987   Explaining the Present: Theoretical Dilemmas in Processual An-
          thropology. American Ethnologist 14(4): 727–751.

1993a   Changing Perspectives on a Changing Africa: The Work of Anthro

Moore, Sally Falk (*continued*)
        pology. In Africa and the Disciplines. Robert H. Bates, V. Y. Mudimbe, and Jean O'Barr, eds. Pp. 3–57. Chicago: University of Chicago Press.
  1993b   The Ethnography of the Present and the Analysis of Process. In Assessing Cultural Anthropology. Robert Borofsky, ed. Pp. 362–376. New York: McGraw-Hill.

Moore, Sally Falk, and Barbara Myerhoff, eds.
  1975   Symbol and Politics in Communal Ideology: Cases and Questions. Ithaca, N.Y.: Cornell University Press.

Morgan, L. H.
  1963[1877] Ancient Society. Cleveland, Ohio: Meridian Books.

Morley, David
  1980   The "Nationwide" Audience. London: British Film Institute.
  1986   Family Television. London: Comedia / Routledge.

Moulton, J. C.
  1914   Zoological Notes on a Collecting Expedition in Borneo. The Zoologist, 4th ser., 18: 361–374, 714–731.

Mudimbe, V. Y.
  1988   The Invention of Africa: Gnosis, Philosophy, and the Order of Knowledge. Bloomington: Indiana University Press.

Muñoz, José
  1995   The Autoethnographic Performance: Reading Richard Fung's Queer Hybridity. Screen 36(2): 83–99.

Murdock, George P.
  1967   The Ethnographic Atlas: A Summary. Pittsburgh: University of Pittsburgh Press.

Myerhoff, Barbara
  1975   Organization and Ecstasy: Deliberate and Accidental Communitas among Huichol Indians and American Youth. In Symbol and Politics in Communal Ideology: Cases and Questions. Sally Falk Moore and Barbara Myerhoff, eds. Pp. 33–67. Ithaca, N.Y.: Cornell University Press.

Nader, Laura
  1964   Talea and Juquila: A Comparison of Zapotec Social Organization. University of California Publications in American Archaeology and Ethnology 48(3): 195–296.
  1965   Choices in Legal Procedure: Shia Moslem and Mexican Zapotec. American Anthropologist 67(2): 394–399.
  1972   Up the Anthropologist: Perspectives Gained from Studying Up. In Reinventing Anthropology. Dell Hymes, ed. Pp. 284–311. New York: Pantheon Books.
  1978   Preface. In The Disputing Process: Law in Ten Societies. L. Nader and Harry F. Todd, Jr., eds. New York: Columbia University Press.

———, ed.
  1965   The Ethnography of Law. American Anthropologist, part 2, 67(6). Special issue.

1969   Law in Culture and Society. Chicago: Aldine.
Nader, Laura, and Duane Metzger
    1963   Conflict Resolution in Two Mexican Communities. American An-
                thropologist 65: 584–592.
Nader, Laura, Klaus Koch, and Bruce Cox
    1966   The Ethnography of Law: A Bibliographic Survey. Current Anthro-
                pology 7(3): 267–294.
Nader, Laura, and Harry F. Todd, Jr., eds.
    1978   The Disputing Process: Law in Ten Societies. New York: Columbia
                University Press.
Narayan, Kirin
    1989   Storytellers, Saints, and Scoundrels: Folk Narrative in Hindu Religious
                Teaching. Philadelphia: University of Pennsylvania Press.
    1993   How Native is the "Native" Anthropologist? American Anthropolo-
                gist 95(3): 19–34.
Nash, June
    1979   Anthropology of the Multinational Corporation. In The Politics of
                Anthropology: From Colonialism and Sexism: Toward a View from
                Below. Gerrit Huizer and Bruce Mannheim, eds. Pp. 421–446. The
                Hague: Mouton Publishers.
Nelson, Cary
    1995   Lessons from the Job Wars: Late Capitalism Arrives on Campus. So-
                cial Text 13(3): 119–134.
Newton, Esther
    1979   Mother Camp: Female Impersonators in America. Chicago: Univer-
                sity of Chicago Press.
    1993a   Cherry Grove, Fire Island: Sixty Years in America's First Gay and Les-
                bian Town. Boston: Beacon Press.
    1993b   Lesbian and Gay Issues in Anthropology: Some Remarks to the Chairs
                of Anthropology Departments. Paper presented at the annual meet-
                ing of the American Anthropological Association, Washington, D.C.,
                November.
    1993c   My Best Informant's Dress: The Erotic Equation in Fieldwork. Cul-
                tural Anthropology 8(1): 3–23.
Nicholson, Linda J., ed.
    1990   Feminism/Postmodernism. New York: Routledge.
Nordstrom, Carolyn, and Antonius Robben, eds.
    1995   Fieldwork under Fire: Contemporary Studies of Violence and Sur-
                vival. Berkeley: University of California Press.
Novick, P.
    1988   That Noble Dream. New York: Cambridge University Press.
Omi, Michael, and Howard Winant
    1986   Racial Formation in the United States from the 1960s to the 1980s.
                New York: Routledge.
Ong, Aihwa
    1995   Women out of China: Traveling Tales and Traveling Theories in

Ong, Aihwa (*continued*)
>colonial Feminism. In Women Writing Culture. Ruth Behar and Deborah A. Gordon, eds. Pp. 350–372. Berkeley: University of California Press.

Ortiz, Fernando
1995   Cuban Counterpoint: Tobacco and Sugar. Durham, N.C.: Duke University Press.

Ortner, Sherry
1984   Theory in Anthropology since the Sixties. Comparative Studies in Society and History 26(1): 126–166.

Owens, L.
1985   Pure and Sound Government: Laboratories, Gymnasia, and Playing-Fields in Nineteenth-Century America. Isis 76: 129–162.

Pang, A.
1993   The Social Event of the Season: Solar Eclipse Expeditions and Victorian Culture. Isis 84: 252–277.

Paredes, Americo
1958   "With His Pistol in His Hand": A Border Ballad and Its Hero. Austin: University of Texas Press.
1978   On Ethnographic Work Among Minority Groups: A Folklorist's Perspective. In New Directions in Chicano Scholarship. Ricardo Romo and Raymund Paredes, eds. La Jolla, Calif.: Chicano Studies Monograph Series.
1993   Folklore and Culture on the Texas-Mexican Border. 1st ed. Austin: Center for Mexican-American Studies Books.

Passaro, Joanne
1996   The Unequal Homeless: Men on the Streets, Women in their Place. New York: Routledge.

Patel, Geeta
In press   Home, Homo, Hybrid: Gender and Sexuality in South Asia. College Literature.

Patton, Cindy
1992   From Nation to Family: Containing "African AIDS." In Nationalisms and Sexualities. Andrew Parker et al., eds. Pp. 218–234. New York: Routledge.

Pedelty, Mark
1995   War Stories: The Culture of Foreign Correspondents. New York: Routledge.

Pietilä, Veikko
1995   TV-uutisista, hyvää iltaa. Tampere, Finland: Vastapaino.

Piña-Cabral, João de
1989   The Mediterranean as a Category of Comparison: A Critical View. Current Anthropology 30(3): 399–406.

Piore, Michael J., and Charles F. Sabel
1984   The Second Industrial Divide: Possibilities for Prosperity. New York: Basic Books.

Pitt Rivers, Julian
    1961   People of the Sierra. Chicago: University of Chicago Press.
Pletsch, Carl
    1981   The Three Worlds, or the Division of Social Scientific Labor Circa
                1950–1975. Comparative Studies in Society and History 23(4):
                505–590.
Porter, Dennis
    1991   Haunted Journeys: Desire and Transgression in European Travel Writ-
                ing. Princeton: Princeton University Press.
Powdermaker, Hortense
    1950   Hollywood, the Dream Factory. New York: Grosset and Dunlap.
Pratt, Mary Louise
    1986   Fieldwork in Common Places. In Writing Culture: The Poetics and
                Politics of Ethnography. James Clifford and George Marcus, eds. Pp.
                27–50. Berkeley: University of California Press.
    1992   Imperial Eyes: Travel Writing and Transculturation. London: Rout-
                ledge.
Pratt, Minnie Bruce
    1984   Identity: Skin, Blood, Heart. In Yours in Struggle: Three Feminist Per-
                spectives on Anti-Semitism and Racism. Elly Burkin, Minnie Bruce
                Pratt, and Barbara Smith, eds. Pp. 11–63. Brooklyn: Long Haul Press.
    1991   Identity: Skin Blood Heart. In Rebellion: Essays 1980–1991. Ithaca,
                N.Y.: Firebrand Books.
    1995   S/he. Ithaca, N.Y.: Firebrand Books.
Price, Richard, and Sally Price
    1992   Equatoria. New York: Routledge.
Price, Sally
    1989   Primitive Art in Civilized Places. Chicago: University of Chicago
                Press.
Quiggin, A. H.
    1942   Haddon the Head Hunter. Cambridge, England: Cambridge Uni-
                versity Press.
Rabinow, Paul
    1977   Reflections on Fieldwork in Morocco. Berkeley: University of Cali-
                fornia Press.
    1991   For Hire: Resolutely Late Modern. In Recapturing Anthropology:
                Working in the Present. Richard G. Fox, ed. Pp. 59–72. Santa Fe,
                N.Mex.: School of American Research Press.
Radcliffe-Brown, A. R.
    1940   Preface. In African Political Systems. M. Fortes and E. E. Evans-
                Pritchard, eds. Pp. xi–xxiii. New York: Oxford University Press.
Radin, Paul
    1966[1933] The Method and Theory of Ethnology: An Essay in Criticism. New
                York: Basic Books.
    1970[1935] The Italians of San Francisco: Their Adjustment and Acculturation.
                San Francisco: R and E Research Associates.

Raiskin, Judith
    1994   Inverts and Hybrids: Lesbian Rewritings of Sexual and Racial Identities. In The Lesbian Postmodern. Laura Doan, ed. Pp. 156–172. New York: Columbia University Press.

Rapp, Rayna
    1988   Chromosomes and Communication: The Discourse of Genetic Counseling. Medical Anthropology Quarterly 2: 143–157.

Rattray, R. S.
    1929   Ashanti Law and Constitution. Oxford: Clarendon Press.

Reagon, Bernice Johnson
    1983   Coalition Politics: Turning the Century. In Home Girls: A Black Feminist Anthology. Barbara Smith, ed. Pp. 356–368. New York: Kitchen Table Press.

Rheingold, Howard
    1991   Virtual Reality. New York: Summit Books.

Rich, Adrienne
    1986   Notes toward a Politics of Location. In Blood, Bread, and Poetry: Selected Prose, 1979–1985. New York: Norton.

Richards, J. L.
    1986   Projective Geometry and Mathematical Progress in Mid-Victorian Britain. Studies in History and Philosophy of Science 17: 297–325.

Rivers, W. H. R.
    1908   The Influence of Alcohol and Other Drugs on Fatigue. London: Edward Arnold.

————, ed.
    1922   Essays on the Depopulation of Melanesia. Cambridge, England: Cambridge University Press.

Roach, Colleen, ed.
    1993   Communication and Culture in War and Peace. Newbury Park, Calif.: Sage.

Robbins, D.
    1987   Sport, Hegemony, and the Middle Class: The Victorian Mountaineers. Theory, Culture, and Society 4: 579–601.

Román, David
    1993   It's My Party and I'll Die if I Want to: Gay Men, AIDS, and the Circulation of Camp in U.S. Theater. In Camp Grounds: Style and Homosexuality. David Bergman, ed. Pp. 206–233. Amherst: University of Massachusetts Press.

Romilly, H. H.
    1887   The Islands of the New Britain Group. Proceedings of the Royal Geographical Society, n.s., 9: 1–18.

Rosaldo, Renato
    1980   Ilongot Headhunting, 1883–1974: A Study in Society and History. Stanford: Stanford University Press.
    1987   Politics, Patriarchs, and Laughter. Cultural Critique 6: 65–86.
    1988   Ideology, Place, and People Without Culture. Cultural Anthropology 3(1): 77–87.

1989a   Culture and Truth: The Remaking of Social Analysis. Boston: Beacon Press.

1989b   Imperialist Nostalgia. In Culture and Truth: The Remaking of Social Analysis. Pp. 68–87. Boston: Beacon Press.

1990   Response to Geertz. New Literary History 21(2): 337–341.

1993   Cultural Citizenship in San Jose, California. Paper presented at an international colloquium, From Local to Global Culture: Perspectives from Anthropology, at Universidad Autónoma Metropolitana-Itztapalapa, Mexico City.

1994   Cultural Citizenship and Educational Democracy. Cultural Anthropology 9(3): 402–411.

Roseberry, William

1989   Anthropologies and Histories: Essays in Culture, History, and Political Economy. New Brunswick, N.J.: Rutgers University Press.

1996   The Unbearable Lightness of Anthropology. Radical History Review 65: 5–25.

Rosenthal, A. M., and Arthur Gelb

1984   Introduction. In The Sophisticated Traveler: Beloved Cities: Europe. A. M. Rosenthal and Arthur Gelb, eds. New York: Penguin Books.

Ross, Andrew

1992   New Age Technoculture. In Cultural Studies. Lawrence Grossberg, Cary Nelson, and Paula A. Treichler, eds. Pp. 531–548. New York: Routledge.

1993   Uses of Camp. In Camp Grounds: Style and Homosexuality. David Bergman, ed. Pp. 54–77. Amherst: University of Massachusetts Press.

Rouse, Roger

1991   Mexican Migration and the Social Space of Postmodernism. Diaspora 1(1): 8–23.

Rozwadowski, H.

1996   Fathoming the Ocean: Discovery and Exploration of the Deep Sea, 1840–1880. Ph.D. diss., University of Pennsylvania.

Sahlins, Marshall

1976   Culture and Practical Reason. Chicago: University of Chicago Press.

1985   Islands of History. Chicago: University of Chicago Press.

1993   Goodbye to Tristes Tropes: Ethnography in the Context of Modern World History. The Journal of Modern History 65(1): 1–25.

Said, Edward

1979   Orientalism. New York: Vintage.

1981   Covering Islam: How the Media and the Experts Determine How We See the Rest of the World. New York: Pantheon Books.

1989   Representing the Colonized: Anthropology's Interlocutors. Critical Inquiry 15: 205–225.

Salazar, Claudia

1991   A Third World Woman's Text: Between the Politics of Criticism and Cultural Politics. In Women's Words: The Feminist Practice of Oral History. Sherna Berger Gluck and Daphne Patai, eds. Pp. 93–106. New York: Routledge.

Sanders, Rickie
  1993   The Last Decade: A Content Analysis of the African Studies Review,
              1982–91. African Studies Review 36(1): 115–126.
Sanjek, Roger, ed.
  1990   Fieldnotes: The Makings of Anthropology. Ithaca, N.Y.: Cornell Uni-
              versity Press.
Sarris, Greg
  1991   "What I'm Talking about When I'm Talking about My Baskets": Con-
              versations with Mabel McKay. In De/Colonizing the Subject. Sidonie
              Smith and Julia Watson, eds. Pp. 20–33. Minneapolis: University of
              Minnesota Press.
  1994   Mabel McKay: Weaving the Dream. Berkeley: University of California
              Press.
Schapera, Isaac
  1938   A Handbook of Tswana Law and Custom. London: Oxford Univer-
              sity Press.
Scheper-Hughes, Nancy
  1992   Death without Weeping: The Violence of Everyday Life in Brazil.
              Berkeley: University of California Press.
  1995   The Primacy of the Ethical: Propositions for a Militant Anthropol-
              ogy. Current Anthropology 36(3): 409–420.
Schiller, Herbert
  1981   Who Knows? Information in the Age of the Fortune 500. Norwood,
              N.J.: Ablex Publishing.
  1989   Culture, Inc.: The Corporate Takeover of Public Expression. Oxford:
              Oxford University Press.
Schneider, David
  1995   Schneider on Schneider: The Conversion of the Jews and Other An-
              thropological Tales. Durham, N.C.: Duke University Press.
Scott, David
  1989   Locating the Anthropological Subject: Postcolonial Anthropologists
              in Other Places. Inscriptions 5: 75–85
  1991   That Event, This Memory: Notes on the Anthropology of African Di-
              asporas in the New World. Diaspora 1(3): 261–284.
Scott, Joan W.
  1992   "Experience." In Feminists Theorize the Political. Judith Butler and
              Joan W. Scott, eds. Pp. 22–40. New York: Routledge.
  1994   The Evidence of Experience. In Questions of Evidence: Proof, Prac-
              tice, and Persuasion across the Disciplines. James Chandler, Arnold
              Davidson, and Harry Harootunian, eds. Pp. 363–387. Chicago: The
              University of Chicago Press.
Secord, A.
  1994   Science in the Pub: Artisan Botanists in Early Nineteenth-Century
              Lancashire. History of Science 32: 269–315.
Secord, J. A.
  1986   The Geological Survey of Great Britain as a Research School,
              1839–1855. History of Science 24: 223–275.

Seiter, Ellen, Hans Borchers, Gabriele Kreutzner, and Eva-Maria Warth, eds.

1989   Remote Control: Television, Audiences, and Cultural Power. New York: Routledge.

Sereno, Paul C.

1995   Dinosaurs and Drifting Continents. Natural History 104(1): 40–47.

Shapin, S.

1984   Pump and Circumstance: Robert Boyle's Literary Technology. Social Studies of Science 14: 481–520.

Shortland, M.

1994   Darkness Visible: Underground Culture in the Golden Age of Geology. History of Science 32: 1–61.

Shostak, Marjorie

1981   Nisa: The Life and Words of a !Kung Woman. Cambridge, Mass.: Harvard University Press.

Skinner, Elliott P.

1983   Afro-Americans in Search of Africa: The Scholars' Dilemma. In Transformation and Resiliency in Africa. Pearl T. Robinson and Elliott P. Skinner, eds. Pp. 3–26. Washington D.C.: Howard University Press.

Sklar, Katherine Kish

1993   Historical Foundations of Women's Power. In Mothers of a New World. Seth Koven and Sonya Michel, eds. New York: Routledge.

Skocpol, Theda

1992   Protecting Soldiers and Mothers. Cambridge, England: Cambridge University Press.

Smith, B.

1960   European Vision and the South Pacific, 1768–1850. Oxford: Clarendon Press.

Smith, Chris

1991   From 1960s' Automation to Flexible Specialization: a Déjà Vu of Technological Panaceas. In Farewell to Flexibility? Anna Pollert, ed. Oxford: Basil Blackwell.

Smith, Stephanie A.

1993   Morphing, Materialism, and the Marketing of Xenogenesis. Genders 18: 67–86.

Society for the Anthropology of North America (SANA)

1996   Anthropology Newsletter 37(3): 31–32.

Sommer, Doris

1988   "Not Just a Personal Story": Women's Testimonios and the Plural Self. In Life/Lines: Theorizing Women's Autobiography. Bella Brodzki and Celeste Schenck, eds. Pp. 107–130. Ithaca, N.Y.: Cornell University Press.

Southall, Aidan

1983   The Contribution of Anthropology to African Studies. African Studies Review 26(September–December): 63–76.

Speck, Dara Culhane

1987   An Error in Judgement: The Politics of Medical Care in an Indian/

Speck, Dara Culhane (*continued*)
      White Community. Vancouver, British Columbia: Talonbooks.
Spicer, Edward H.
   1968   International Encyclopedia of the Social Sciences. Vol. 1. S.v. Accul-
           turation. New York: Macmillan and The Free Press.
Spitulnik, Debra
   1993   Anthropology and Mass Media. Annual Review of Anthropology 22:
           293–315.
   1994   Radio Culture in Zambia: Audiences, Public Words, and the Nation-
           State. Ph.D. diss. University of Chicago.
Spivak, Gayatri Chakravorty
   1988   Can the Subaltern Speak? In Marxism and the Interpretation of Cul-
           ture. Cary Nelson and Lawrence Grossberg, eds. Pp. 271–313. Urbana:
           University of Illinois Press.
   1990   The Post-Colonial Critic. New York: Routledge.
Stafford, R. A.
   1984   Geological Surveys, Mineral Discoveries, and British Expansion. Jour-
           nal of Imperial and Commonwealth History 12: 5–32.
Stein, Rebecca
   1995   "In the Pleasure of the Landscape": On Malinowski and Specular Pro-
           duction. Unpublished paper.
Stocking, George W., Jr.
   1968   From Physics to Ethnology. In Race, Culture, and Evolution: Essays
           in the History of Anthropology. Pp. 133–160. New York: The Free
           Press.
   1976   Ideas and Institutions in American Anthropology: Thoughts toward
           a History of the Interwar Years. In Selected Papers from the Ameri-
           can Anthropologist: 1921–1945. Pp. 1–53. Washington, D.C.: Ameri-
           can Anthropological Association.
   1983   The Ethnographer's Magic: Fieldwork in British Anthropology from
           Tylor to Malinowski. In Observers Observed: Essays on Ethnographic
           Fieldwork. George W. Stocking, ed. Pp. 70–120. Madison: University
           of Wisconsin Press.
   1988   Guardians of the Sacred Bundle: The American Anthropological As-
           sociation and the Representation of Holistic Anthropology. In
           Learned Societies and the Evolution of the Disciplines. ACLS Occa-
           sional Paper, no. 5. Pp. 17–25. New York: American Council of
           Learned Societies.
   1992a   The Ethnographer's Magic and Other Essays in the History of An-
           thropology. Madison: University of Wisconsin Press.
   1992b   Philanthropoids and Vanishing Cultures: Rockefeller Funding and
           the End of the Museum Era in Anglo-American Anthropology. In The
           Ethnographer's Magic and Other Essays in the History of Anthro-
           pology. Pp. 178–211. Madison: University of Wisconsin Press.
————, ed.
   1974   The Shaping of American Anthropology, 1883–1911: A Franz Boas
           Reader. New York: Basic Books.

1983   Observers Observed: Essays on Ethnographic Fieldwork. Madison: University of Wisconsin Press.

1991   Colonial Situations: Essays on the Contextualization of Ethnographic Knowledge. Madison: University of Wisconsin Press.

1995   After Tylor. Madison: University of Wisconsin Press.

Tansley, A. G.

1947   The Early History of Modern Plant Ecology in Britain. Journal of Ecology 35: 130–137.

Tate, Greg

1992   Flyboy in the Buttermilk: Essays on Contemporary America: An Eye-Opening Look at Race, Politics, Literature, and Music. New York: Simon and Schuster.

Tax, Sol

1975   In Honour of Sol Tax. Current Anthropology 16(4): 507–540.

Teaiwa, Teresia

1993   Between Traveler and Native: The Traveling Native as Performative/ Informative Figure. Paper presented at the University of California Humanities Research Institute's Minority Discourse 2 Conference. Irvine, Calif., June.

Tedlock, Dennis

1983   The Spoken Word and the Work of Interpretation. Philadelphia: University of Pennsylvania Press.

Third World Network

1993   Modern Science in Crisis: A Third World Response. In The Racial Economy of Science: Toward a Democratic Future. Sandra Harding, ed. Pp. 484–518. Bloomington: Indiana University Press.

Thomas, Nicholas

1989a   The Force of Ethnology: Origins and Significance of the Melanasia/ Polynesia Division. Current Anthropology 30(1): 27–41.

1989b   Out of Time: History and Evolution in Anthropological Discourse. Cambridge, England: Cambridge University Press.

1991   Against Ethnography. Cultural Anthropology 6(3): 306–322.

Tishkov, Valery A.

1992   The Crisis in Soviet Ethnography. Current Anthropology 33(4): 371–394.

Tobey, R. C.

1981   Saving the Prairies. Berkeley: University of California Press.

Tomas, David

1991   Tools of the Trade: The Production of Ethnographic Observations on the Andaman Islands, 1858–1922. In Colonial Situations: Essays on the Contextualization of Ethnographic Knowledge. George W. Stocking, Jr., ed. Pp. 75–108. Madison: University of Wisconsin Press.

Trattner, Walter I.

1979   From Poor Law to Welfare State. New York: Free Press.

Traweek, Sharon

1988   Beamtimes and Lifetimes: The World of High Energy Physics. Cambridge, Mass.: Harvard University Press.

Traweek, Sharon (*continued*)

1992   Border Crossings: Narrative Strategies in Science Studies and among Physicists in Tsukuba Science City, Japan. In Science as Practice and Culture. A. Pickering, ed. Pp. 429–465. Chicago: University of Chicago Press.

1993   An Introduction to Cultural and Social Studies of Sciences and Technologies. Culture, Medicine and Psychiatry 17: 3–25.

Trinh, T. Minh-ha

1989   Woman, Native, Other. Bloomington: Indiana University Press.

Trouillot, Michel-Rolph

1991   Anthropology and the Savage Slot: The Poetics and Politics of Otherness. In Recapturing Anthropology: Working in the Present. Richard G. Fox, ed. Pp. 17–44. Santa Fe, N.Mex.: School of American Research Press.

Tsing, Anna Lowenhaupt

1993   In the Realm of the Diamond Queen: Marginality in an Out-of-the-way Place. Princeton: Princeton University Press.

1994a   Discussant's comments at the conference, Anthropology and "the Field," Stanford University, 18 February.

1994b   From the Margins. Cultural Anthropology 9(3): 279–297.

Tunstall, Elizabeth

1995   "Reach Out and Touch Someone": The Continuum of Intimacy in Phone Sex Culture. Paper presented at the meeting of the American Anthropological Association, Washington, D.C.

Turner, Victor

1957   Schism and Continuity in an African Society: A Study of Ndembu Village Life. Rhodes-Livingstone Institute, Northern Rhodesia. Manchester, England: Manchester University Press.

1969   The Ritual Process: Structure and Anti-Structure. Chicago: Aldine.

Uberoi, J.P.S.

1984   The Other Mind of Europe. Delhi: Oxford University Press.

Urbain, Jean-Didier

1991   L'idiot du voyage: Histoires de touristes. Paris: Plon.

Vail, Leroy, ed.

1989   The Creation of Tribalism in Southern Africa. Berkeley: University of California Press.

Van Maanen, John

1988   Tales of the Field: On Writing Ethnography. Chicago: University of Chicago Press.

Vansina, Jan

1965   Oral Tradition: A Study in Historical Methodology. H. M. Wright, trans. Chicago: Aldine.

1985   Oral Tradition as History. Madison: University of Wisconsin Press.

1994   Living with Africa. Madison: University of Wisconsin Press.

Van Velsen, Jaap

1979   The Extended-Case Method and Situational Analysis. In The Craft of

Social Anthropology. A. L. Epstein, ed. Pp. 129–149. Oxford: Perga-
mon Press.

Vidich, Arthur J.
1966[1933]   Introduction. In The Method and Theory of Ethnology: An Essay in
Criticism, by Paul Radin. New York: Basic Books.

Vincent, Joan
1990   Anthropology and Politics: Visions, Traditions, and Trends. Tucson:
University of Arizona Press.
1991   Engaging Historicism. In Recapturing Anthropology: Working in the
Present. Richard G. Fox, ed. Pp. 45–58. Santa Fe, N.Mex.: School of
American Research Press.

Visweswaran, Kamala
1994   Fictions of Feminist Ethnography. Minneapolis: University of Minnesota Press.

Vizenor, Gerald
1990   Crossbloods: Bone Courts, Bingo, and Other Reports. Minneapolis:
University of Minnesota Press.

Wach, Howard
1993   Unitarian Philanthropy and Cultural Hegemony in Comparative Perspective. Journal of Social History 26(3): 539–557.

Wagner, David
1993   Checkerboard Square: Culture and Resistance in a Homeless Community. Boulder, Colo.: Westview Press.

Wagner, Roy
1981   The Invention of Culture. Chicago: University of Chicago Press.

Wallace, Michelle
1989   The Politics of Location. Framework 36: 42–55.

Wallerstein, Immanuel
1976   The Modern World System. New York: Academic Press.

Warren, Kay
Forth-   Enduring Tensions and Changing Identities: Mayan Family Struggles
coming   in Guatemala. In History in Person: The Mutual Constitution of En-
demic Struggles and Enduring Identities. Dorothy Holland and Jean
Lave, eds. Pp. 1–35. Santa Fe, N.Mex.: School of American Research
Press.

Wellman, David
1995   The Union Makes Us Strong: Radical Unionism on the San Francisco
Waterfront. Cambridge, England: Cambridge University Press.

West, Cornel
1993   Race Matters. Boston: Beacon Press.

Weston, Kath
1991   Families We Choose: Lesbians, Gays, Kinship. New York: Columbia
University Press.
1993   Lesbian/Gay Studies in the House of Anthropology. Annual Review
of Anthropology 22: 339–367.
1995   Get Thee to a Big City: Sexual Imaginary and the Great Gay Migra-

Weston, Kath (*continued*)
        tion. GLQ: A Journal of Lesbian and Gay Studies 2(3): 253–277.
White, Francis E.
    1990   Africa on my Mind: Gender, Counter Discourse and African-American
                Nationalism. Journal of Women's History 2(1): 73–97.
White, R.
    1992   Discovering Nature in North America. Journal of American History
                79: 874–891.
Willis, Paul
    1977   Learning to Labour: How Working Class Kids Get Working Class Jobs.
                Farnborough, England: Saxon House.
Willis, William S., Jr.
    1972   Skeletons in the Anthropological Closet. In Reinventing Anthropol-
                ogy. Dell Hymes, ed. Pp. 121–152. New York: Pantheon Books.
Wilson, Godfrey
    1941–1942   An Essay on the Economics of Detribalization in Northern Rhodesia.
                Rhodes-Livingstone Papers nos. 5–6. Manchester, England: Man-
                chester University Press for Rhodes-Livingstone Institute.
Wilson, Monica Hunter
    1936   Reaction to Conquest: Effects of Contact with Europeans on the
                Pondo of South Africa. Oxford: Oxford University Press.
Wissler, Clark
    1923   Man and Culture. New York: Thomas Y. Crowell.
Wolf, Eric
    1964   Anthropology. New York: Norton.
    1982   Europe and the People without History. Berkeley: University of Cal-
                ifornia Press.
Woolley, Benjamin
    1992   Virtual Worlds: A Journey in Hype and Hyperreality. Oxford: Basil
                Blackwell.
Worster, Donald
    1993   The Wealth of Nature: Environmental History and the Ecological
                Imagination. New York: Oxford University Press.
Wright, G.
    1987   Tradition in the Service of Modernity: Architecture and Urbanism
                in French Colonial Policy, 1900–1930. Journal of Modern History 59:
                291–316.
Yanagisako, Sylvia, and Carol Delaney
    1995   Naturalizing Power: Essays in Feminist Cultural Analysis. New York:
                Routledge.
Young, Robert J. C.
    1995   Colonial Desire: Hybridity in Theory, Culture and Race. New York:
                Routledge.
Zalewski, Daniel
    1995   Can This Journal Be Saved? Lingua Franca 5(5): 15–16.

Zavella, Patricia
    1993   Feminist Insider Dilemmas: Constructing Ethnic Identity with "Chi-
cana" Informants. Frontiers 13(3): 53–76.
Zeleza, Tiyambe
    1993   CODESRIA Bulletin (1 November): 20–22.

CONTRIBUTORS

Deborah Amory is assistant professor in the Anthropology Board of Study at the State University of New York–Purchase. Her research focuses on identity, performance, and gender issues on the East African Swahili-speaking coast.

Mary Des Chene taught at the University of British Columbia and Bryn Mawr College after receiving her Ph.D. in anthropology from Stanford University. She is editor of the journal *Studies in Nepali History and Society* and is currently affiliated with the Nepal Studies Group of the Centre for Social Research and Development in Kathmandu, Nepal. Her current research, funded by Wenner-Gren Foundation, concerns the uses of literature and folklore studies in the crafting of a state-sponsored unitary national culture during Nepal's Panchayat era (1962–90).

James Clifford is professor in the History of Consciousness Program at the University of California, Santa Cruz. He is author of *The Predicament of Culture: Twentieth-Century Ethnography, Literature and Art* (Harvard University Press, 1988) and co-editor (with George Marcus) of *Writing Culture: The Poetics and Politics of Ethnography* (University of California Press, 1986). His most recent book is entitled *Routes: Travel and Translation in the Late Twentieth Century* (Harvard University Press, 1997).

Jane F. Collier is professor of anthropology at Stanford University. She teaches the history of anthropological theory and has written books about indigenous law, social inequality, and kinship theory. Her forthcoming book on family change in Spain is entitled *From Duty to Desire: Remaking Families in a Spanish Village* (Princeton University Press).

James Ferguson is associate professor in the Department of Anthropology at the University of California, Irvine. He is author of *The Anti-Politics Machine: 'Development,' Depoliticization, and Bureaucratic Power in Lesotho* (Cambridge University Press, 1990). He is co-editer (with Akhil Gupta) of the forthcoming book *Culture, Power, Place: Explorations in Critical Anthropology* (Duke University Press). He is currently completing a manuscript on urban-rural relations and conceptions of modernity in the Zambian Copperbelt.

Akhil Gupta is assistant professor in the Department of Anthropology at Stanford University. His forthcoming book is entitled *Postcolonial Developments: Agriculture in the Making of Modern India* (Duke University Press). He has co-edited (with James Ferguson) the forthcoming book *Culture, Power, Place: Explorations in Critical Anthropology* (Duke University Press). He is currently working on a manuscript that ethnographically investigates the state in northern India.

Henrika Kuklick is professor in the Department of History and Sociology of Science at the University of Pennsylvania, where she teaches the history of the human sciences and the sociology of knowledge. She is author of *The Savage Within: The Social History of British Anthropology, 1885–1945* (Cambridge University Press, 1991) and co-editor (with Robert Kohler) of *Science in the Field* (special issue of *Osiris*, 1996). She is currently writing a comparative analysis of early twentieth-century understandings of the relationship between people and places.

Liisa H. Malkki is assistant professor of anthropology at the University of California, Irvine. She is author of *Purity and Exile: Violence, Memory, and National Cosmology Among Hutu Refugees in Tanzania* (University of Chicago Press, 1995), which won the Royal Anthropological Institute's 1996 Amaury Talbot Prize for the best book on Africa. She teaches and writes on nationalism and xenophobia, racism and violence, and internationalism and practices of humanitarianism. She is currently studying the social imagination of the future in the aftermath of genocide among exiles from Rwanda and Burundi.

Emily Martin is professor of anthropology at Princeton University. Beginning with *The Woman in the Body: A Cultural Analysis of Reproduction* (Beacon Press, 1987), which won the Society for Medical Anthropology's Eileen Basker Memorial Prize, she explored the anthropology of science and reproduction in the United States. In *Flexible Bodies: Tracking Immunity in America from the Days of Polio to the Age of AIDS* (Beacon Press, 1994), she focused on the interplay between scientific and popular conceptions of the immune system. Her present work is on the theories of normalization and the evolving constitution of selfhood in contemporary society.

Joanne Passaro is assistant professor of anthropology at the Center for Liberal Studies at Clarkson University, Potsdam, New York. She is author of *The Unequal Homeless: Men on the Streets, Women in Their Place* (Routledge, 1996) and is currently at work on a comparative study of rural poverty.

Kath Weston is associate professor of anthropology in the Department of Social and Behavioral Sciences at Arizona State University West. She is author of *Families We Choose: Lesbians, Gays, Kinship* (Columbia University Press, 1991) and co-editor (with Estelle Freedman, Barbara Gelpi, and Susan Johnson) of *The Lesbian Issue: Essays from Signs* (University of Chicago Press, 1985). Her most recent book is entitled *Render Me, Gender Me* (Columbia University Press, 1996).

INDEX

Compositor:	Integrated Composition Systems
Text:	10/12 Baskerville
Display:	Baskerville
Printer:	IBT
Binder:	IBT